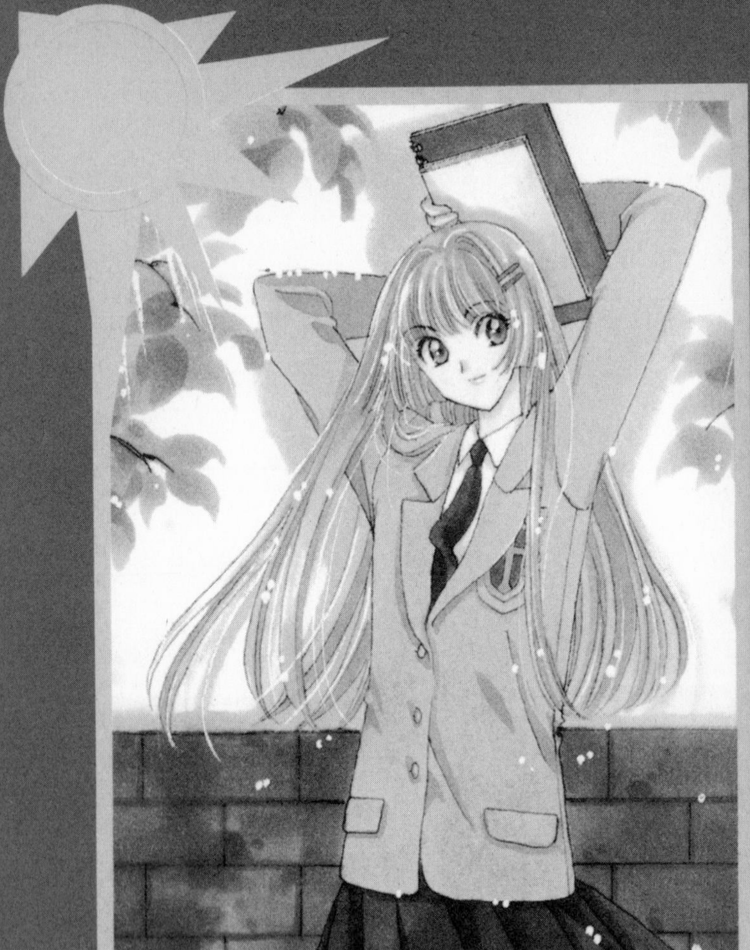

CLAMP

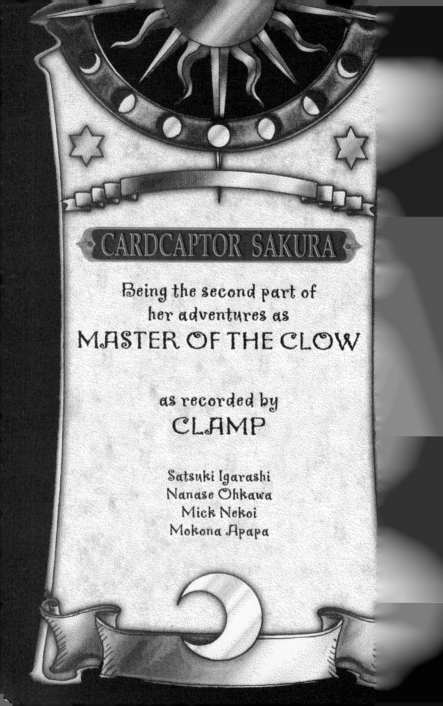

CARDCAPTOR SAKURA

Being the second part of
her adventures as
MASTER OF THE CLOW

as recorded by
CLAMP

Satsuki Igarashi
Nanase Ohkawa
Mick Nekoi
Mokona Apapa

Translator - Anita Sengupta
English Adaption - Carol Fox
Copy Editor - Jodi Bryson
Retouch & Lettering - Faun Lau
Cover Artist - Raymond Swanland
Cover Layout - Gary Shum

Senior Editor - Jake Forbes
Managing Editor - Jill Freshney
Production Coordinator - Antonio DePietro
Production Managers - Jennifer Miller, Mutsumi Miyazaki
Art Director - Matt Alford
Editorial Director - Jeremy Ross
VP of Production - Ron Klamert
President & C.O.O. - John Parker
Publisher & C.E.O. - Stuart Levy

Email: editor@TOKYOPOP.com
Come visit us online at www.TOKYOPOP.com

A 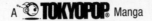 Manga

TOKYOPOP Inc.
5900 Wilshire Blvd. Suite 2000
Los Angeles, CA 90036

Cardcaptor Sakura: Master of the Clow Vol. 2

ISBN: 1-892213-76-1

First TOKYOPOP® printing: December 2002

10 9 8 7 6 5 4

Printed in USA

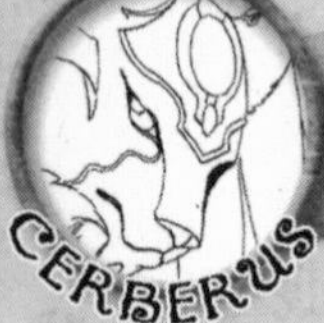

CERBERUS

Kero's true form is a lot... bigger. Unlike Yukito, Kero knows about his true form. His symbol of power is the sun.

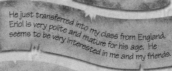

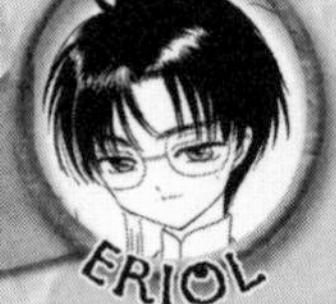

He just transferred into my class from England. Eriol is very polite and mature for his age. He seems to be very interested in me and my friends.

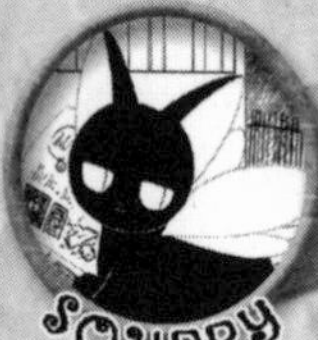

ERIOL

SOUPPY

He's a talking cat-like creature that lives with Eriol. He's very wise and likes his peace and quiet. I've never met him.

This fearsome winged panther appears in my dreams. [Sakura doesn't know this, but Spinnel Sun is Souppy's true form!]

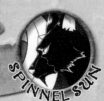

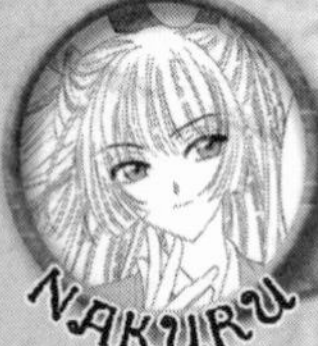

SPINNEL SUN

NAKURU

This obnoxious girl just transferred into Toya's class. I think she has a crush on him. She doesn't like Yukito at all. Talk about bad taste!

This beautiful woman with butterfly wings also keeps appearing in my dreams. [Actually, she's not male or female but is Nakuru's true form.]

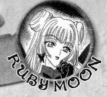

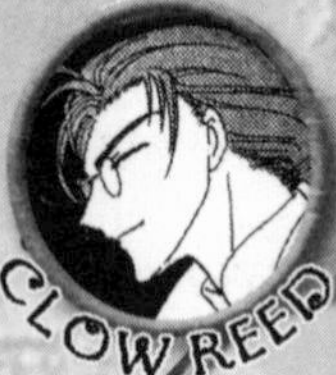

RUBY MOON

CLOW REED

He made the Clow Cards and created Kero and Yue. Even though he's been dead for many years, his presence is still hovering over Tomoeda.

THE STORY SO FAR...

Hey there! Thanks for coming back to hear about more of my adventures. Strange things are happening here in Tomoeda, and this time it's not because of Clow Cards. First there was this weird rain that kept pouring only on my hometown. Clow Cards alone aren't enough to fight this new enemy, but that's okay. It turns out I have the power to transform the cards into what Tomoyo has named "Sakura Cards" (how embarrassing!). With these new cards made by my own magic, I was able to stop the attacks. Kero and Yue don't know what's behind the incidents, but they do sense the presence of Clow Reed nearby. But that's impossible, right? He's been dead for years! Maybe those dreams I've been having lately have something to do with it...

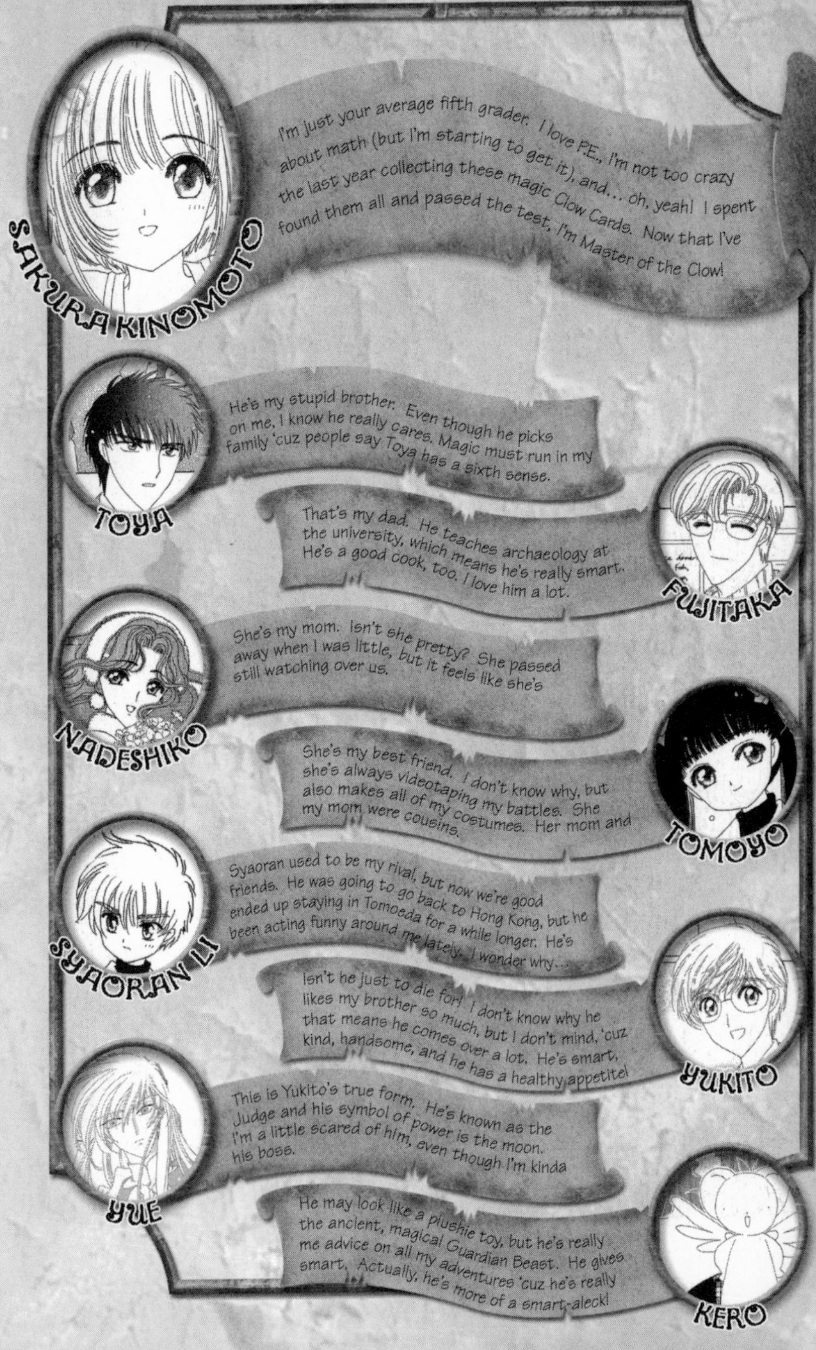
SAKURA KINOMOTO
I'm just your average fifth grader. I love P.E., I'm not too crazy about math (but I'm starting to get it), and... oh, yeah! I spent the last year collecting these magic Clow Cards. Now that I've found them all and passed the test, I'm Master of the Clow!
TOYA
He's my stupid brother. Even though he picks on me, I know he really cares. Magic must run in my family 'cuz people say Toya has a sixth sense.
FUJITAKA
That's my dad. He teaches archaeology at the university, which means he's really smart. He's a good cook, too. I love him a lot.
NADESHIKO
She's my mom. Isn't she pretty? She passed away when I was little, but it feels like she's still watching over us.
TOMOYO
She's my best friend. I don't know why, but she's always videotaping my battles. She also makes all of my costumes. Her mom and my mom were cousins.
SYAORAN LI
Syaoran used to be my rival, but now we're good friends. He was going to go back to Hong Kong, but he ended up staying in Tomoeda for a while longer. He's been acting funny around me lately. I wonder why...
YUKITO
Isn't he just to die for! I don't know why he likes my brother so much, but I don't mind, 'cuz that means he comes over a lot. He's smart, kind, handsome, and he has a healthy appetite!
YUE
This is Yukito's true form. He's known as the Judge and his symbol of power is the moon. I'm a little scared of him, even though I'm kinda his boss.
KERO
He may look like a plushie toy, but he's really the ancient, magical Guardian Beast. He gives me advice on all my adventures 'cuz he's really smart. Actually, he's more of a smart-aleck!

I FEAR I MIGHT MAKE THINGS DIFFICULT FOR YOU,
YOUNG SAKURA...

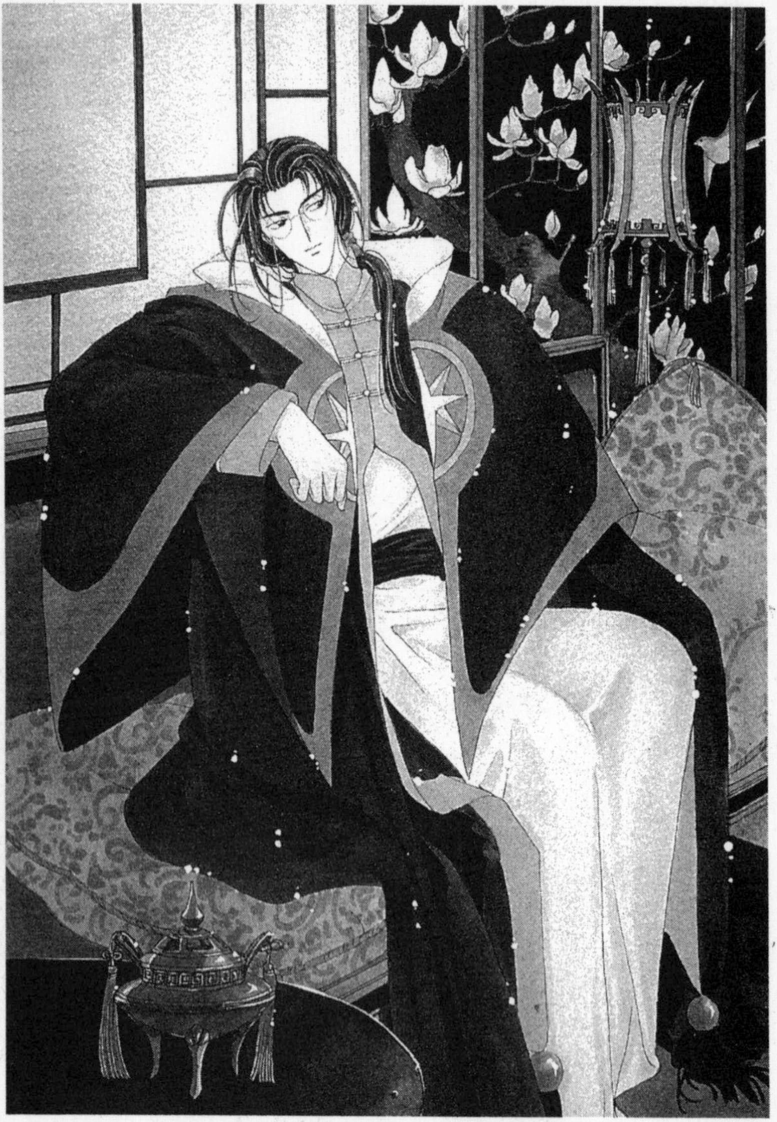

BUT I'M SURE YOU'LL BE ALL RIGHT.

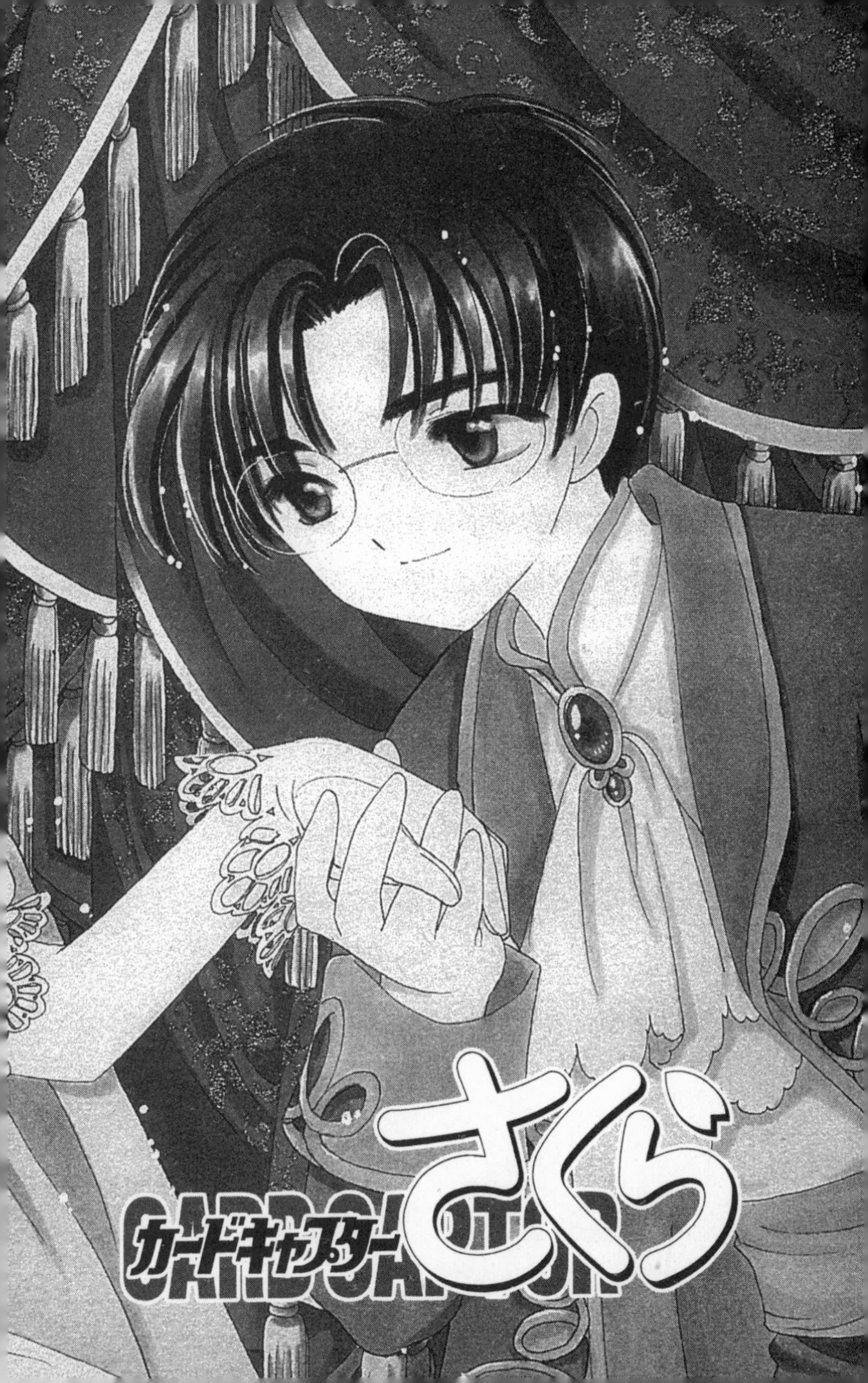
カードキャプター
さくら
CARD CAPTOR

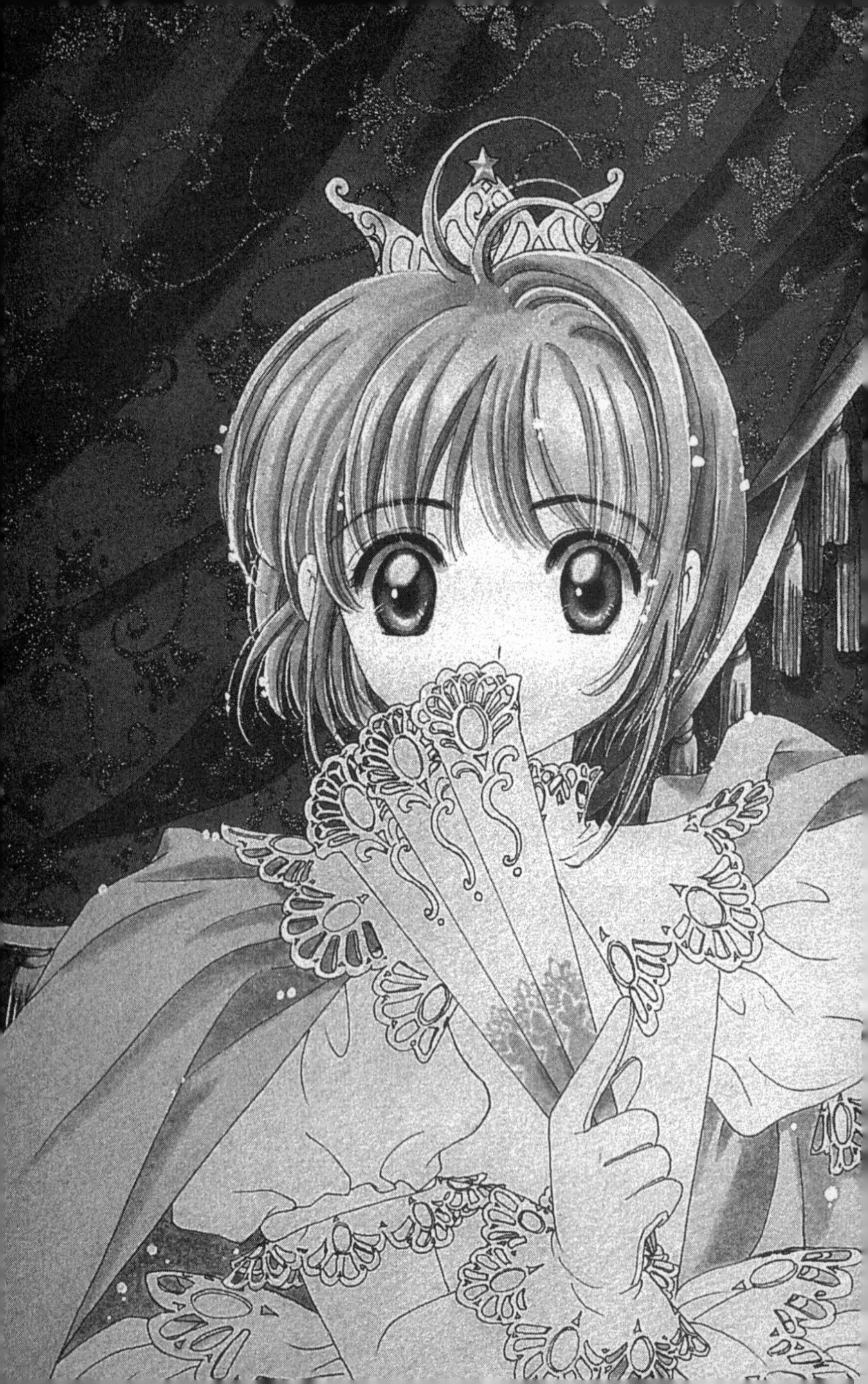

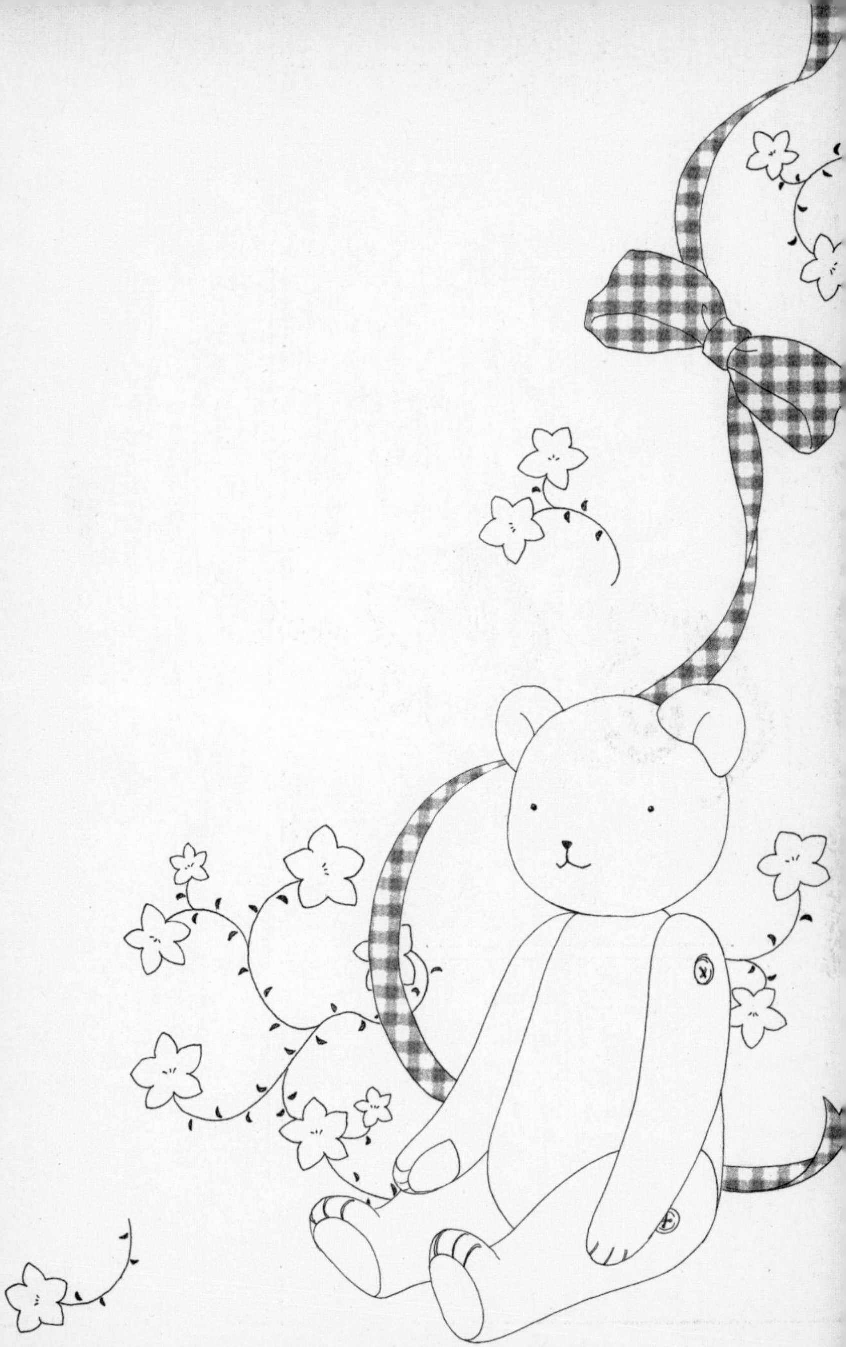

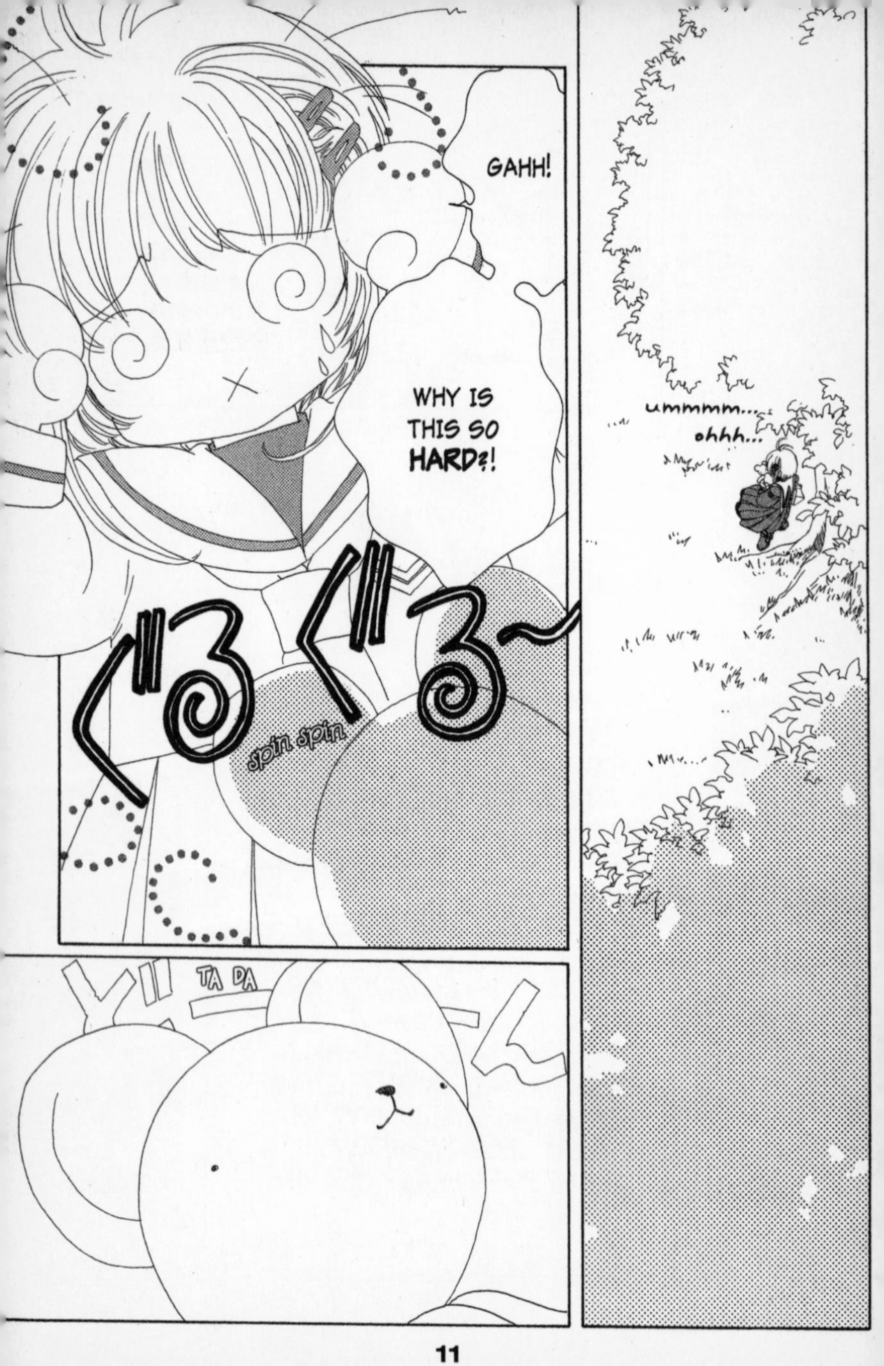
ummmm...
ohhh...
GAHH!
WHY IS THIS SO HARD?!
ぐるぐる~
spin spin
TA DA

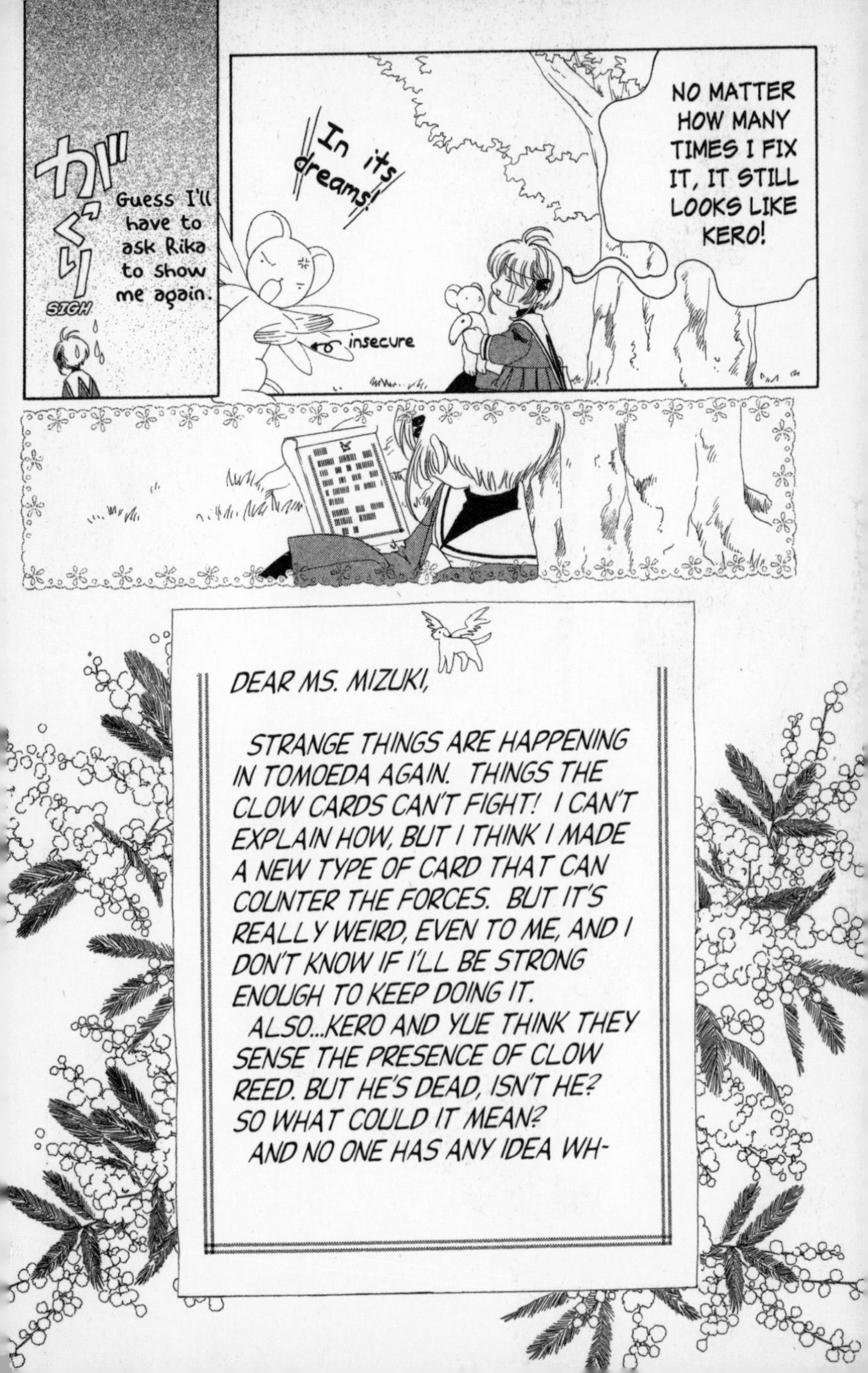
NO MATTER HOW MANY TIMES I FIX IT, IT STILL LOOKS LIKE KERO!
In its dreams!
insecure
がっくり
SIGH
Guess I'll have to ask Rika to show me again.

DEAR MS. MIZUKI,

STRANGE THINGS ARE HAPPENING IN TOMOEDA AGAIN. THINGS THE CLOW CARDS CAN'T FIGHT! I CAN'T EXPLAIN HOW, BUT I THINK I MADE A NEW TYPE OF CARD THAT CAN COUNTER THE FORCES. BUT IT'S REALLY WEIRD, EVEN TO ME, AND I DON'T KNOW IF I'LL BE STRONG ENOUGH TO KEEP DOING IT.

ALSO...KERO AND YUE THINK THEY SENSE THE PRESENCE OF CLOW REED. BUT HE'S DEAD, ISN'T HE? SO WHAT COULD IT MEAN?

AND NO ONE HAS ANY IDEA WH-

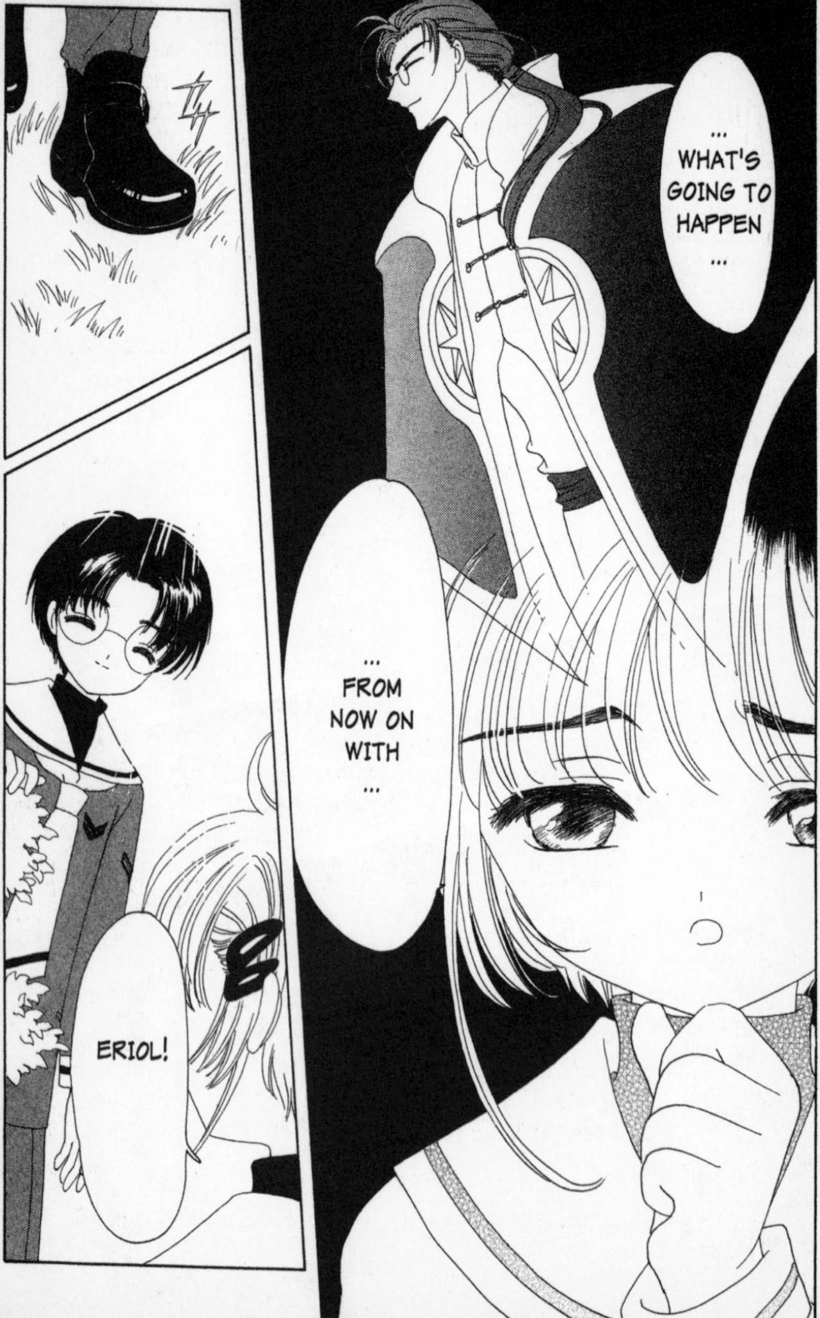
... WHAT'S GOING TO HAPPEN ...
... FROM NOW ON WITH ...
ERIOL!

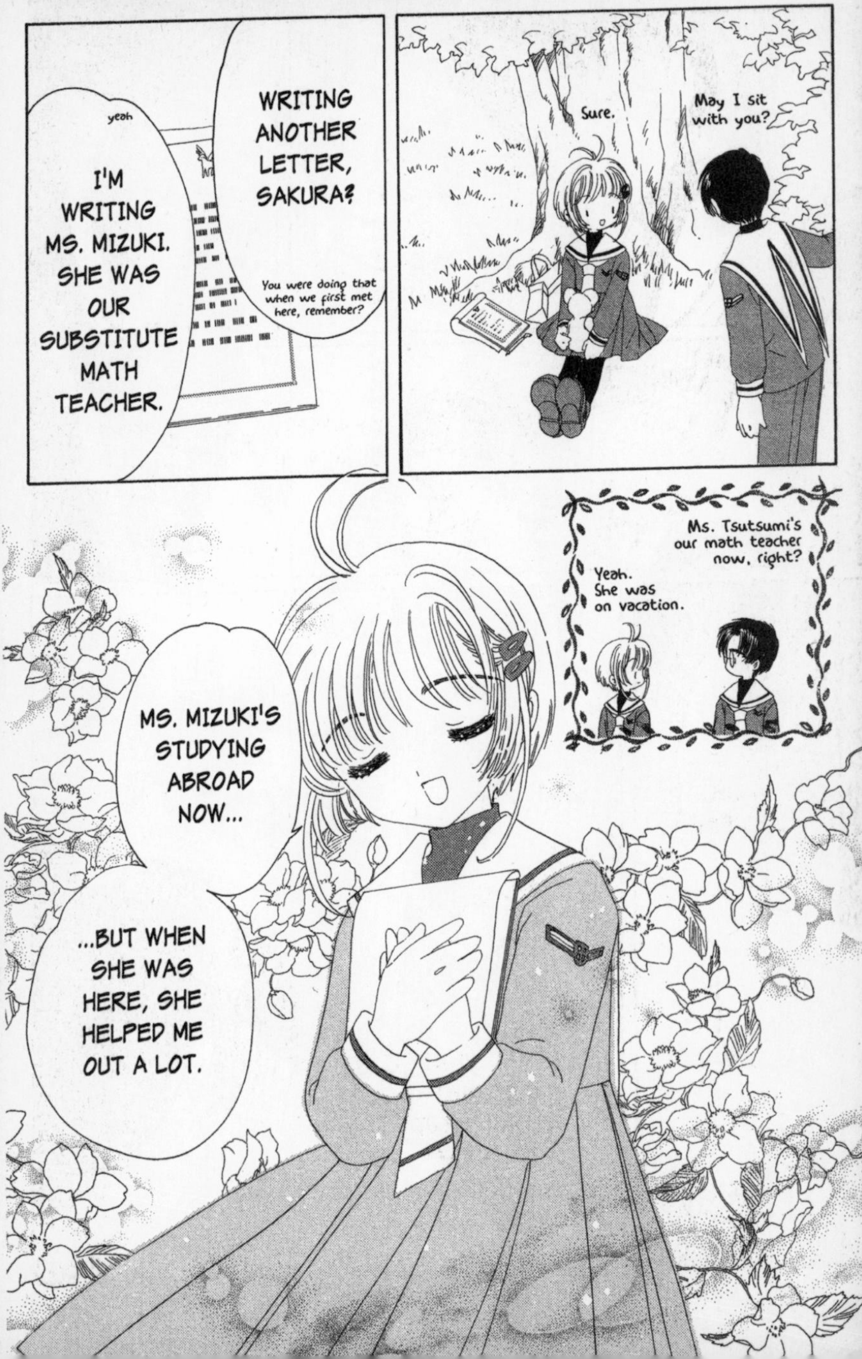
May I sit with you?
Sure.
WRITING ANOTHER LETTER, SAKURA?
You were doing that when we first met here, remember?
yeah
I'M WRITING MS. MIZUKI. SHE WAS OUR SUBSTITUTE MATH TEACHER.
Ms. Tsutsumi's our math teacher now, right?
Yeah. She was on vacation.
MS. MIZUKI'S STUDYING ABROAD NOW...
...BUT WHEN SHE WAS HERE, SHE HELPED ME OUT A LOT.

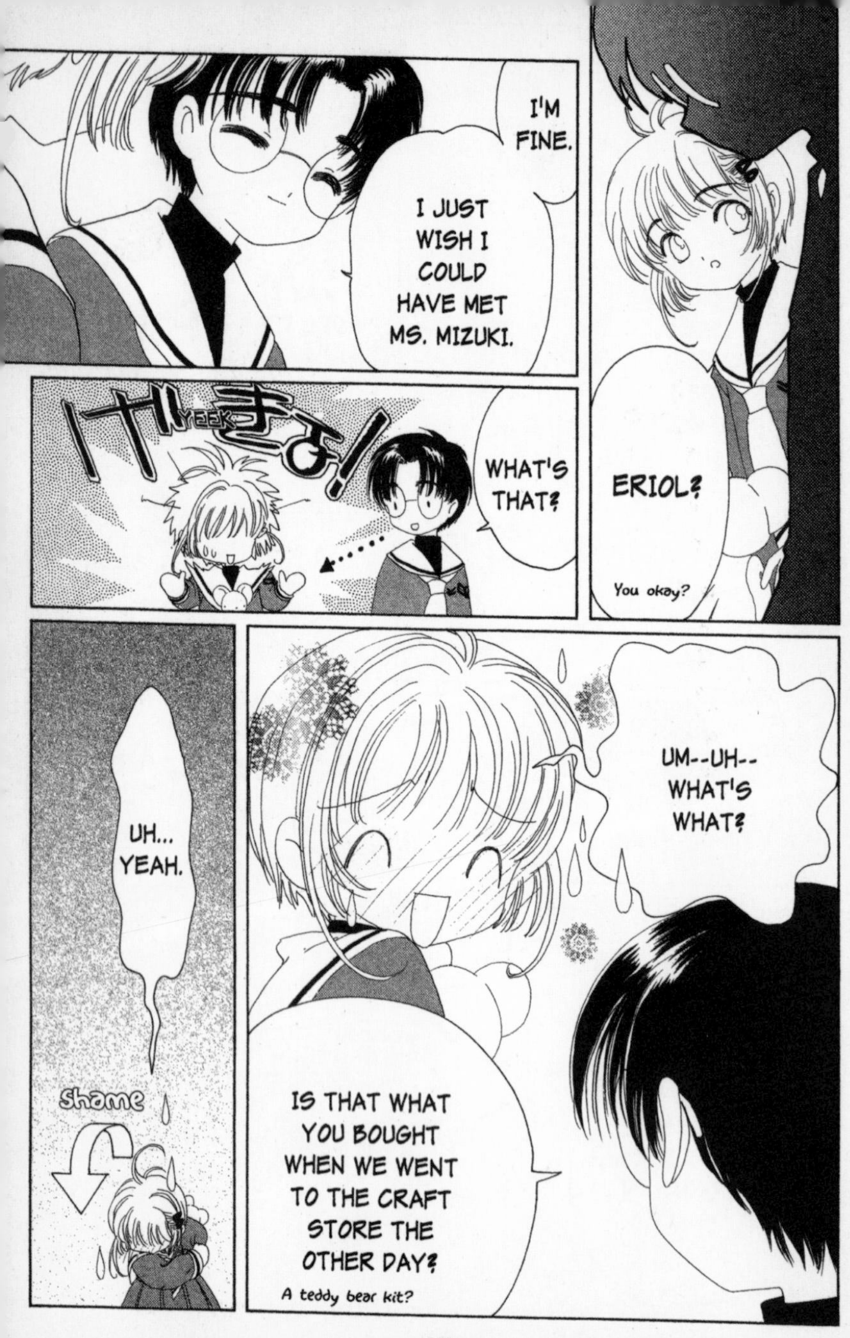
ERIOL?
You okay?
I'M FINE.
I JUST WISH I COULD HAVE MET MS. MIZUKI.
YEEK
WHAT'S THAT?
UM--UH-- WHAT'S WHAT?
IS THAT WHAT YOU BOUGHT WHEN WE WENT TO THE CRAFT STORE THE OTHER DAY?
A teddy bear kit?
UH... YEAH.
shame

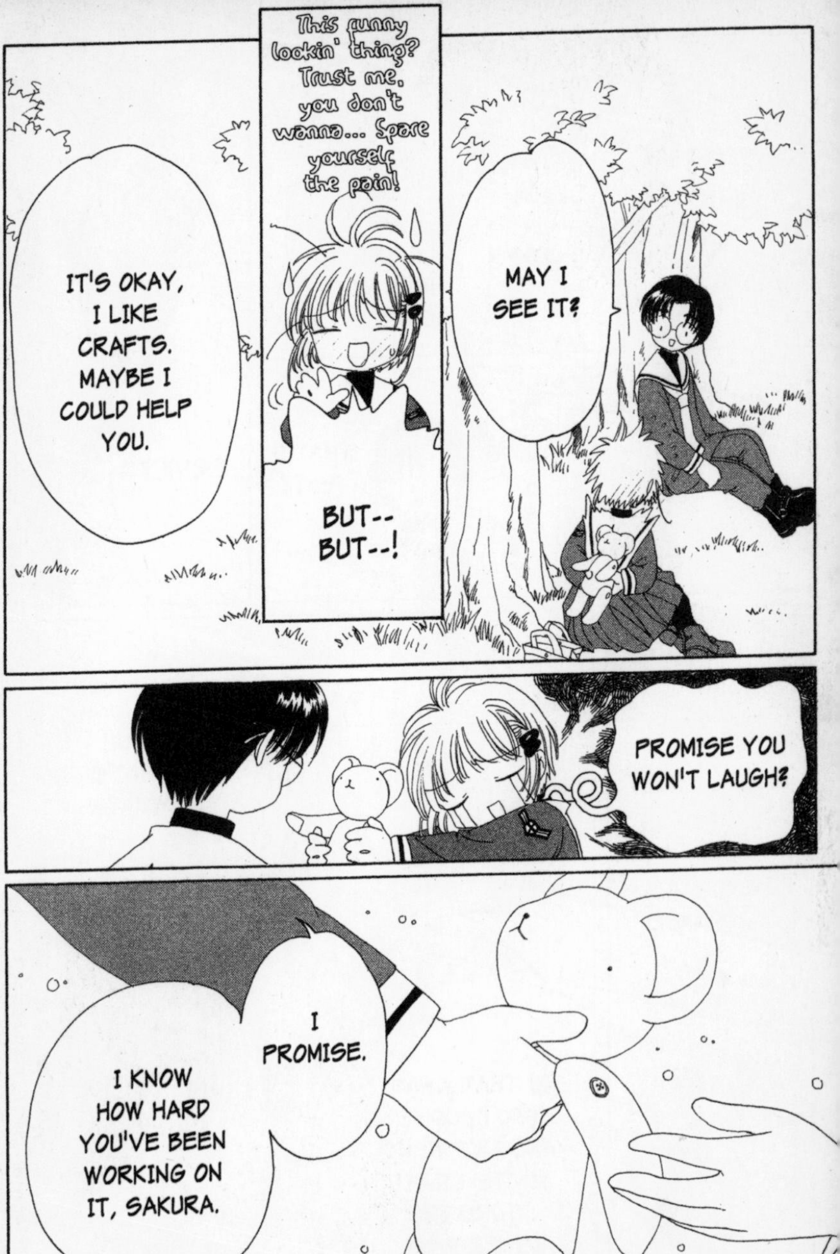
MAY I SEE IT?
This funny lookin' thing? Trust me, you don't wanna... Spare yourself the pain!
BUT-- BUT--!
IT'S OKAY, I LIKE CRAFTS. MAYBE I COULD HELP YOU.
PROMISE YOU WON'T LAUGH?
I PROMISE.
I KNOW HOW HARD YOU'VE BEEN WORKING ON IT, SAKURA.

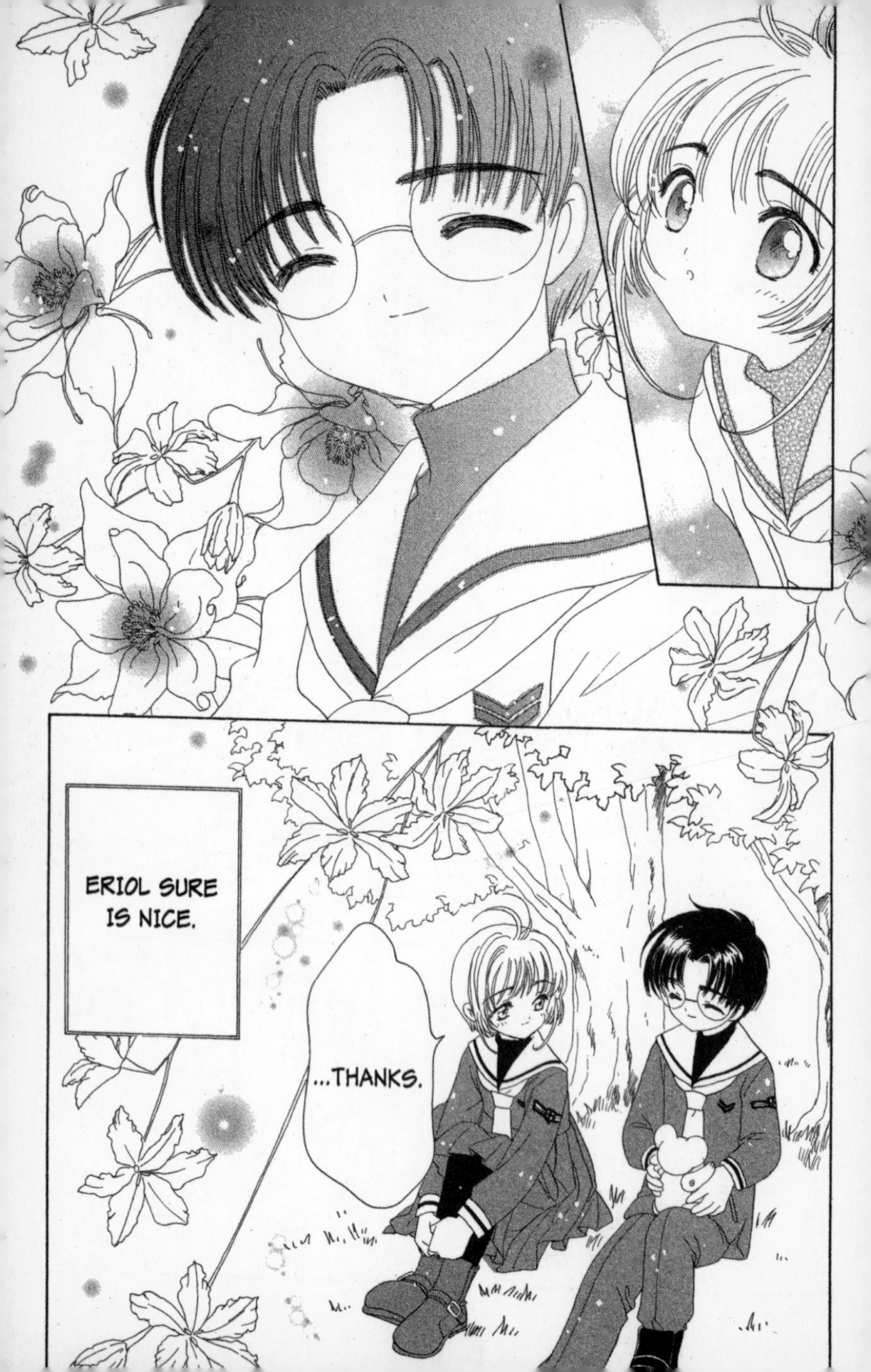
ERIOL SURE IS NICE.
...THANKS.

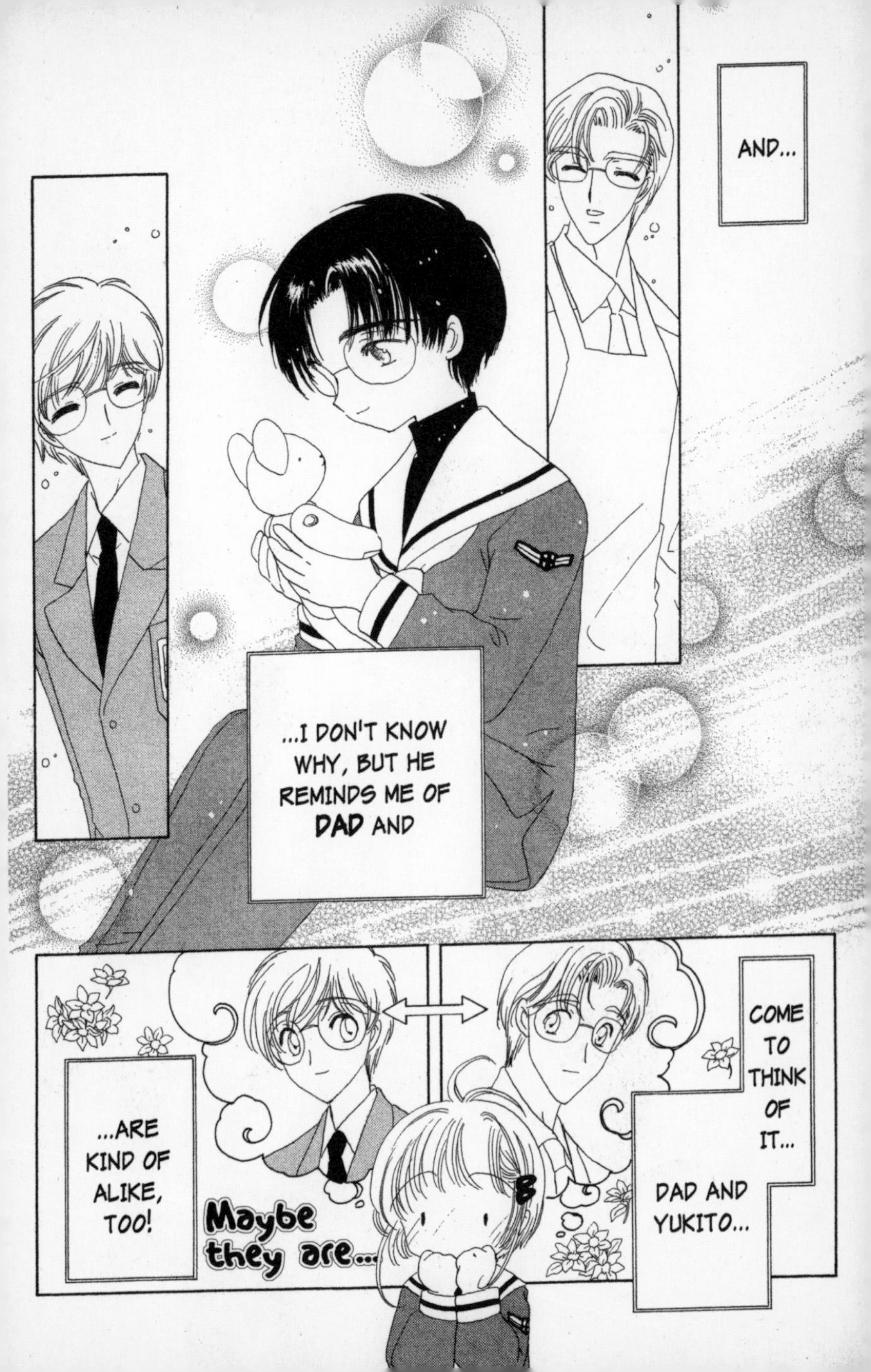
AND...
...I DON'T KNOW WHY, BUT HE REMINDS ME OF DAD AND
COME TO THINK OF IT...
DAD AND YUKITO...
Maybe they are...
...ARE KIND OF ALIKE, TOO!

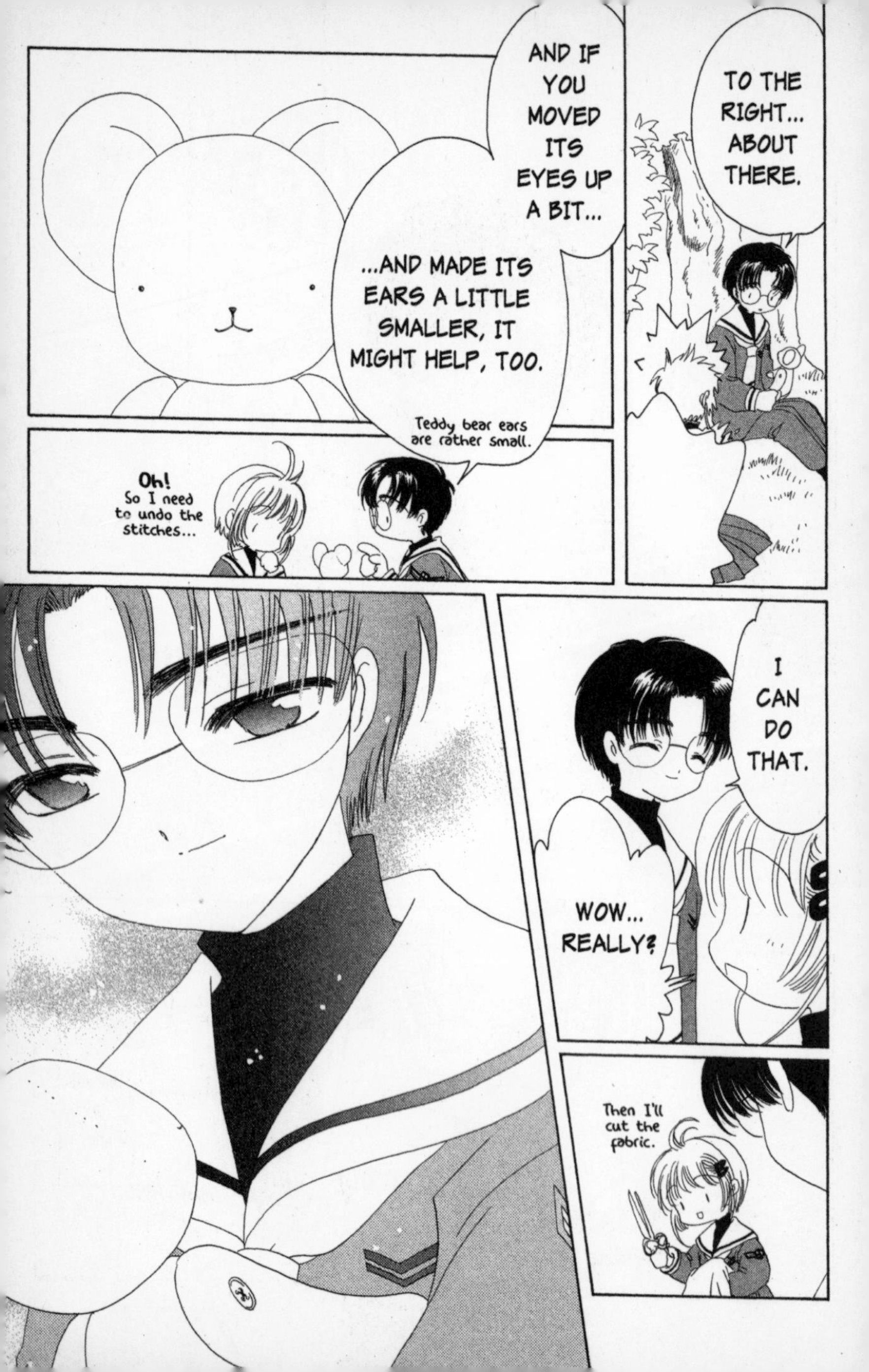
TO THE RIGHT... ABOUT THERE.
AND IF YOU MOVED ITS EYES UP A BIT...
...AND MADE ITS EARS A LITTLE SMALLER, IT MIGHT HELP, TOO.
Teddy bear ears are rather small.
Oh! So I need to undo the stitches...
I CAN DO THAT.
WOW... REALLY?
Then I'll cut the fabric.

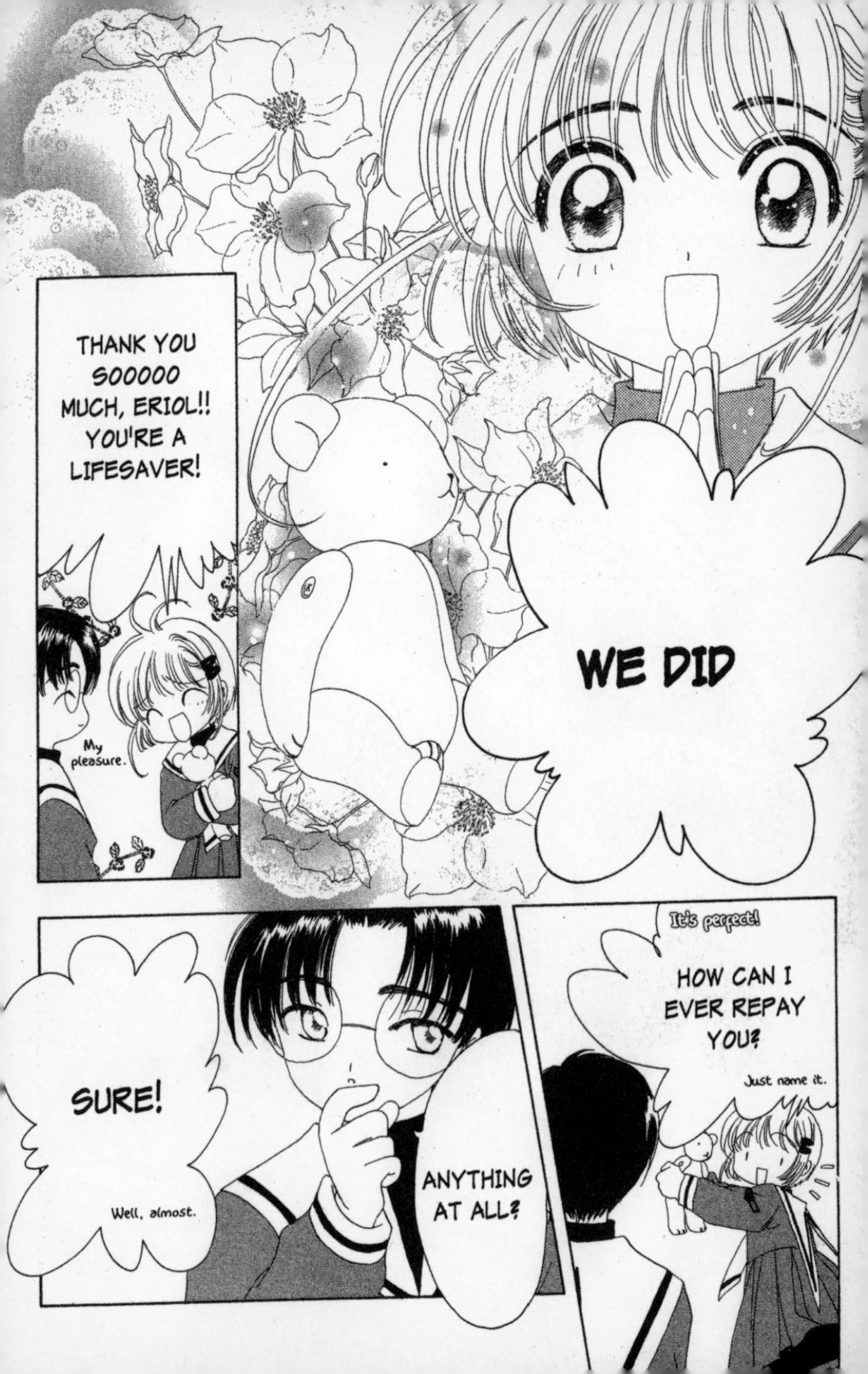
WE DID
THANK YOU SOOOOO MUCH, ERIOL!! YOU'RE A LIFESAVER!
My pleasure.
It's perfect!
HOW CAN I EVER REPAY YOU?
Just name it.
ANYTHING AT ALL?
SURE!
Well, almost.

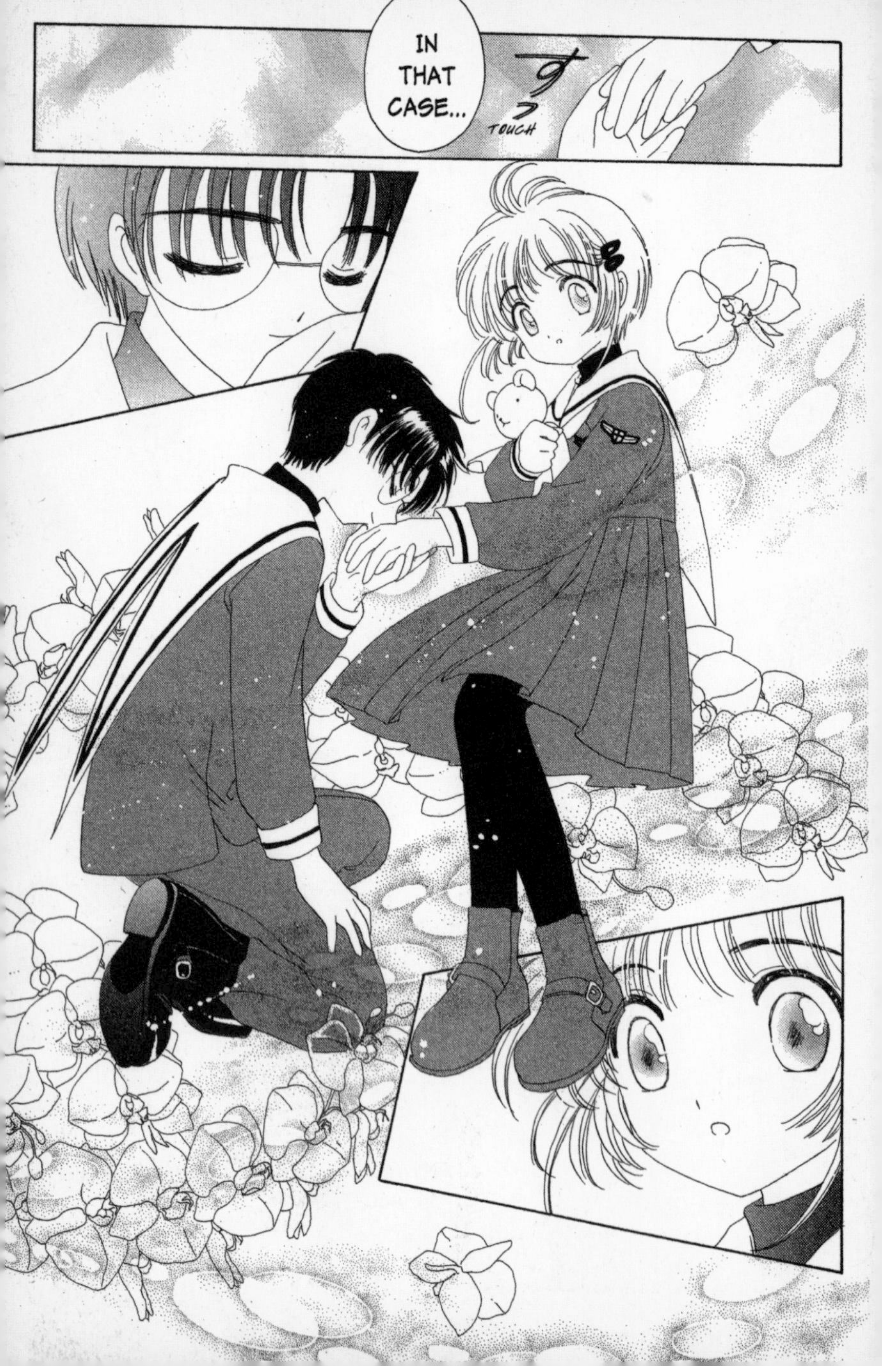
IN THAT CASE...
すっ
TOUCH

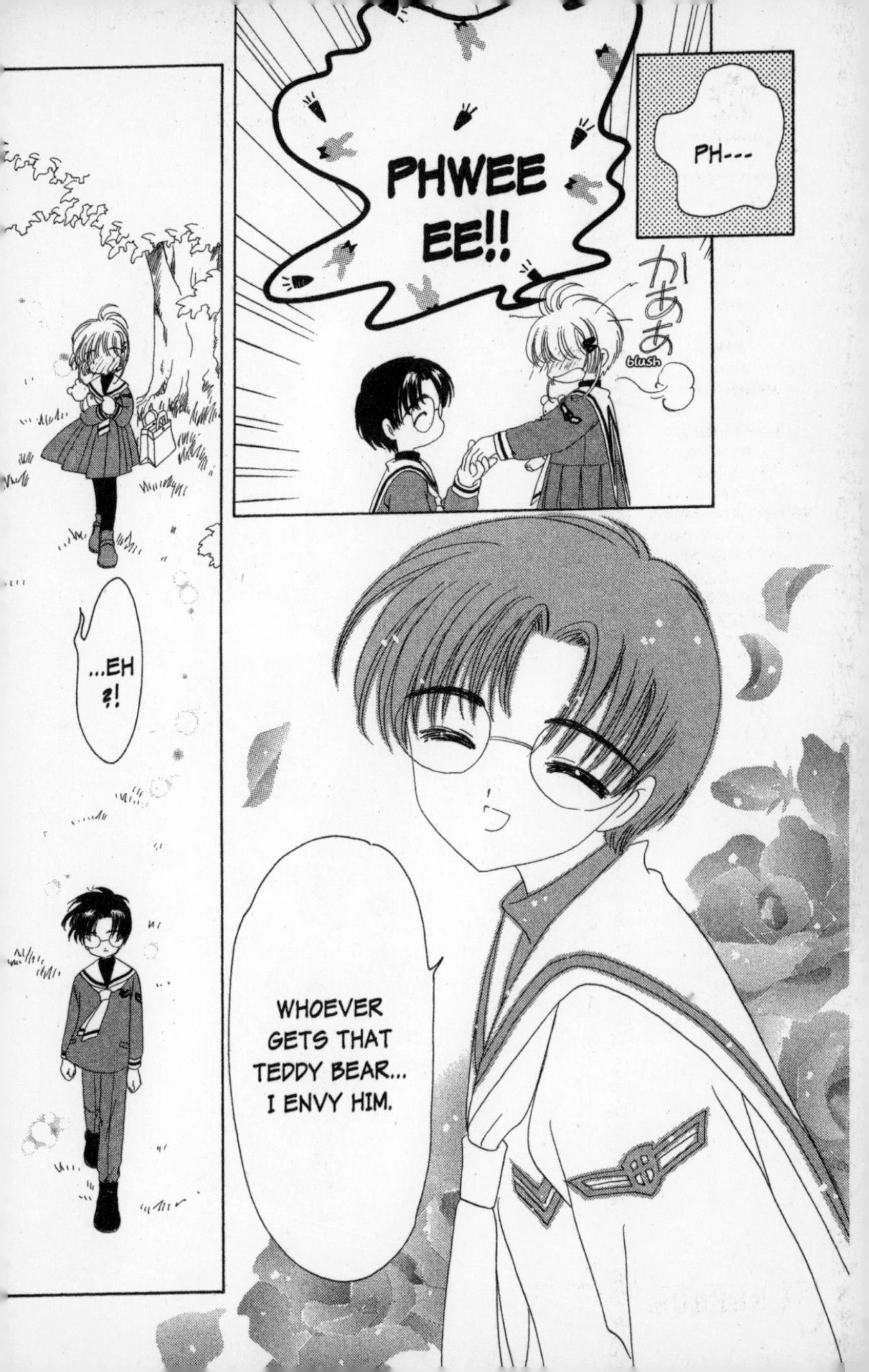
PH---
PHWEE EE!!
かああ
blush
WHOEVER GETS THAT TEDDY BEAR... I ENVY HIM.
...EH ?!

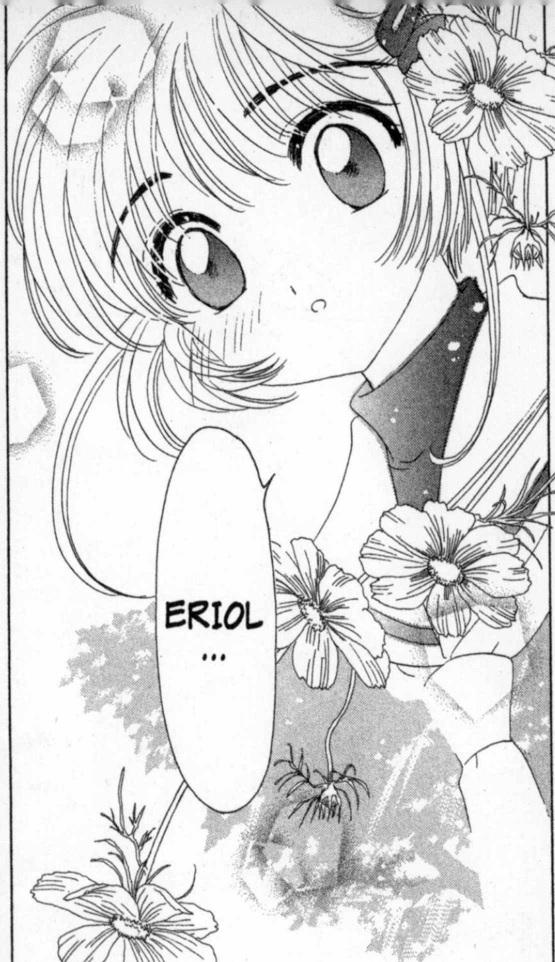
ERIOL ...

21

CERBERUS

MASTER:
SAKURA KINOMOTO

BIRTHDAY:
SECRET

SYMBOL:
SUN

ASPECT:
LIGHT

EYES:
GOLD

BODY:
ORANGE-GOLD

MAGIC:
WESTERN MAGIC

FAVORITE FOOD:
SWEET STUFF

FAVORITE THING:
ANYTHING NOISY AND FUN

LEAST FAVORITE THING:
ANYTHING SAD

TEMPORARY FORM:
ORANGE STUFFED ANIMAL WITH WHITE WINGS

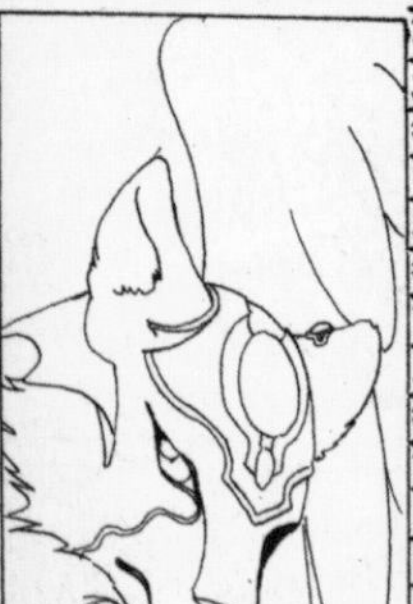

CERBERUS

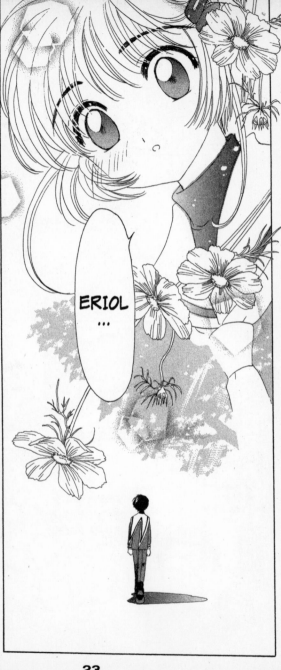

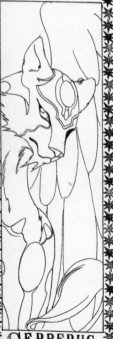

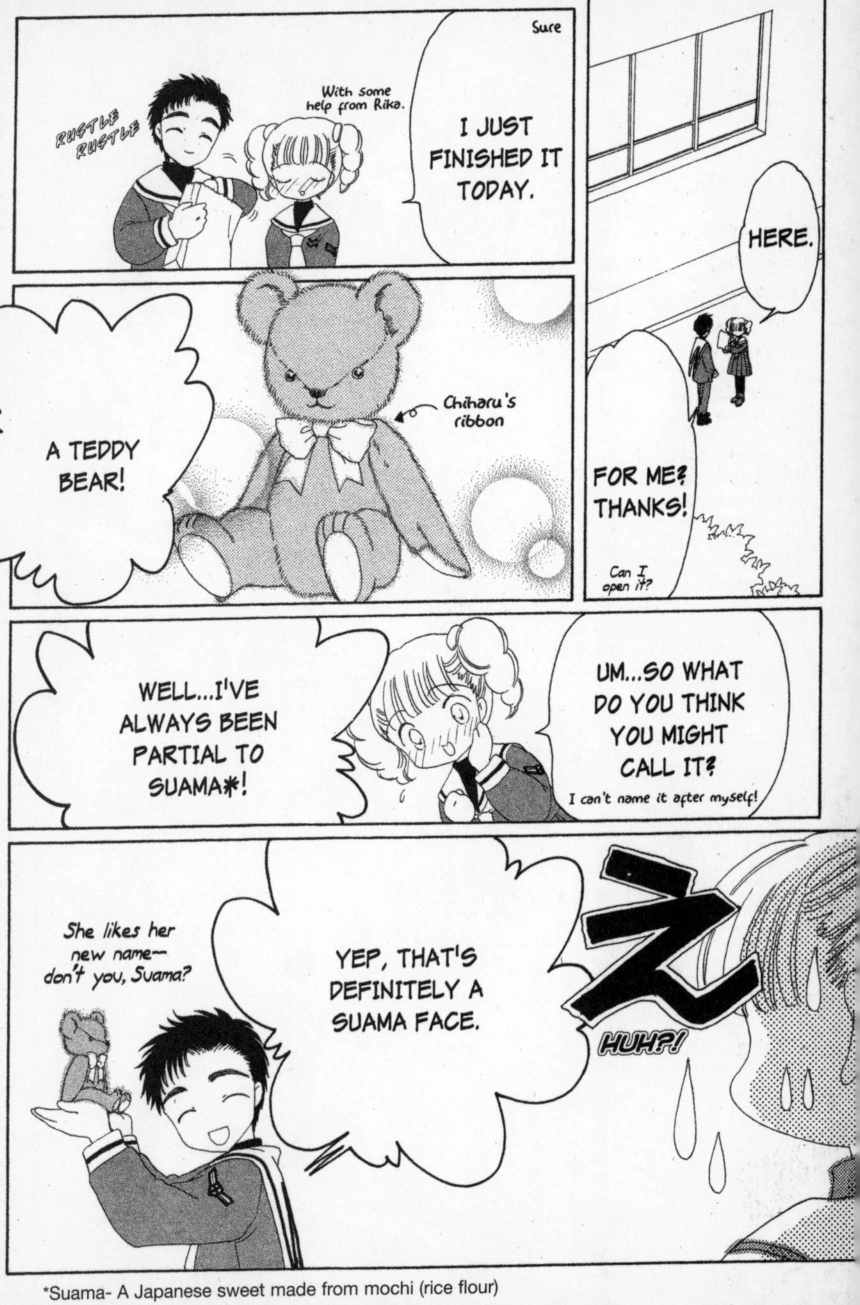
HERE.
FOR ME? THANKS!
Can I open it?
Sure
I JUST FINISHED IT TODAY.
With some help from Rika.
RUSTLE RUSTLE
Chiharu's ribbon
A TEDDY BEAR!
UM...SO WHAT DO YOU THINK YOU MIGHT CALL IT?
I can't name it after myself!
WELL...I'VE ALWAYS BEEN PARTIAL TO SUAMA*!
HUH?!
YEP, THAT'S DEFINITELY A SUAMA FACE.
She likes her new name— don't you, Suama?

*Suama- A Japanese sweet made from mochi (rice flour)

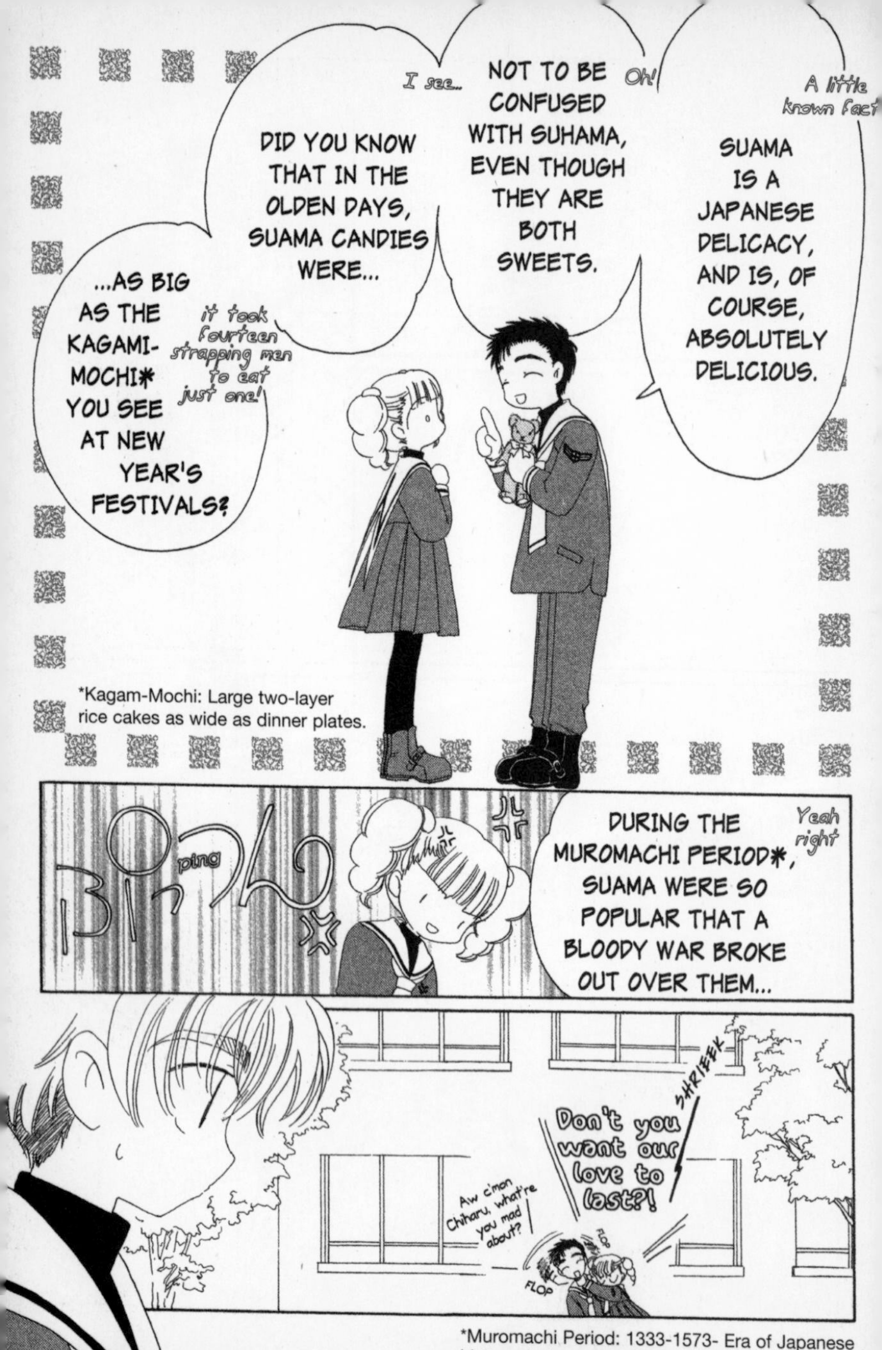
A little known fact
SUAMA IS A JAPANESE DELICACY, AND IS, OF COURSE, ABSOLUTELY DELICIOUS.
Oh!
NOT TO BE CONFUSED WITH SUHAMA, EVEN THOUGH THEY ARE BOTH SWEETS.
I see..
DID YOU KNOW THAT IN THE OLDEN DAYS, SUAMA CANDIES WERE...
...AS BIG AS THE KAGAMI-MOCHI* YOU SEE AT NEW YEAR'S FESTIVALS?
it took fourteen strapping men to eat just one!
Yeah right
DURING THE MUROMACHI PERIOD*, SUAMA WERE SO POPULAR THAT A BLOODY WAR BROKE OUT OVER THEM...
ping
Don't you want our love to last?!
SHRIEEK
Aw c'mon Chiharu, what're you mad about?
FLOP
FLOP

*Kagam-Mochi: Large two-layer rice cakes as wide as dinner plates.

*Muromachi Period: 1333-1573- Era of Japanese history during which the feudal system emerged.

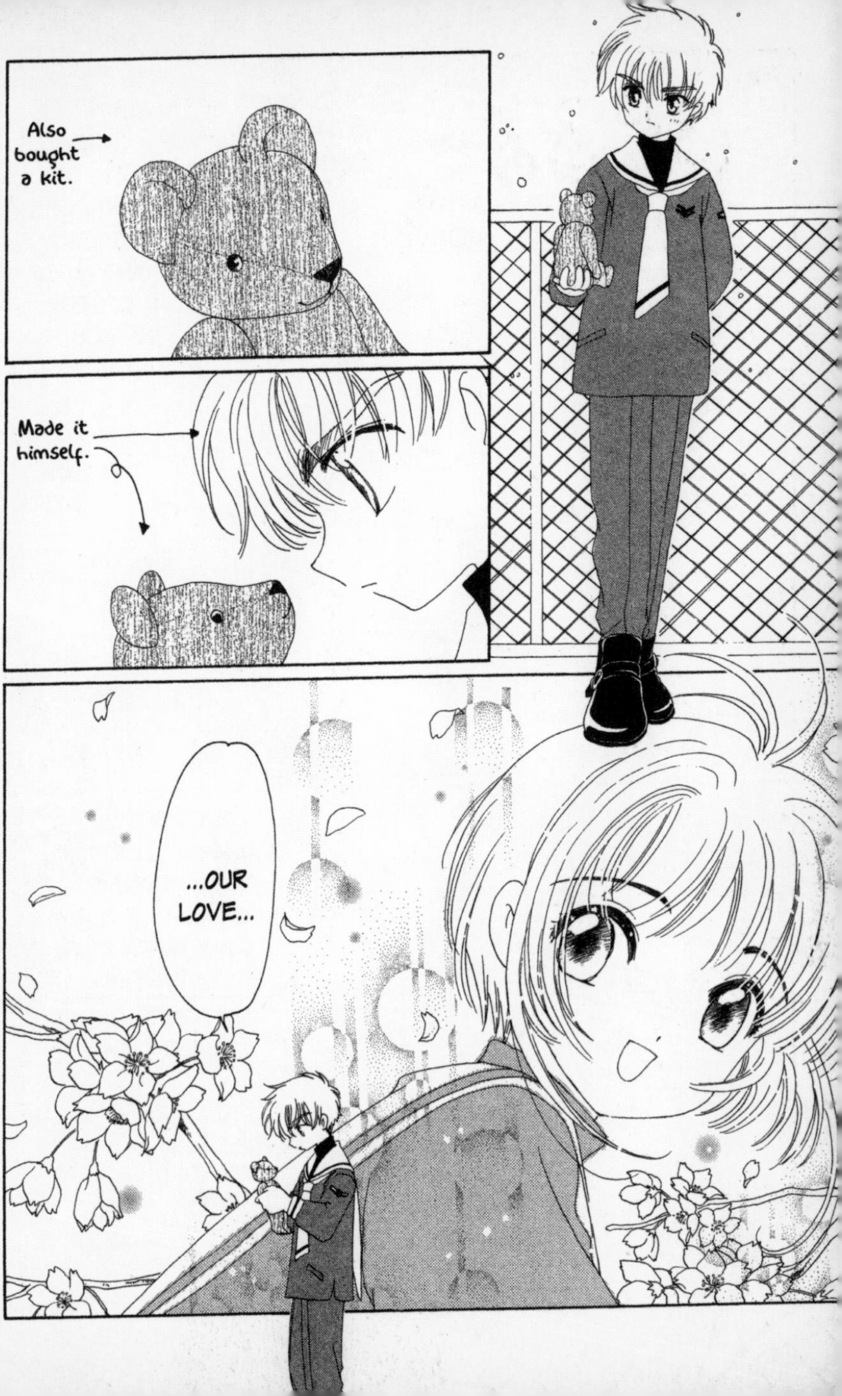
Also bought a kit.
Made it himself.
...OUR LOVE...

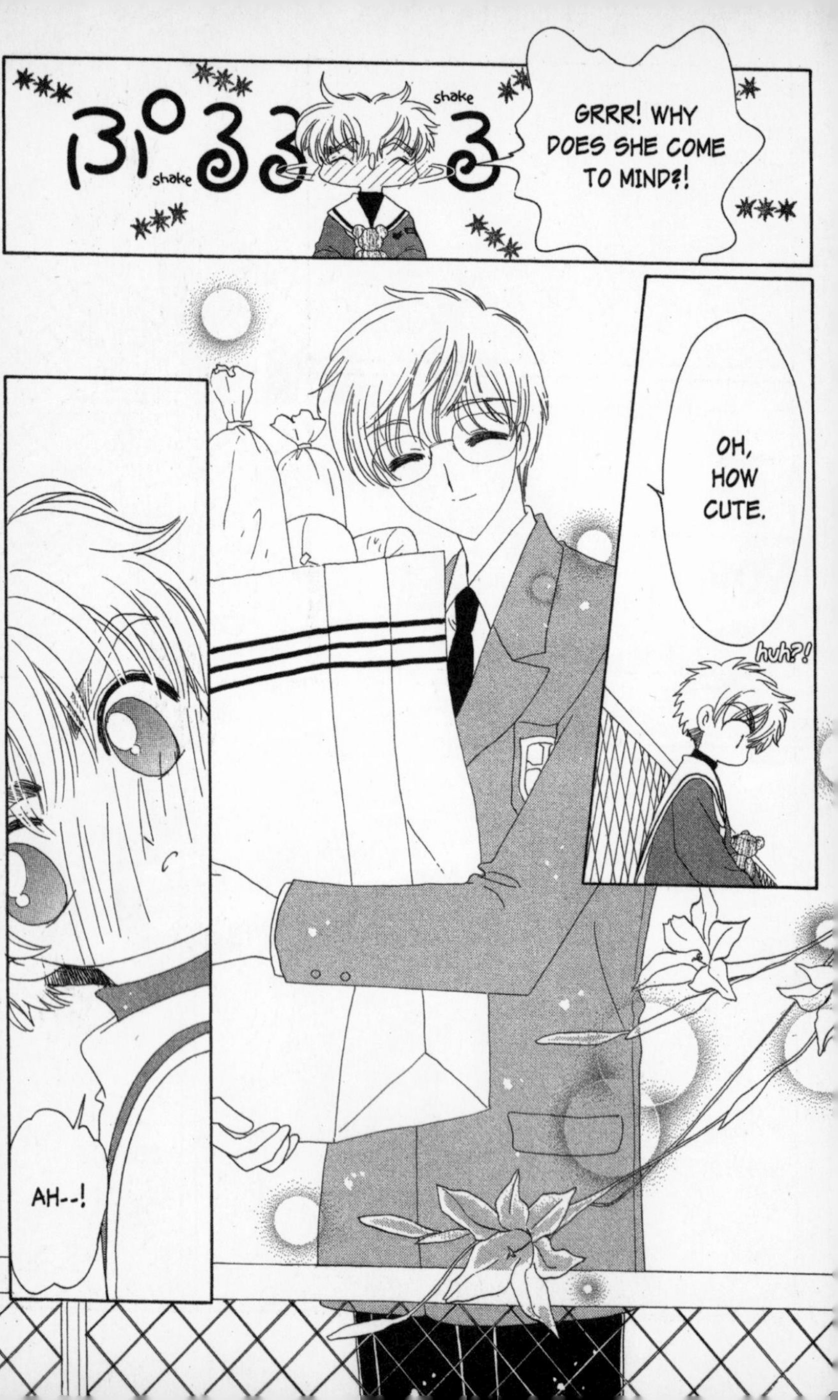

GRRR! WHY DOES SHE COME TO MIND?!
shake
shake
OH, HOW CUTE.
huh?!
AH--!

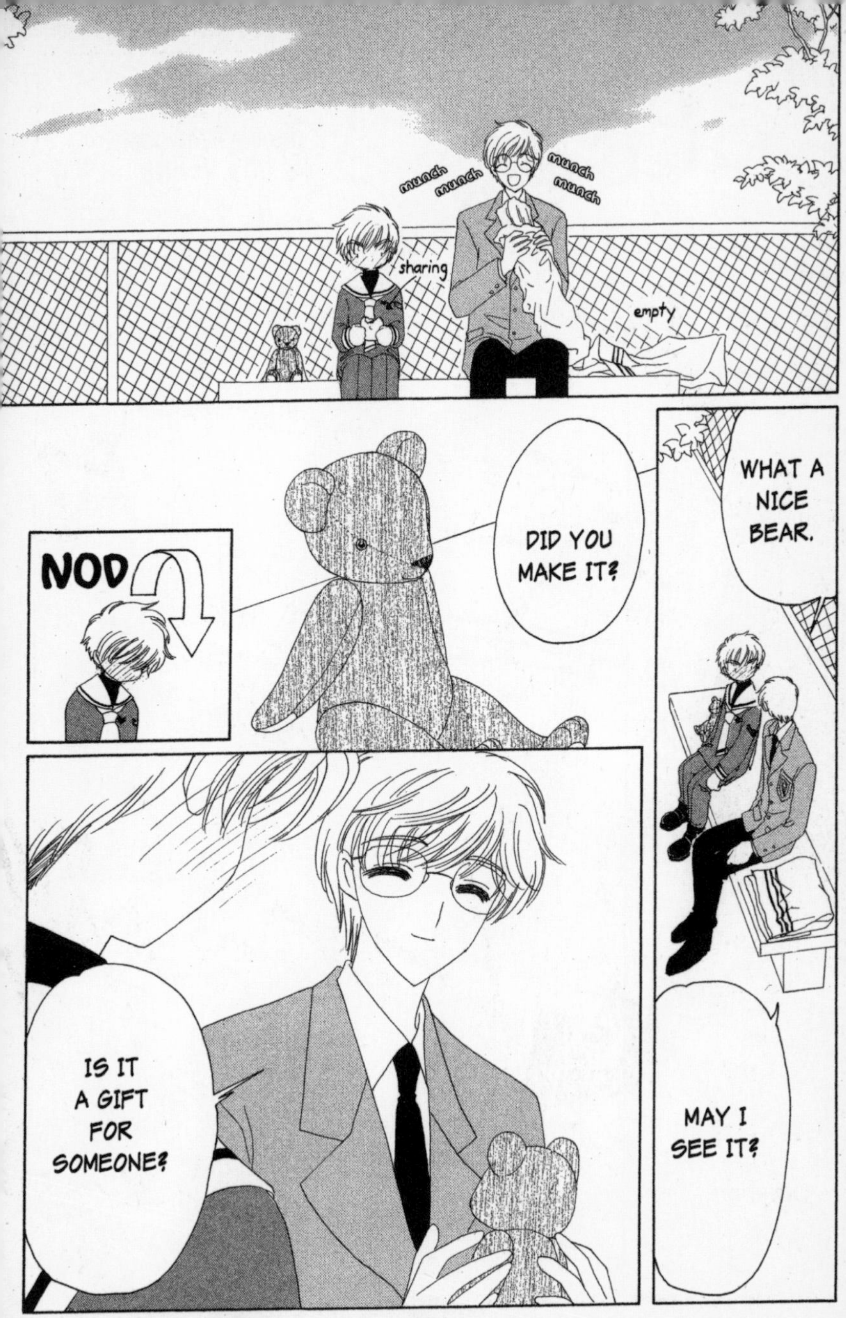
munch munch
empty
munch munch
sharing
WHAT A NICE BEAR.
MAY I SEE IT?
DID YOU MAKE IT?
NOD
IS IT A GIFT FOR SOMEONE?

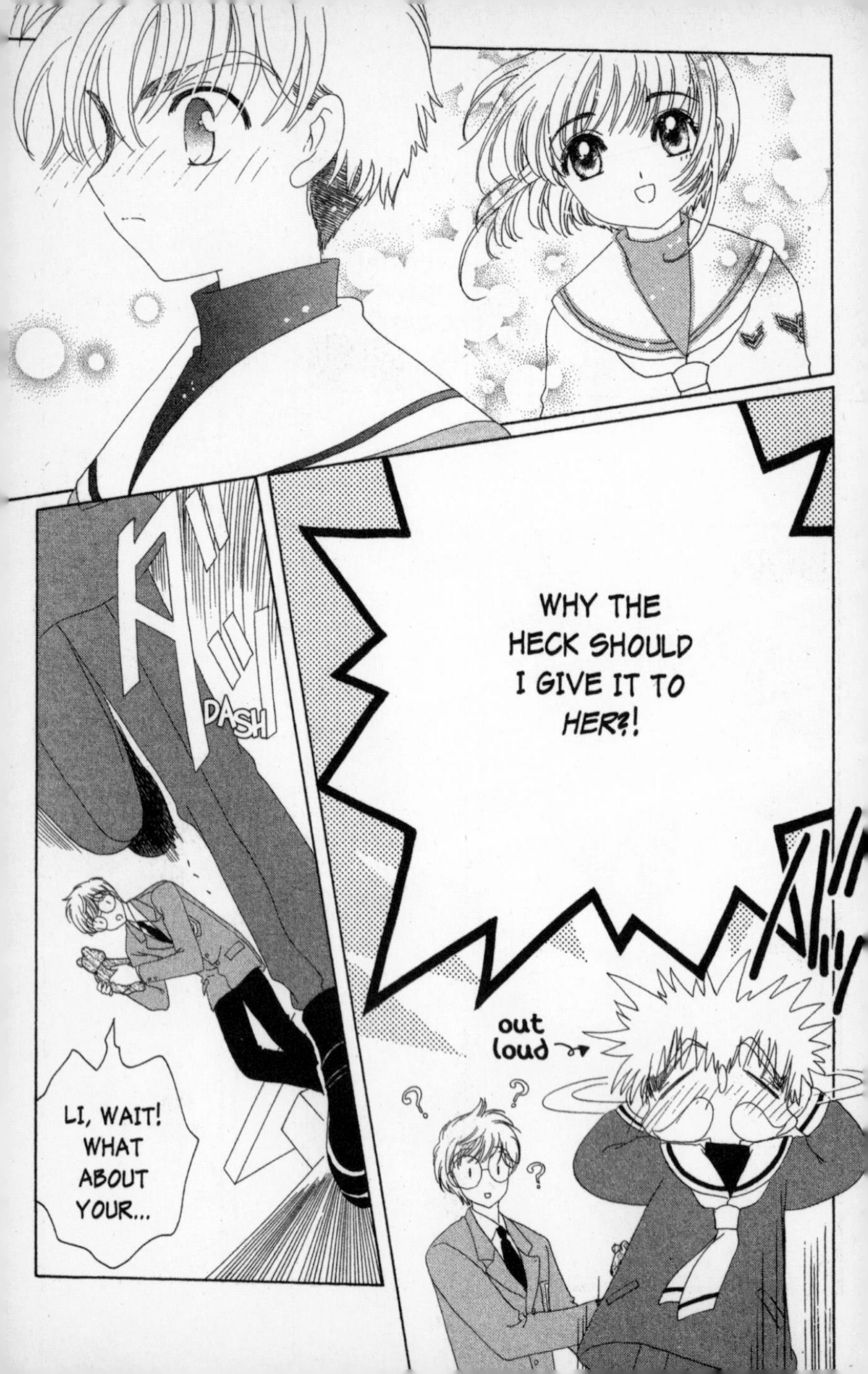
WHY THE HECK SHOULD I GIVE IT TO HER?!
out loud
DASH
LI, WAIT! WHAT ABOUT YOUR...

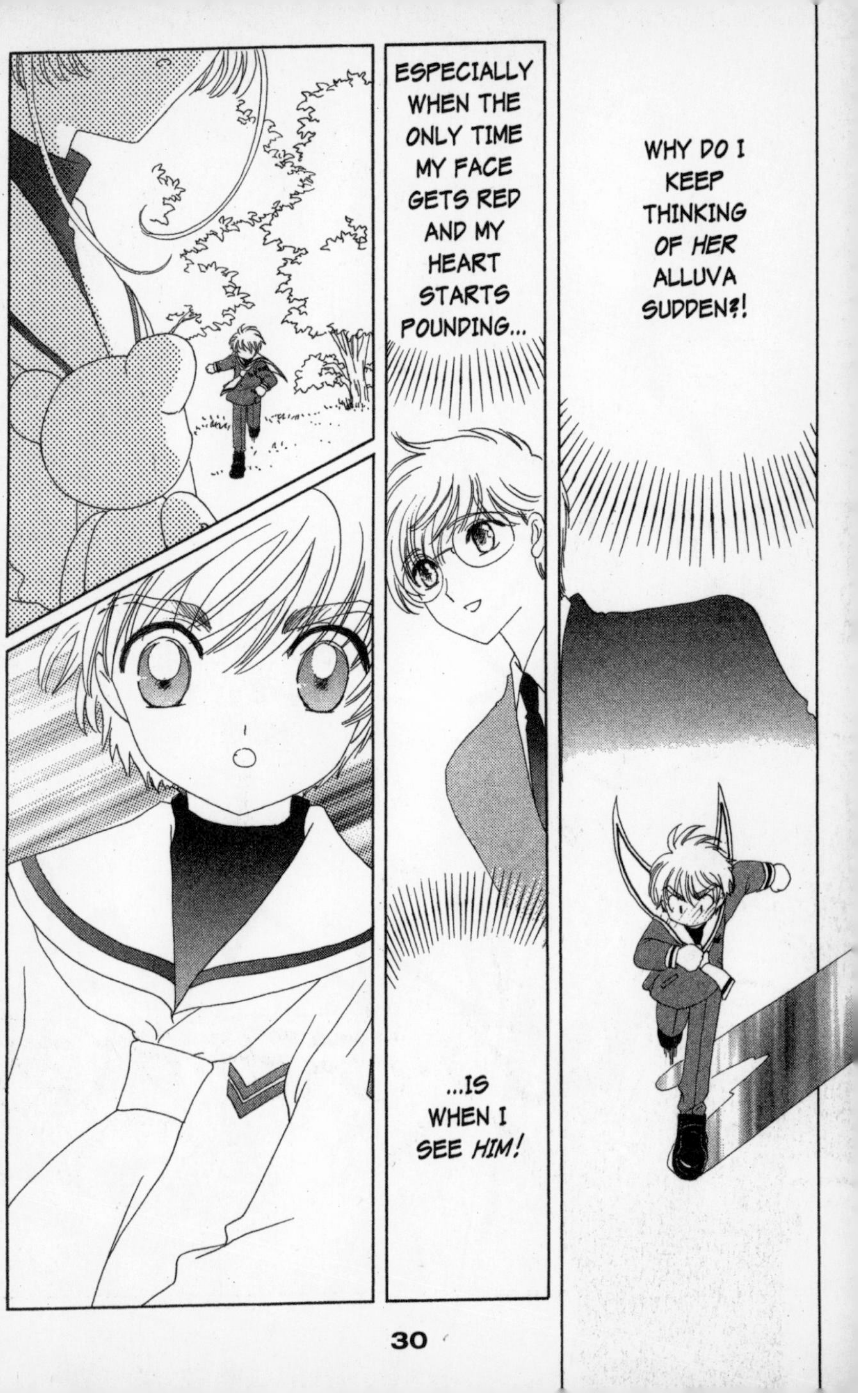
WHY DO I KEEP THINKING OF HER ALLUVA SUDDEN?!
ESPECIALLY WHEN THE ONLY TIME MY FACE GETS RED AND MY HEART STARTS POUNDING...
...IS WHEN I SEE *HIM*!

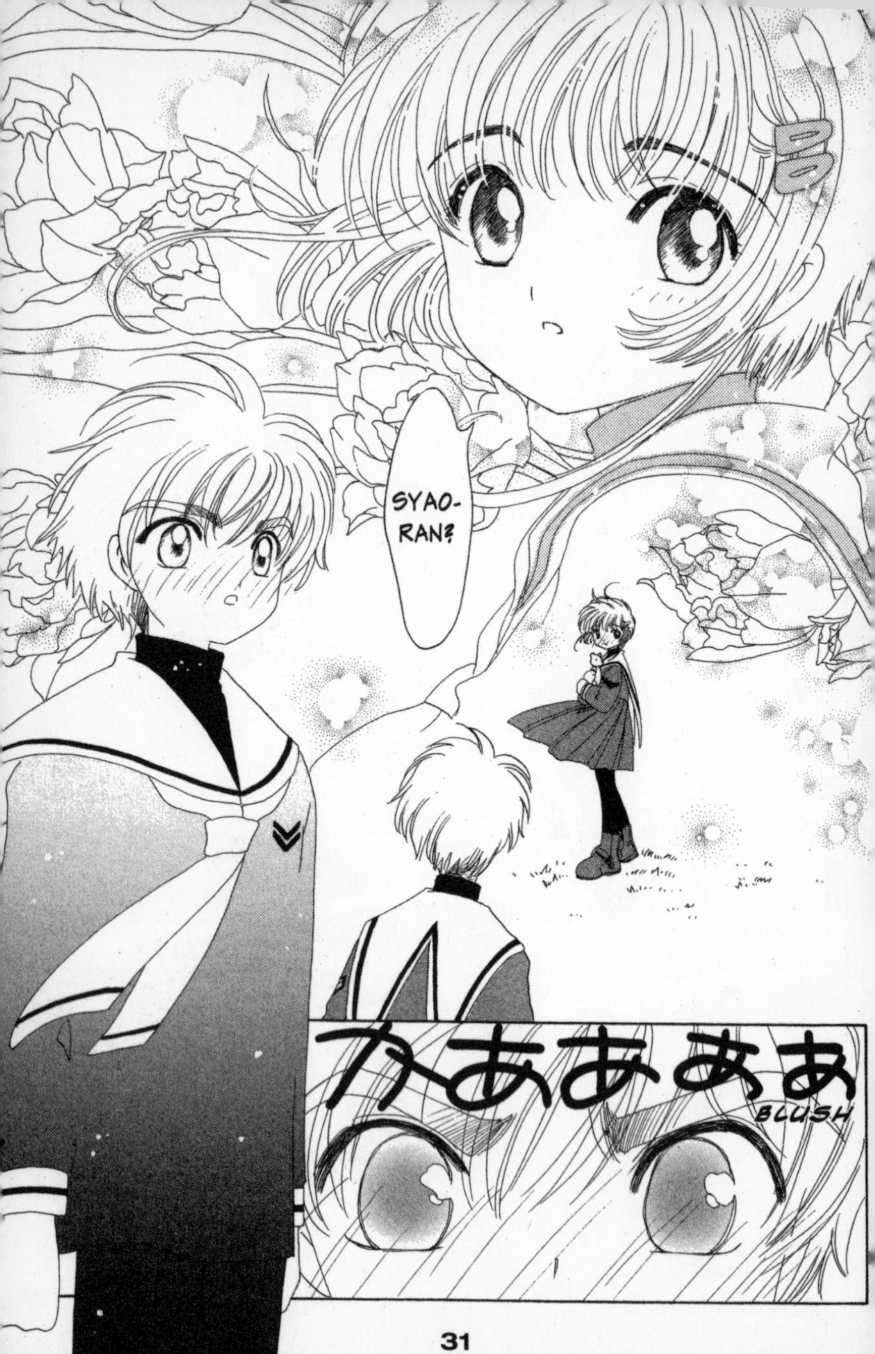
SYAO-RAN?
かあああああ
BLUSH

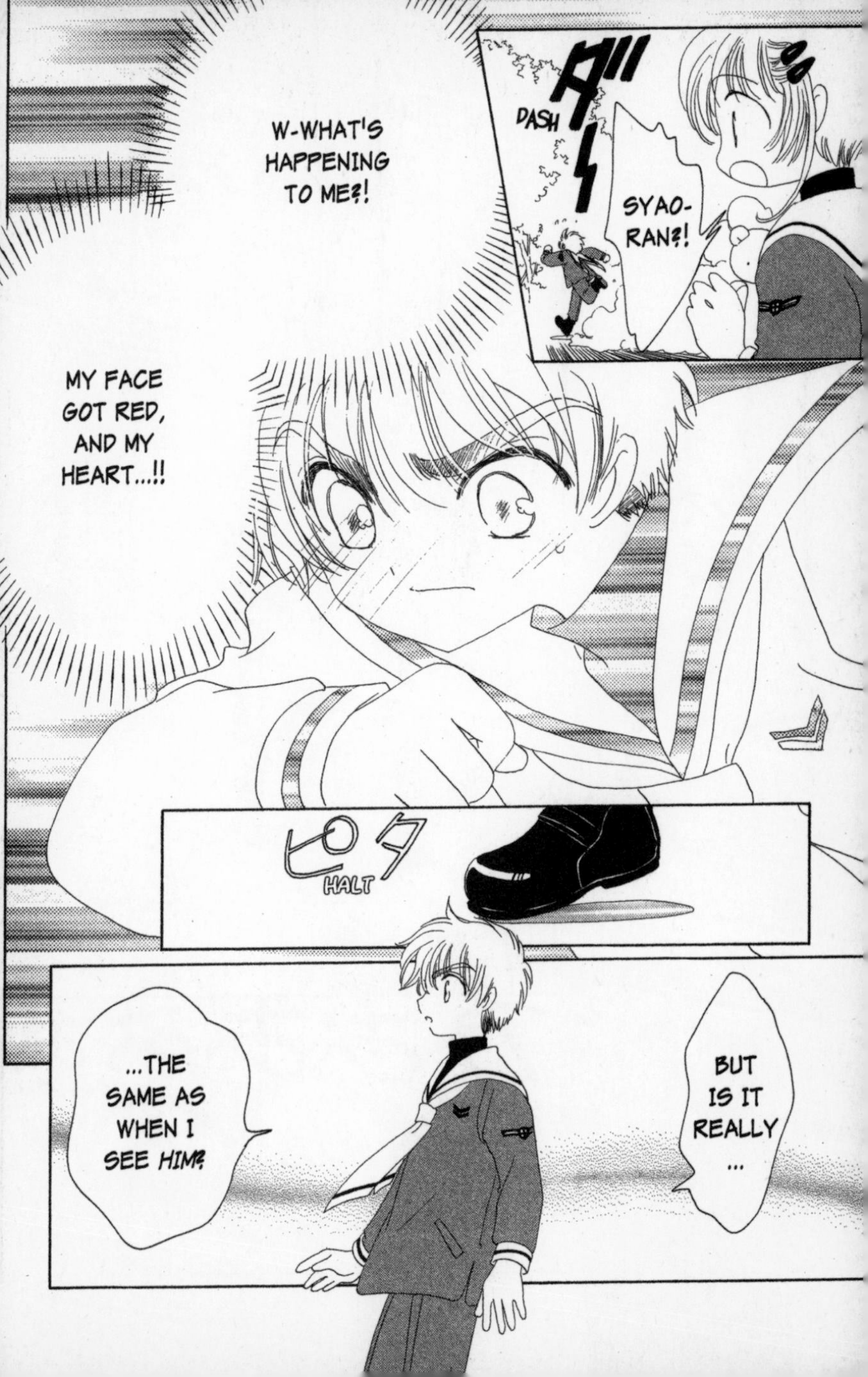
ダッ
DASH
SYAO-RAN?!
W-WHAT'S HAPPENING TO ME?!
MY FACE GOT RED, AND MY HEART...!!
ピタ
HALT
BUT IS IT REALLY ...
...THE SAME AS WHEN I SEE HIM?

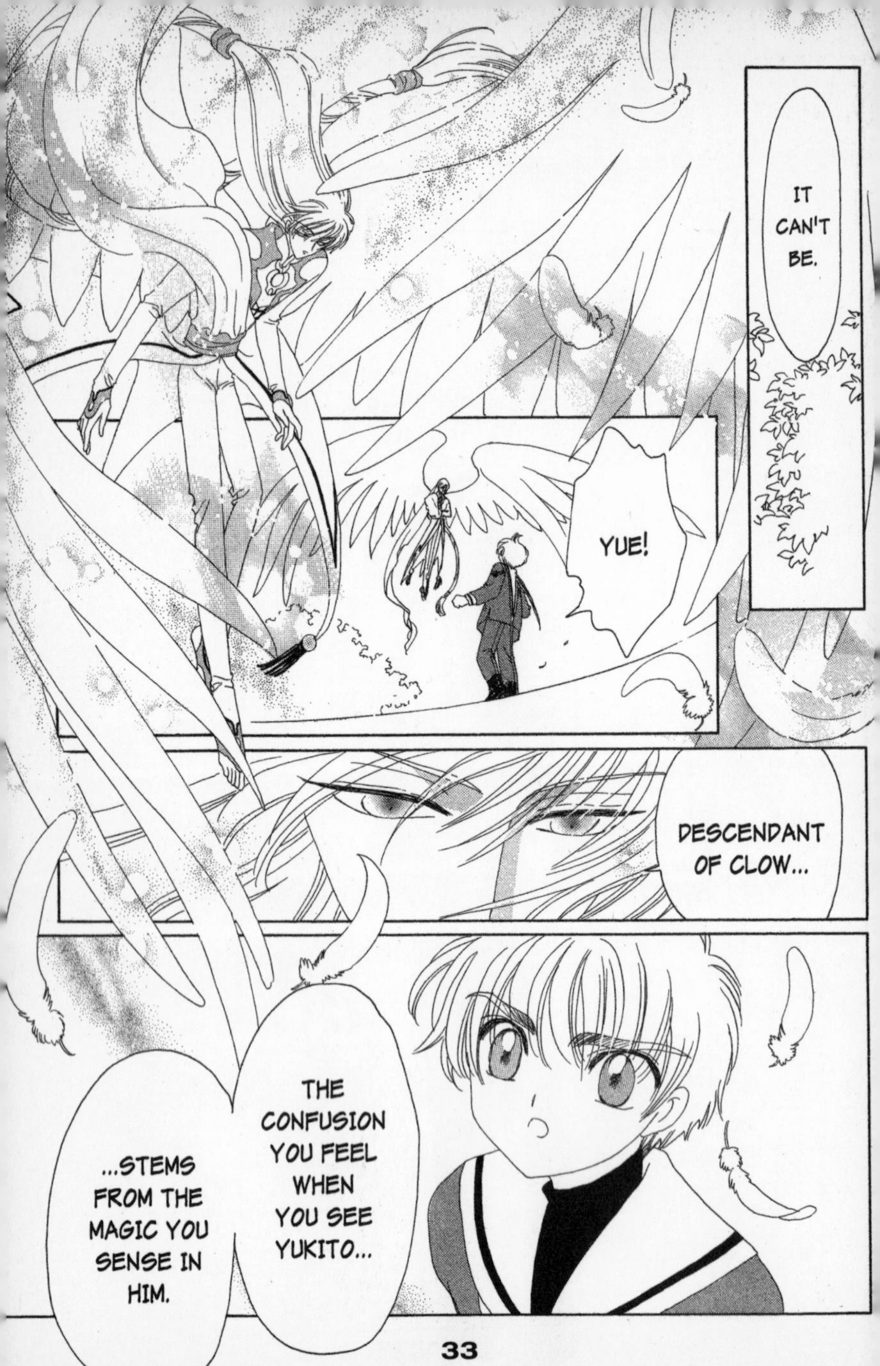
IT CAN'T BE.
YUE!
DESCENDANT OF CLOW...
THE CONFUSION YOU FEEL WHEN YOU SEE YUKITO...
...STEMS FROM THE MAGIC YOU SENSE IN HIM.

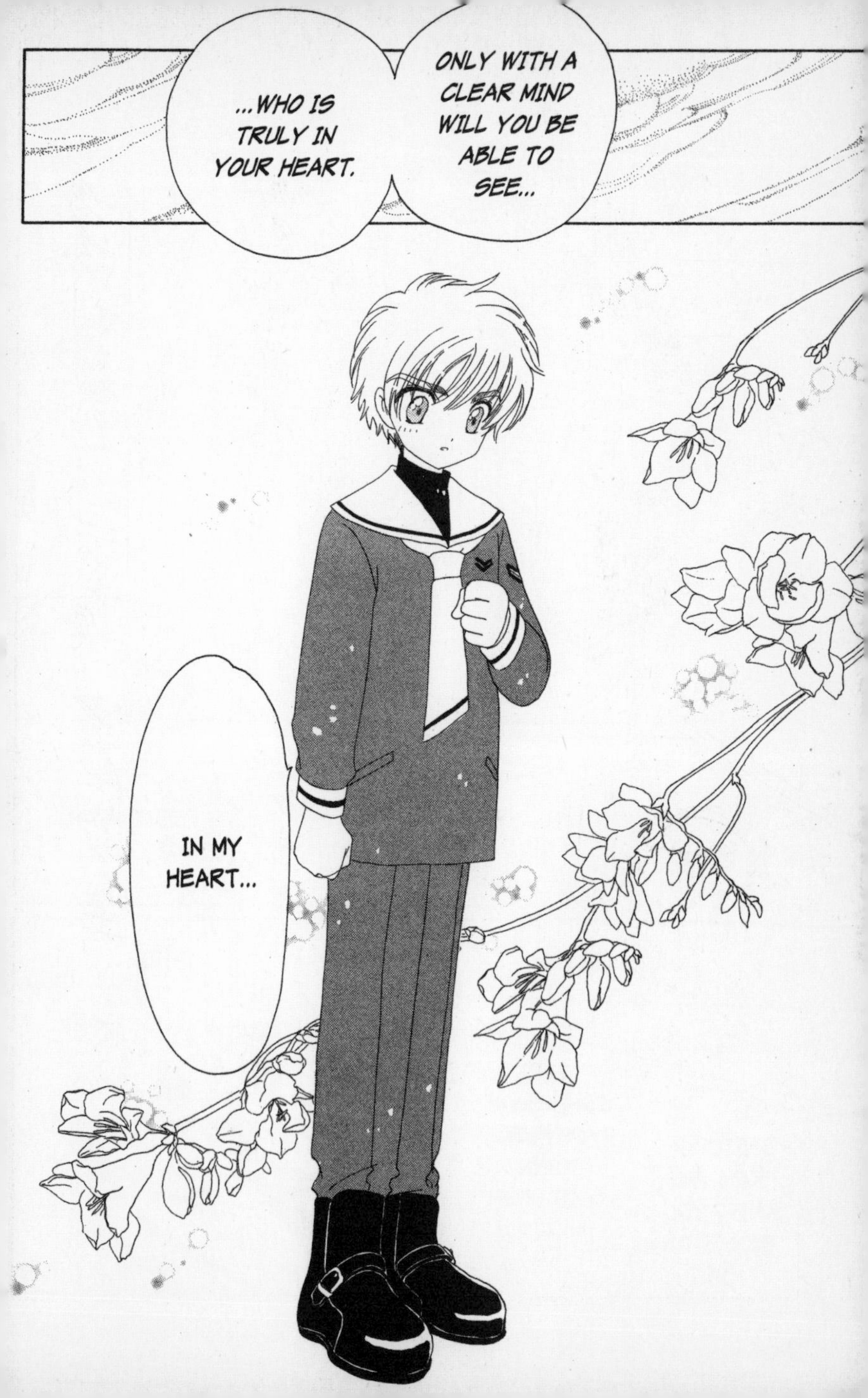
ONLY WITH A CLEAR MIND WILL YOU BE ABLE TO SEE...
...WHO IS TRULY IN YOUR HEART.
IN MY HEART...

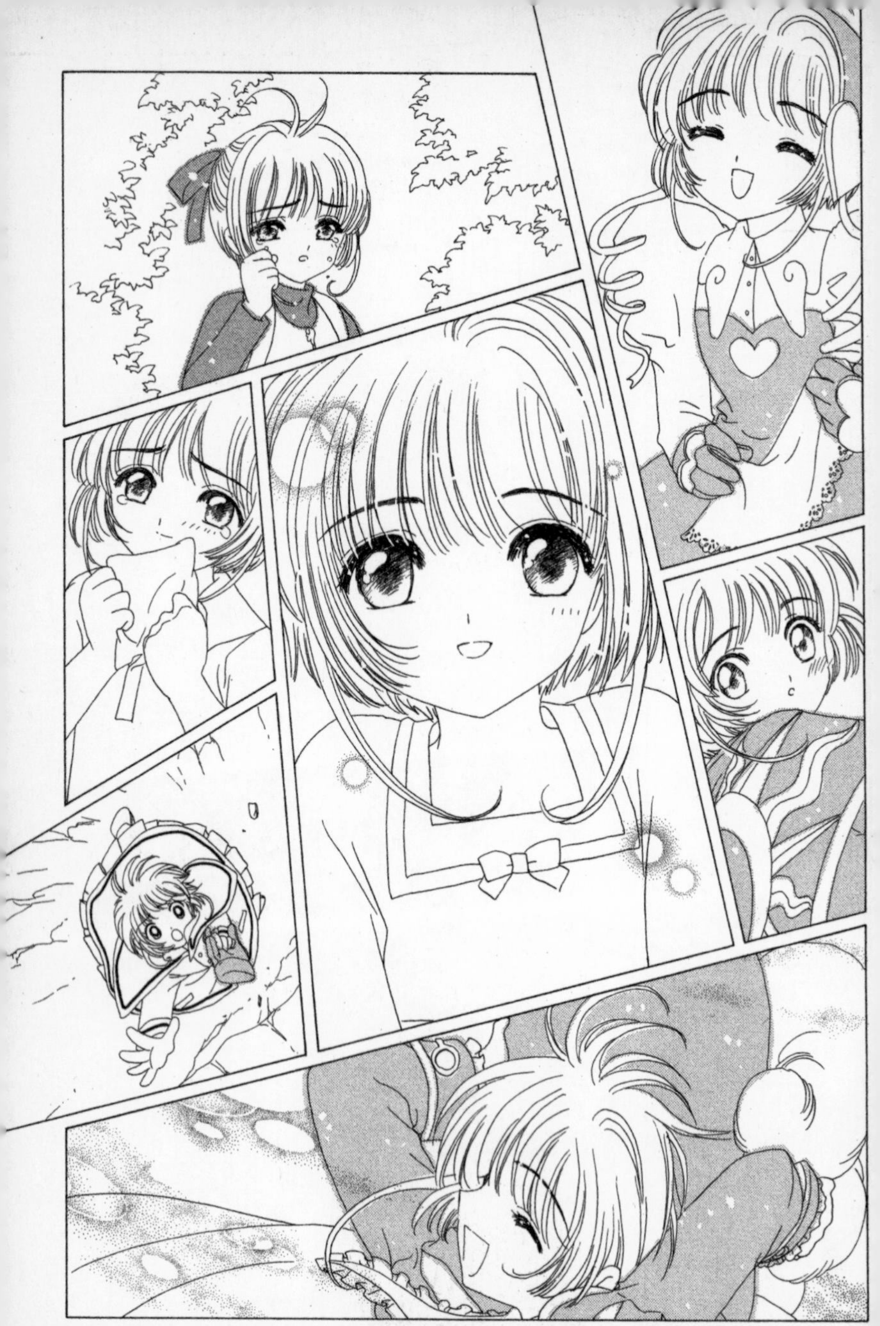

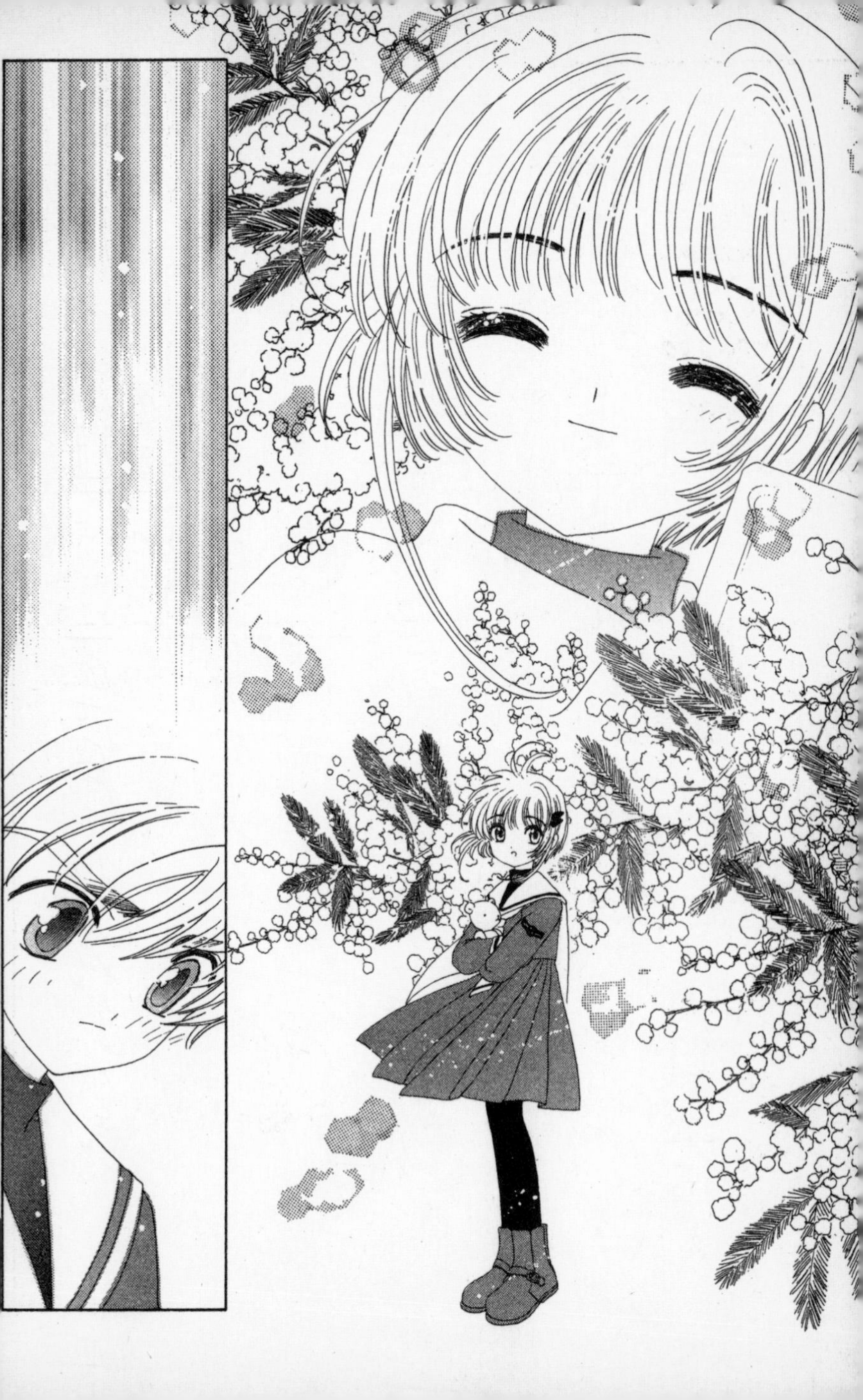

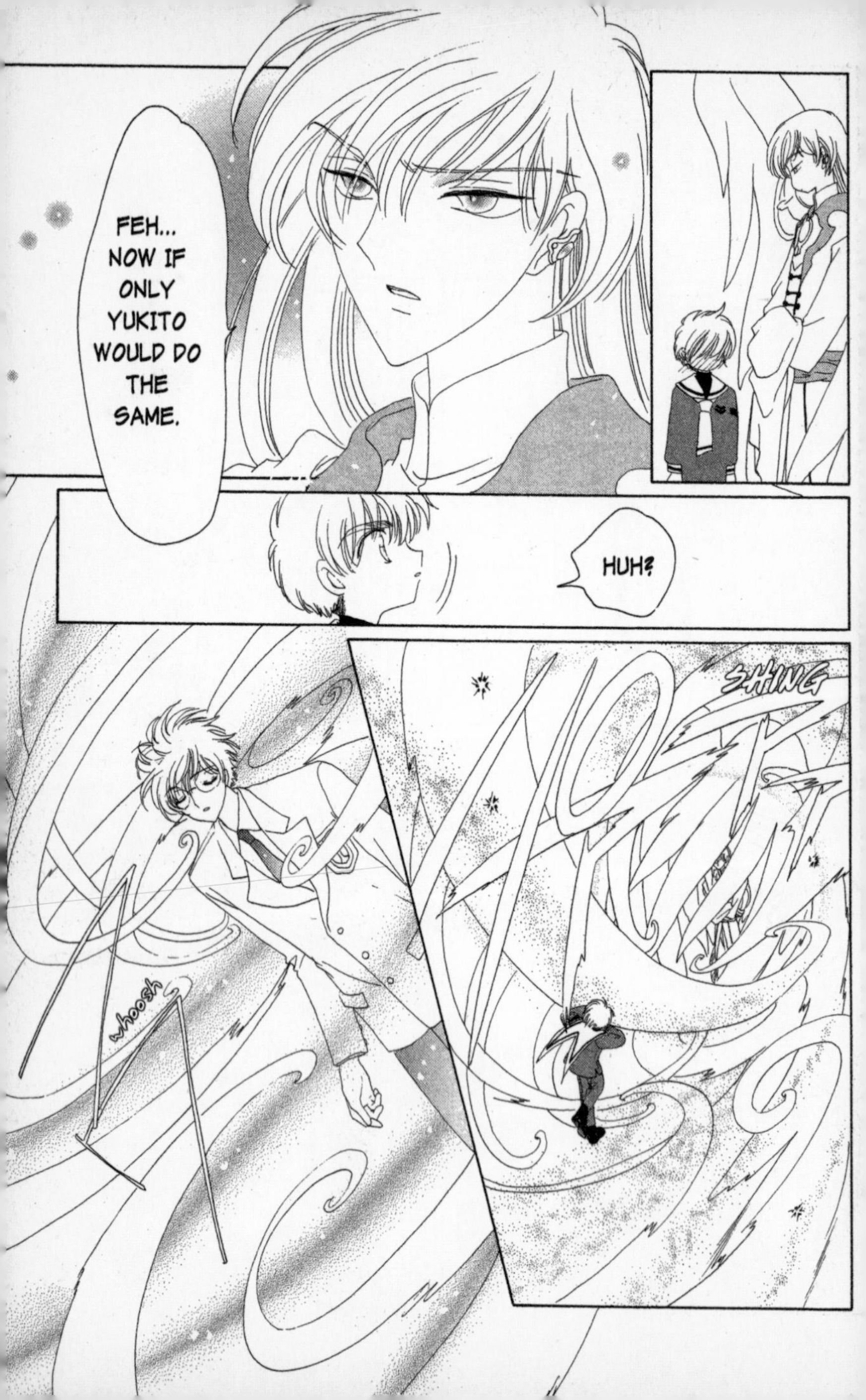
FEH... NOW IF ONLY YUKITO WOULD DO THE SAME.
HUH?
SHING
whoosh

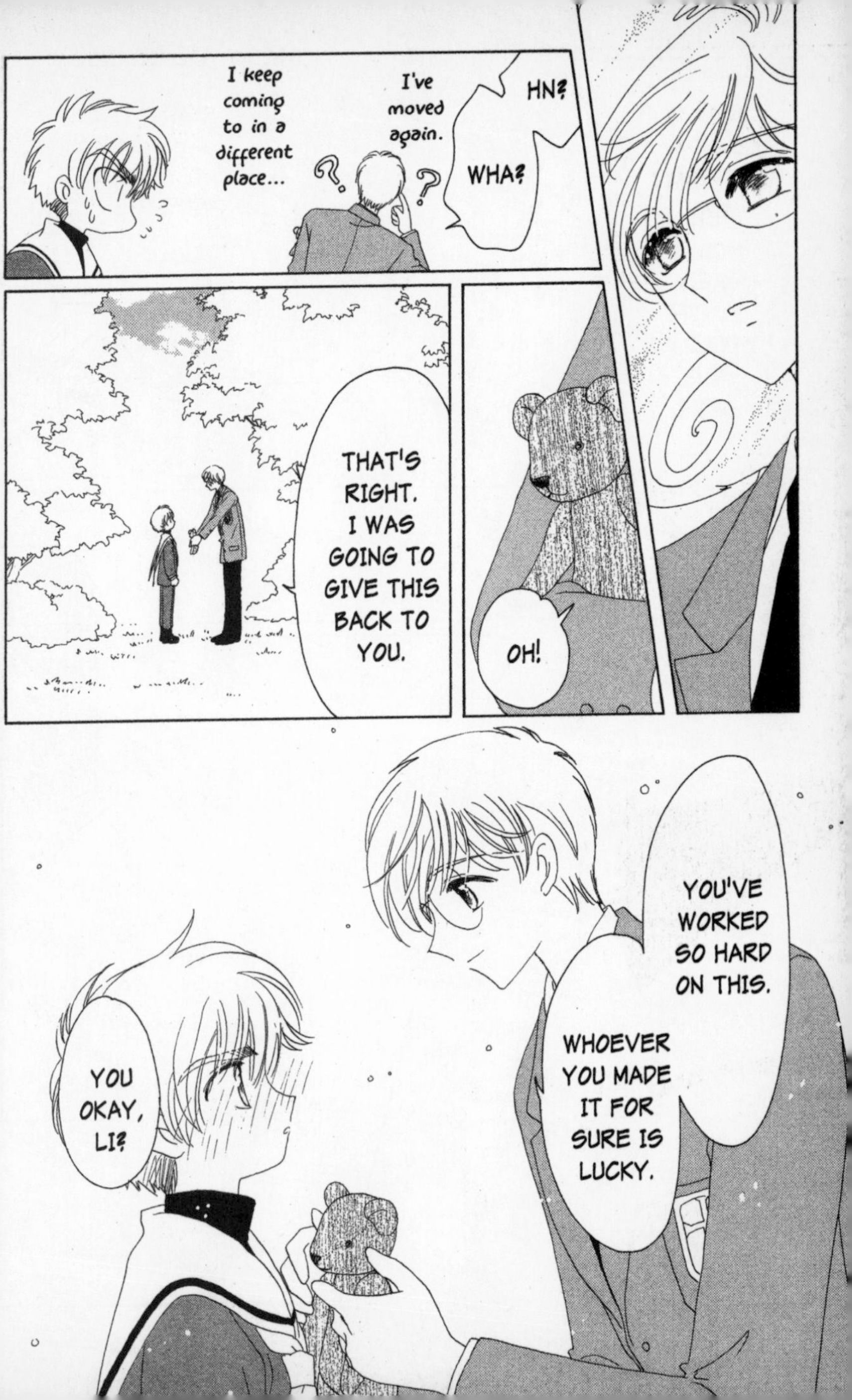
HN?
WHA?
I've moved again.
I keep coming to in a different place...
OH!
THAT'S RIGHT. I WAS GOING TO GIVE THIS BACK TO YOU.
YOU'VE WORKED SO HARD ON THIS.
WHOEVER YOU MADE IT FOR SURE IS LUCKY.
YOU OKAY, LI?

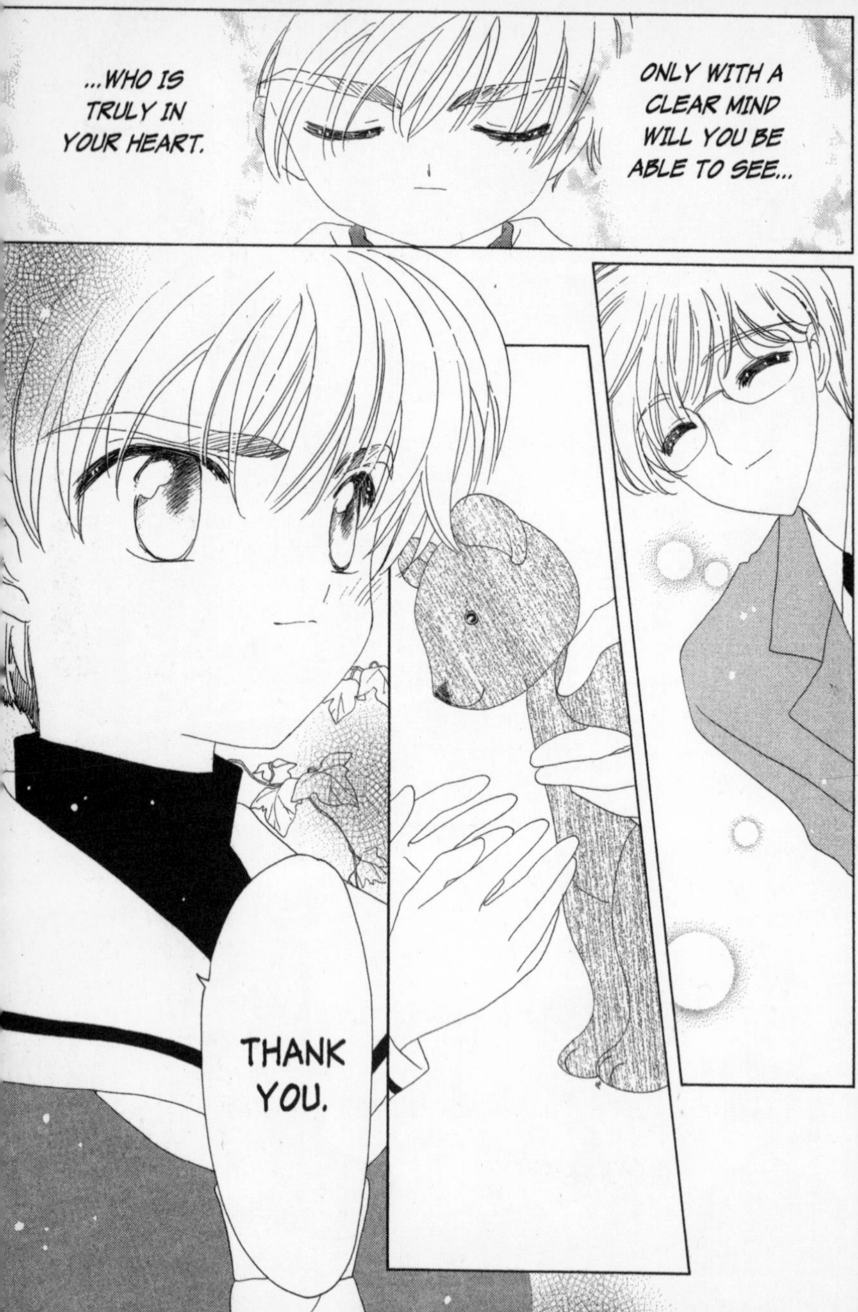
ONLY WITH A CLEAR MIND WILL YOU BE ABLE TO SEE...
...WHO IS TRULY IN YOUR HEART.
THANK YOU.

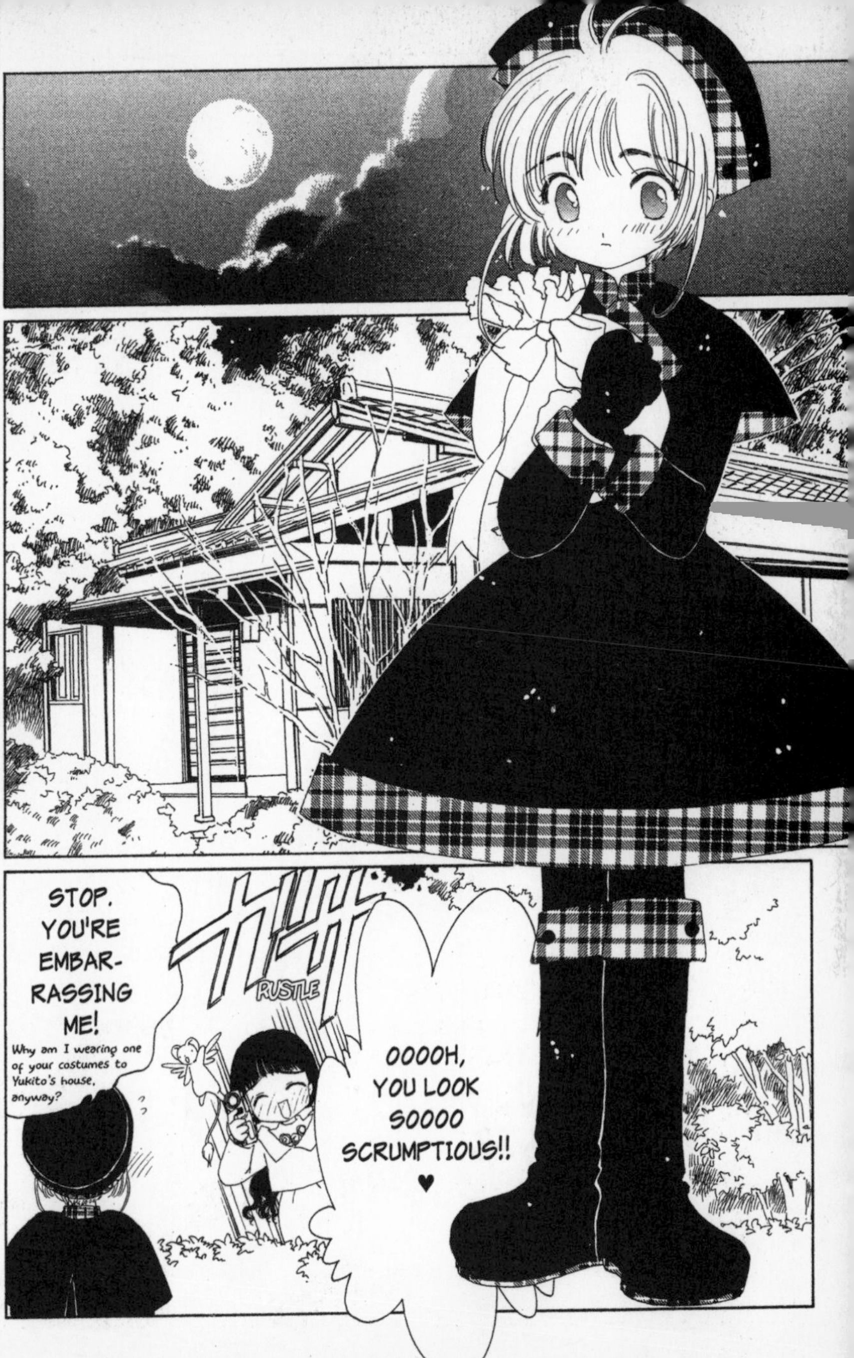

RUSTLE
OOOOH, YOU LOOK SOOOO SCRUMPTIOUS!! ♥
STOP. YOU'RE EMBAR-RASSING ME!
Why am I wearing one of your costumes to Yukito's house, anyway?

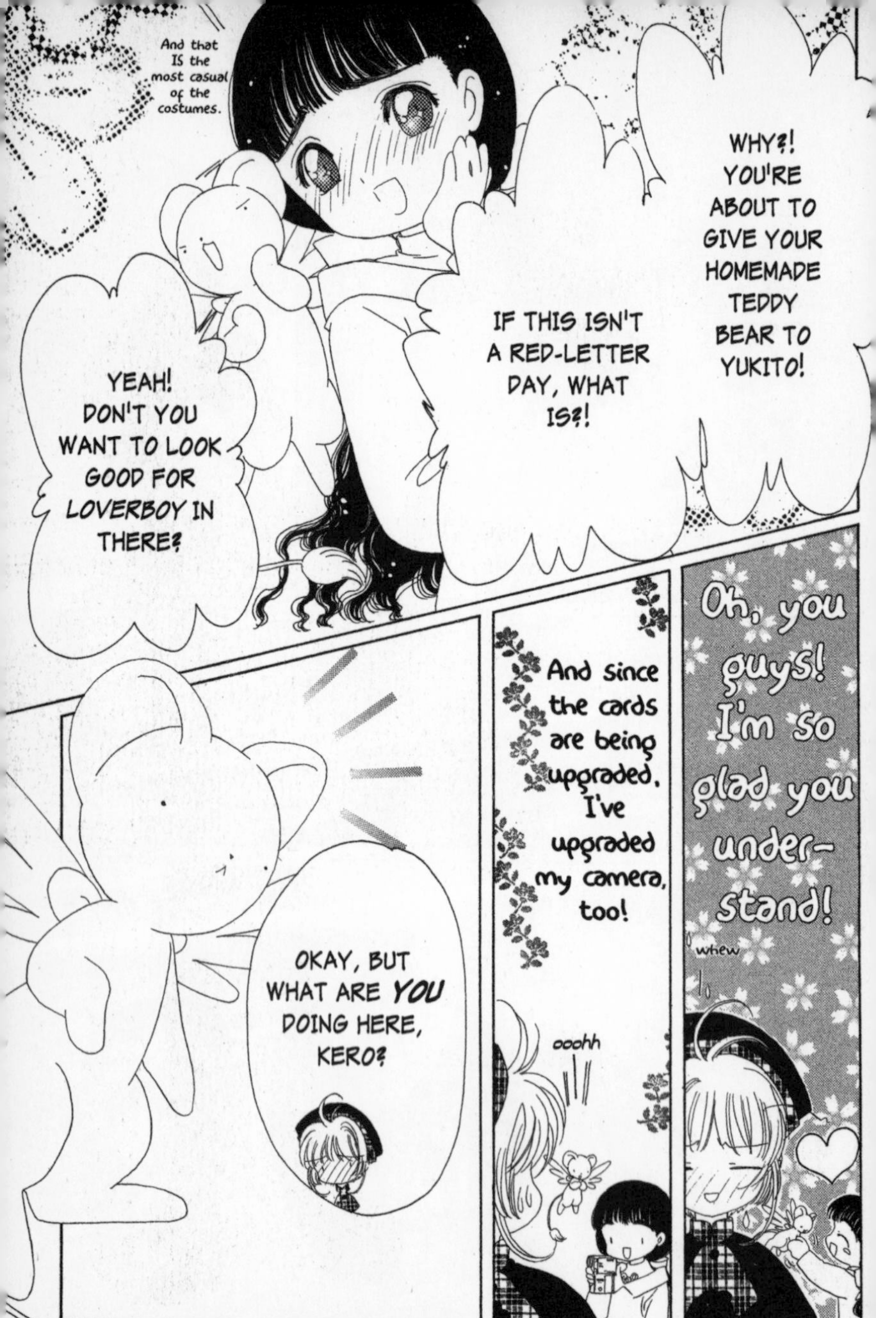

WHY?! YOU'RE ABOUT TO GIVE YOUR HOMEMADE TEDDY BEAR TO YUKITO!
IF THIS ISN'T A RED-LETTER DAY, WHAT IS?!
And that IS the most casual of the costumes.
YEAH! DON'T YOU WANT TO LOOK GOOD FOR LOVERBOY IN THERE?
Oh, you guys! I'm so glad you under-stand!
whew
And since the cards are being upgraded, I've upgraded my camera, too!
ooohh
OKAY, BUT WHAT ARE *YOU* DOING HERE, KERO?

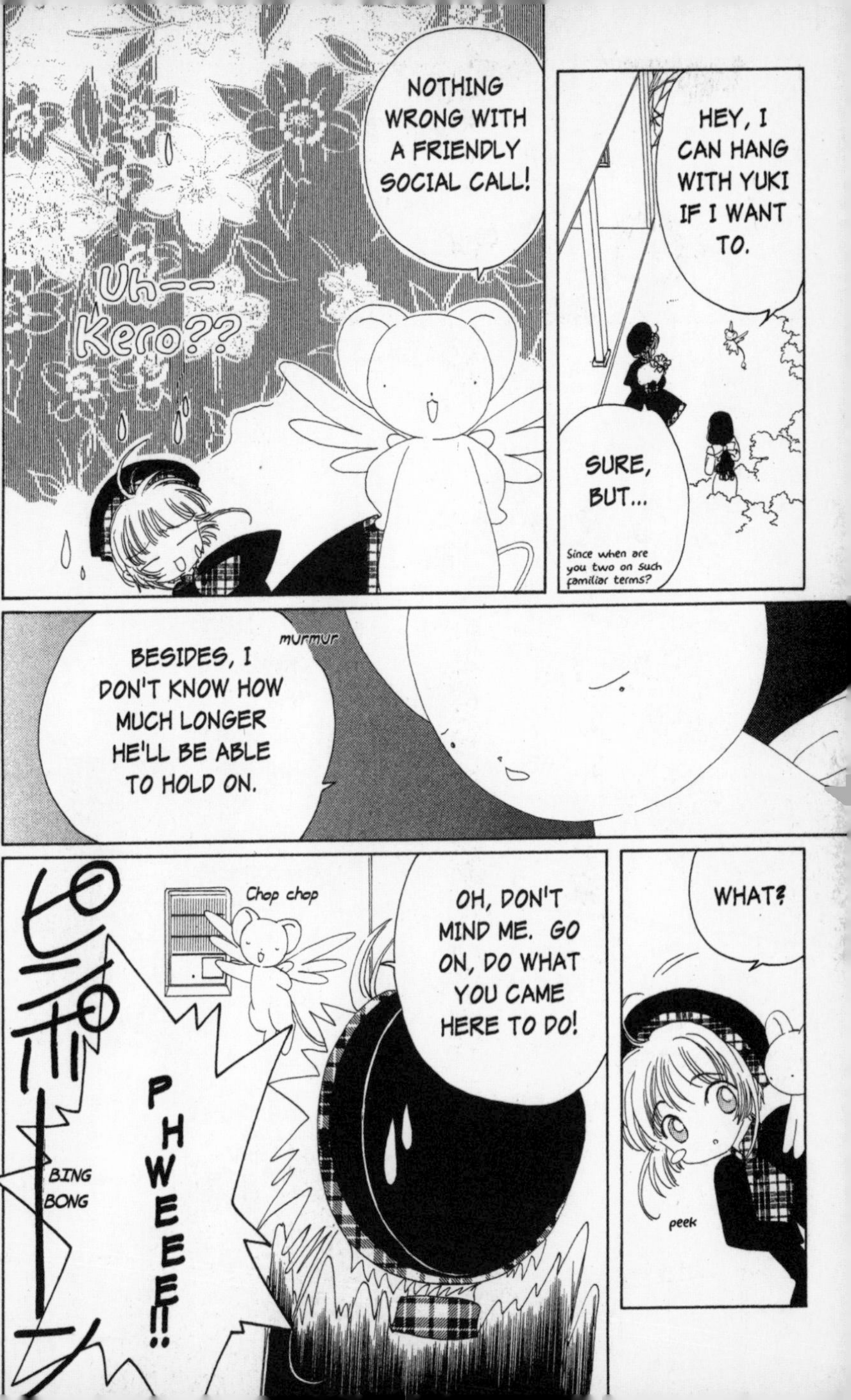
HEY, I CAN HANG WITH YUKI IF I WANT TO.
SURE, BUT...
Since when are you two on such familiar terms?
NOTHING WRONG WITH A FRIENDLY SOCIAL CALL!
Uh-- Kero??
murmur
BESIDES, I DON'T KNOW HOW MUCH LONGER HE'LL BE ABLE TO HOLD ON.
WHAT?
peek
OH, DON'T MIND ME. GO ON, DO WHAT YOU CAME HERE TO DO!
Chop chop
PHWEEE!!
BING BONG

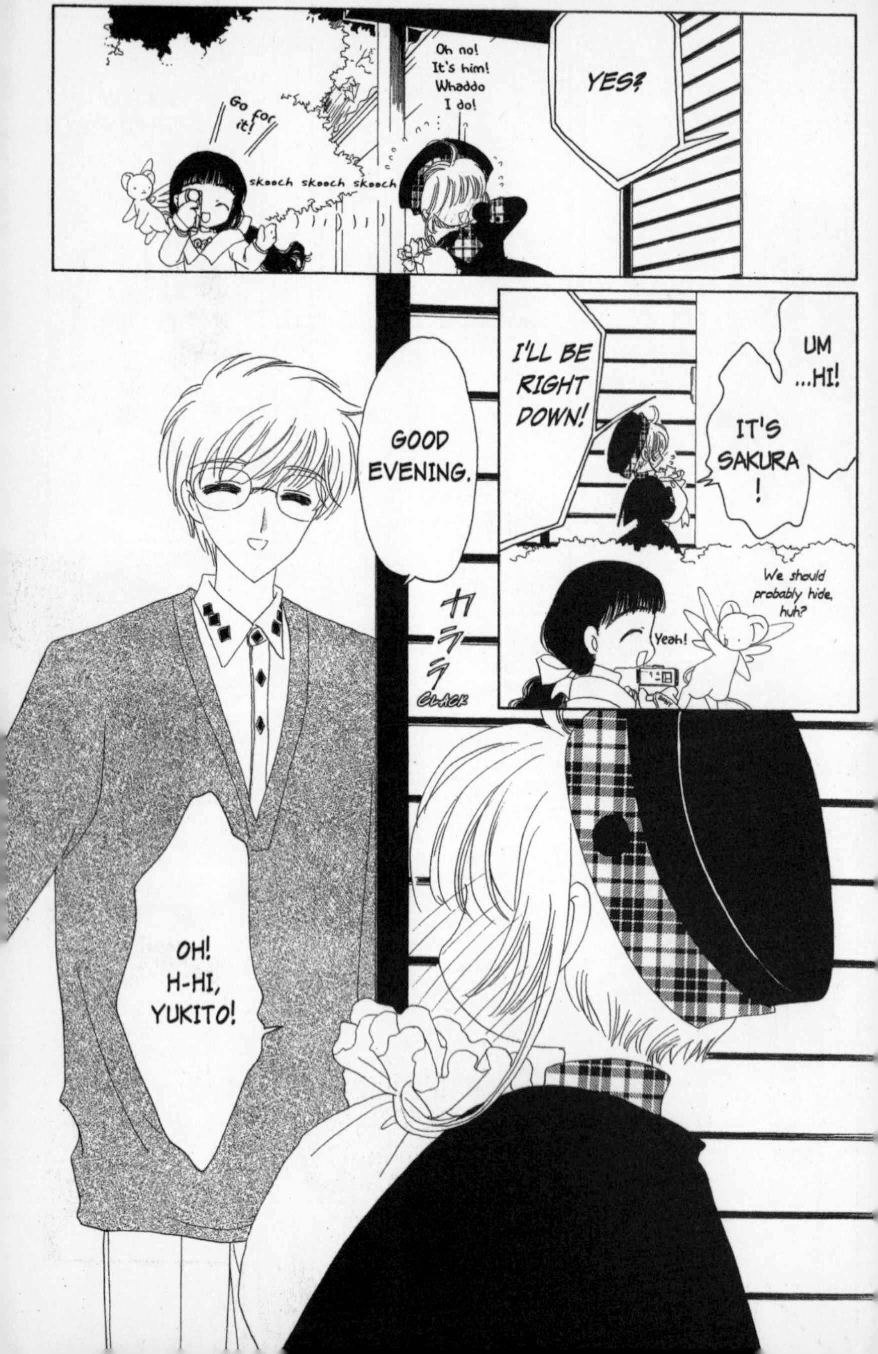
YES?
Oh no! It's him! Whaddo I do!
Go for it!
skooch skooch skooch
UM ...HI!
IT'S SAKURA!
I'LL BE RIGHT DOWN!
We should probably hide, huh?
Yeah!
カララ
CLACK
GOOD EVENING.
OH! H-HI, YUKITO!

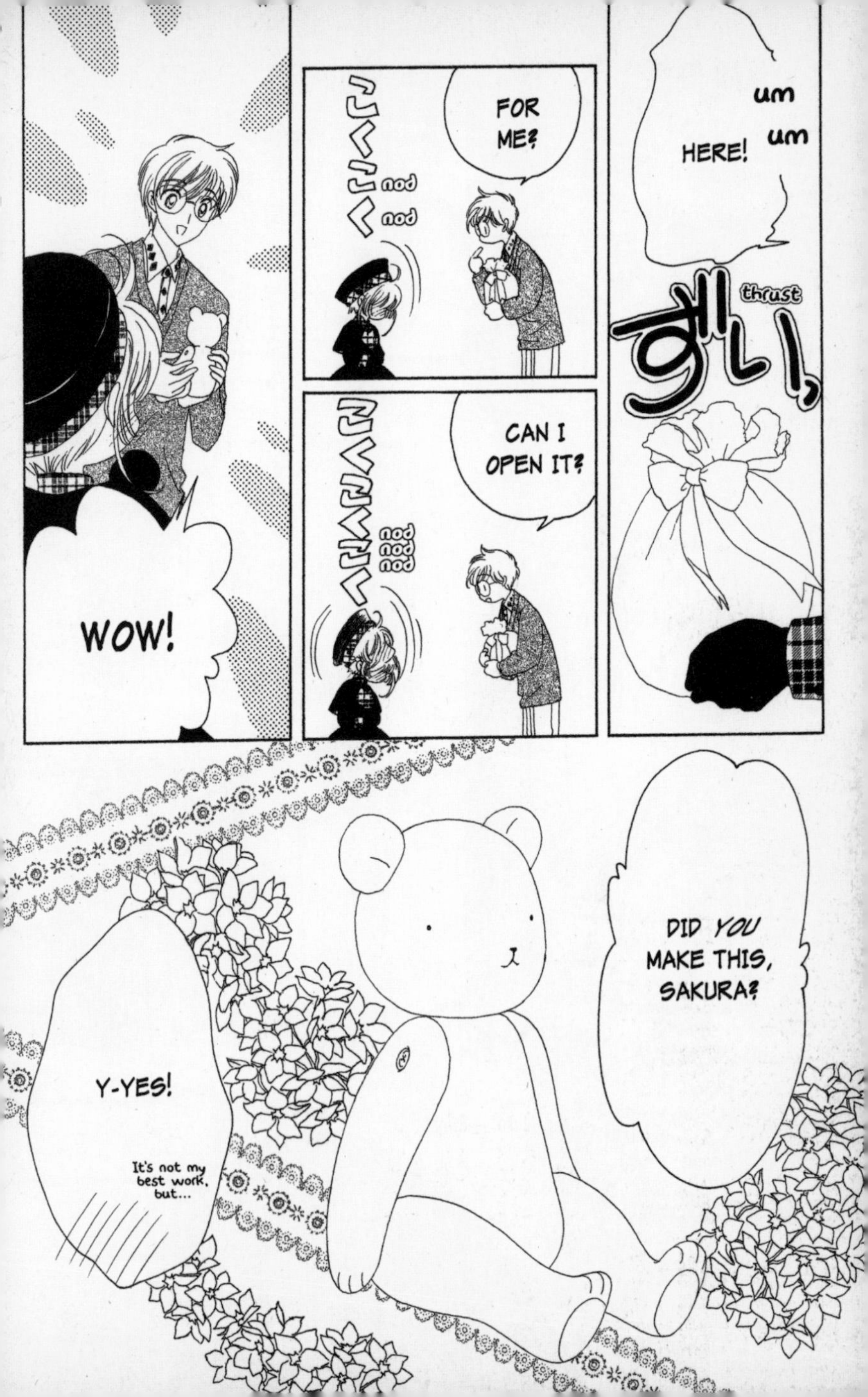
um um
HERE!
すい
thrust
FOR ME?
こくこく
nod nod
CAN I OPEN IT?
こくこくこく
nod nod nod
WOW!
DID YOU MAKE THIS, SAKURA?
Y-YES!
It's not my best work, but...

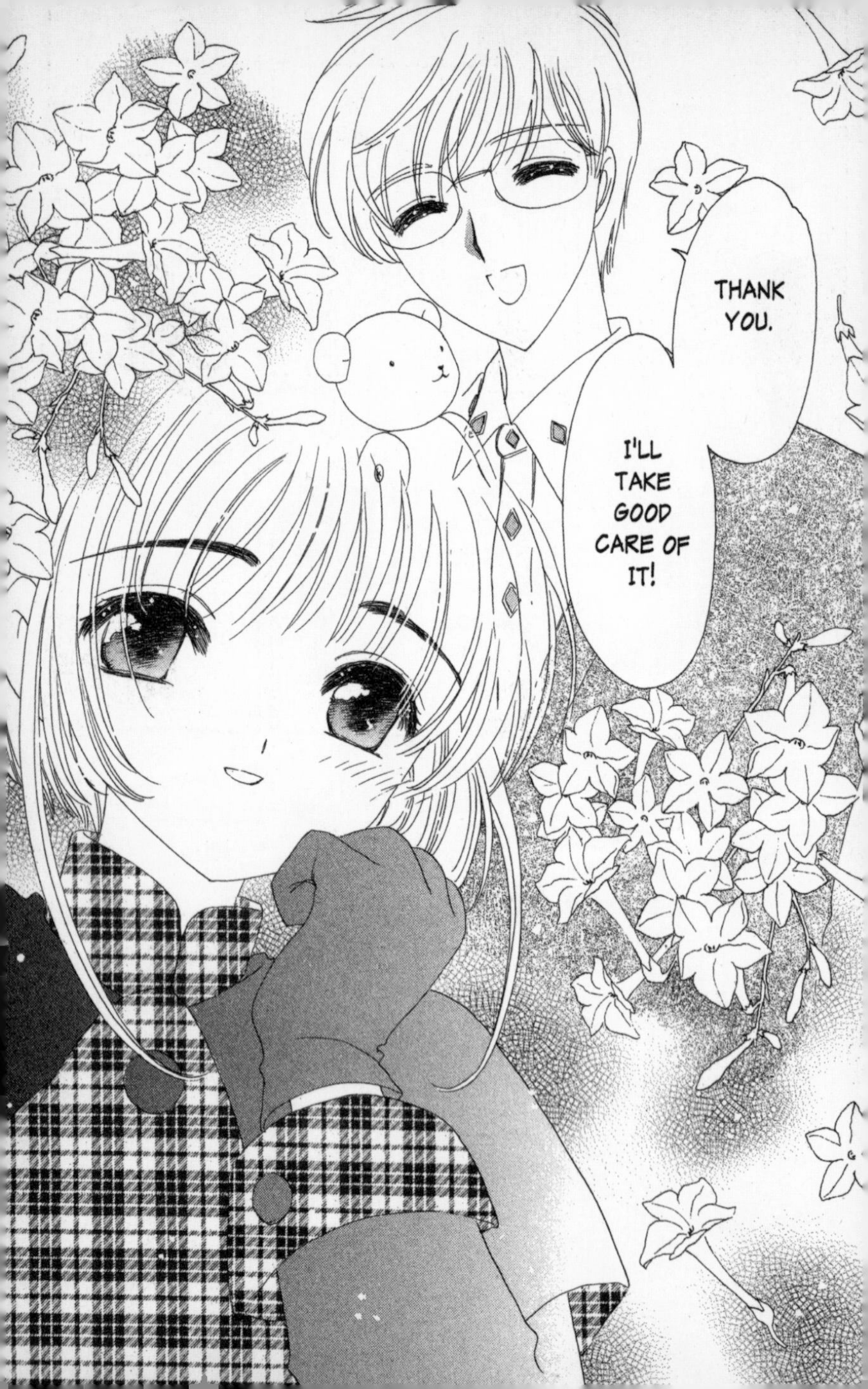
THANK YOU.
I'LL TAKE GOOD CARE OF IT!

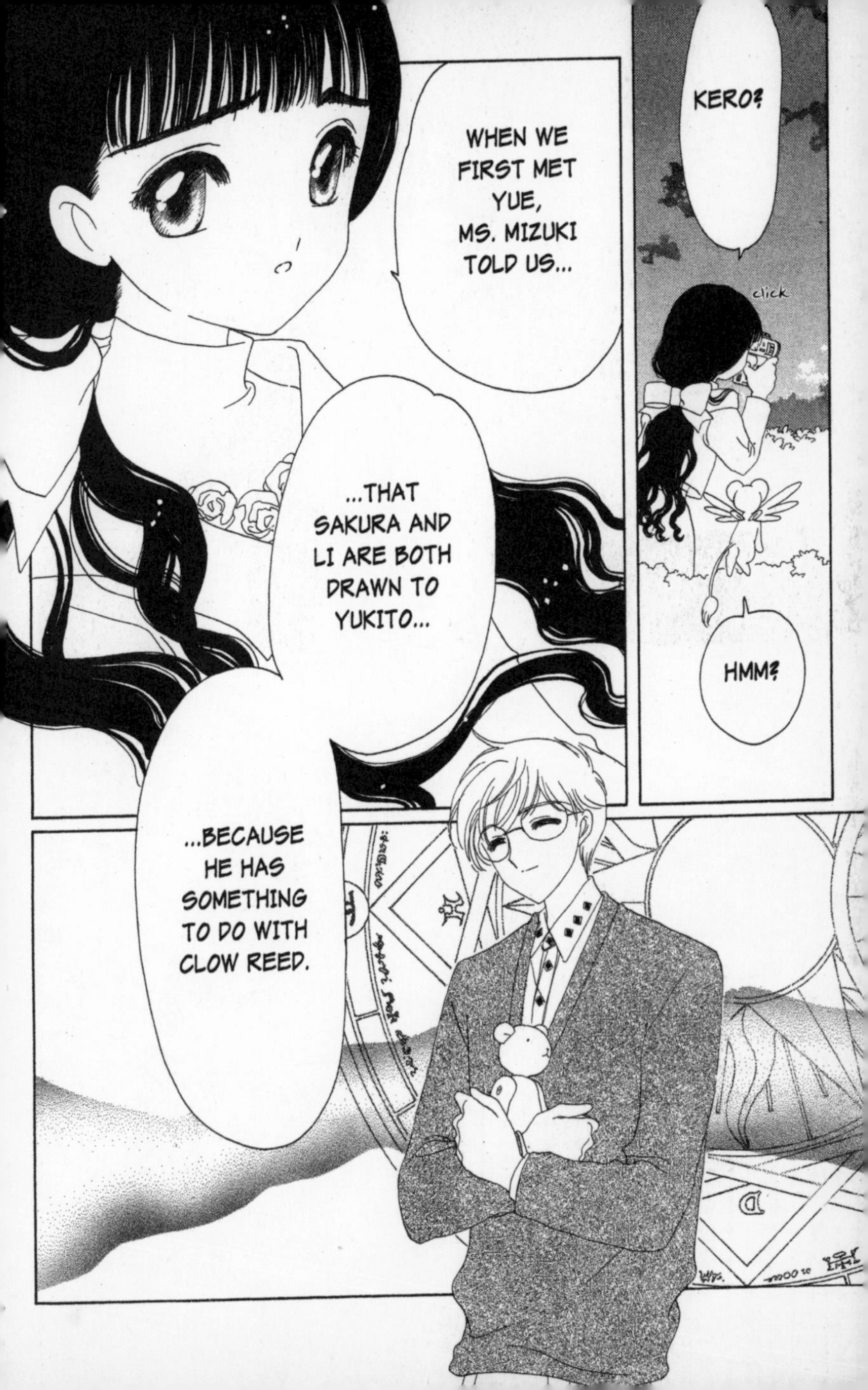
KERO?
click
HMM?
WHEN WE FIRST MET YUE, MS. MIZUKI TOLD US...
...THAT SAKURA AND LI ARE BOTH DRAWN TO YUKITO...
...BECAUSE HE HAS SOMETHING TO DO WITH CLOW REED.

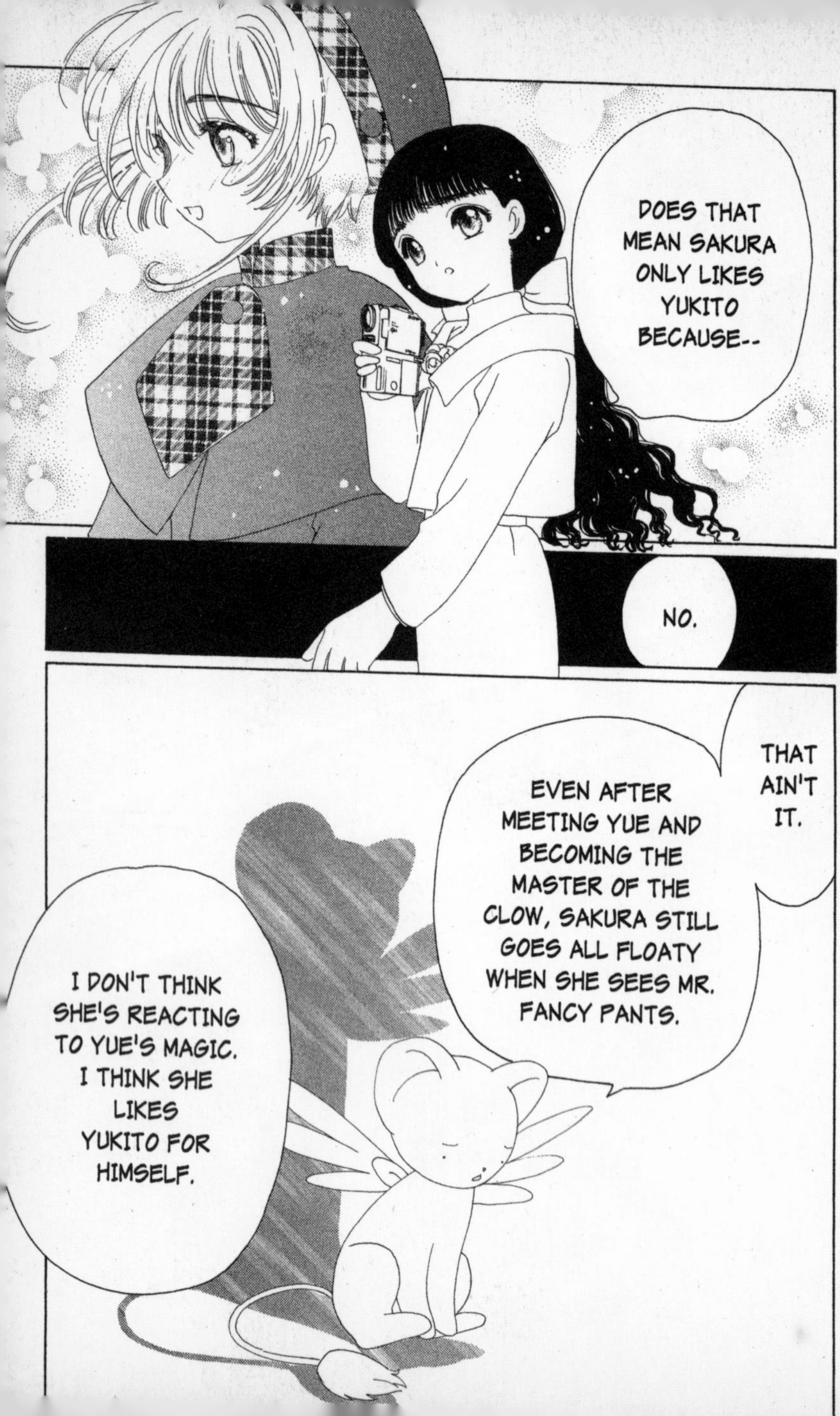
DOES THAT MEAN SAKURA ONLY LIKES YUKITO BECAUSE--
NO.
THAT AIN'T IT.
EVEN AFTER MEETING YUE AND BECOMING THE MASTER OF THE CLOW, SAKURA STILL GOES ALL FLOATY WHEN SHE SEES MR. FANCY PANTS.
I DON'T THINK SHE'S REACTING TO YUE'S MAGIC. I THINK SHE LIKES YUKITO FOR HIMSELF.

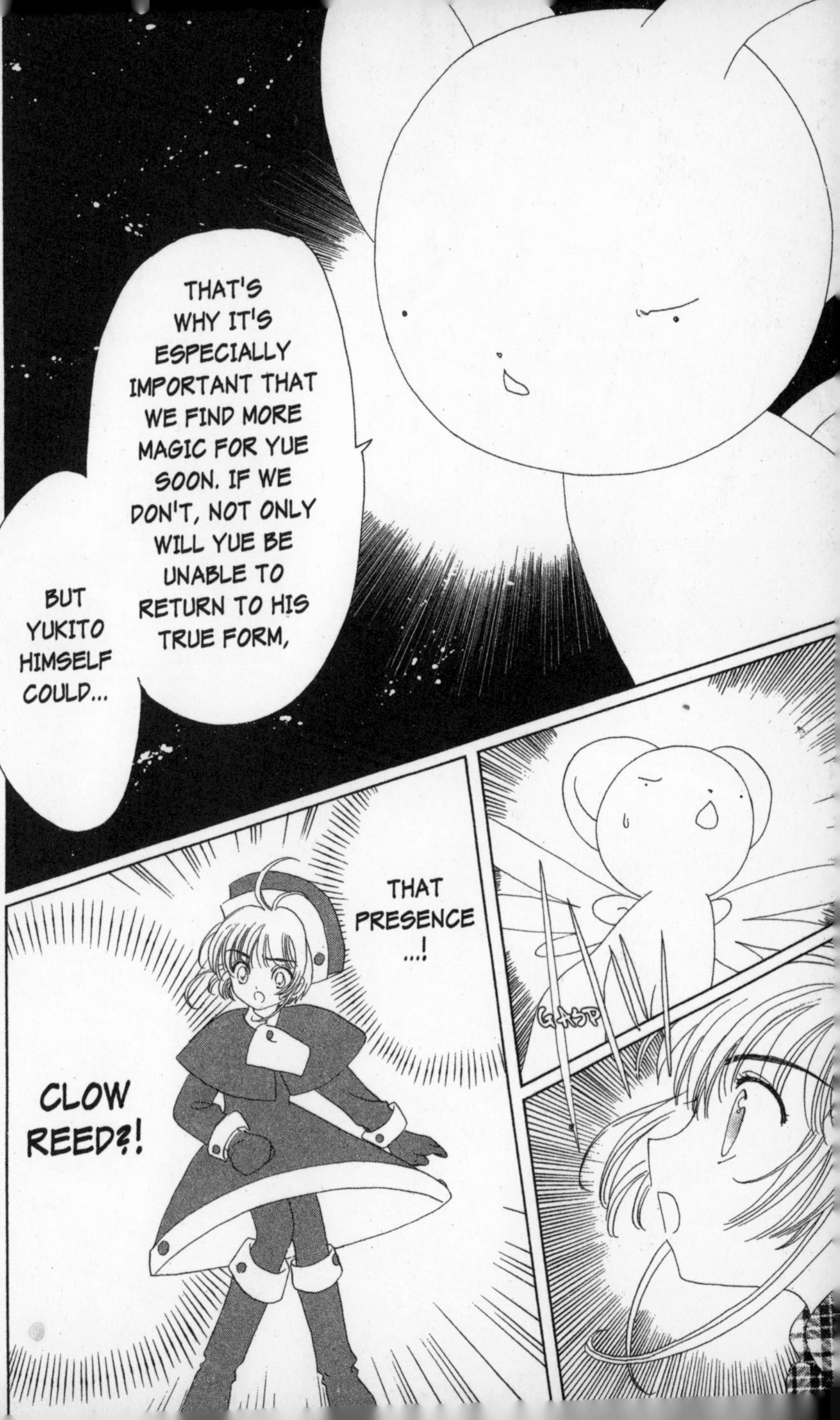
THAT'S WHY IT'S ESPECIALLY IMPORTANT THAT WE FIND MORE MAGIC FOR YUE SOON. IF WE DON'T, NOT ONLY WILL YUE BE UNABLE TO RETURN TO HIS TRUE FORM,
BUT YUKITO HIMSELF COULD...
GASP
THAT PRESENCE ...!
CLOW REED?!

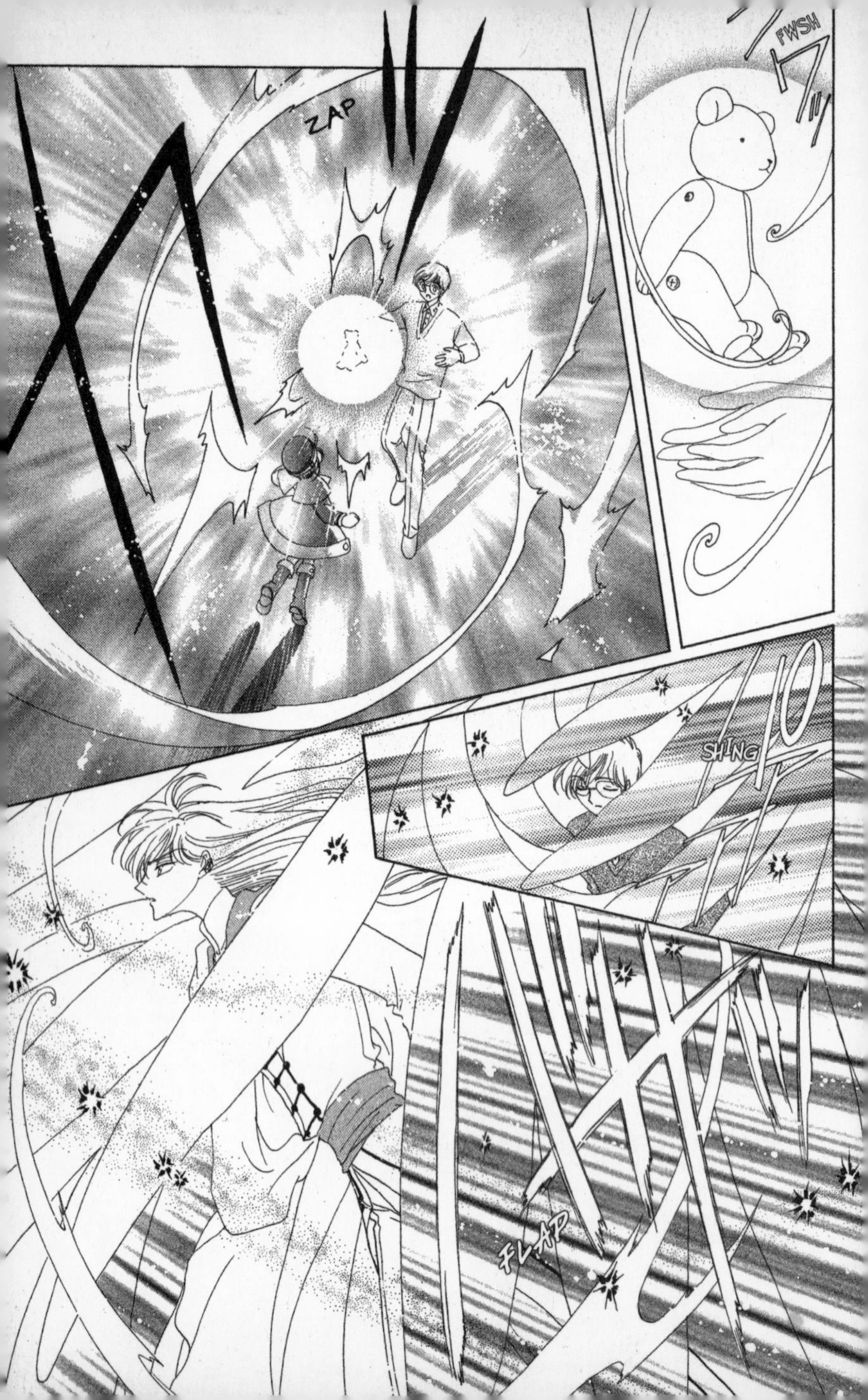
FWSH
ZAP
SHING
FLAP

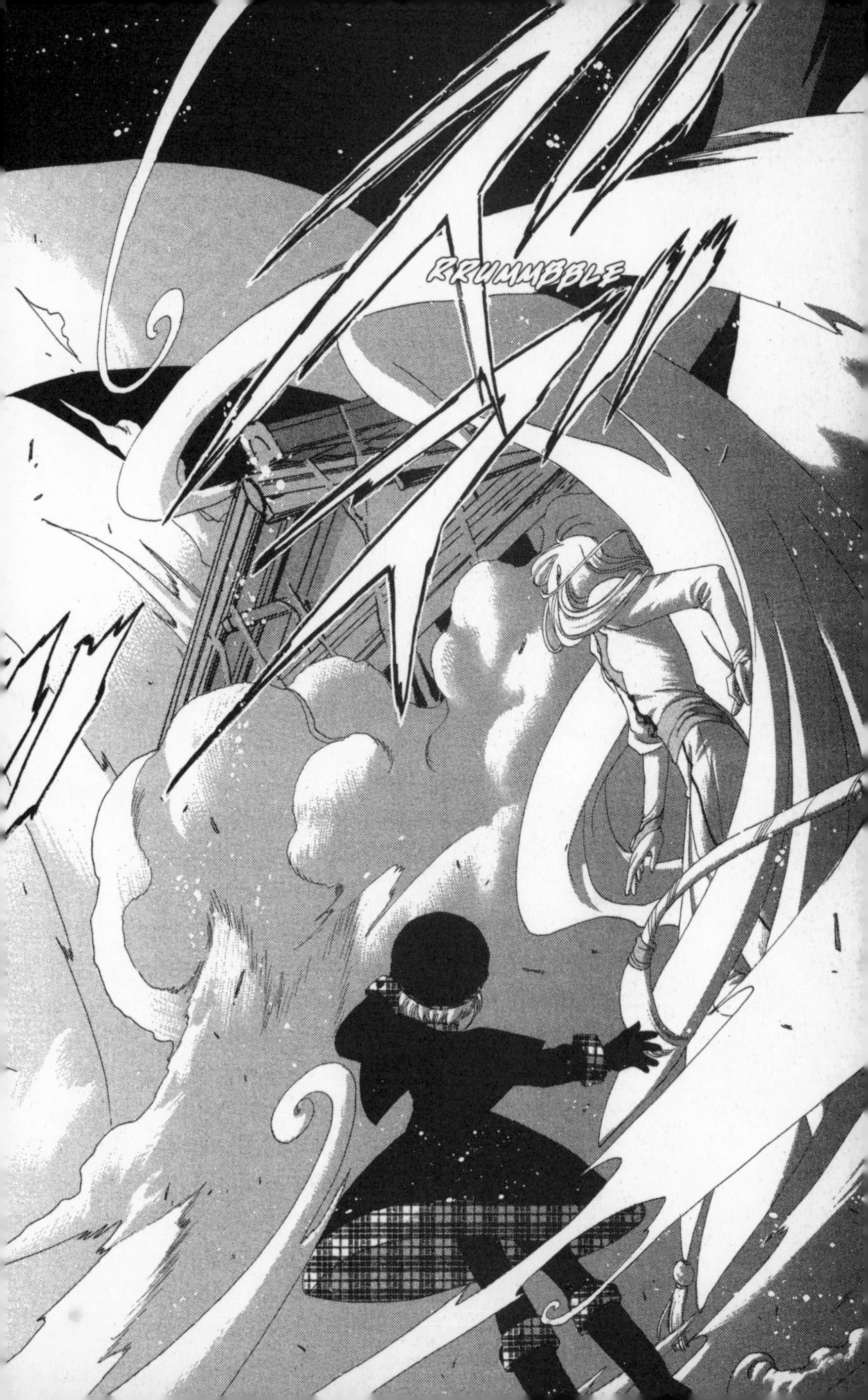
RRUMMBBLE

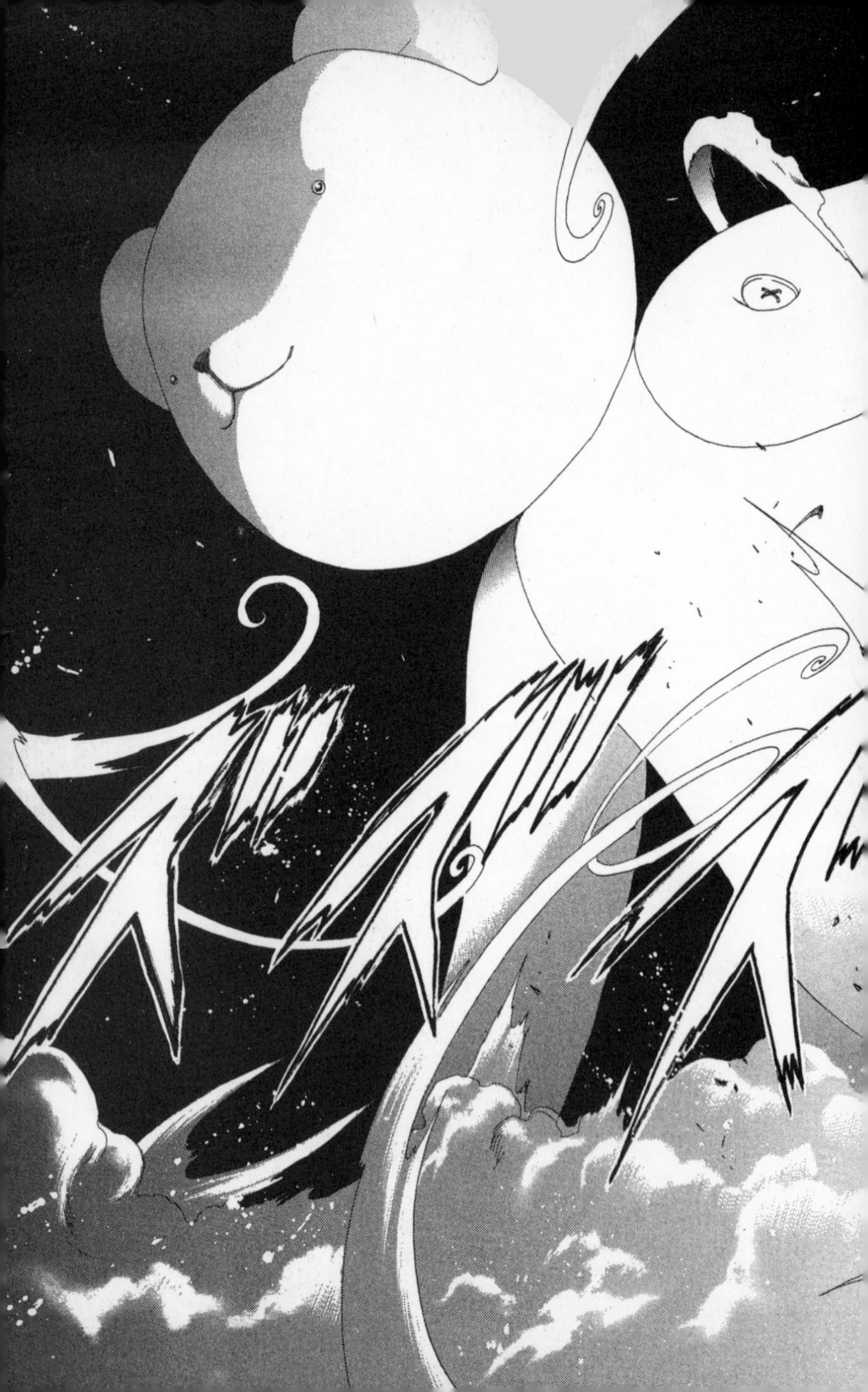

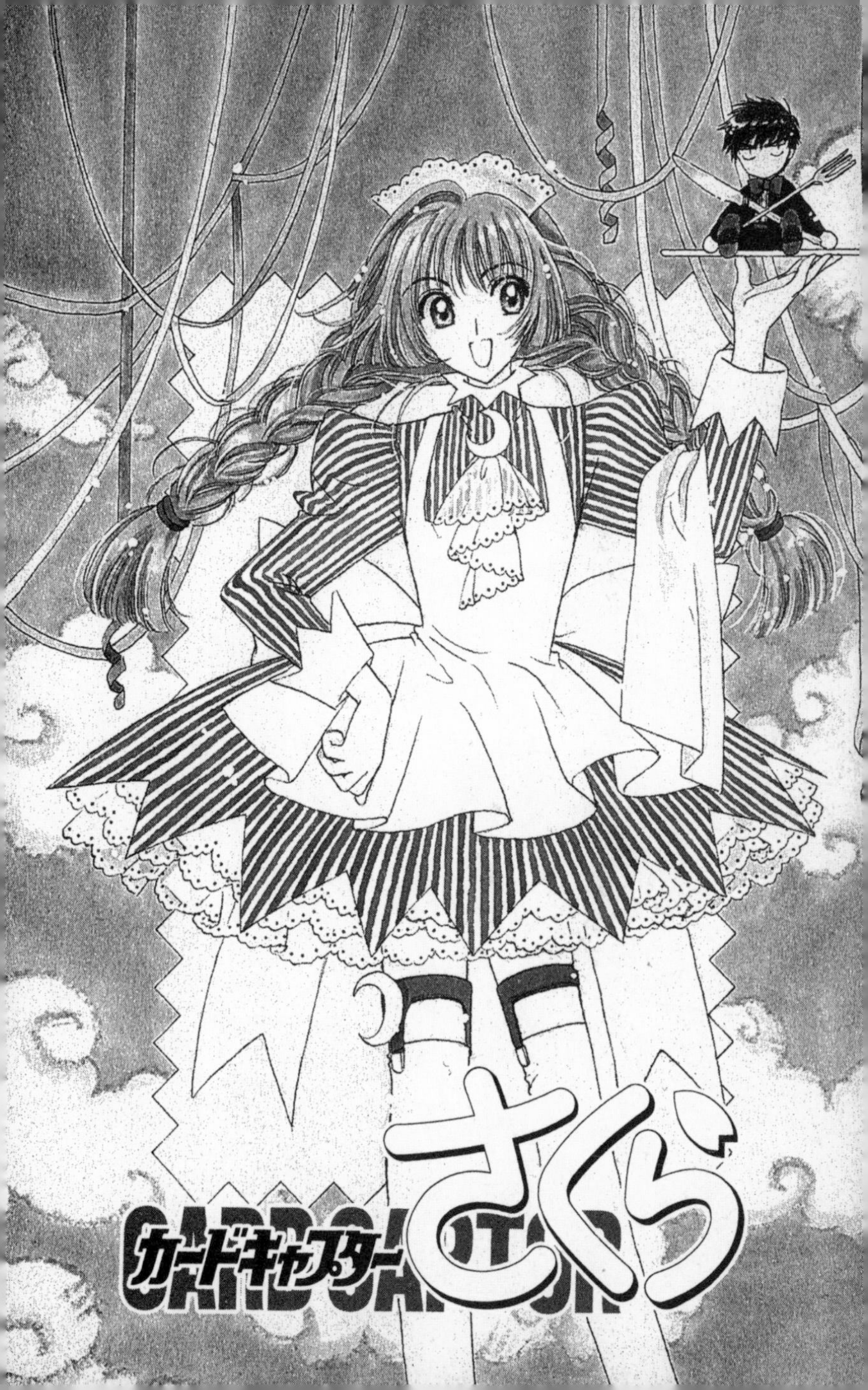
カードキャプターさくら
CARD CAPTOR

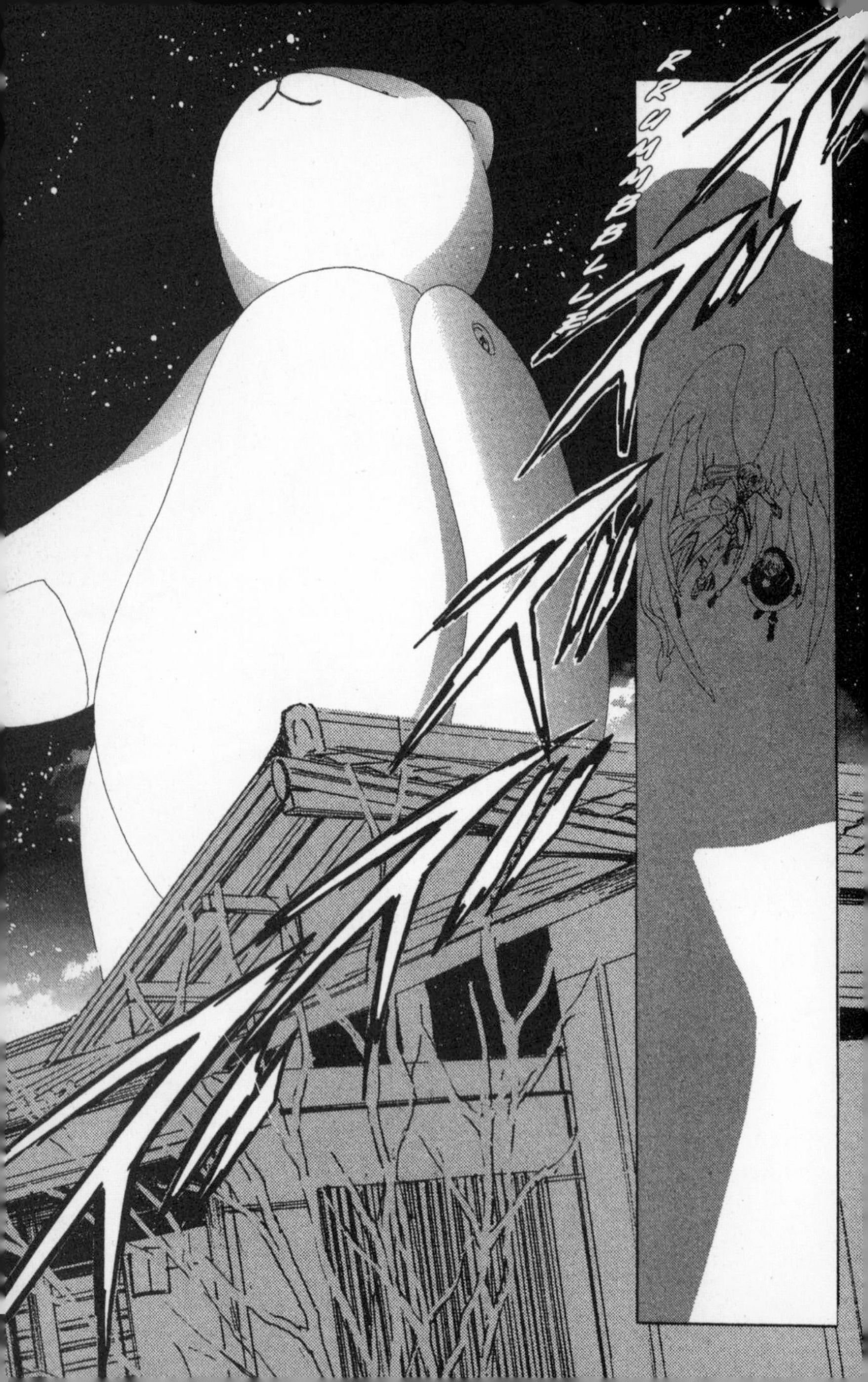
RRUMMBBLLE

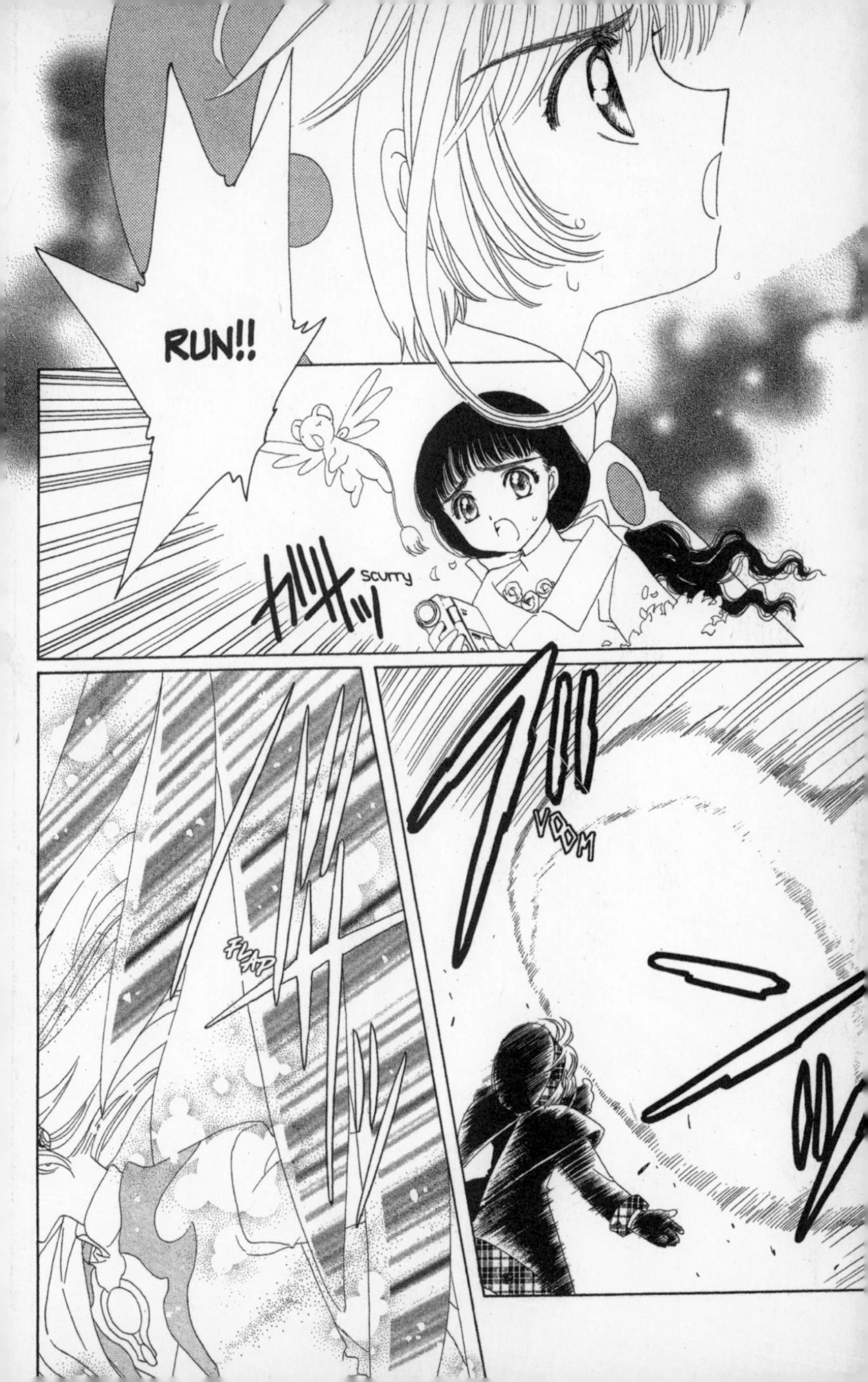
RUN!!
SCURRY
VOOM
FLAP

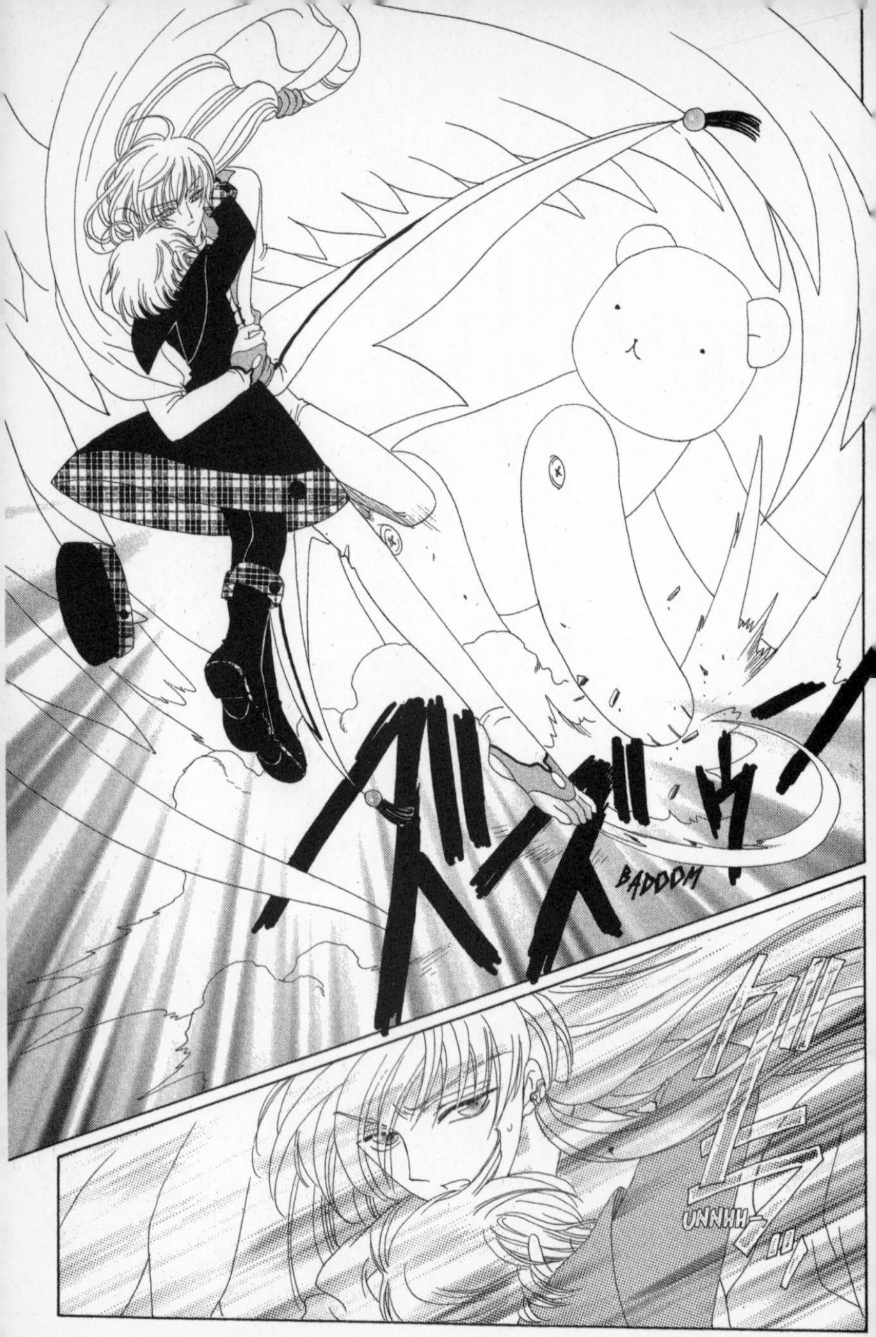
BADOOM
UNNHH—

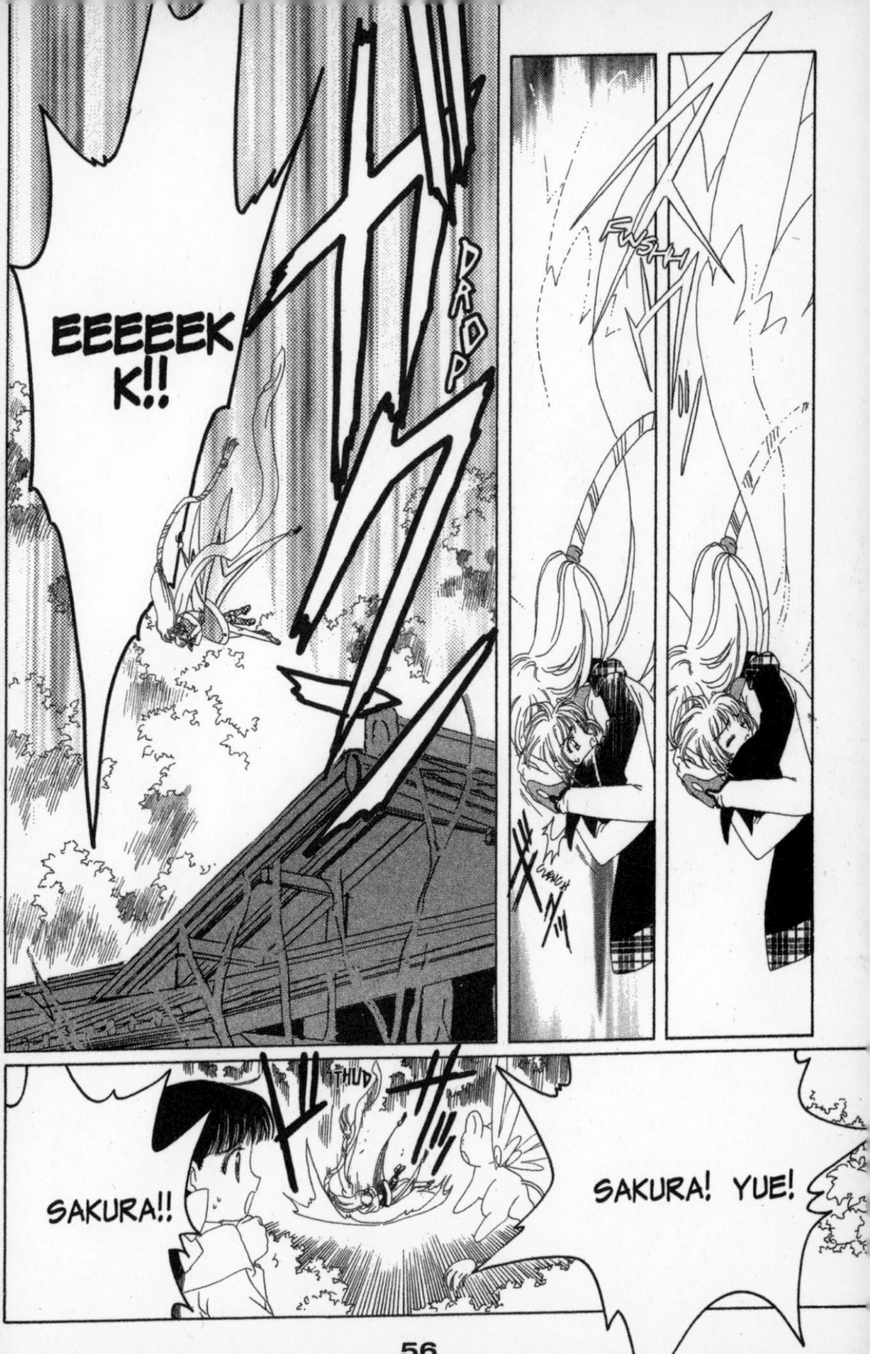
FWSHH
CLENCH
DROP
EEEEEK
K!!
SAKURA! YUE!
THUD
SAKURA!!

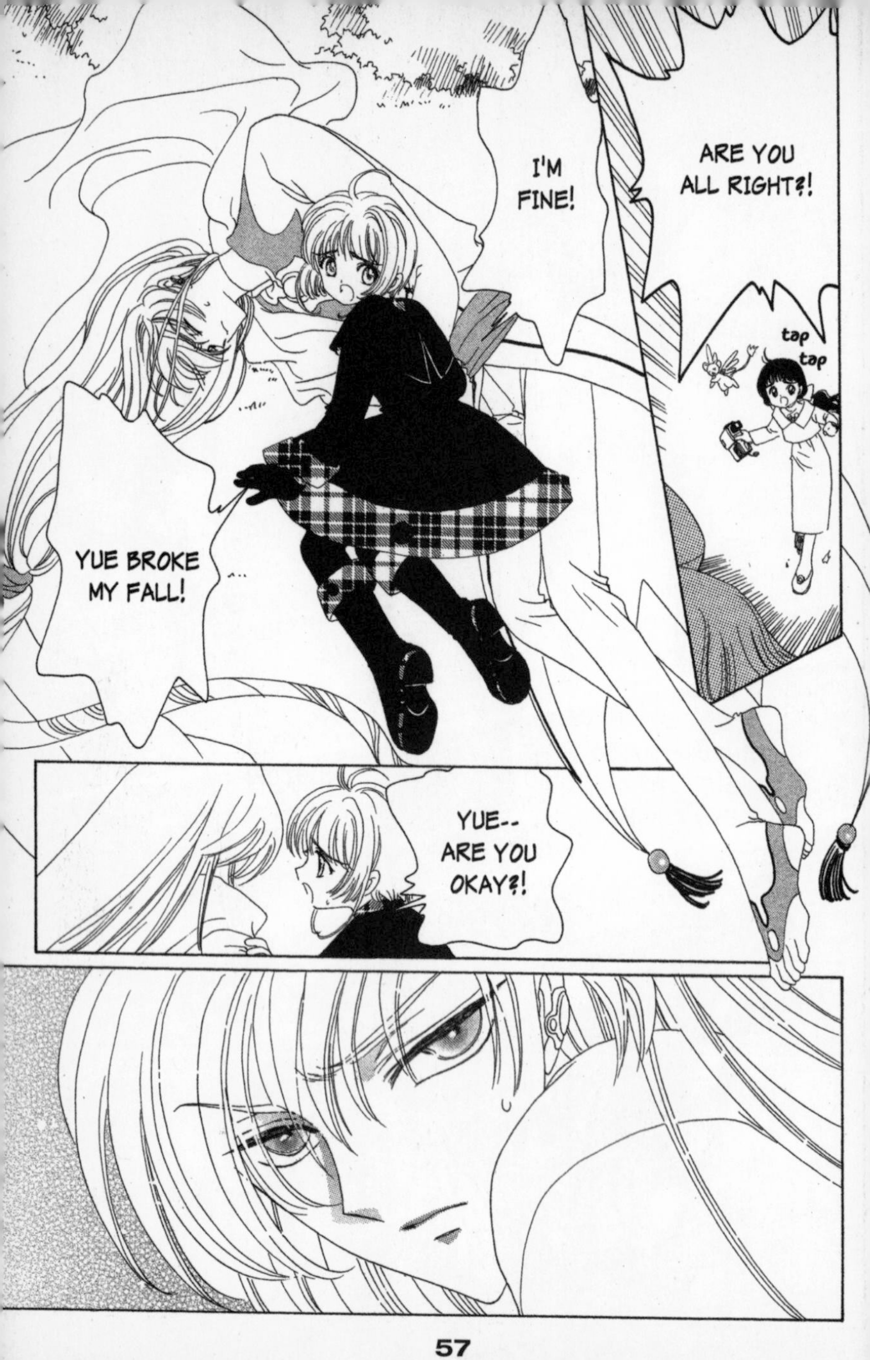
ARE YOU ALL RIGHT?!
tap tap
I'M FINE!
YUE BROKE MY FALL!
YUE--
ARE YOU
OKAY?!

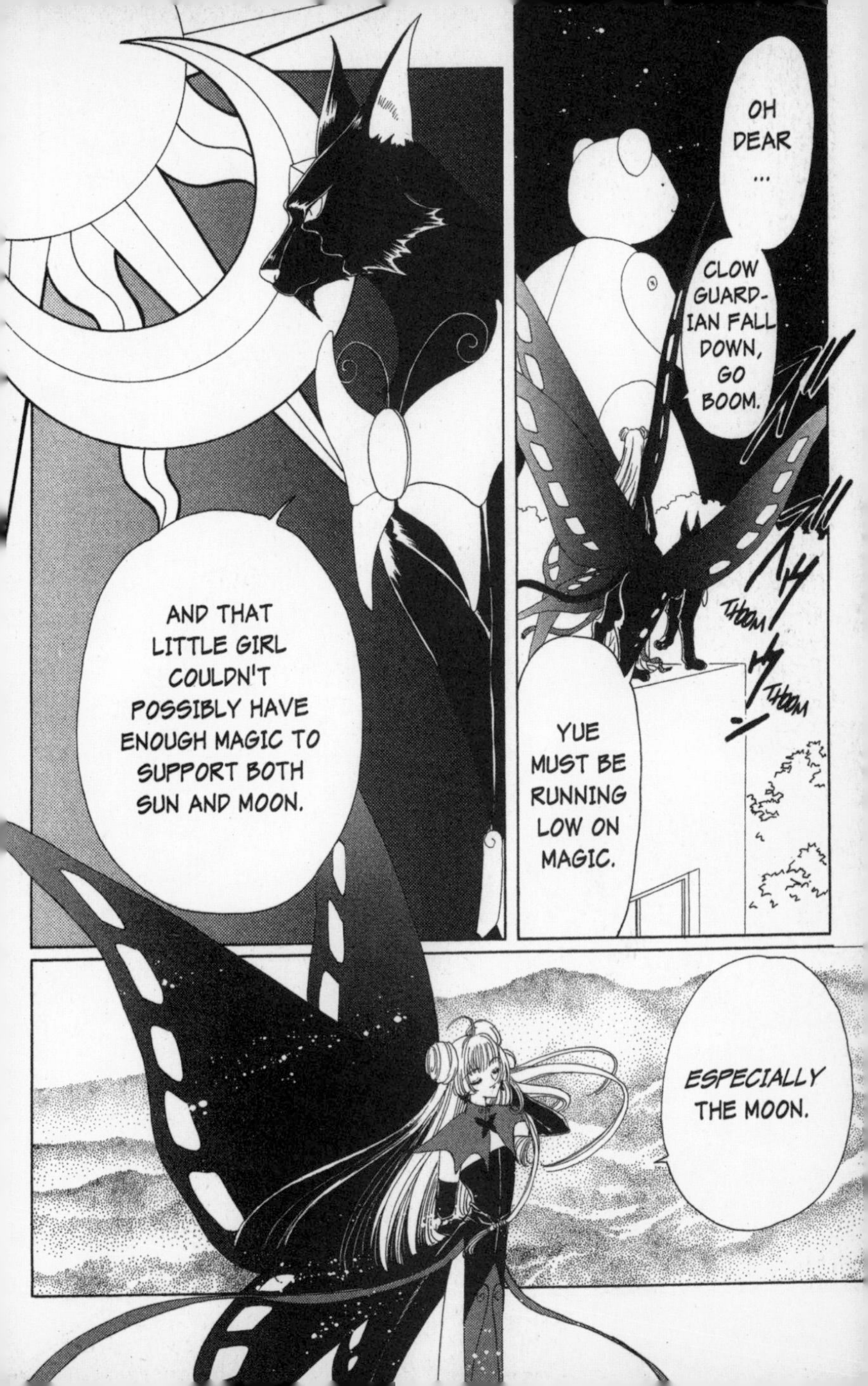
OH DEAR ...
CLOW GUARDIAN FALL DOWN, GO BOOM.
THOOM
THOOM
YUE MUST BE RUNNING LOW ON MAGIC.
AND THAT LITTLE GIRL COULDN'T POSSIBLY HAVE ENOUGH MAGIC TO SUPPORT BOTH SUN AND MOON.
ESPECIALLY THE MOON.

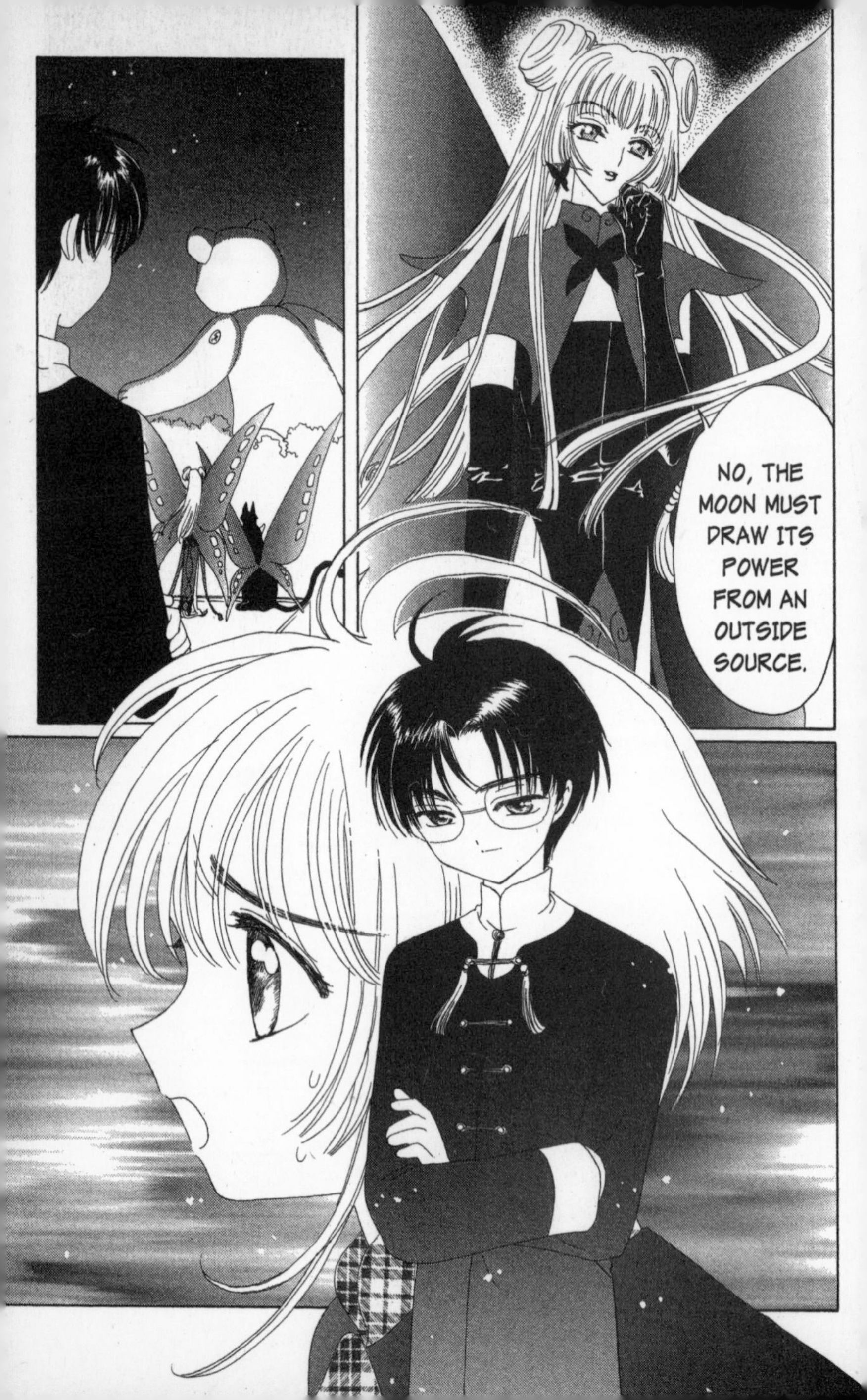
NO, THE MOON MUST DRAW ITS POWER FROM AN OUTSIDE SOURCE.

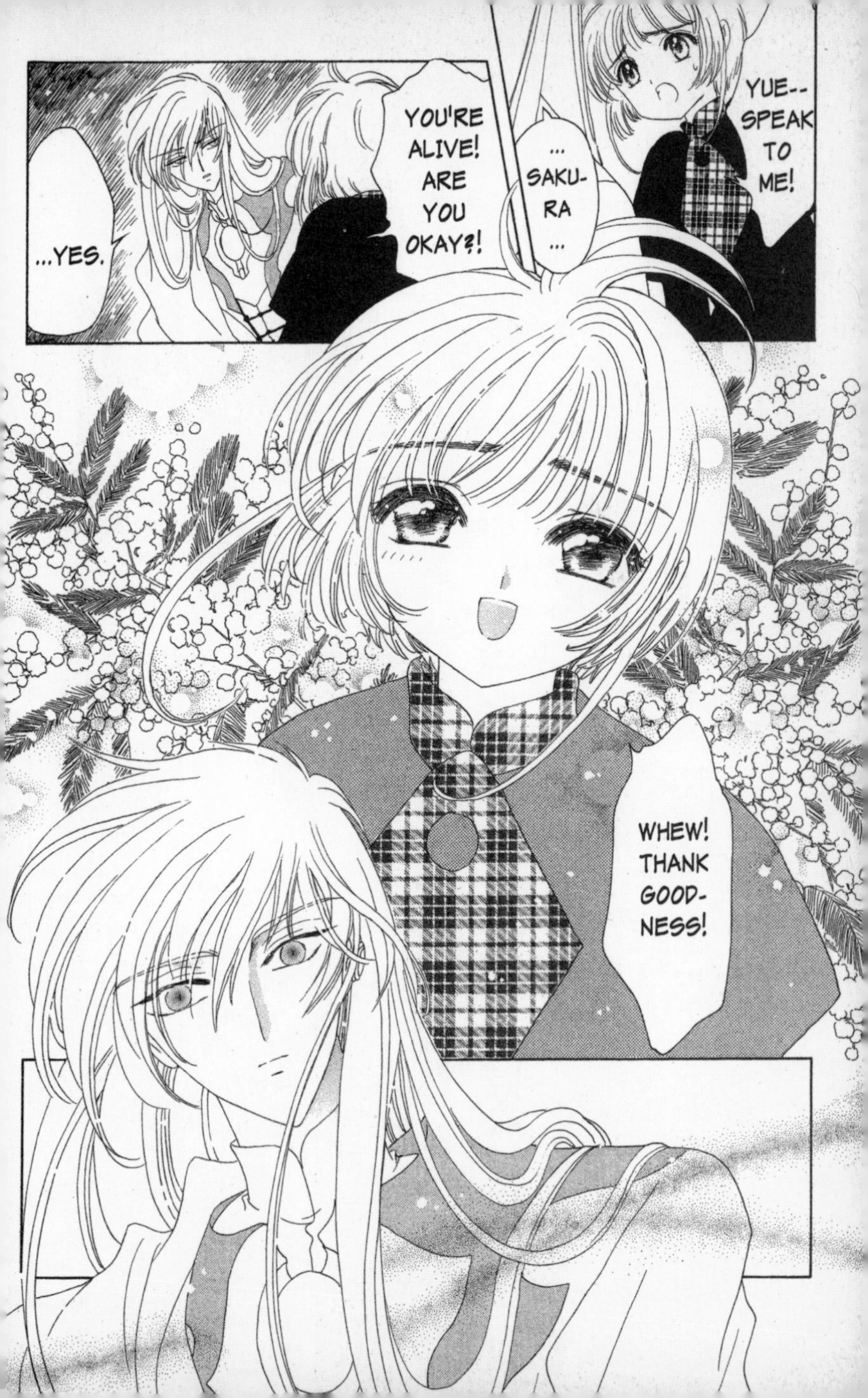
YUE-- SPEAK TO ME!
... SAKURA ...
YOU'RE ALIVE! ARE YOU OKAY?!
...YES.
WHEW! THANK GOODNESS!

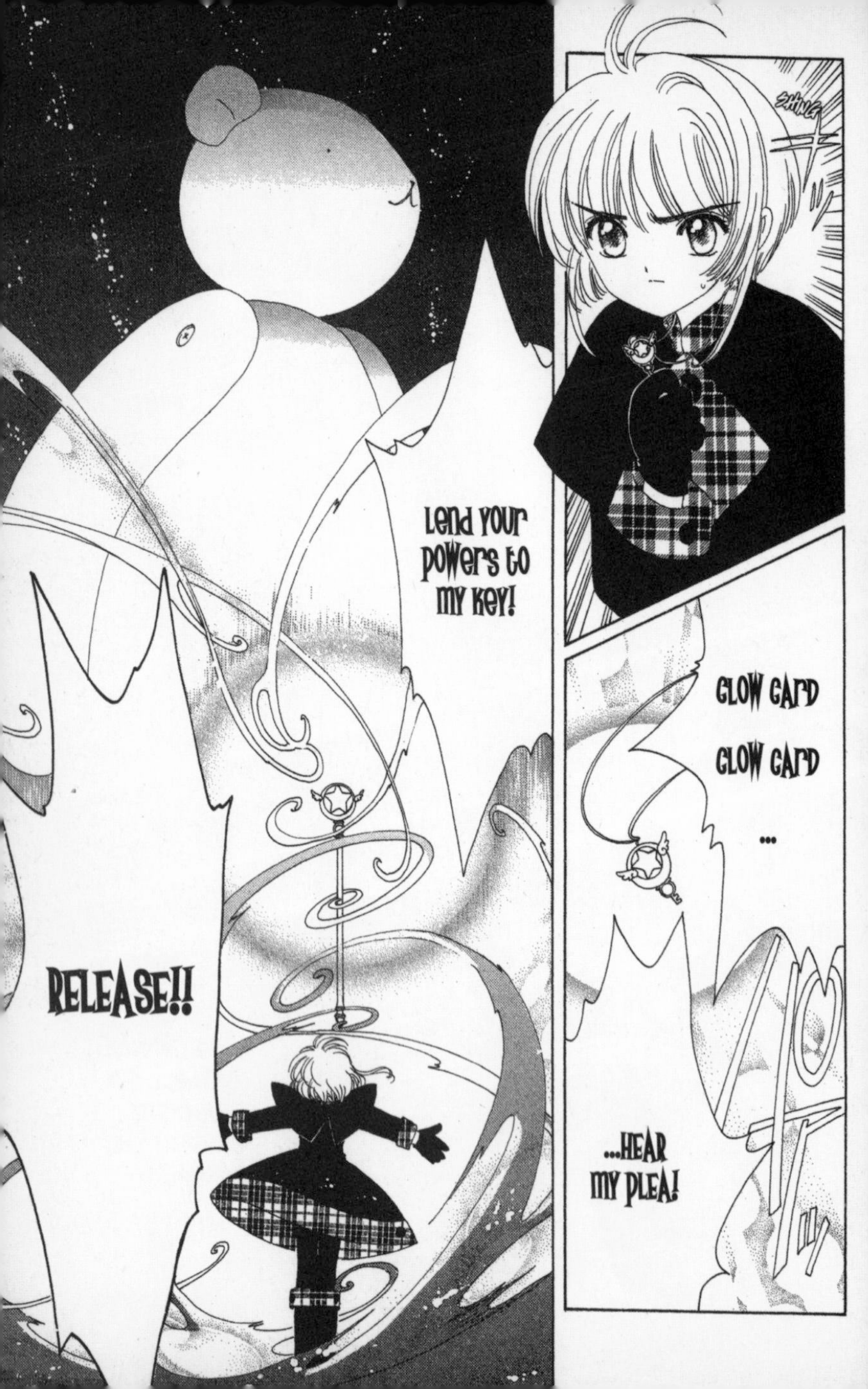
SHING
GLOW CARD
GLOW CARD
...
...HEAR MY PLEA!
LEND YOUR POWERS TO MY KEY!
RELEASE!!

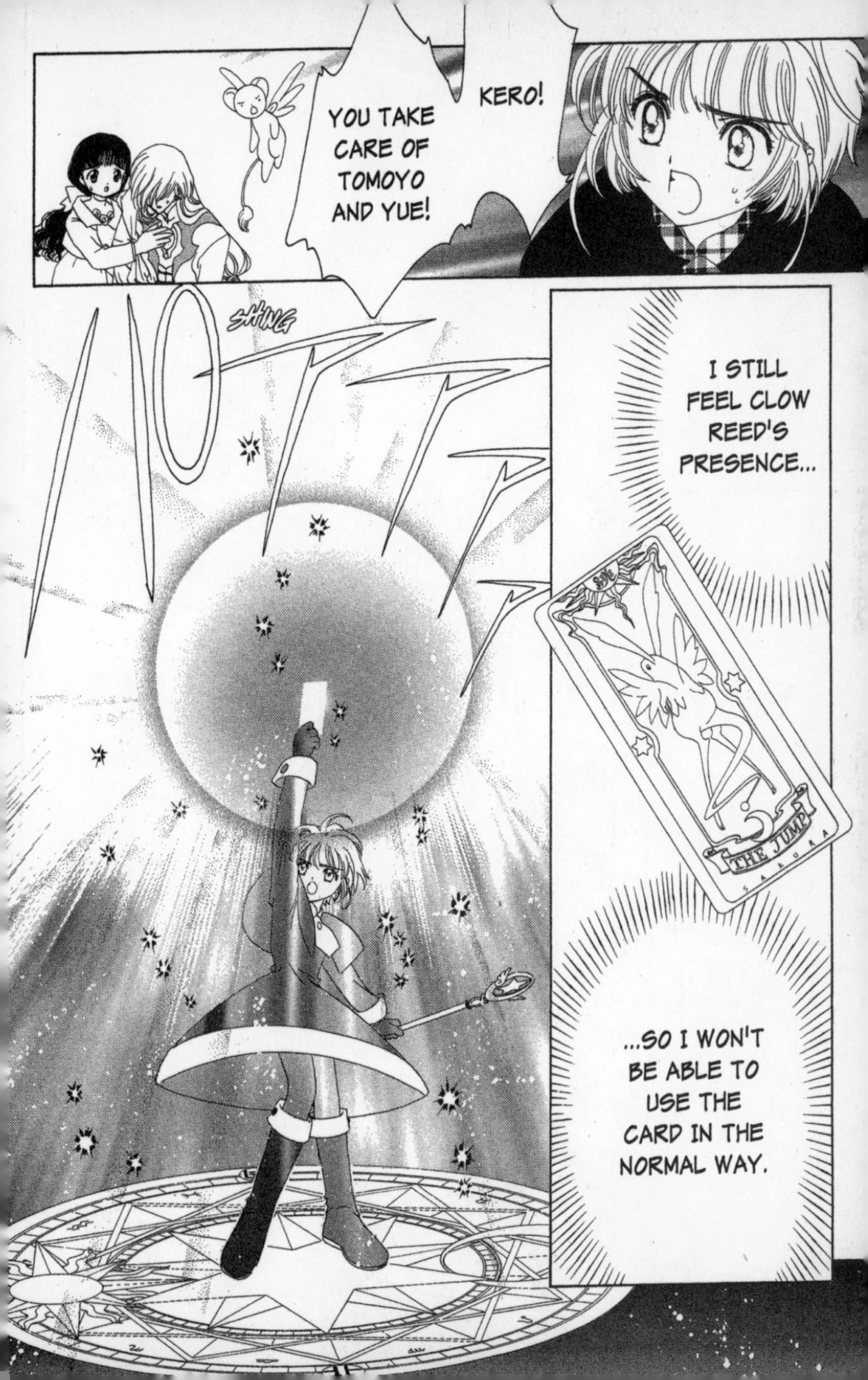
KERO!
YOU TAKE CARE OF TOMOYO AND YUE!
I STILL FEEL CLOW REED'S PRESENCE...
THE JUMP
SAKURA
...SO I WON'T BE ABLE TO USE THE CARD IN THE NORMAL WAY.
SHING

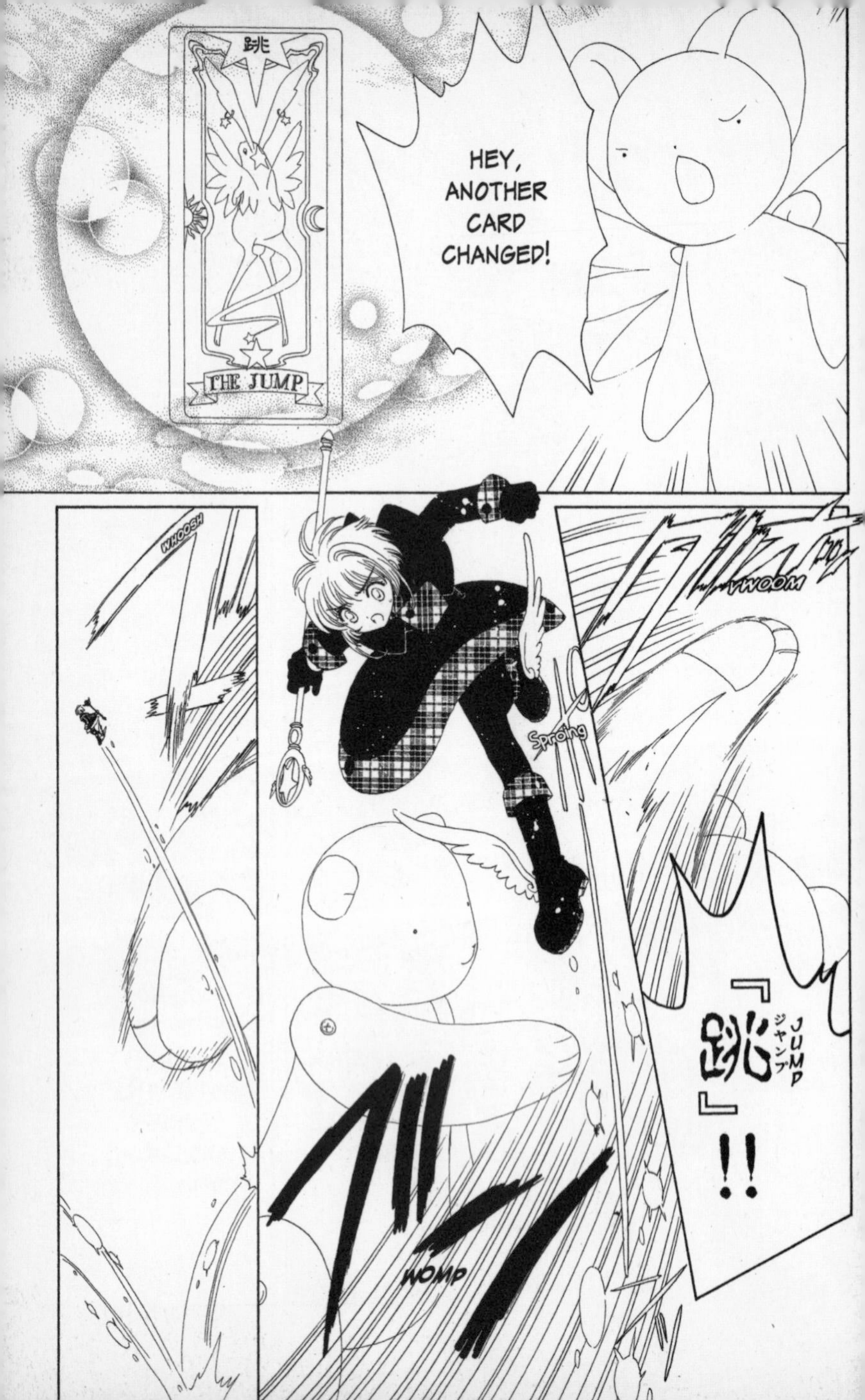
HEY, ANOTHER CARD CHANGED!
跳
THE JUMP
VWOOM
「跳ジャンプ」!!
JUMP
Sproing
WOMP
WHOOSH

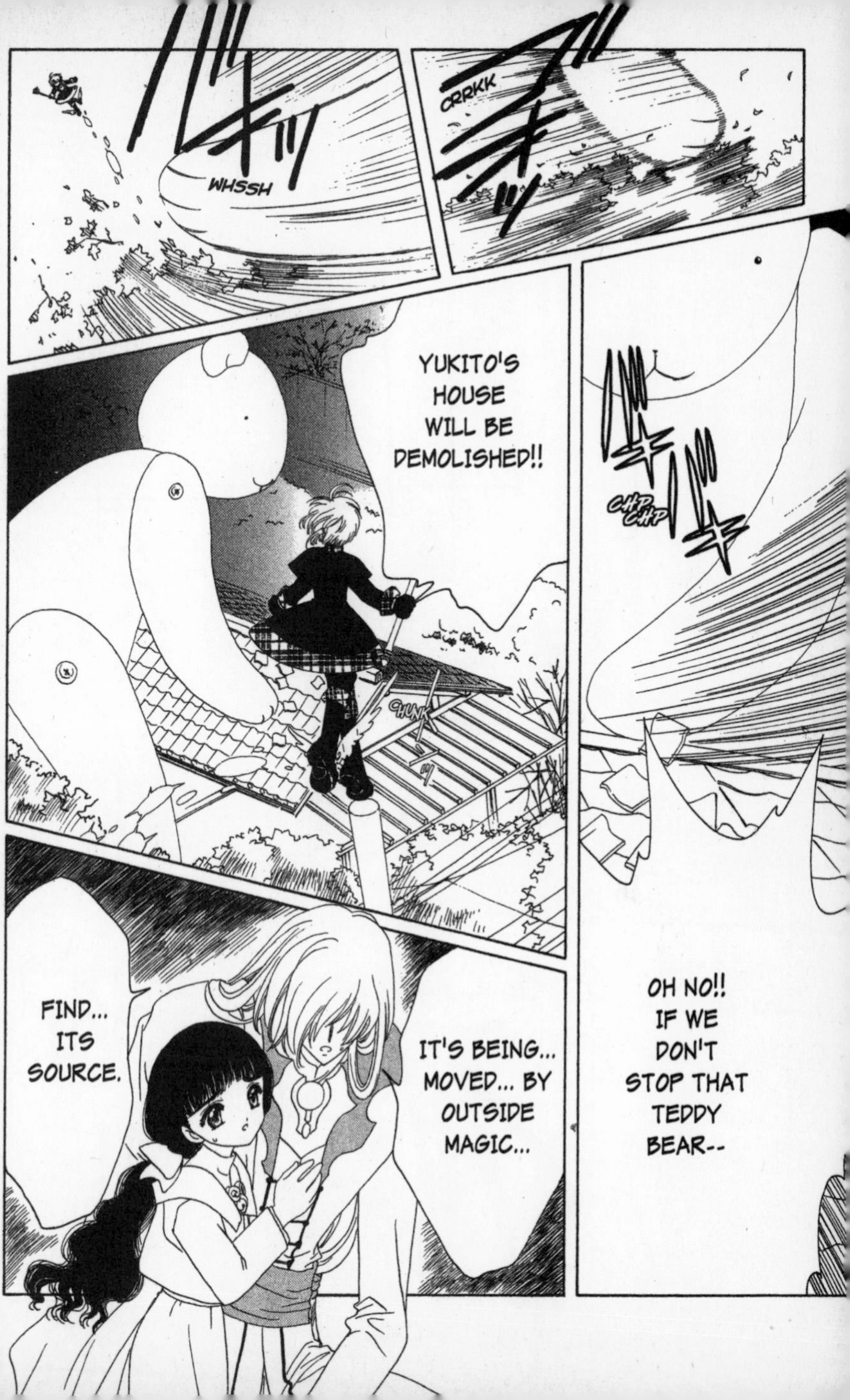
CRRKK
WHSSH
CHP CHP
OH NO!! IF WE DON'T STOP THAT TEDDY BEAR--
YUKITO'S HOUSE WILL BE DEMOLISHED!!
CHUNK
IT'S BEING... MOVED... BY OUTSIDE MAGIC...
FIND... ITS SOURCE.

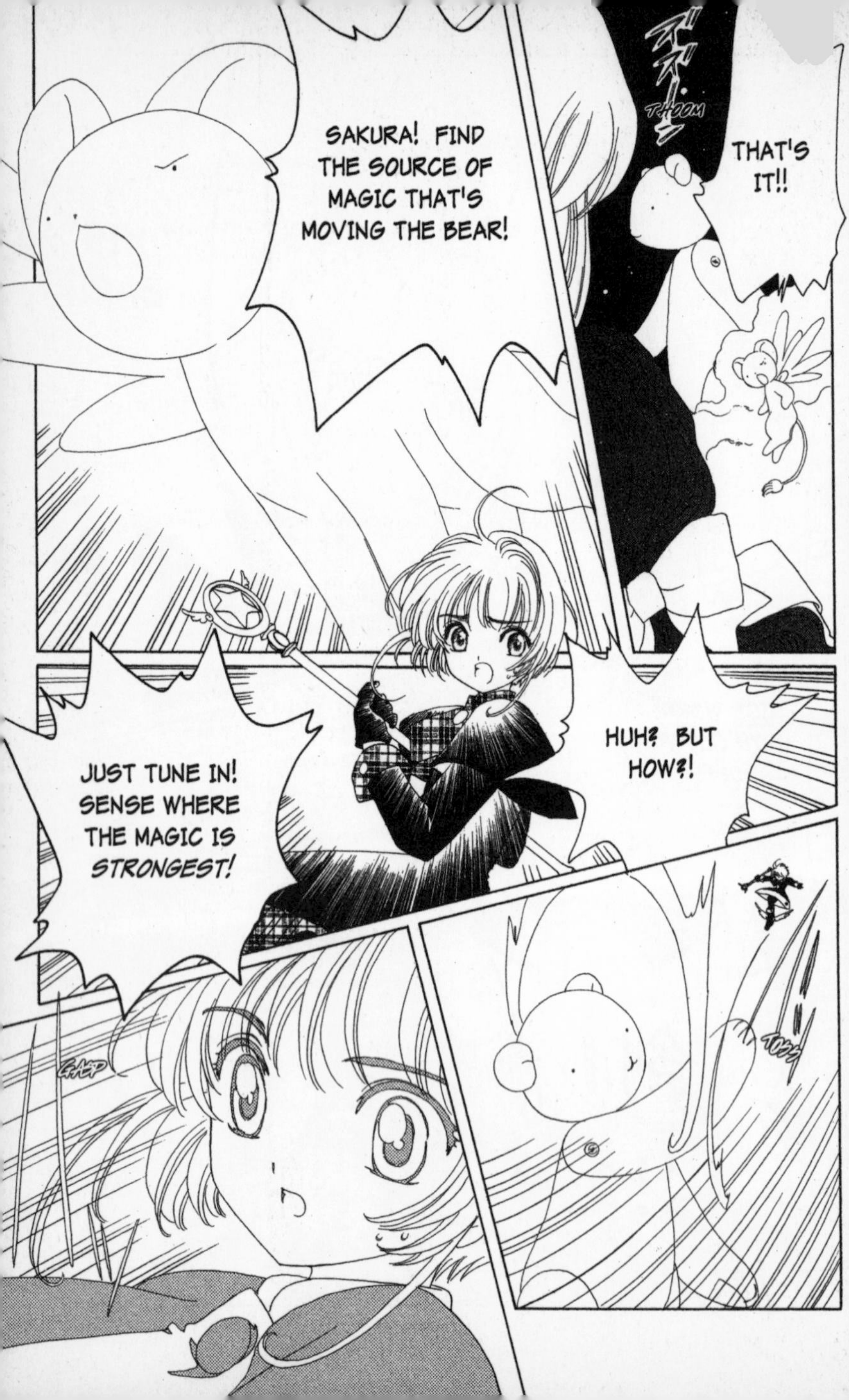
THOOM
THAT'S IT!!
SAKURA! FIND THE SOURCE OF MAGIC THAT'S MOVING THE BEAR!
HUH? BUT HOW?!
JUST TUNE IN! SENSE WHERE THE MAGIC IS *STRONGEST!*
TOSS
GASP

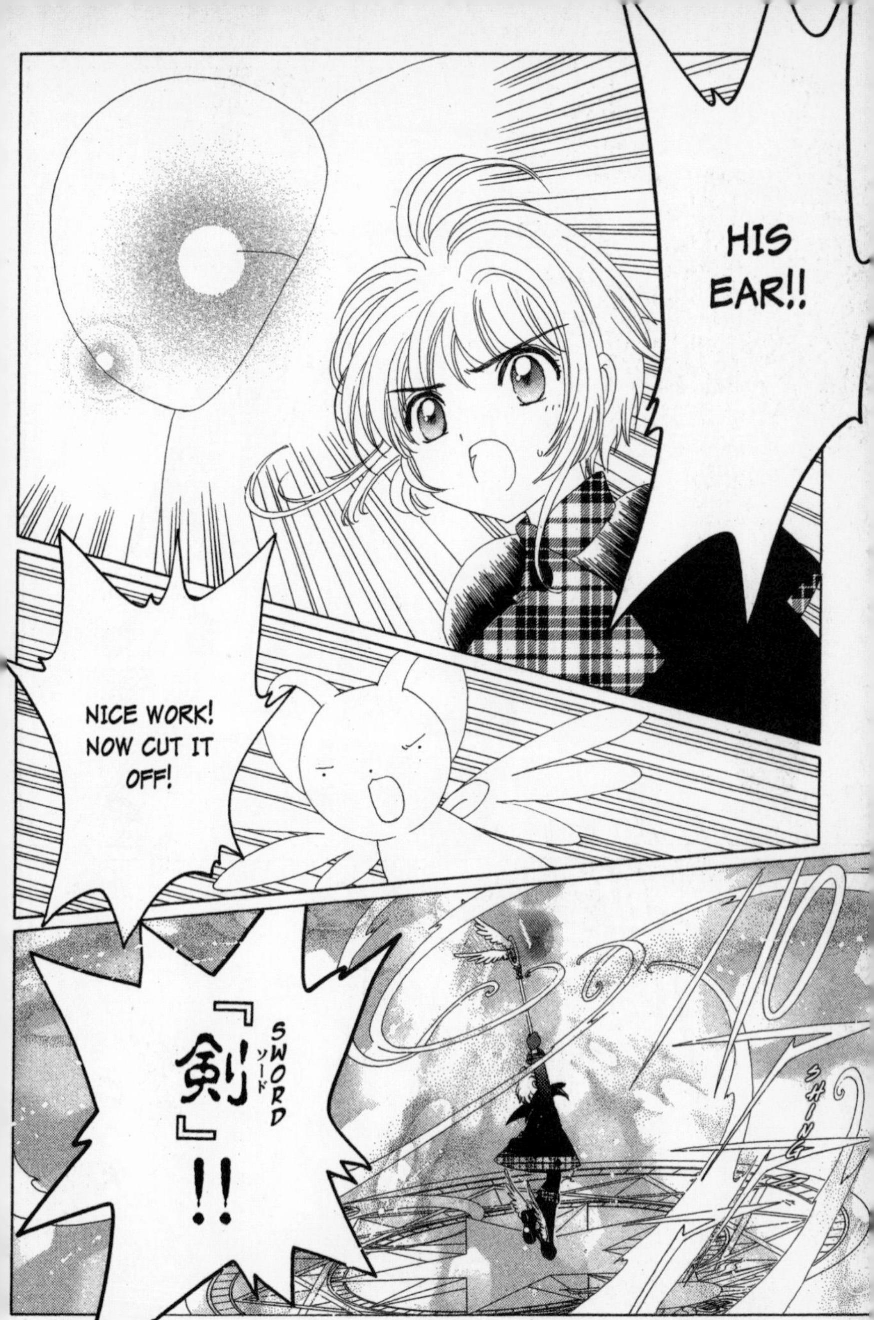
HIS EAR!!
NICE WORK! NOW CUT IT OFF!
『剣』!!
SWORD
ソード
SHING

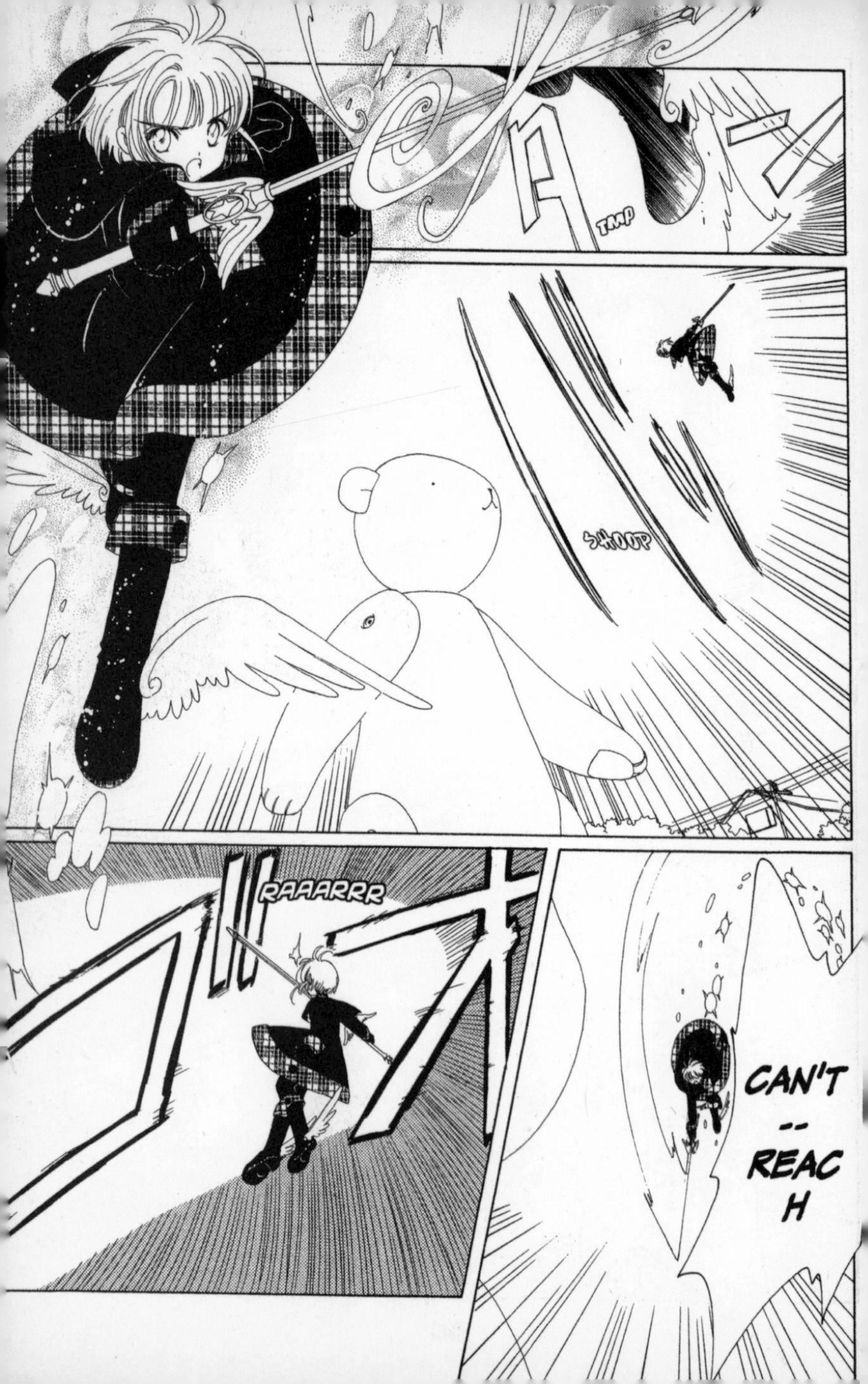
TMP
SHOOP
CAN'T
--
REAC
H
RAAARRR

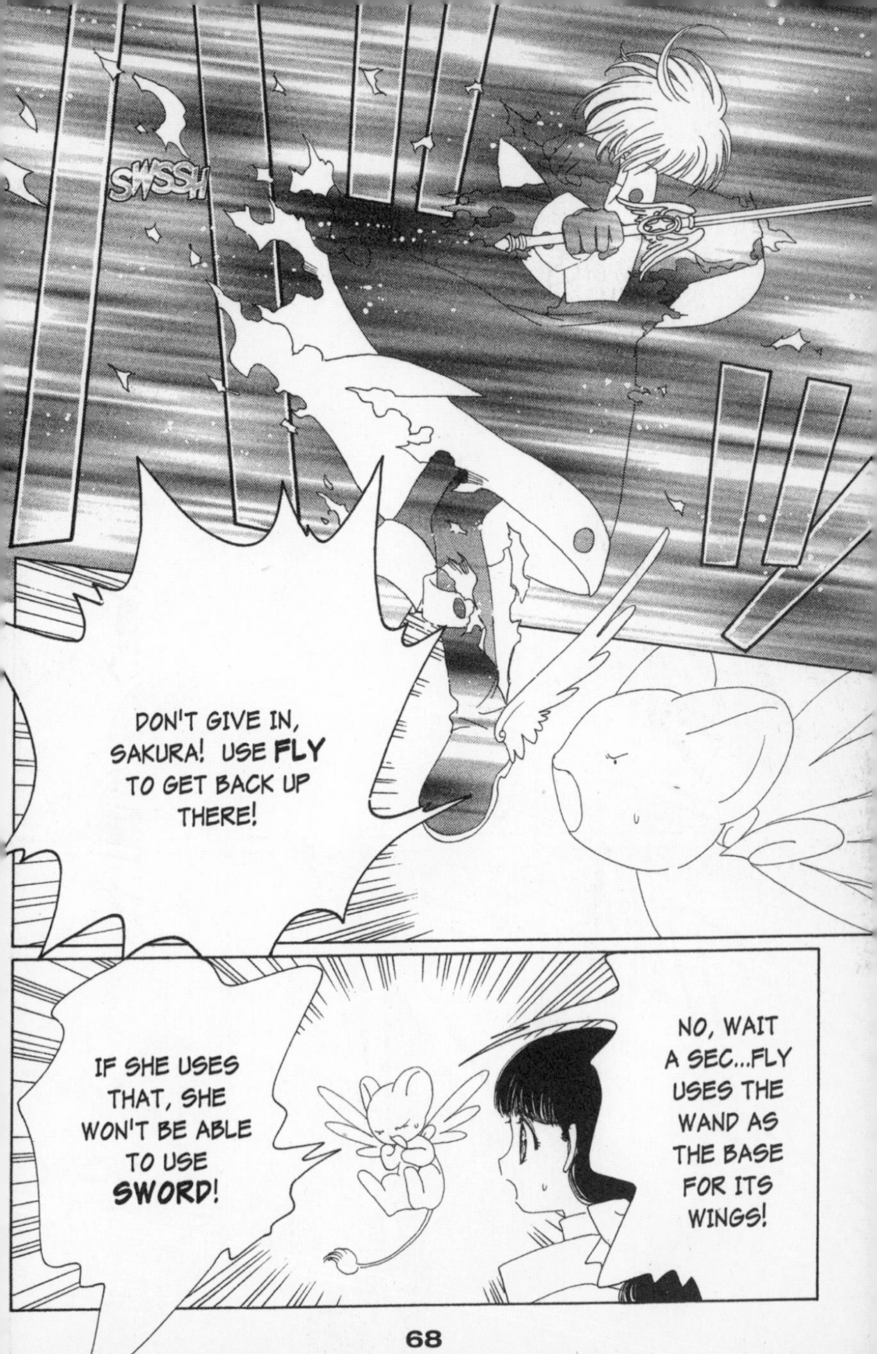
SWSSH
DON'T GIVE IN, SAKURA! USE FLY TO GET BACK UP THERE!
NO, WAIT A SEC...FLY USES THE WAND AS THE BASE FOR ITS WINGS!
IF SHE USES THAT, SHE WON'T BE ABLE TO USE SWORD!

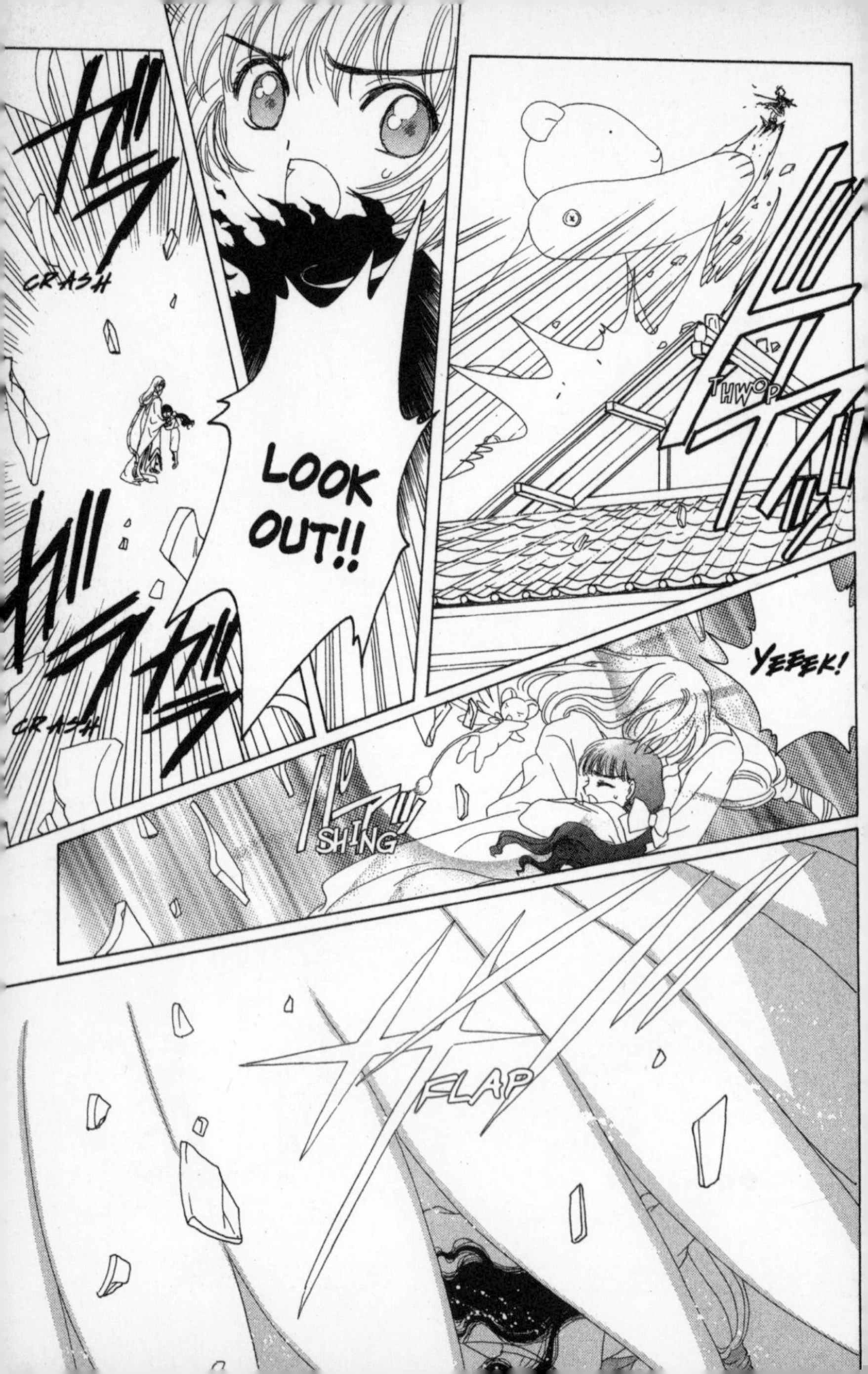
THWOP
LOOK OUT!!
CRASH
CRASH
YEEEK!
SHING
FLAP

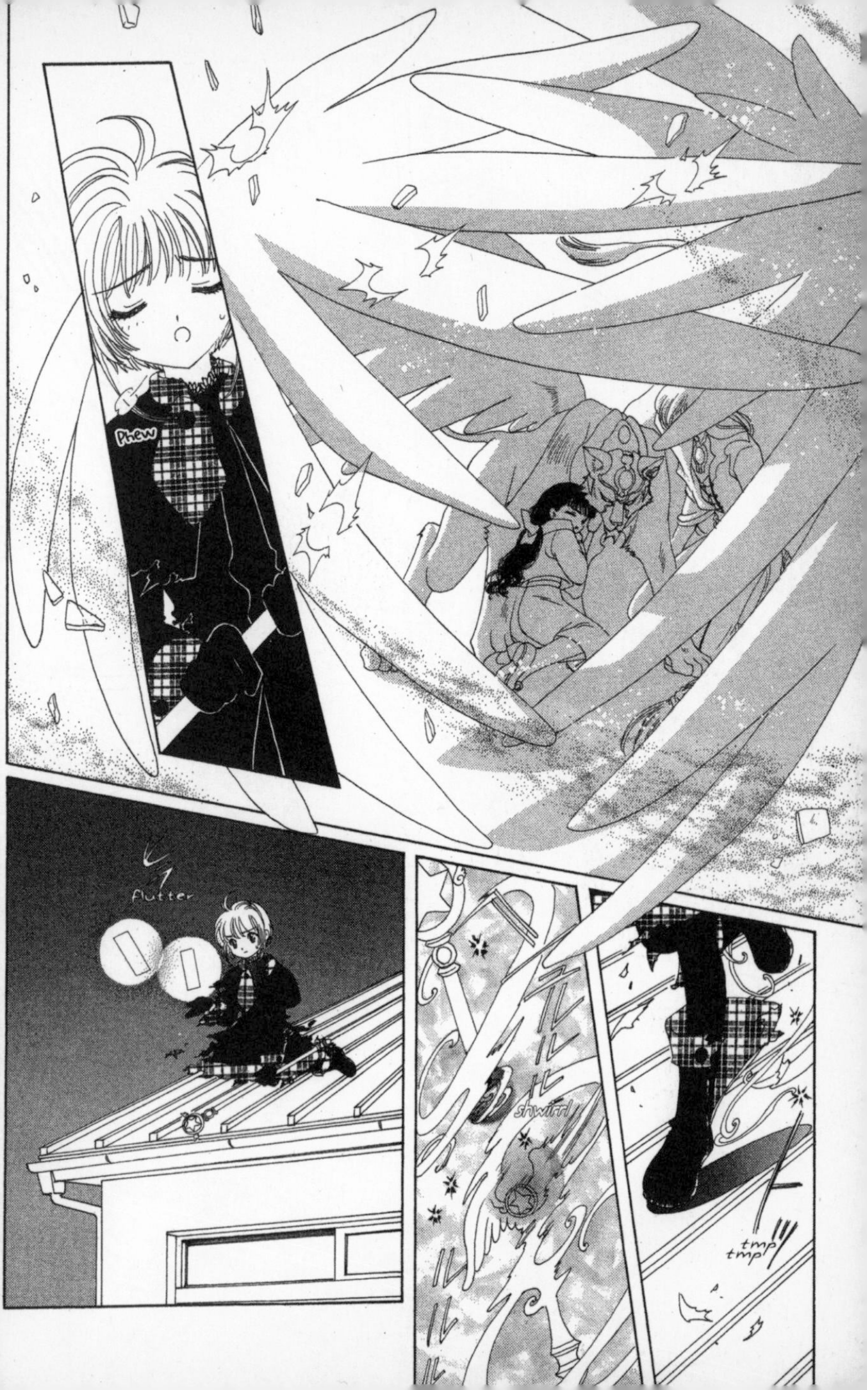
Phew
tmp tmp
shwirrl
flutter

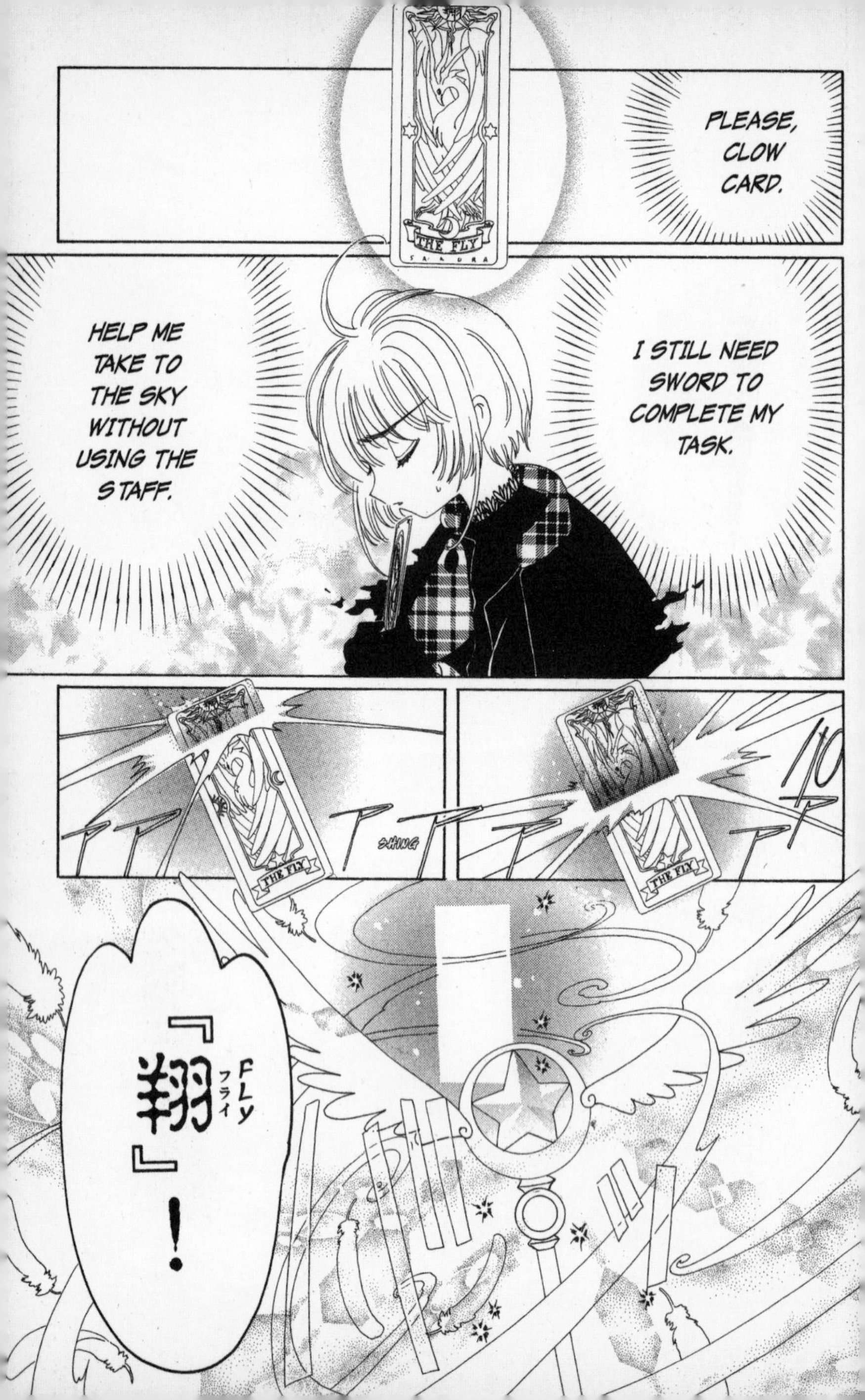
THE FLY
PLEASE, CLOW CARD.
I STILL NEED SWORD TO COMPLETE MY TASK.
HELP ME TAKE TO THE SKY WITHOUT USING THE STAFF.
THE FLY
SHING
THE FLY
『翔』!
FLY
フライ

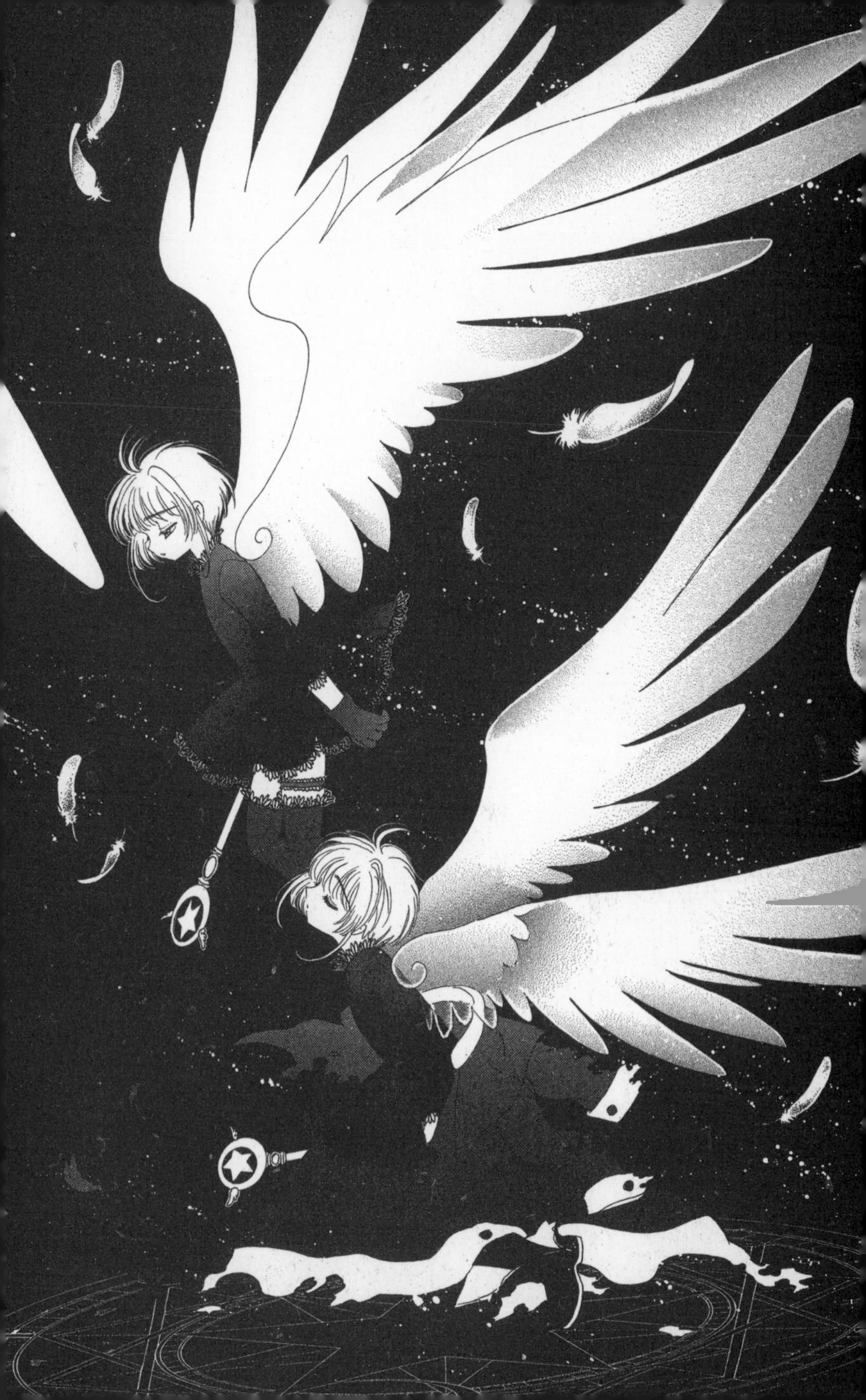

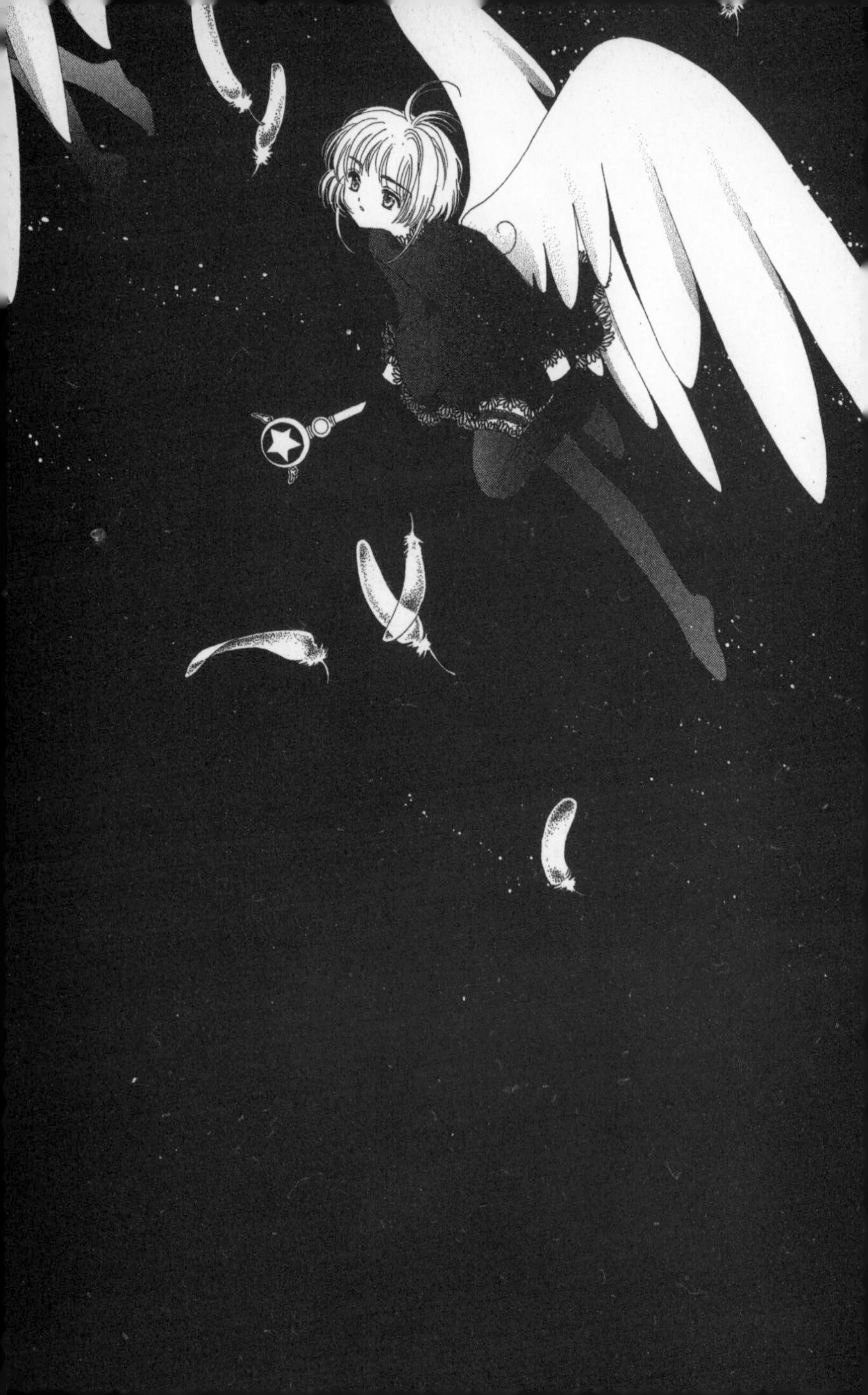

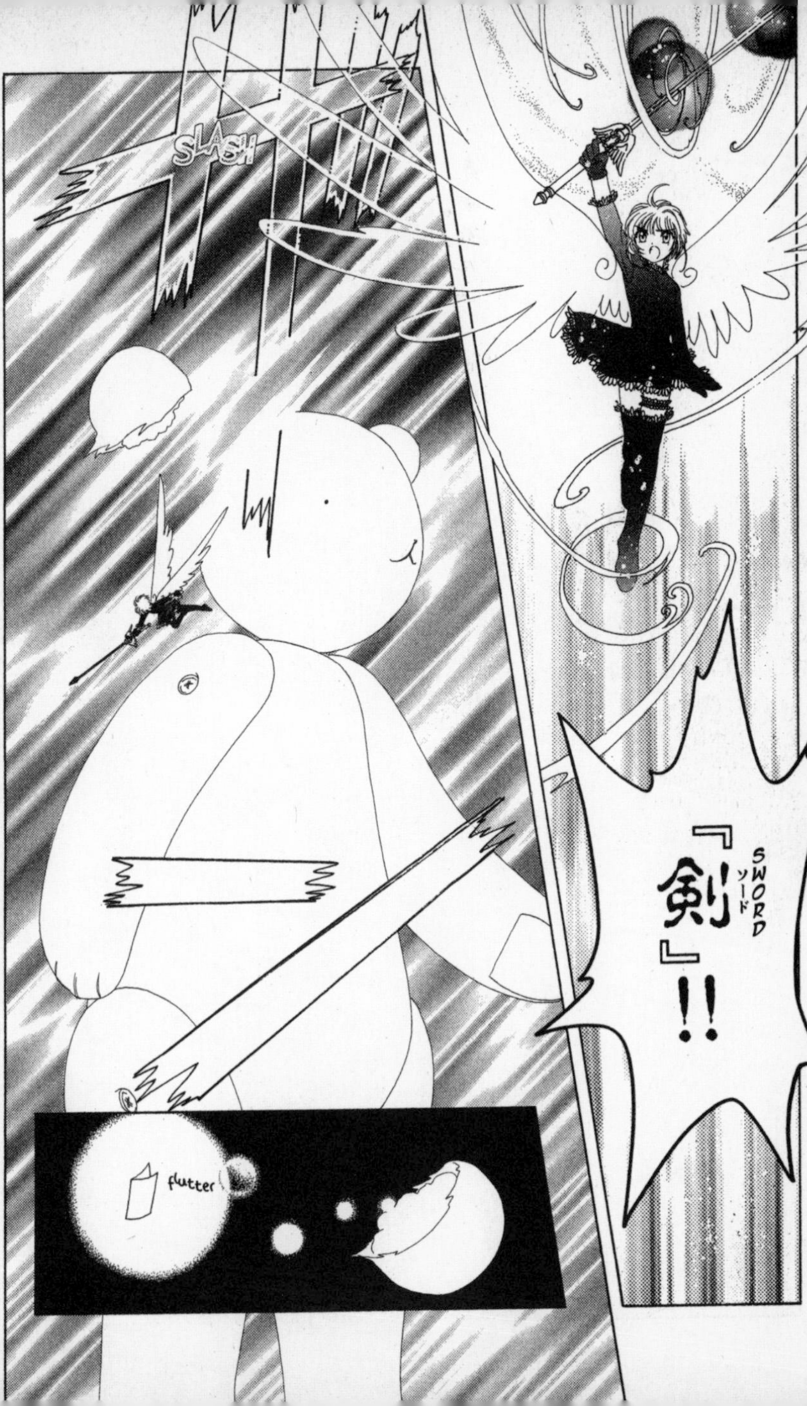
『剣 ソード SWORD』!!
SLASH
flutter

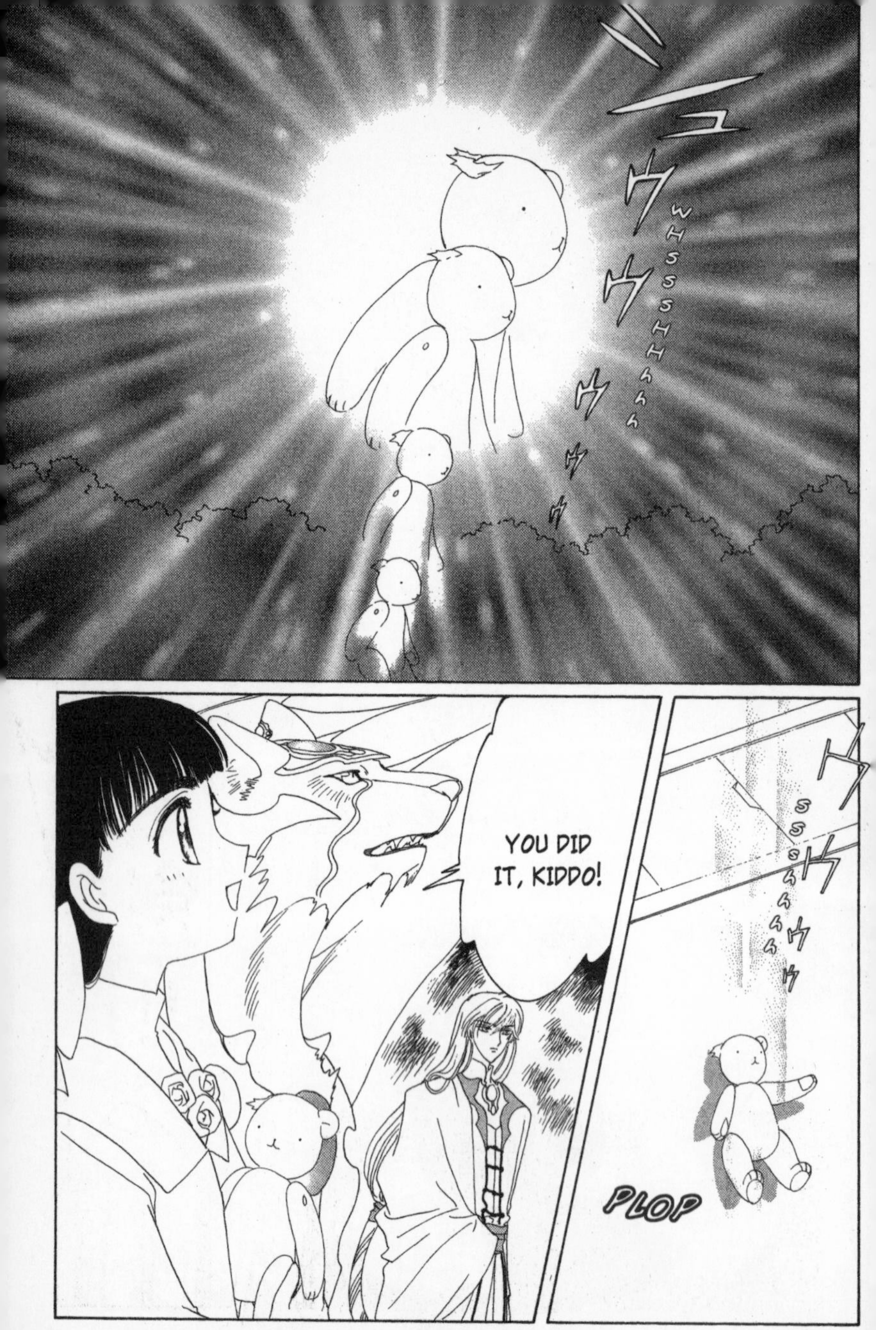
WHSSSHHhhhh
SSShhhh
PLOP
YOU DID IT, KIDDO!

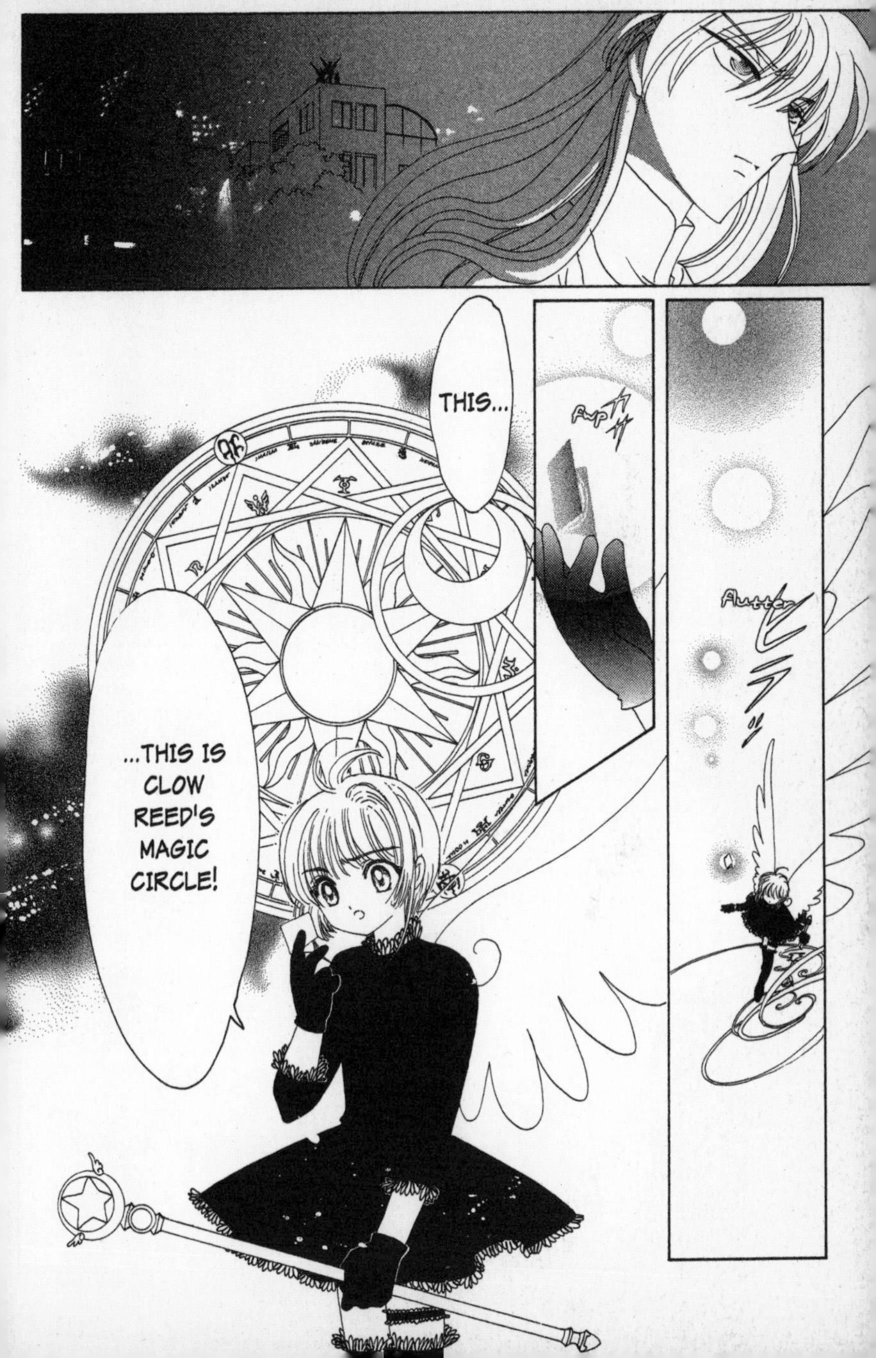
Flutter
Fwp
THIS...
...THIS IS CLOW REED'S MAGIC CIRCLE!

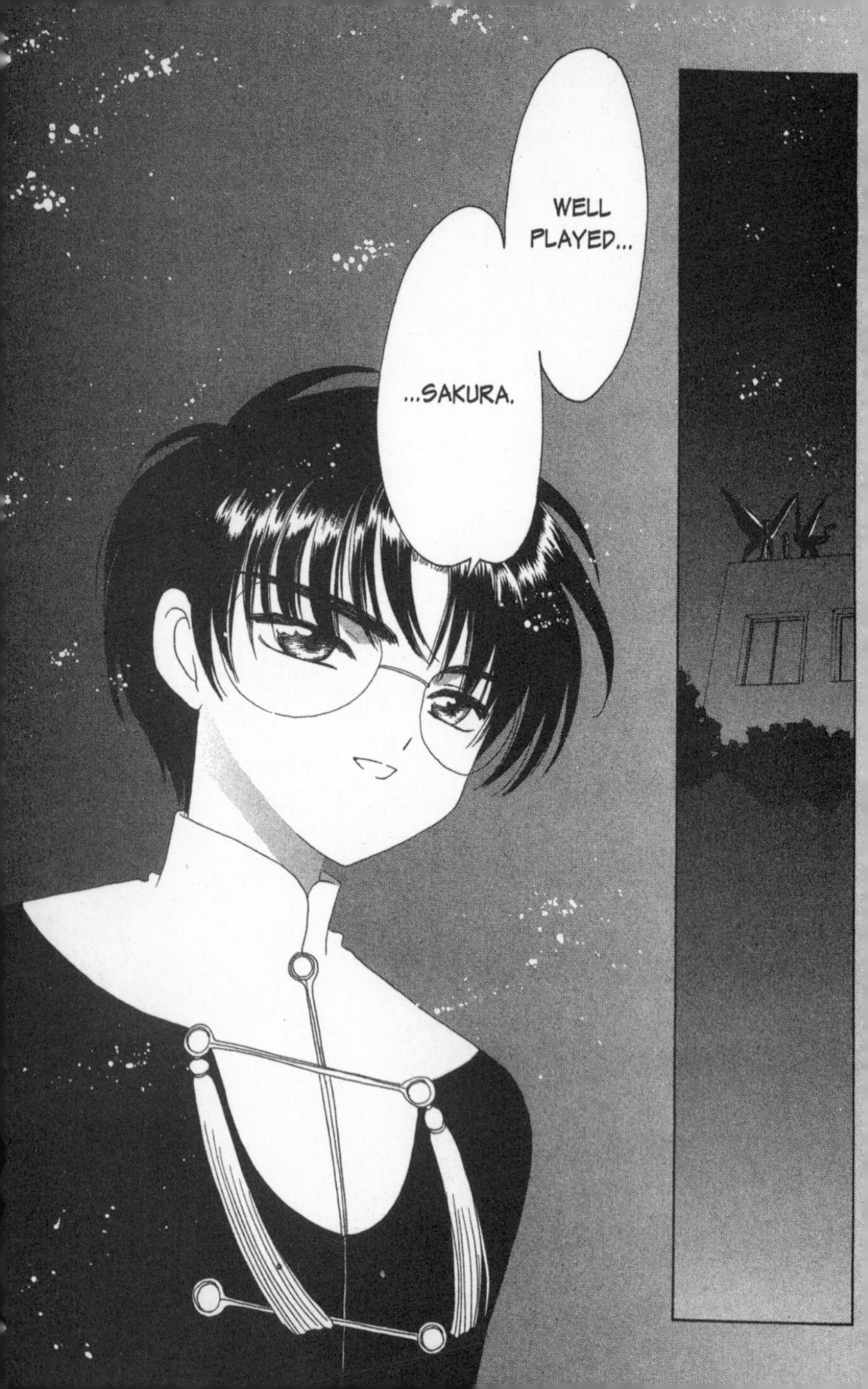
WELL PLAYED...
...SAKURA.

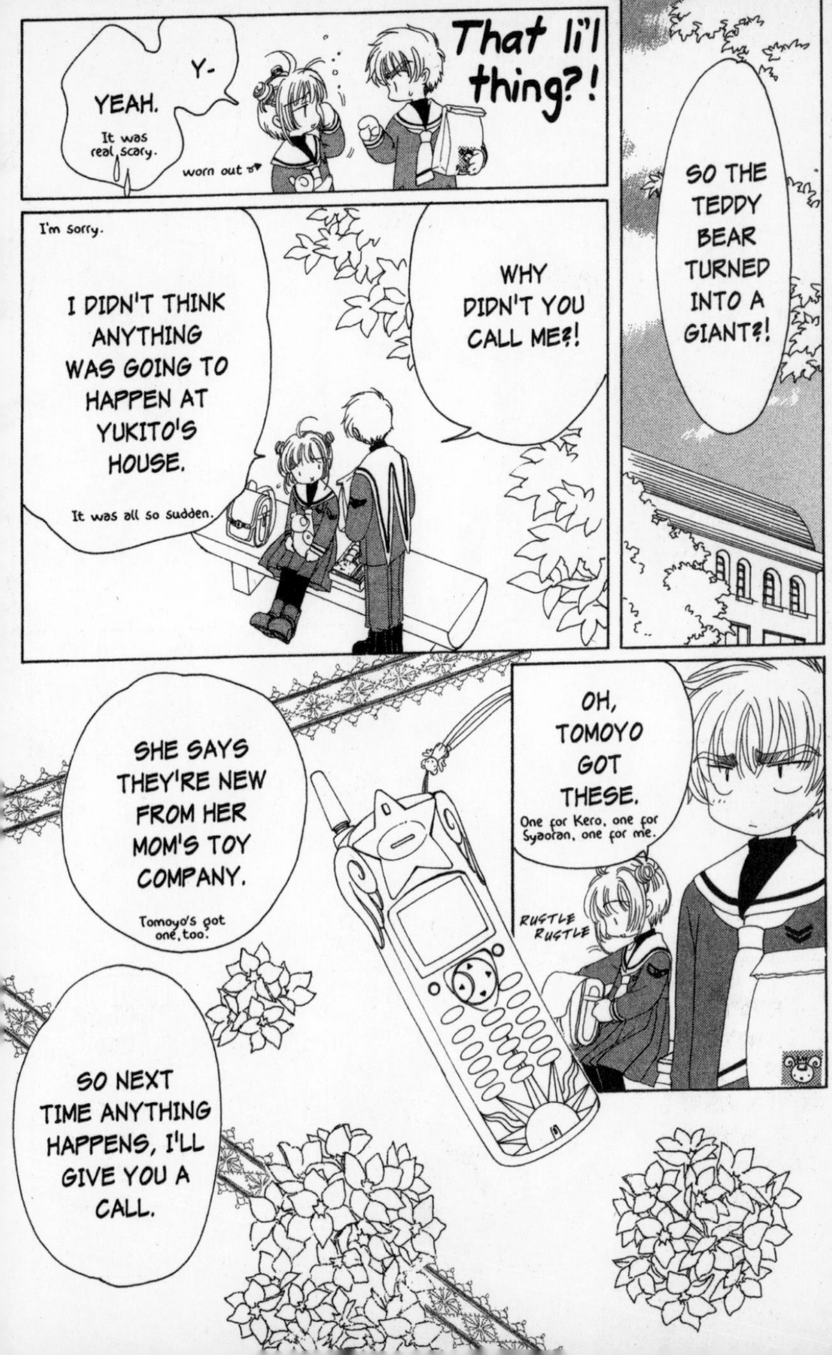
SO THE TEDDY BEAR TURNED INTO A GIANT?!
That li'l thing?!
Y- YEAH.
It was real scary.
worn out
WHY DIDN'T YOU CALL ME?!
I'm sorry.
I DIDN'T THINK ANYTHING WAS GOING TO HAPPEN AT YUKITO'S HOUSE.
It was all so sudden.
OH, TOMOYO GOT THESE.
One for Kero, one for Syaoran, one for me.
RUSTLE RUSTLE
SHE SAYS THEY'RE NEW FROM HER MOM'S TOY COMPANY.
Tomoyo's got one, too.
SO NEXT TIME ANYTHING HAPPENS, I'LL GIVE YOU A CALL.

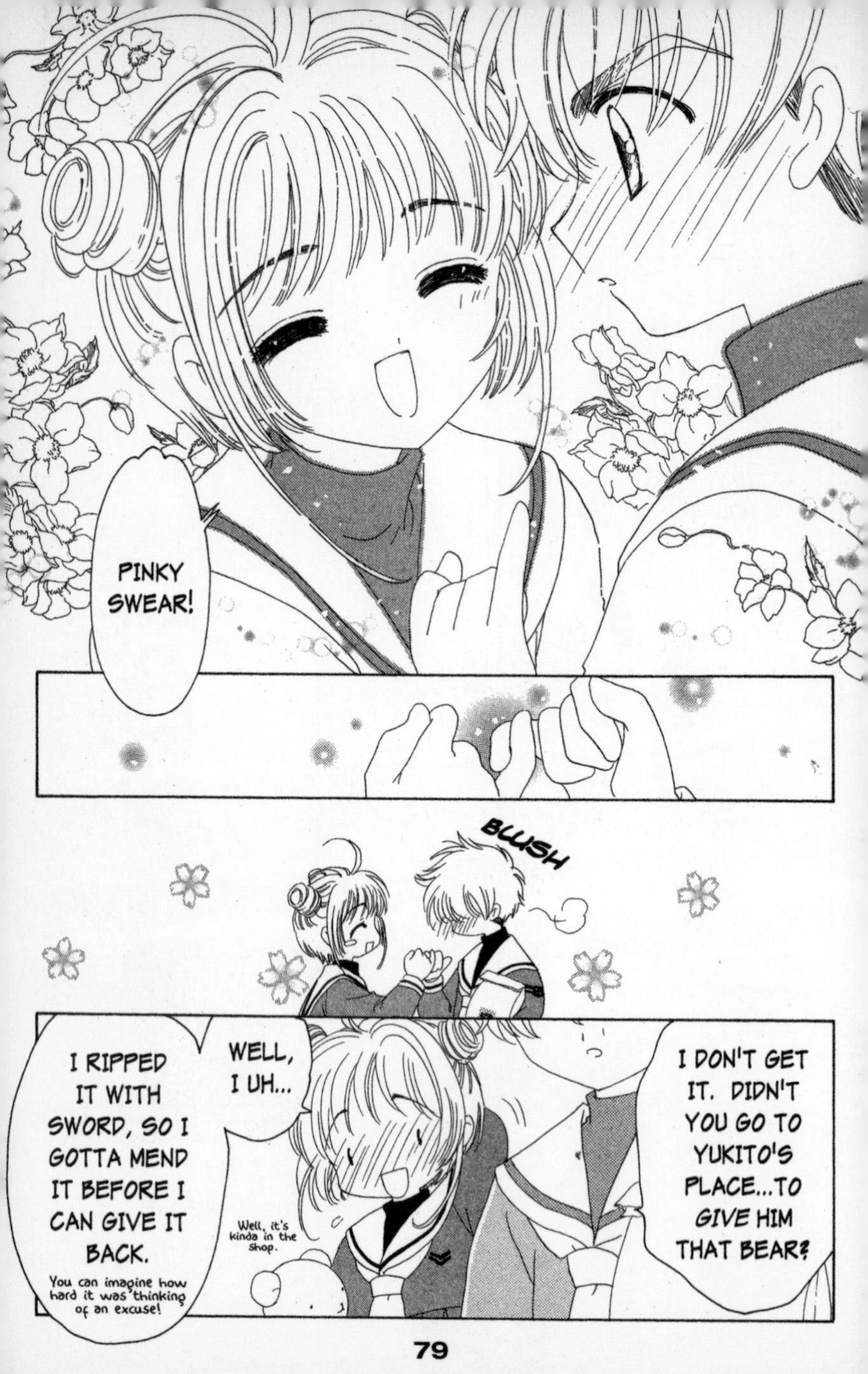
PINKY SWEAR!
BLUSH
I DON'T GET IT. DIDN'T YOU GO TO YUKITO'S PLACE...TO *GIVE* HIM THAT BEAR?
WELL, I UH...
Well, it's kinda in the shop.
I RIPPED IT WITH SWORD, SO I GOTTA MEND IT BEFORE I CAN GIVE IT BACK.
You can imagine how hard it was thinking of an excuse!

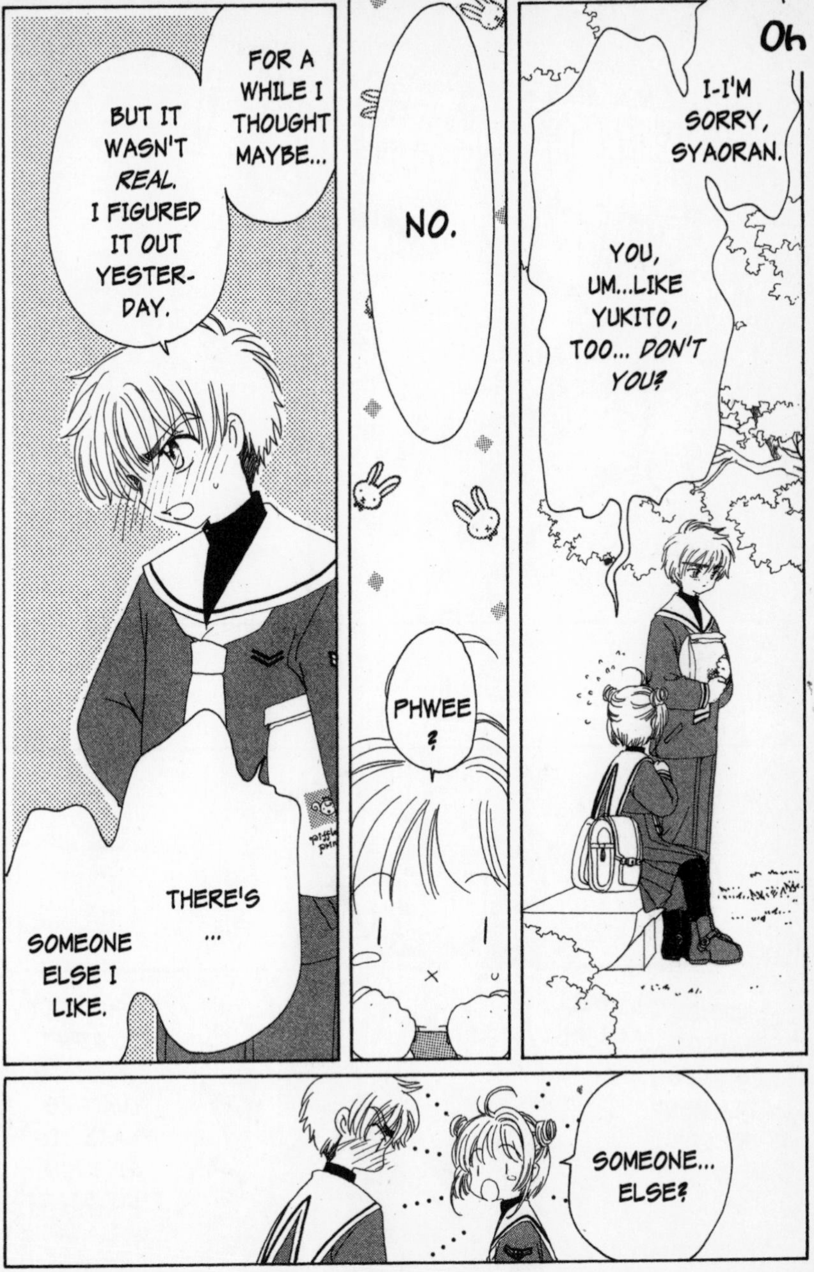
Oh
I-I'M SORRY, SYAORAN.
YOU, UM...LIKE YUKITO, TOO... *DON'T YOU?*
NO.
PHWEE?
FOR A WHILE I THOUGHT MAYBE...
BUT IT WASN'T *REAL.* I FIGURED IT OUT YESTER-DAY.
THERE'S ...
SOMEONE ELSE I LIKE.
SOMEONE... ELSE?

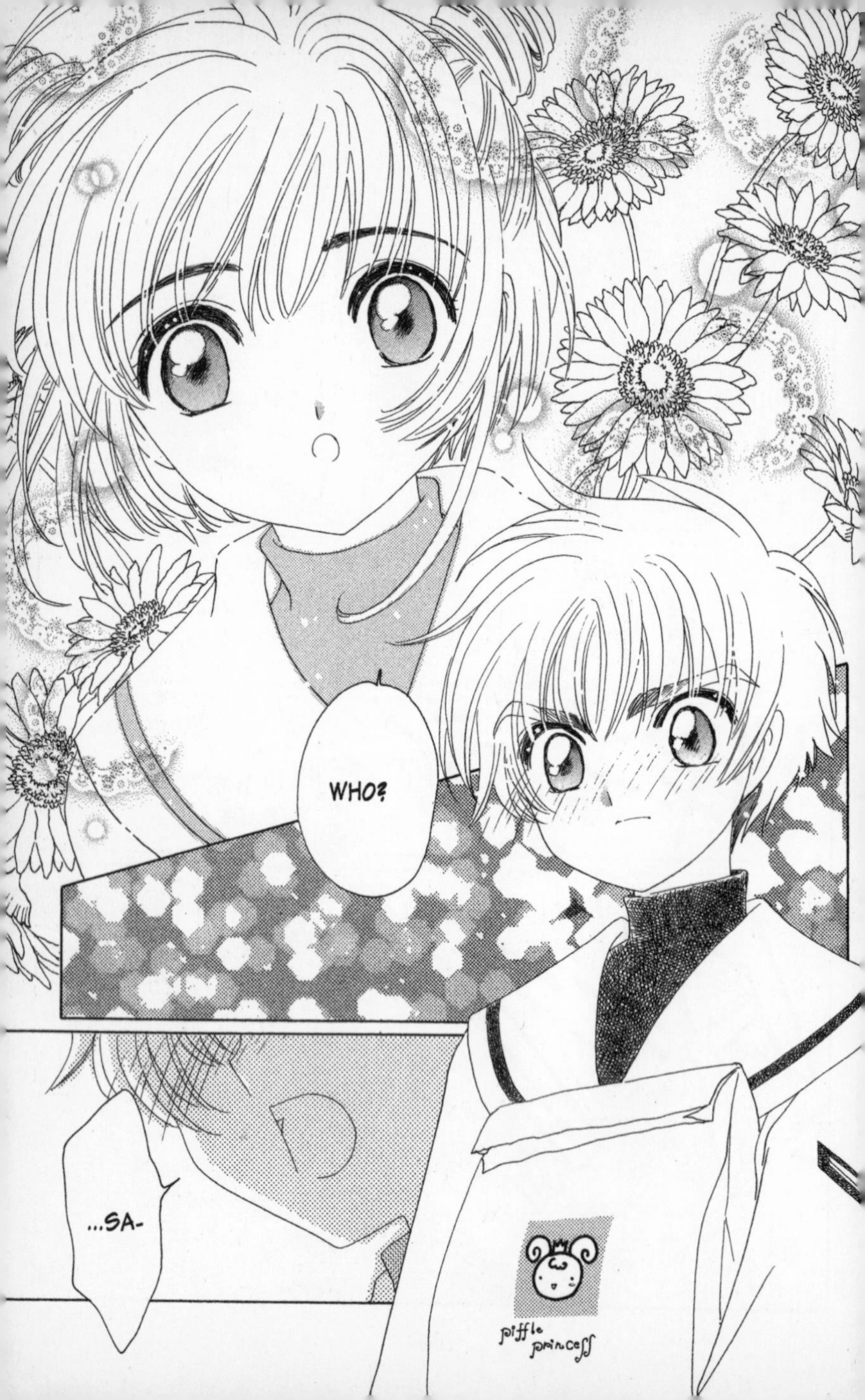
WHO?
...SA-
piffle princess

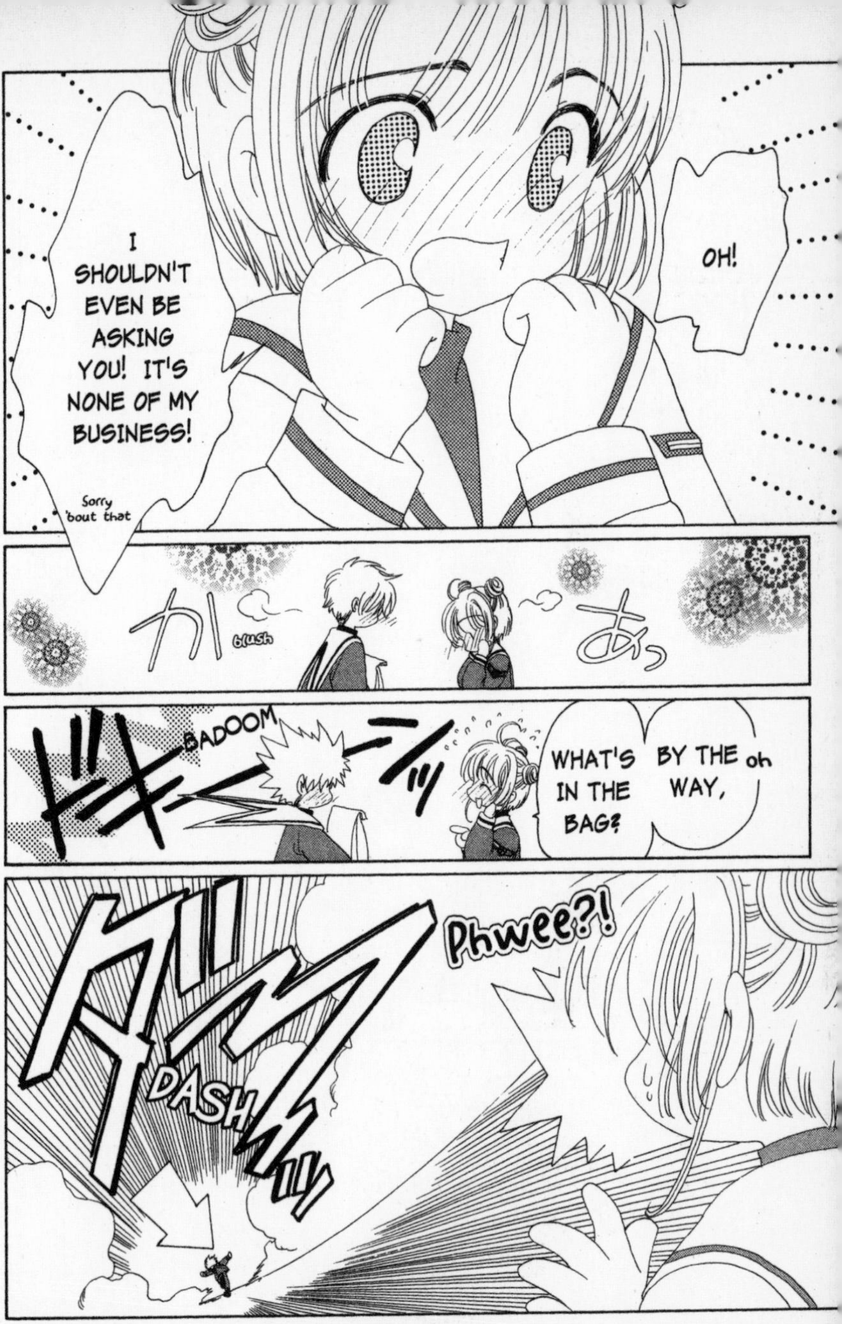
OH!
I SHOULDN'T EVEN BE ASKING YOU! IT'S NONE OF MY BUSINESS!
Sorry 'bout that
あっ
blush
oh
BY THE WAY,
WHAT'S IN THE BAG?
BADOOM
Phwee?!
DASH

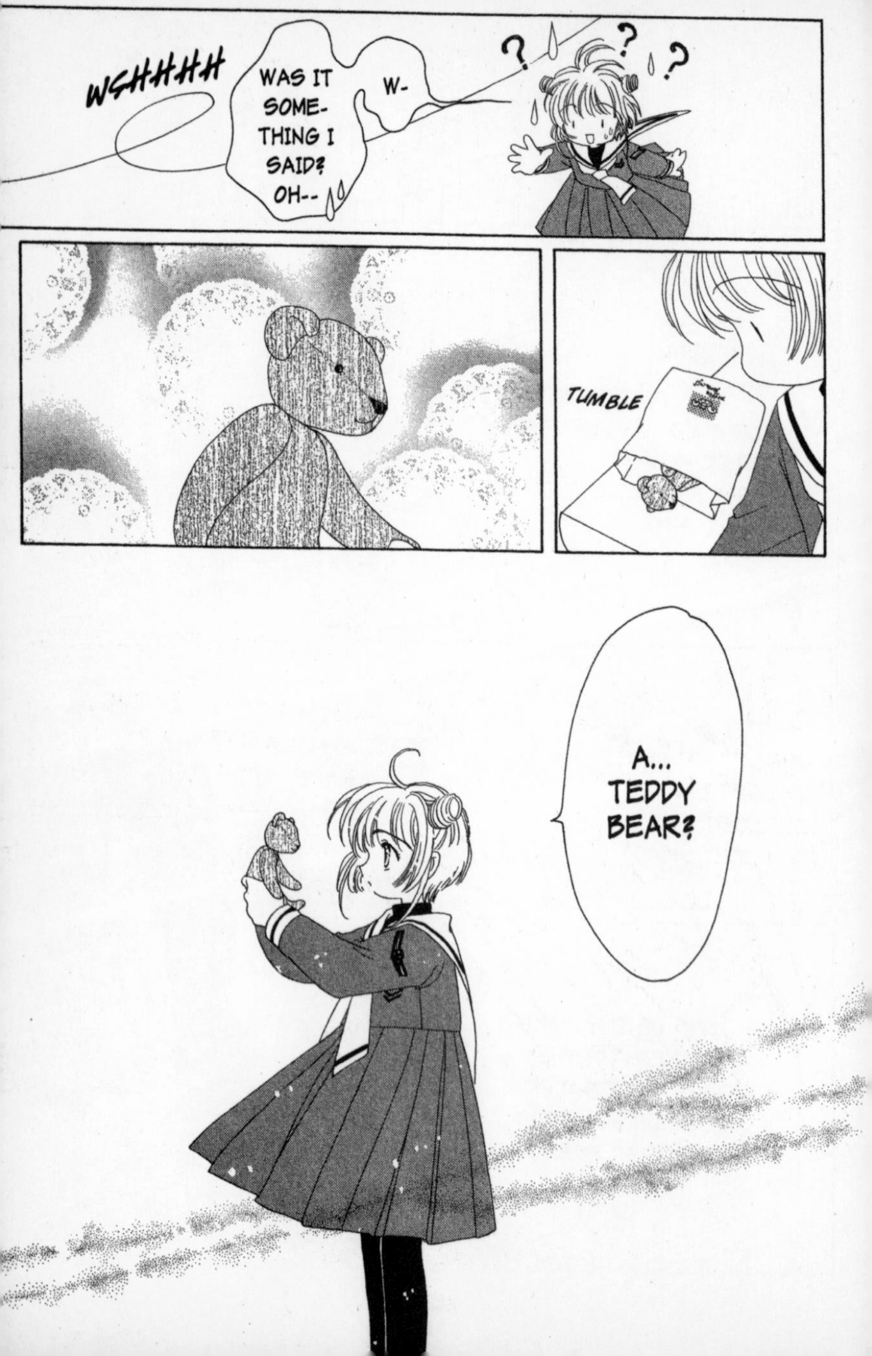
W-
WAS IT SOME-THING I SAID? OH--
WSHHHH
TUMBLE
A... TEDDY BEAR?

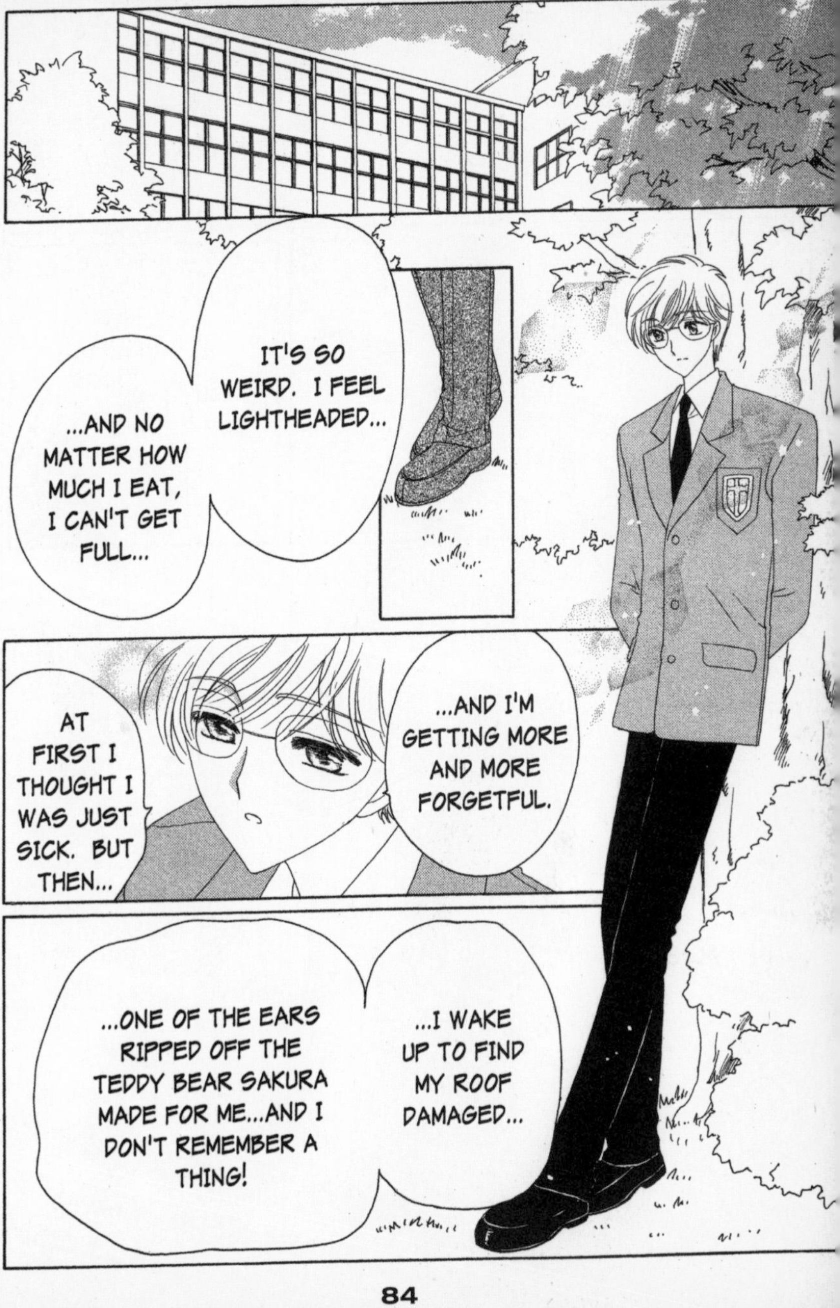
IT'S SO WEIRD. I FEEL LIGHTHEADED...
...AND NO MATTER HOW MUCH I EAT, I CAN'T GET FULL...
...AND I'M GETTING MORE AND MORE FORGETFUL.
AT FIRST I THOUGHT I WAS JUST SICK. BUT THEN...
...I WAKE UP TO FIND MY ROOF DAMAGED...
...ONE OF THE EARS RIPPED OFF THE TEDDY BEAR SAKURA MADE FOR ME...AND I DON'T REMEMBER A THING!

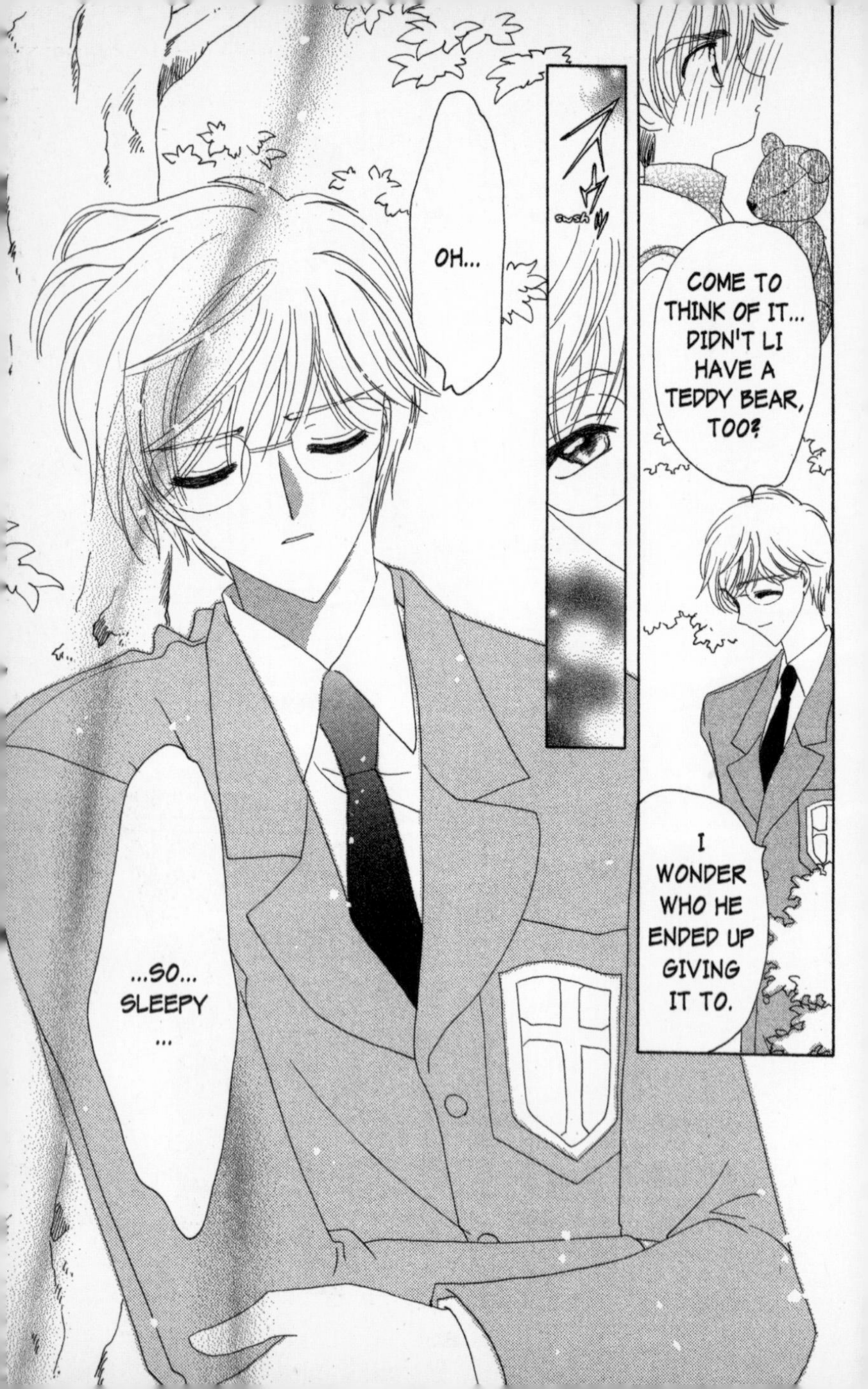
COME TO THINK OF IT... DIDN'T LI HAVE A TEDDY BEAR, TOO?
I WONDER WHO HE ENDED UP GIVING IT TO.
swsh
OH...
...SO... SLEEPY ...

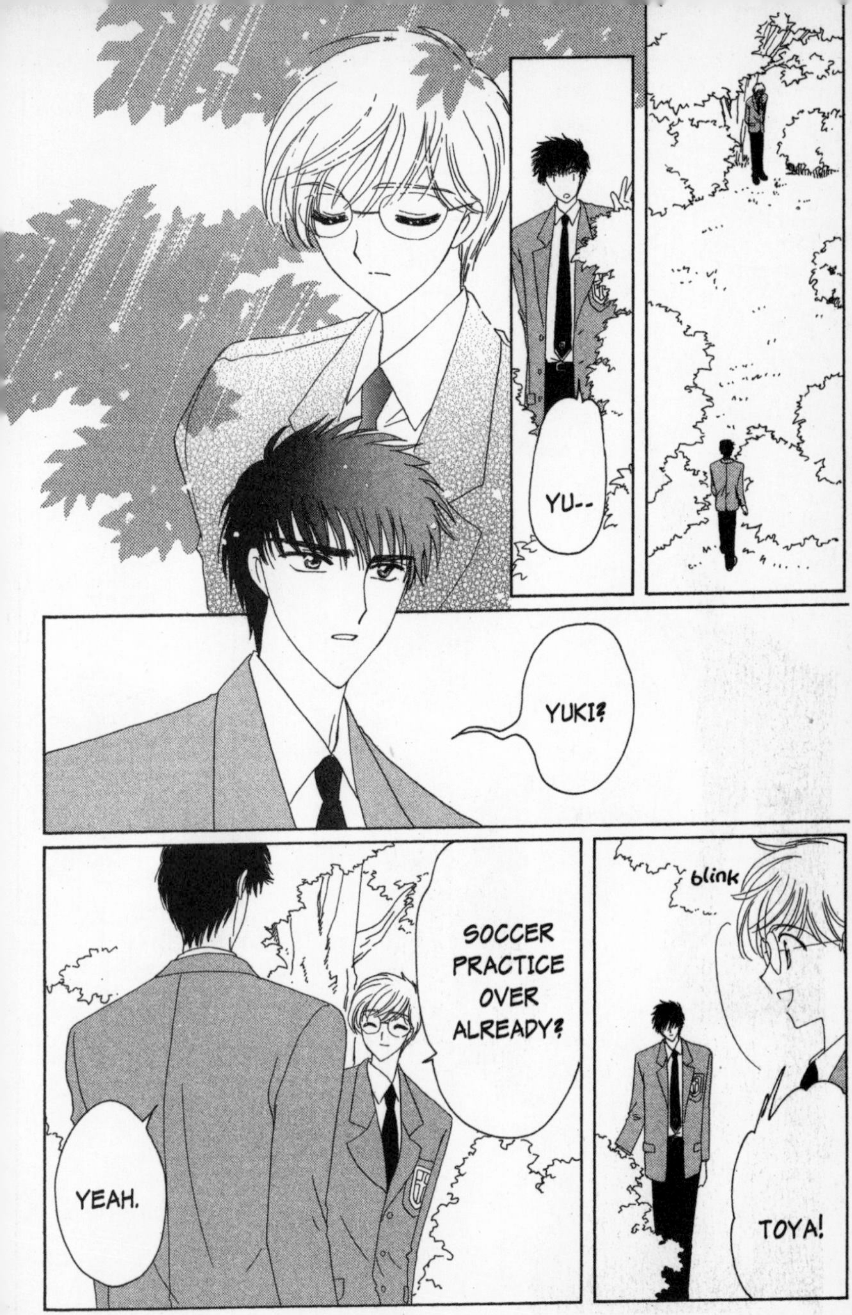
YU--
YUKI?
blink
TOYA!
SOCCER PRACTICE OVER ALREADY?
YEAH.

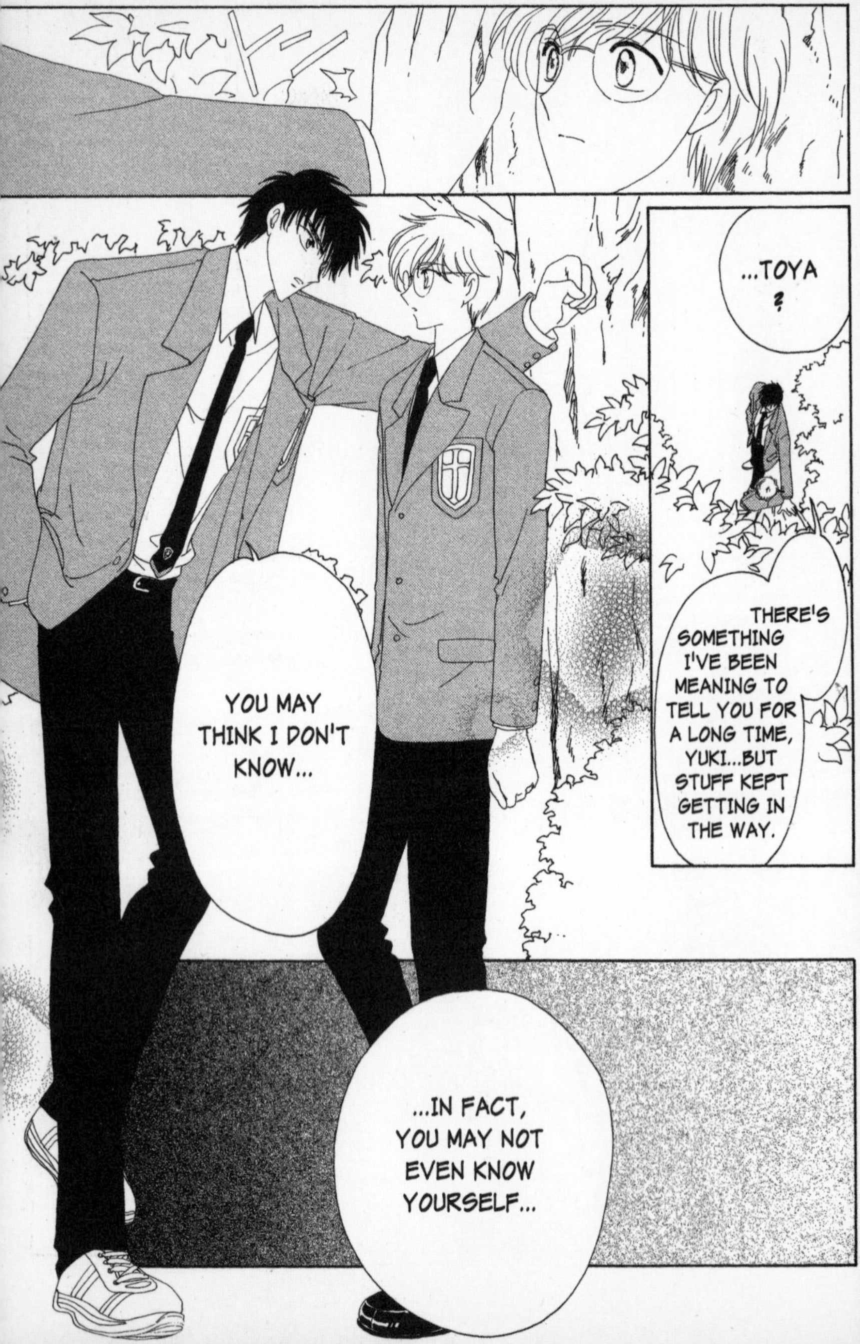
...TOYA?
THERE'S SOMETHING I'VE BEEN MEANING TO TELL YOU FOR A LONG TIME, YUKI...BUT STUFF KEPT GETTING IN THE WAY.
YOU MAY THINK I DON'T KNOW...
...IN FACT, YOU MAY NOT EVEN KNOW YOURSELF...

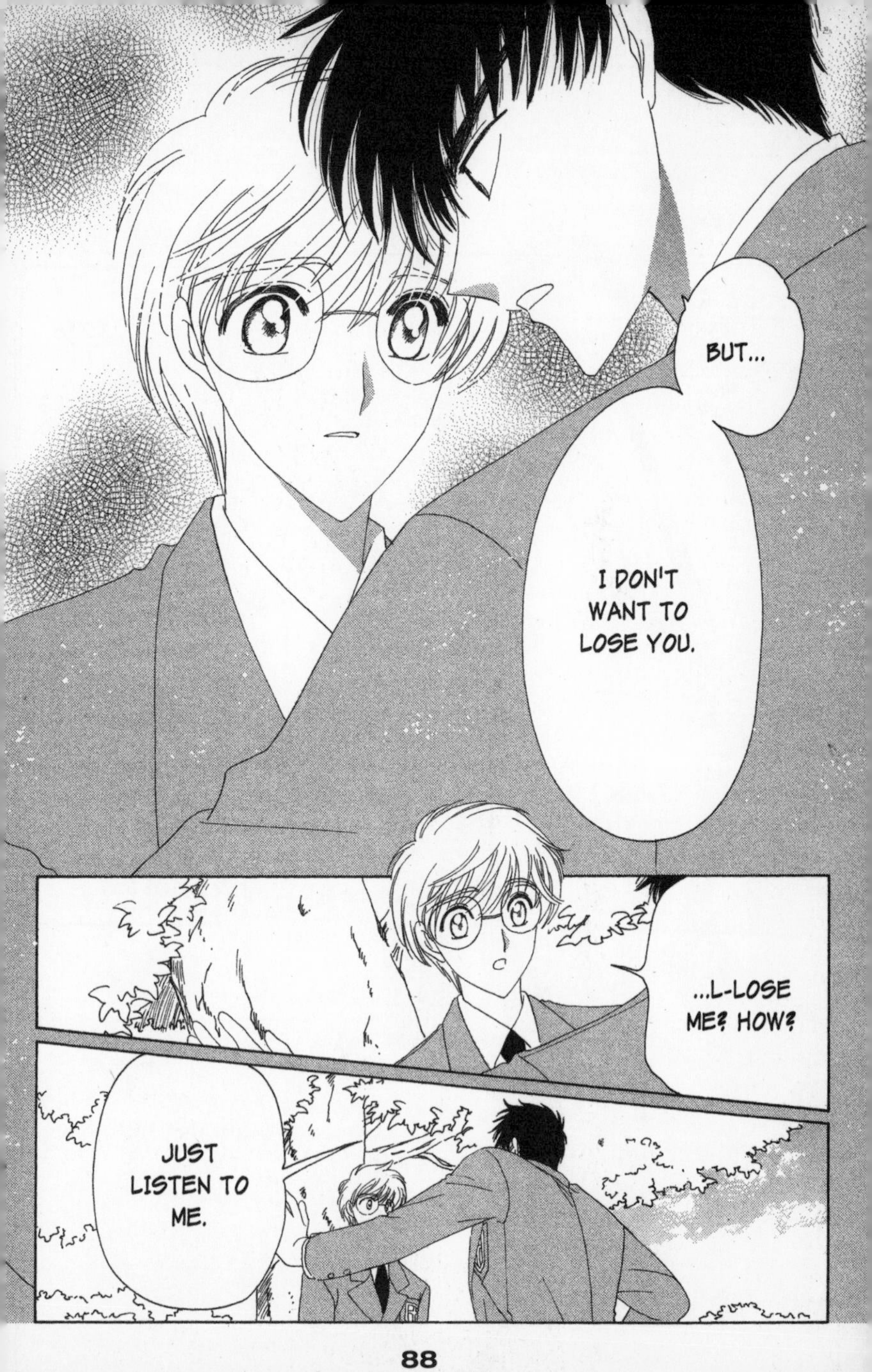
BUT...
I DON'T WANT TO LOSE YOU.
...L-LOSE ME? HOW?
JUST LISTEN TO ME.

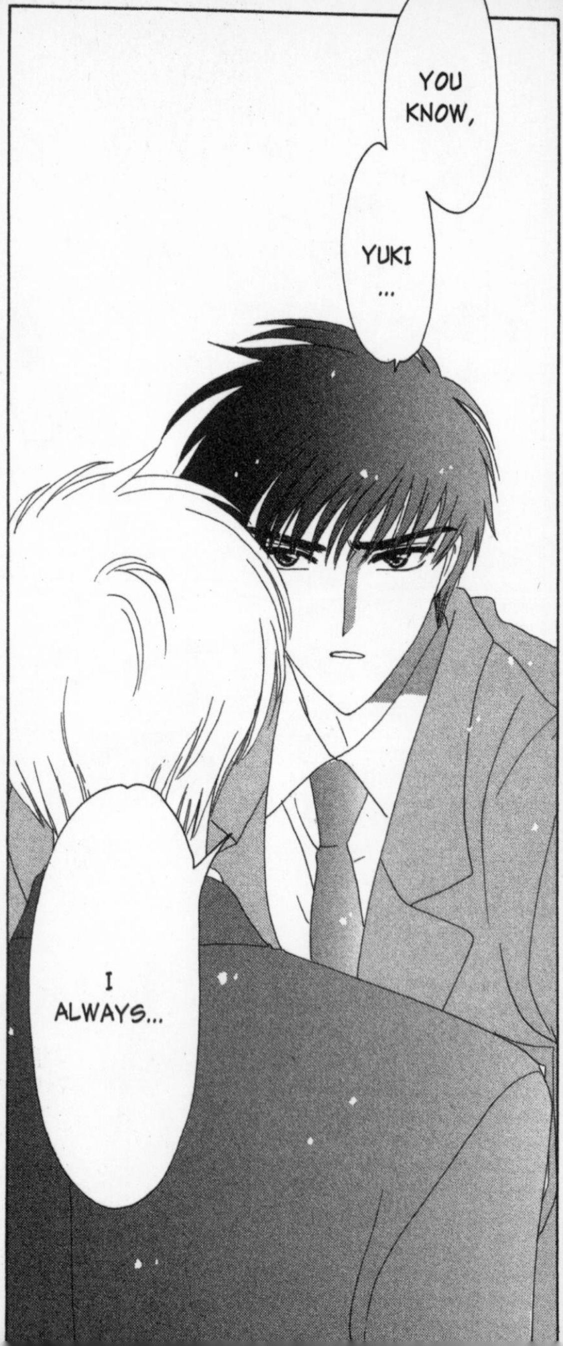
YOU KNOW,
YUKI ...
I ALWAYS...

22

YUE
MASTER:
SAKURA KINOMOTO
BIRTHDAY:
SECRET (DIFFERENT FROM YUKI'S)
SYMBOL:
MOON
ASPECT:
DARK
EYES:
VIOLET-SILVER
HAIR:
SILVER
MAGIC:
EASTERN MAGIC
FAVORITE FOOD:
DOESN'T EAT
FAVORITE THING:
SLEEPING
LEAST FAVORITE THING:
ANYTHING OBNOXIOUS
TEMPORARY FORM:
YUKITO TSUKISHIRO

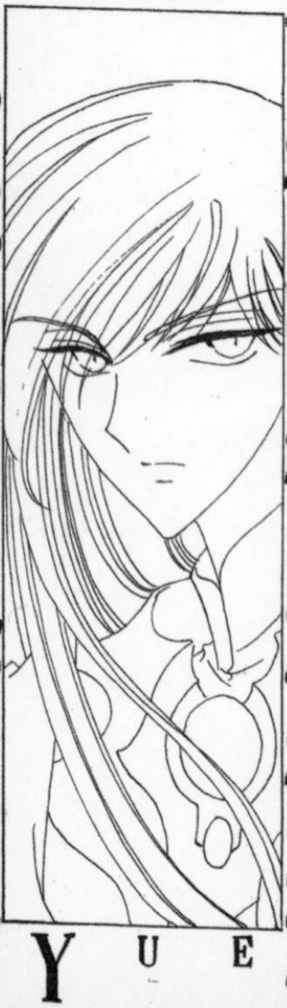

Y U E

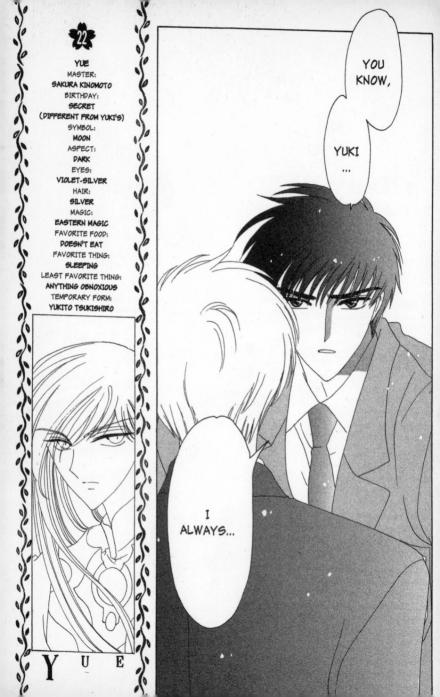

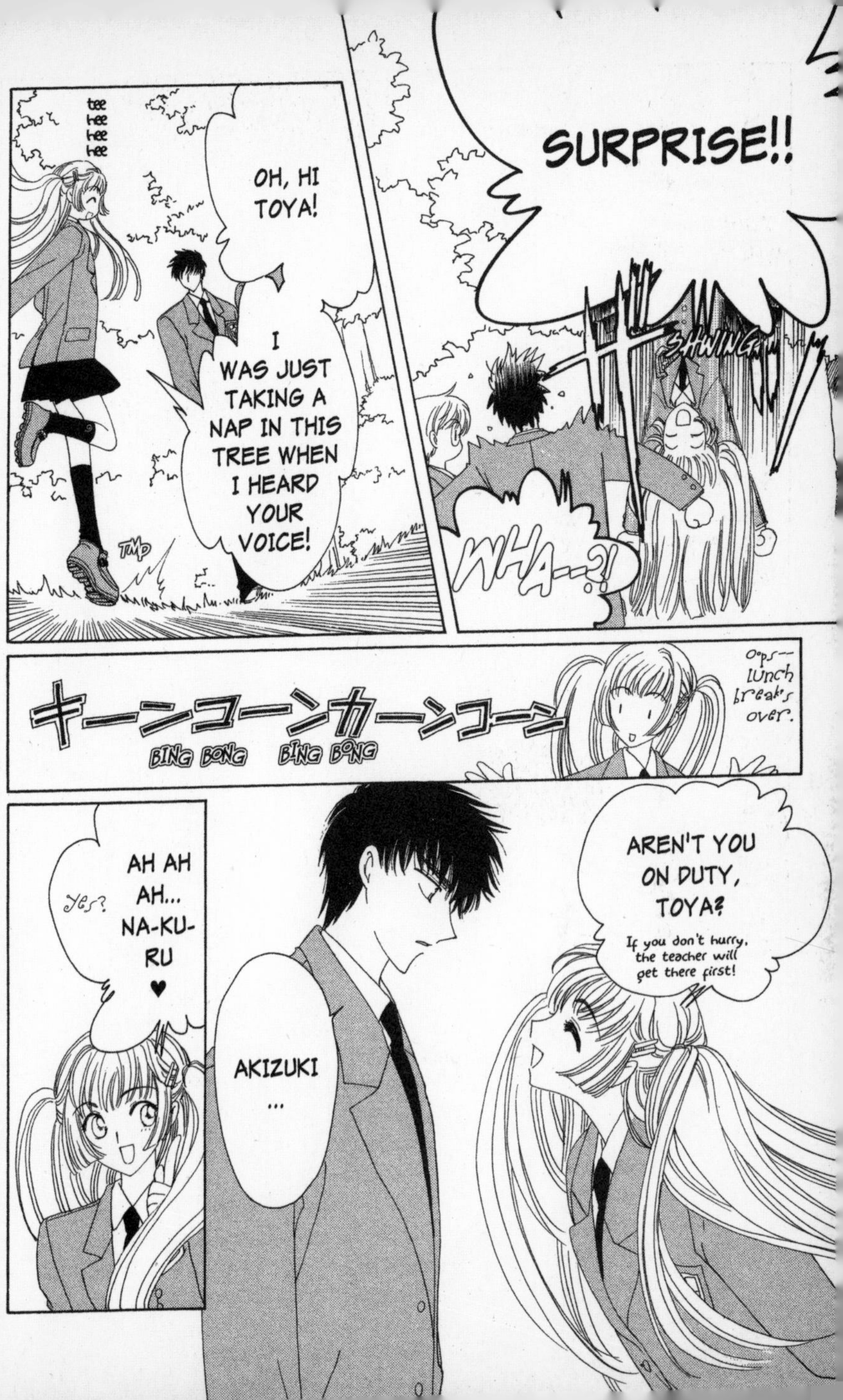
SURPRISE!!
SHWING
WHA--?!
tee hee hee hee
OH, HI TOYA!
I WAS JUST TAKING A NAP IN THIS TREE WHEN I HEARD YOUR VOICE!
TMP
Oops-- lunch break's over.
キーンコーンカーンコーン
BING BONG BING BONG
AREN'T YOU ON DUTY, TOYA?
If you don't hurry, the teacher will get there first!
AKIZUKI ...
AH AH AH... NA-KU-RU ♥
yes?

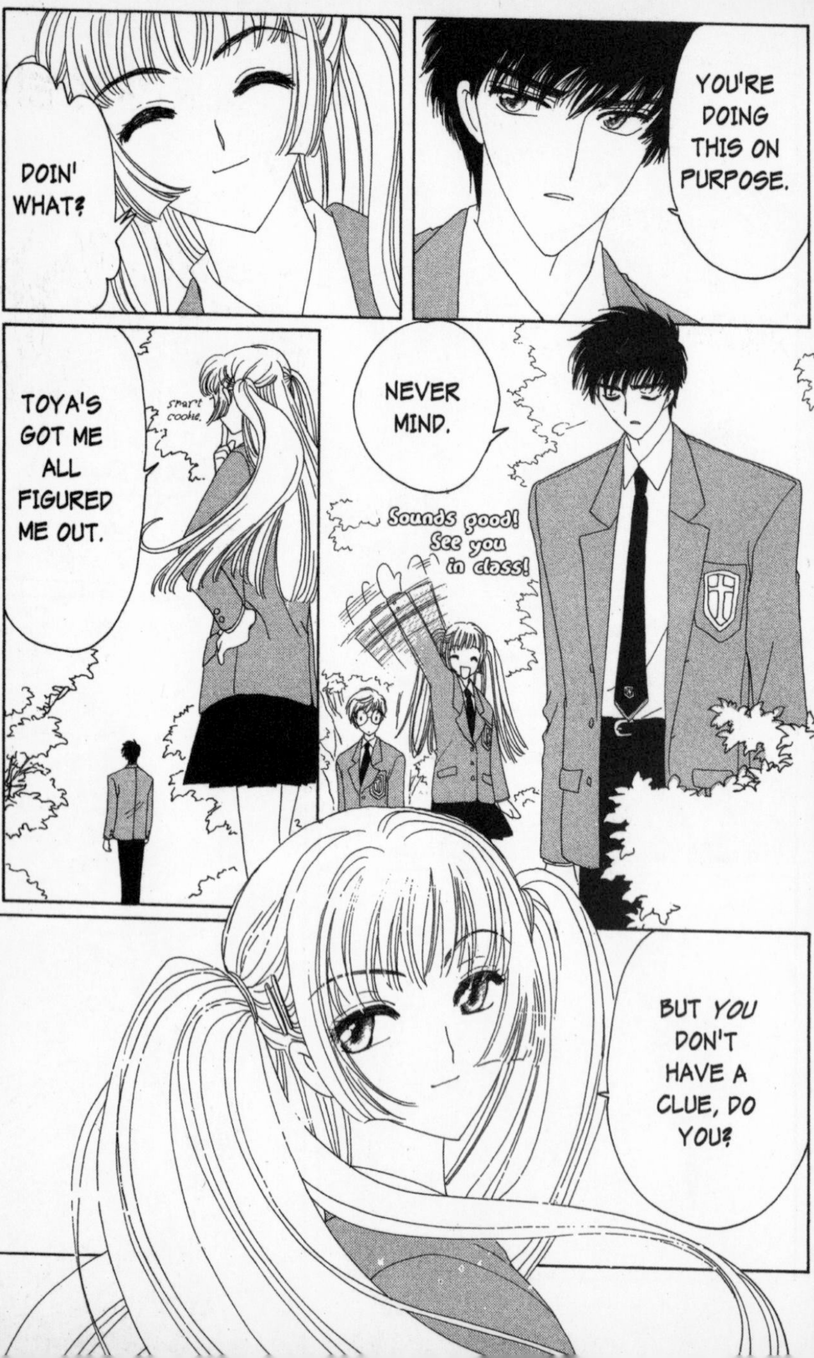
YOU'RE DOING THIS ON PURPOSE.
DOIN' WHAT?
NEVER MIND.
Sounds good! See you in class!
smart cookie.
TOYA'S GOT ME ALL FIGURED ME OUT.
BUT *YOU* DON'T HAVE A CLUE, DO YOU?

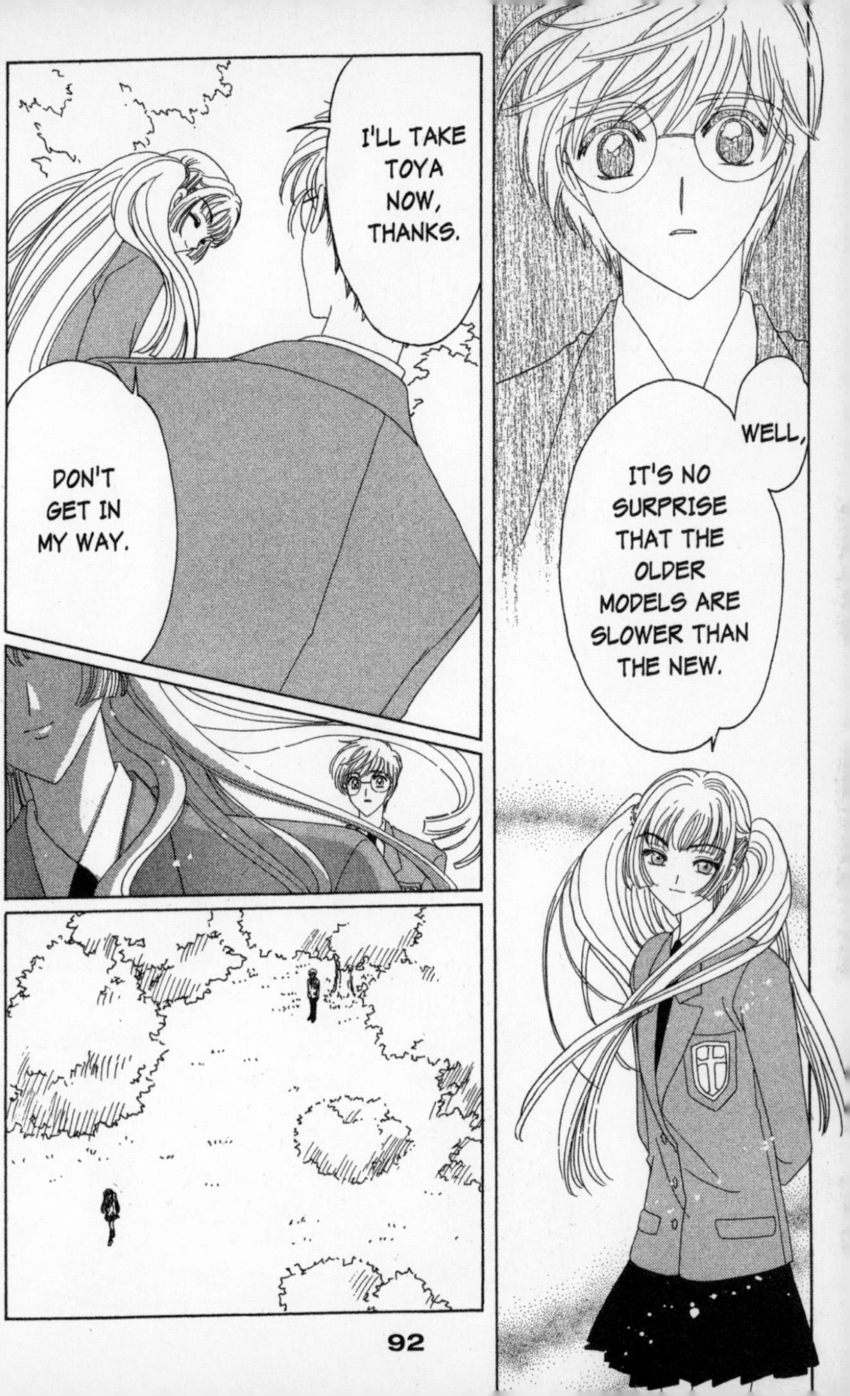
WELL,
IT'S NO SURPRISE THAT THE OLDER MODELS ARE SLOWER THAN THE NEW.
I'LL TAKE TOYA NOW, THANKS.
DON'T GET IN MY WAY.

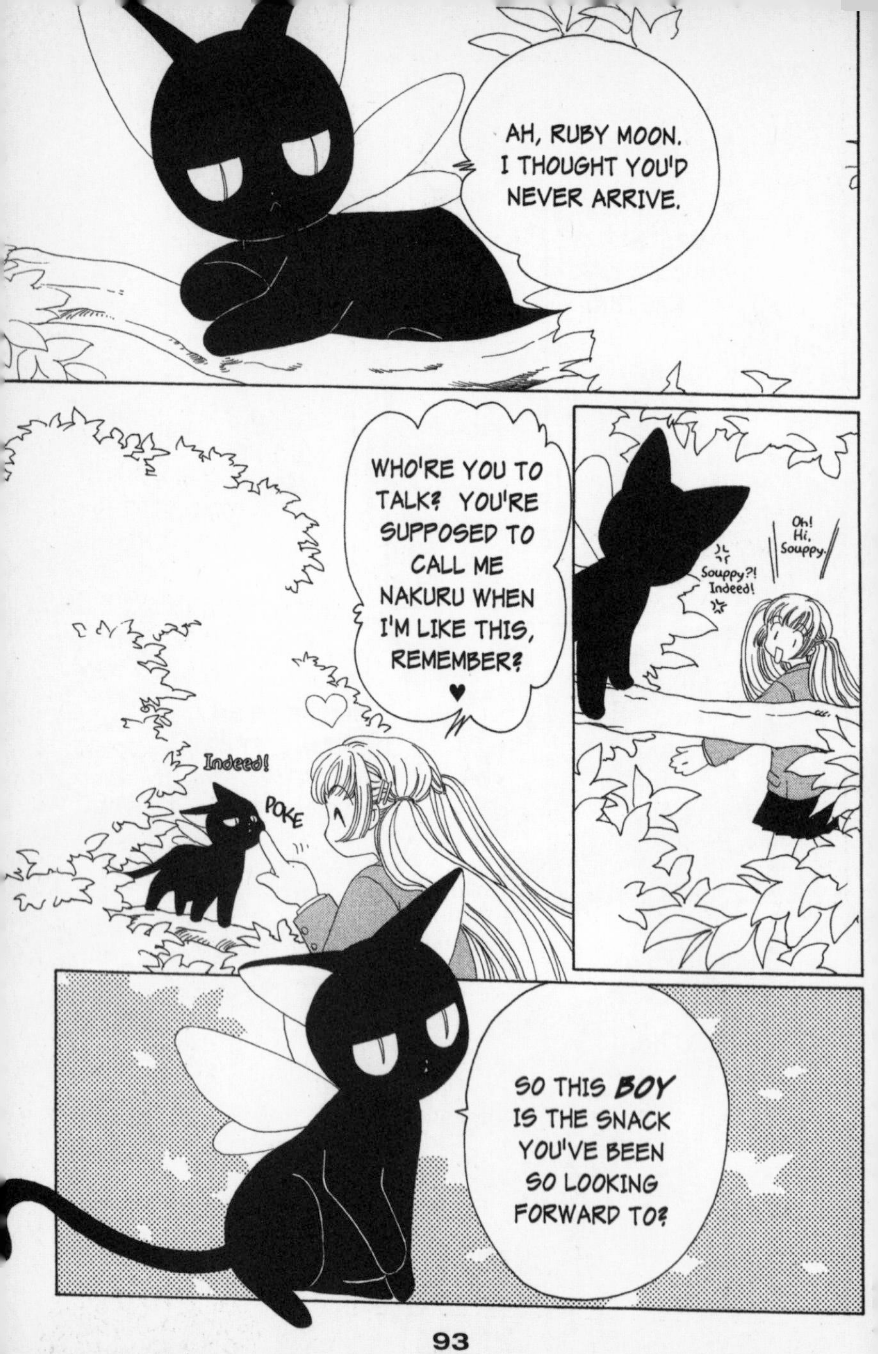
AH, RUBY MOON. I THOUGHT YOU'D NEVER ARRIVE.
Oh! Hi, Souppy.
Souppy?! Indeed!
WHO'RE YOU TO TALK? YOU'RE SUPPOSED TO CALL ME NAKURU WHEN I'M LIKE THIS, REMEMBER? ♥
Indeed!
POKE
SO THIS *BOY* IS THE SNACK YOU'VE BEEN SO LOOKING FORWARD TO?

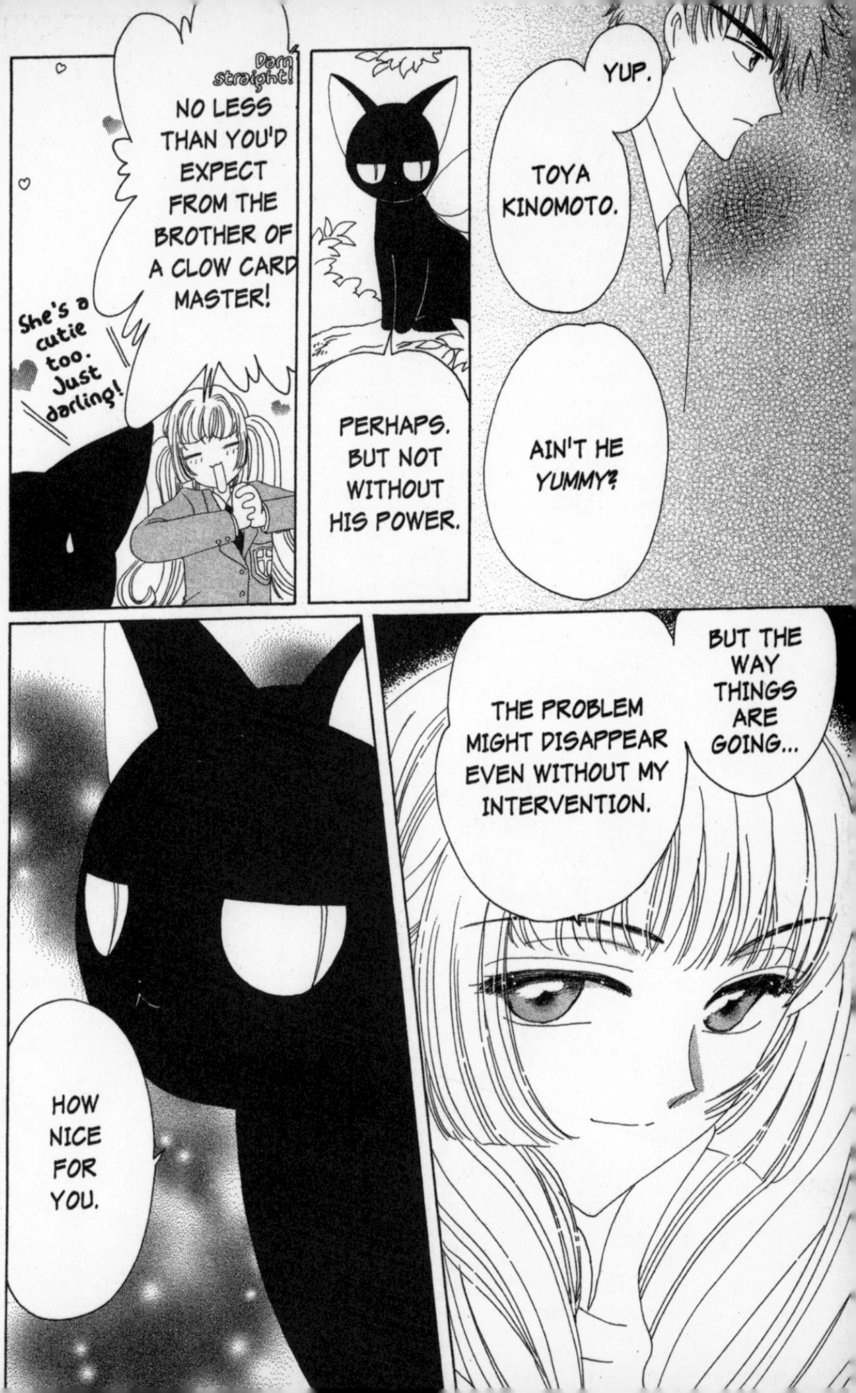
YUP.
TOYA KINOMOTO.
AIN'T HE YUMMY?
PERHAPS. BUT NOT WITHOUT HIS POWER.
Darn straight!
NO LESS THAN YOU'D EXPECT FROM THE BROTHER OF A CLOW CARD MASTER!
She's a cutie too. Just darling!
BUT THE WAY THINGS ARE GOING...
THE PROBLEM MIGHT DISAPPEAR EVEN WITHOUT MY INTERVENTION.
HOW NICE FOR YOU.

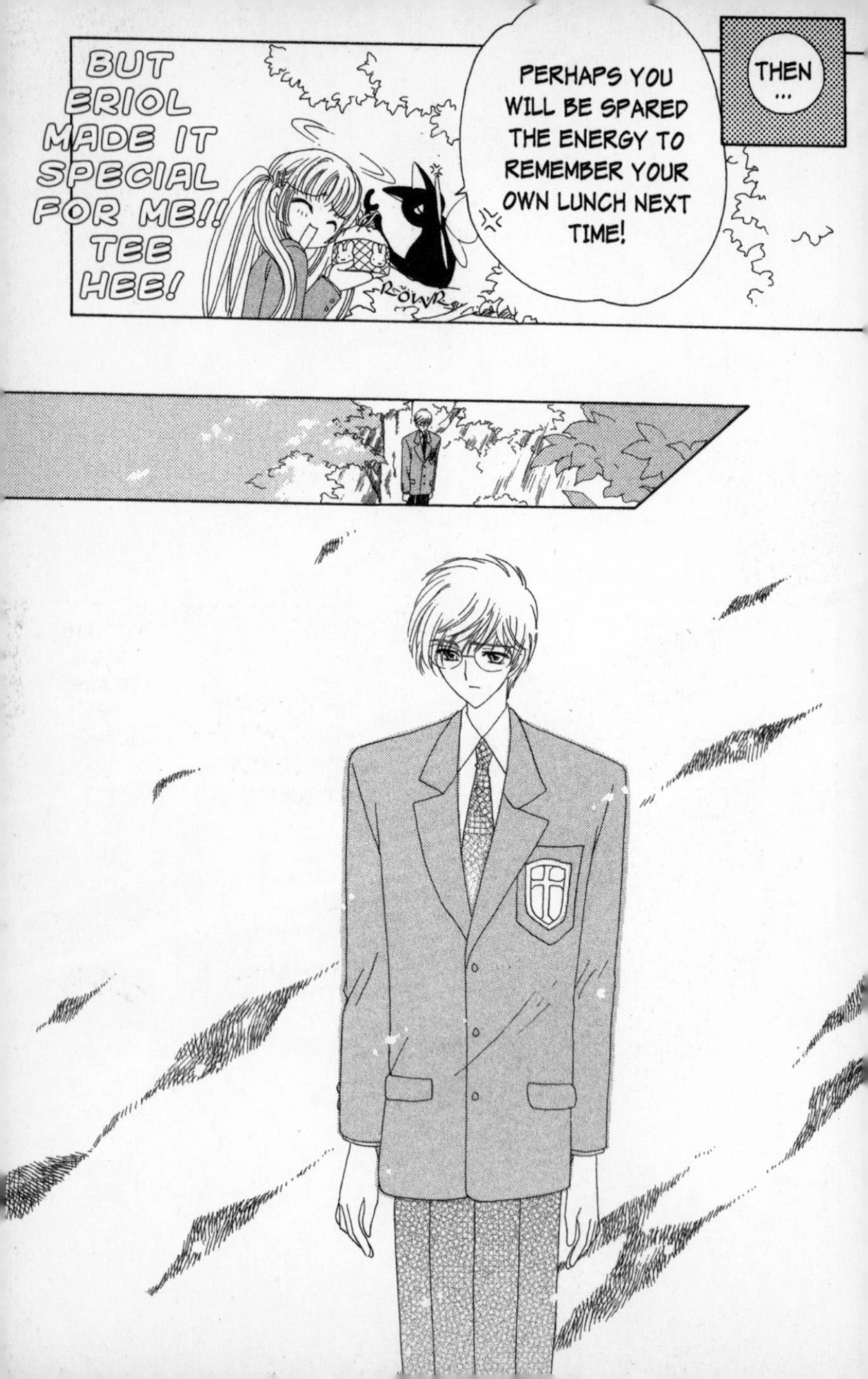
THEN ...
PERHAPS YOU WILL BE SPARED THE ENERGY TO REMEMBER YOUR OWN LUNCH NEXT TIME!
BUT ERIOL MADE IT SPECIAL FOR ME!! TEE HEE!
ROWR

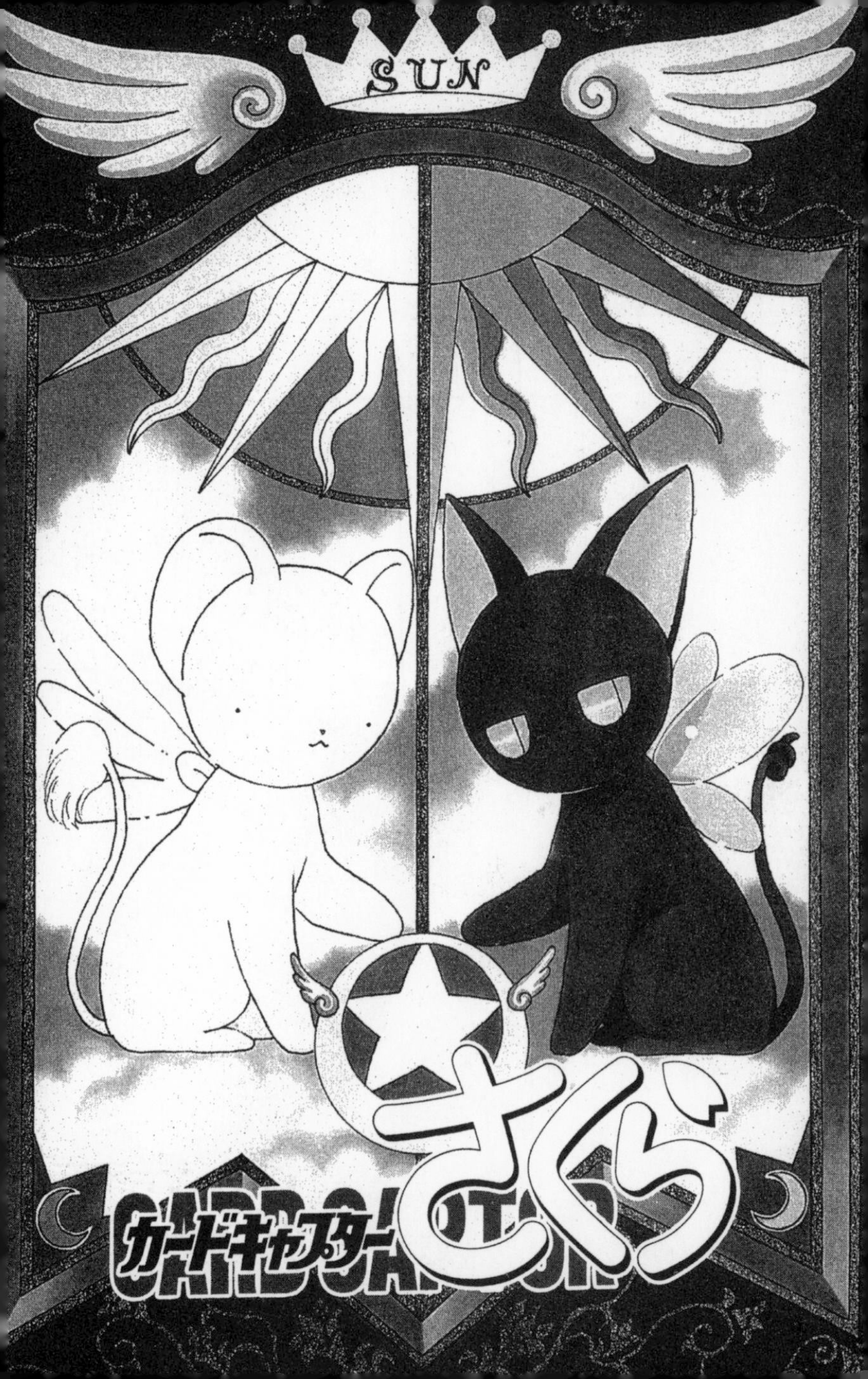
SUN
カードキャプターさくら

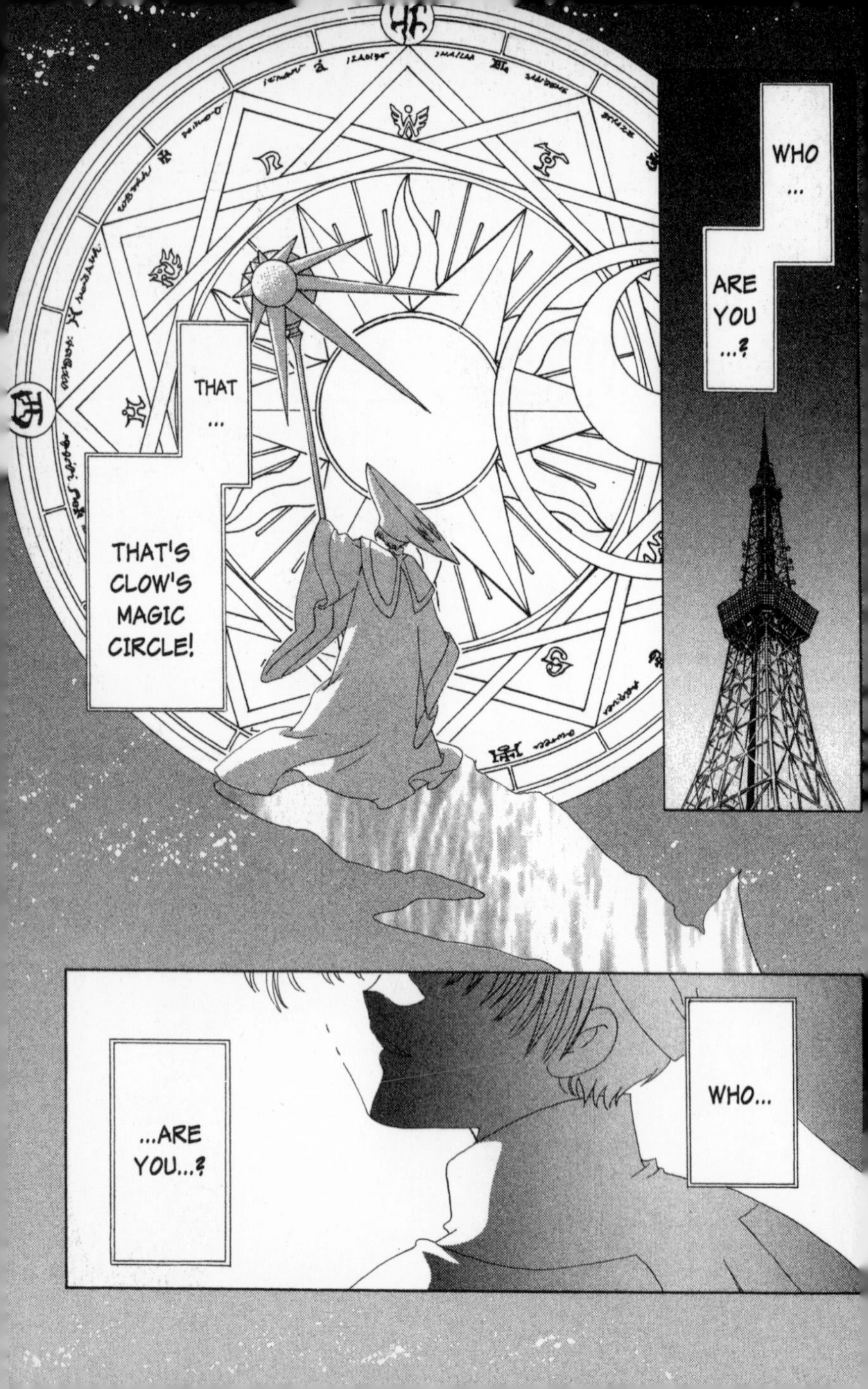
WHO ... ARE YOU ...?
THAT ...
THAT'S CLOW'S MAGIC CIRCLE!
WHO...
...ARE YOU...?

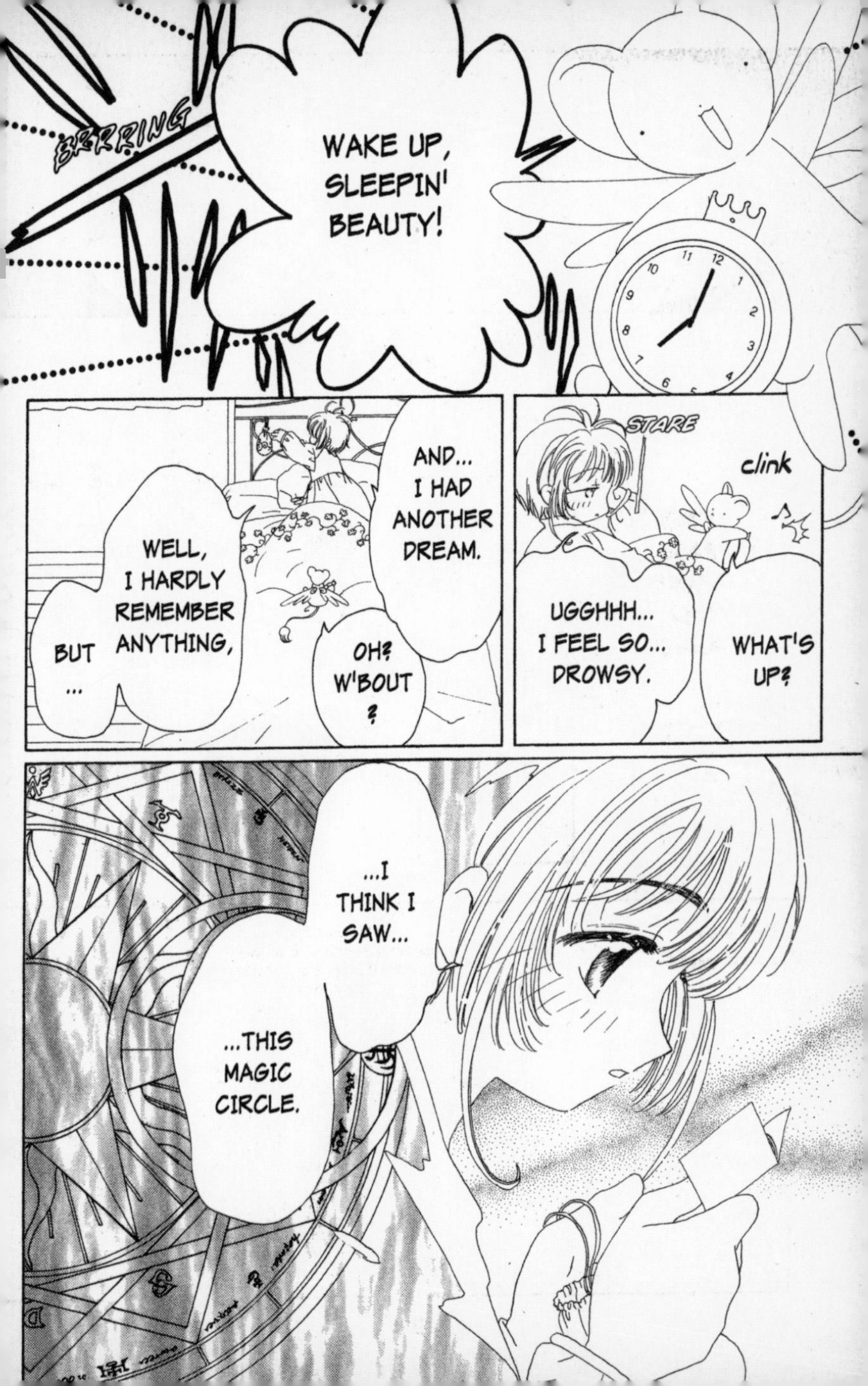
WAKE UP, SLEEPIN' BEAUTY!
BRRRING
STARE
clink
WHAT'S UP?
UGGHHH... I FEEL SO... DROWSY.
AND... I HAD ANOTHER DREAM.
OH? W'BOUT?
WELL, I HARDLY REMEMBER ANYTHING,
BUT ...
...I THINK I SAW...
...THIS MAGIC CIRCLE.

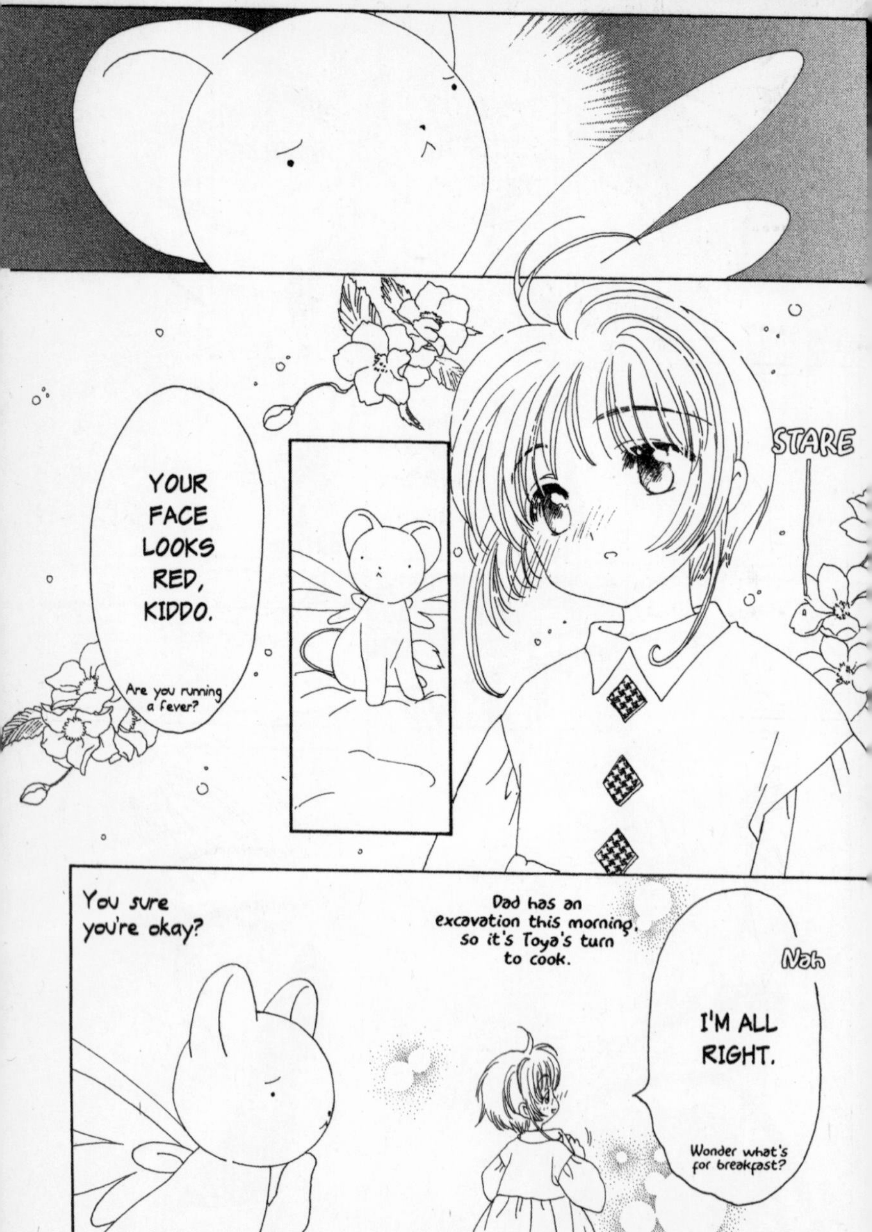
STARE
YOUR FACE LOOKS RED, KIDDO.
Are you running a fever?
Nah
I'M ALL RIGHT.
Wonder what's for breakfast?
Dad has an excavation this morning, so it's Toya's turn to cook.
You sure you're okay?

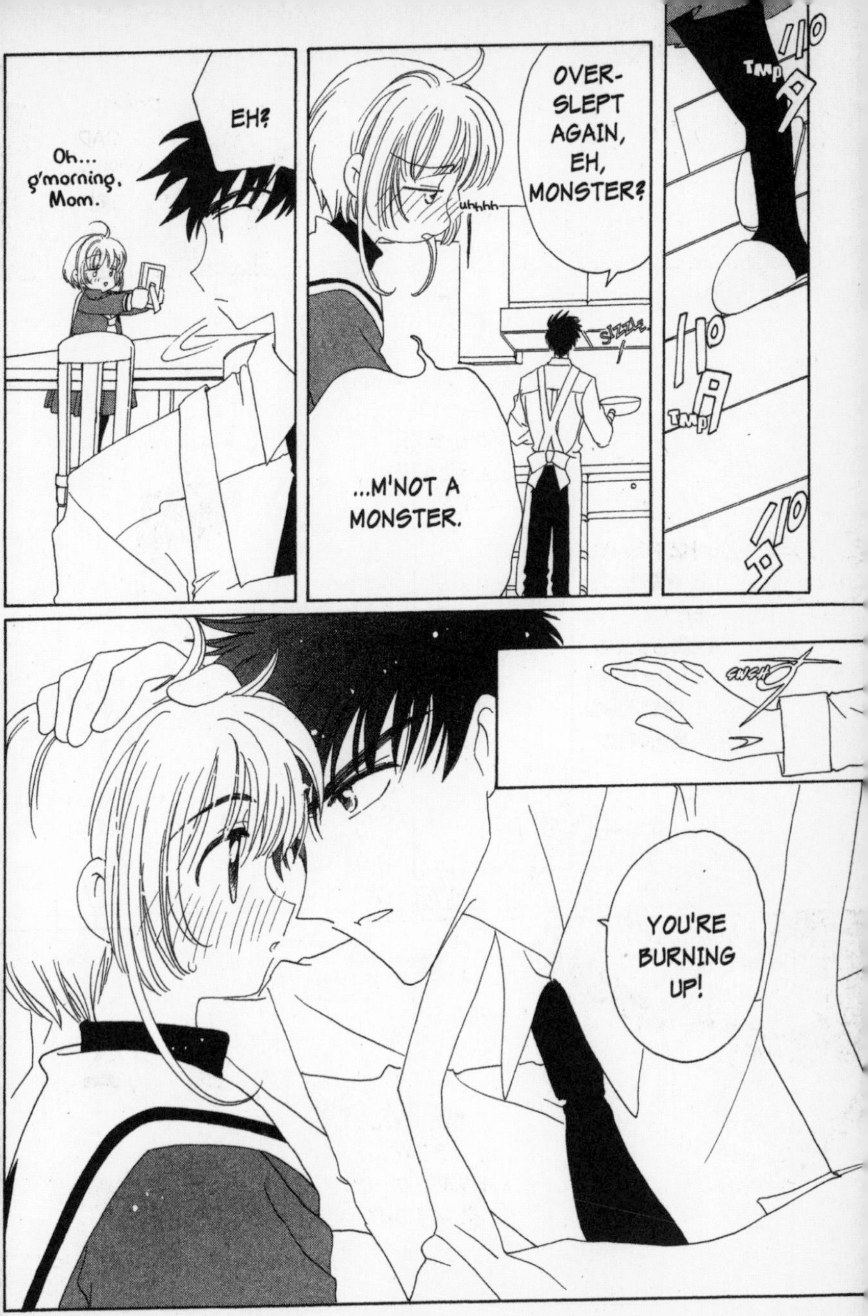
TMP
TMP
OVER-SLEPT AGAIN, EH, MONSTER?
uhhhh
SIZZLE
...M'NOT A MONSTER.
EH?
Oh... g'morning, Mom.
YOU'RE BURNING UP!

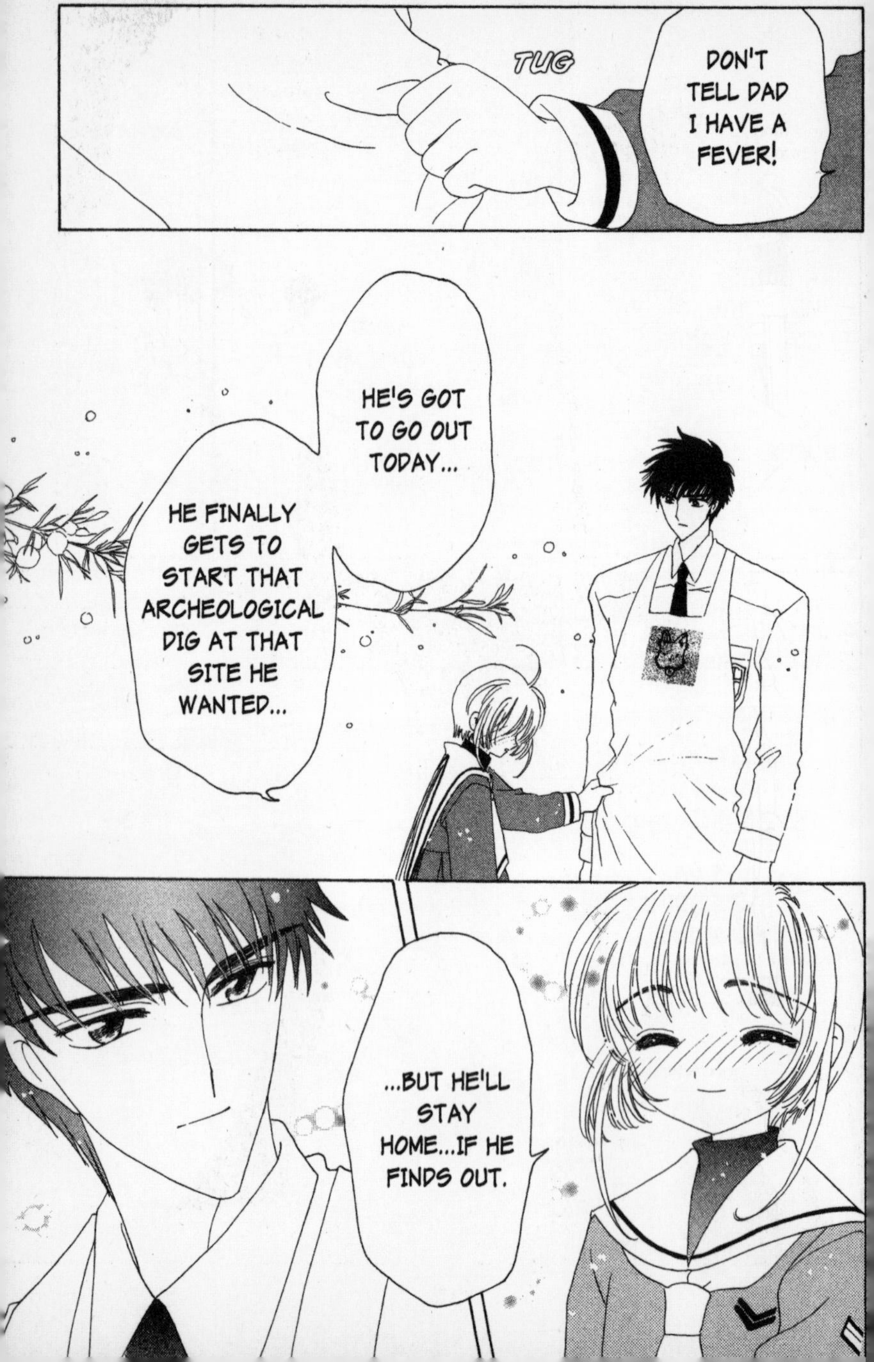

DON'T TELL DAD I HAVE A FEVER!
TUG
HE'S GOT TO GO OUT TODAY...
HE FINALLY GETS TO START THAT ARCHEOLOGICAL DIG AT THAT SITE HE WANTED...
...BUT HE'LL STAY HOME...IF HE FINDS OUT.

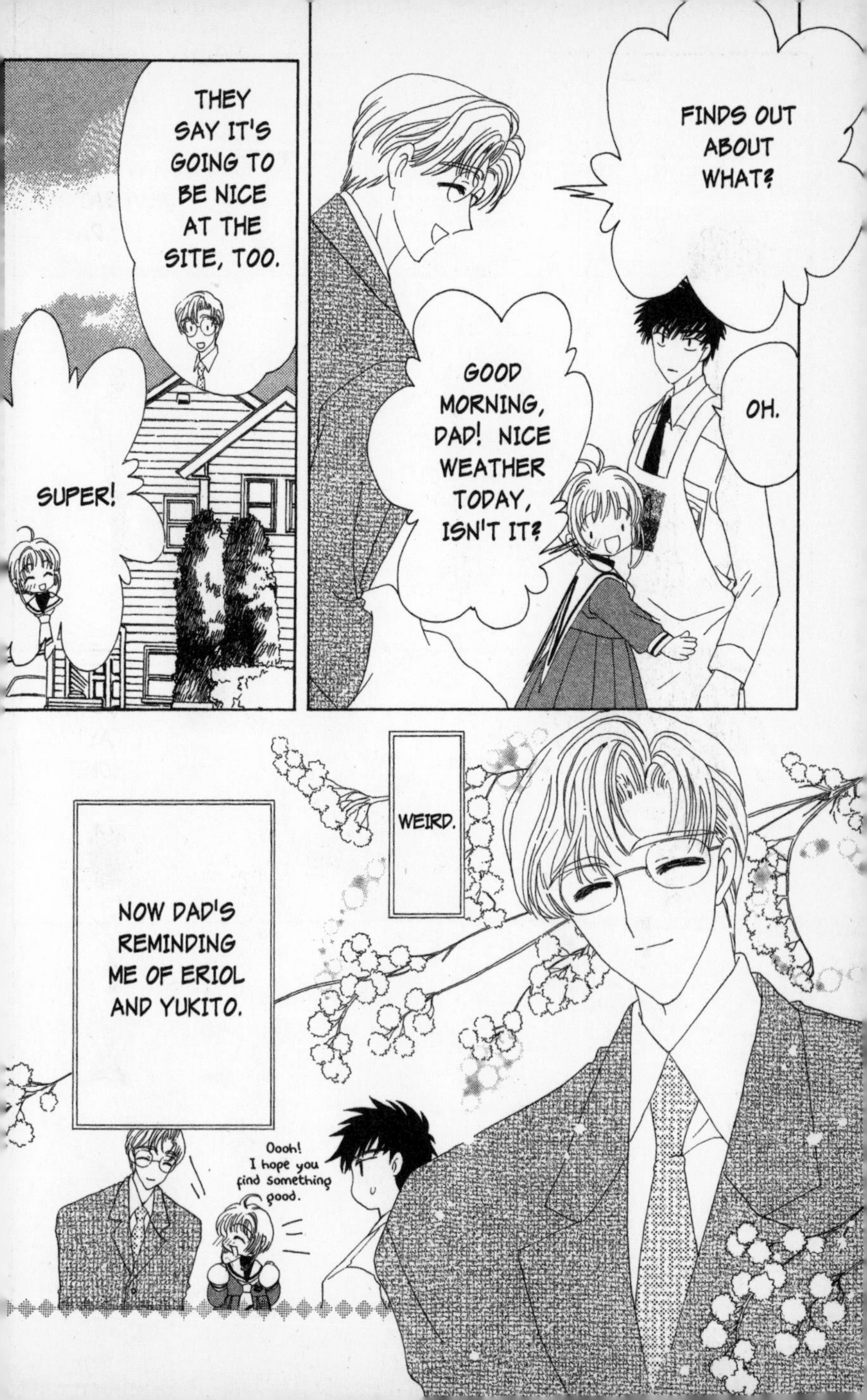
FINDS OUT ABOUT WHAT?
OH.
GOOD MORNING, DAD! NICE WEATHER TODAY, ISN'T IT?
THEY SAY IT'S GOING TO BE NICE AT THE SITE, TOO.
SUPER!
WEIRD.
NOW DAD'S REMINDING ME OF ERIOL AND YUKITO.
Oooh! I hope you find something good.

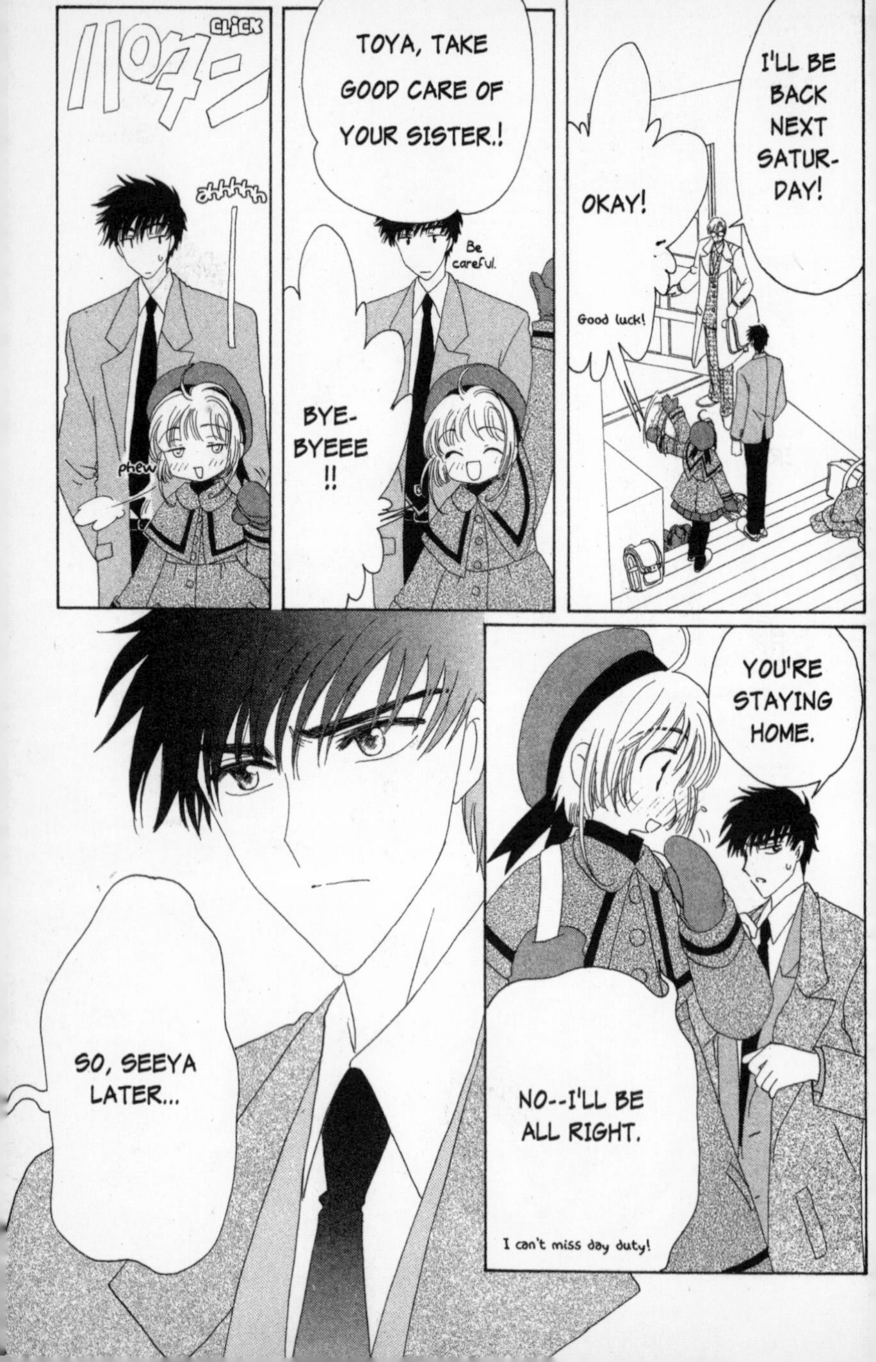
I'LL BE BACK NEXT SATUR-DAY!
OKAY!
Good luck!
TOYA, TAKE GOOD CARE OF YOUR SISTER.!
Be careful.
BYE-BYEEE !!
CLICK
phew
YOU'RE STAYING HOME.
NO--I'LL BE ALL RIGHT.
I can't miss day duty!
SO, SEEYA LATER...

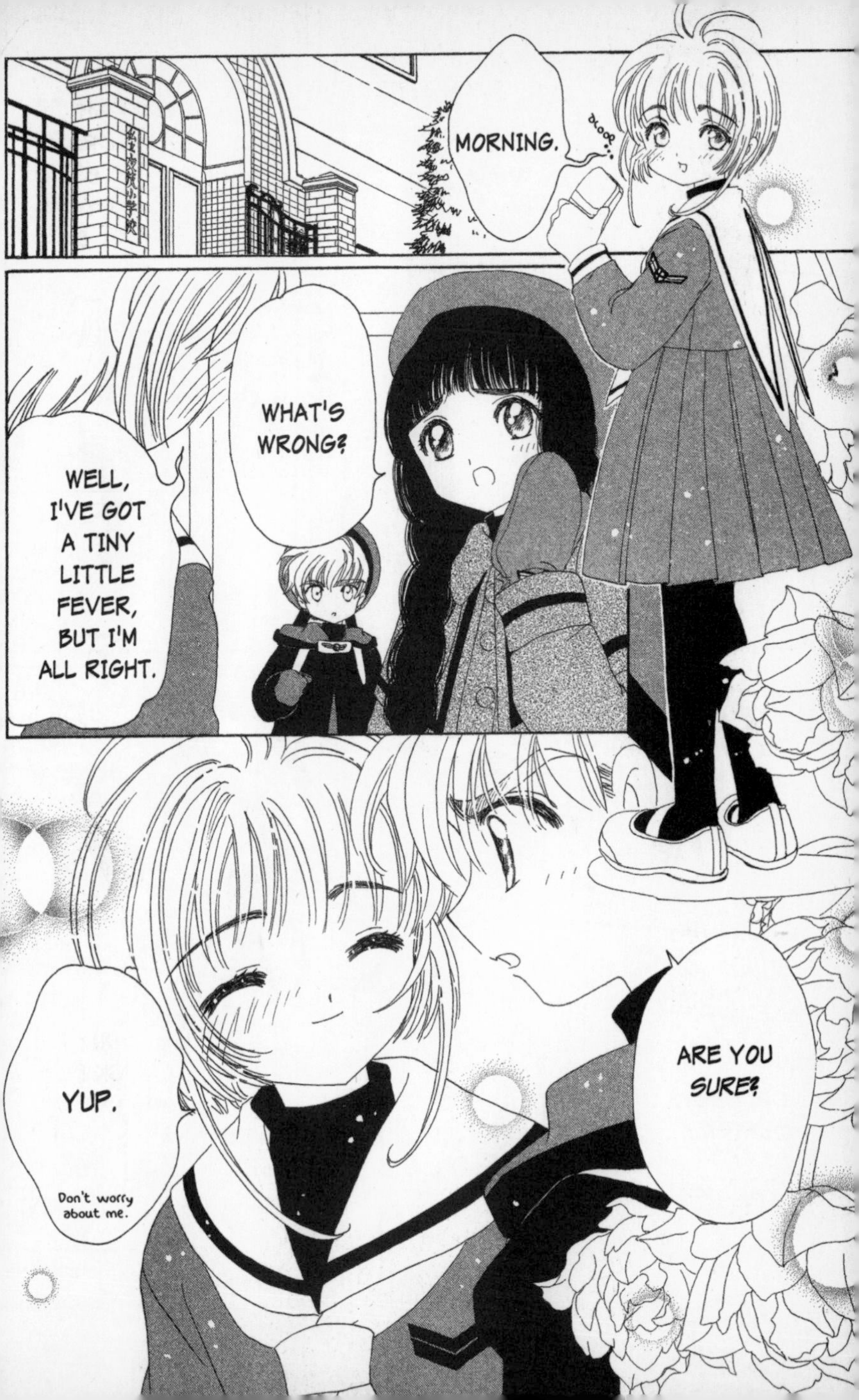

MORNING.
bloop...
WHAT'S WRONG?
WELL, I'VE GOT A TINY LITTLE FEVER, BUT I'M ALL RIGHT.
ARE YOU SURE?
YUP.
Don't worry about me.

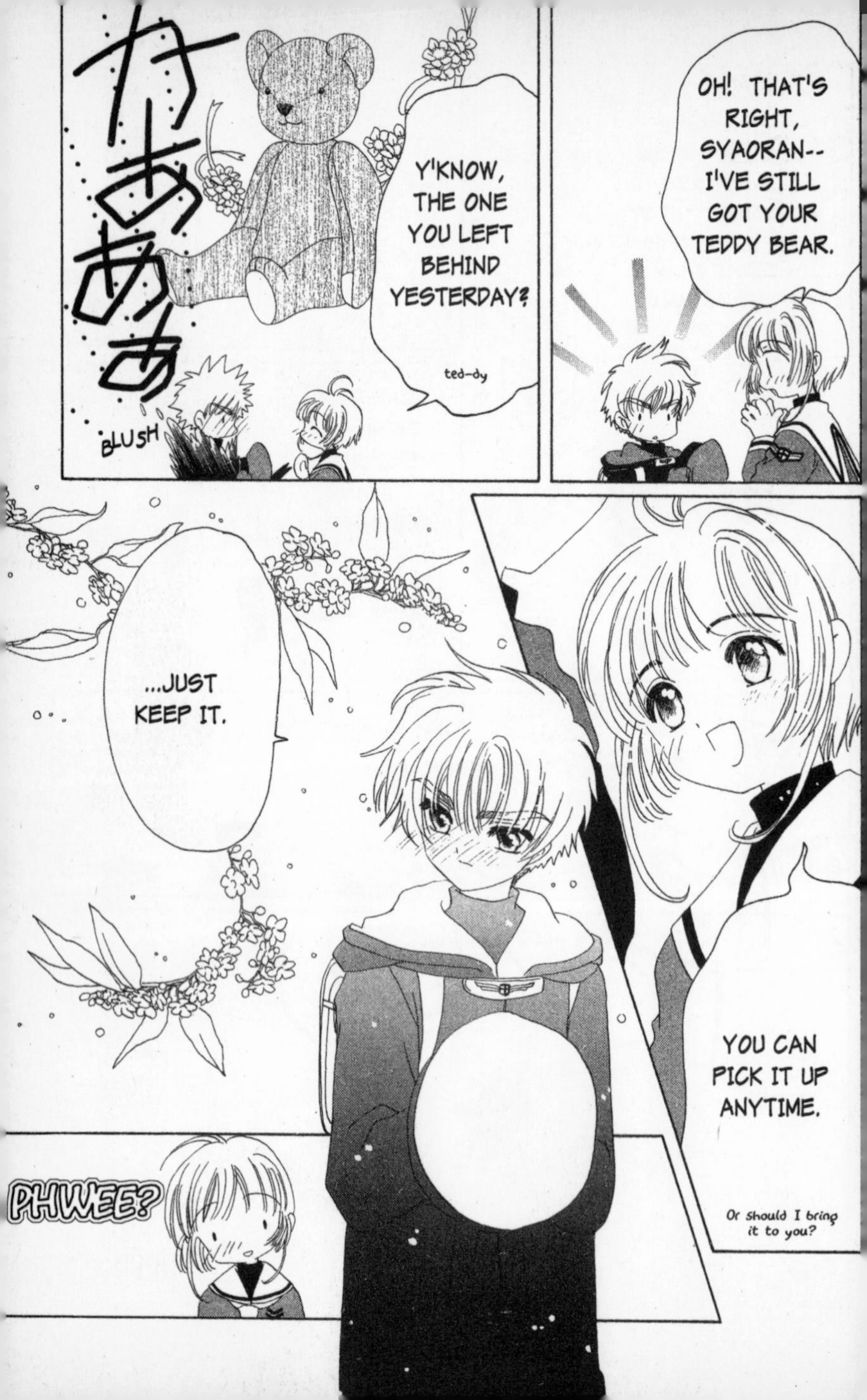
OH! THAT'S RIGHT, SYAORAN-- I'VE STILL GOT YOUR TEDDY BEAR.
Y'KNOW, THE ONE YOU LEFT BEHIND YESTERDAY?
ted-dy
かあああ
BLUSH
YOU CAN PICK IT UP ANYTIME.
Or should I bring it to you?
...JUST KEEP IT.
PHWEE?

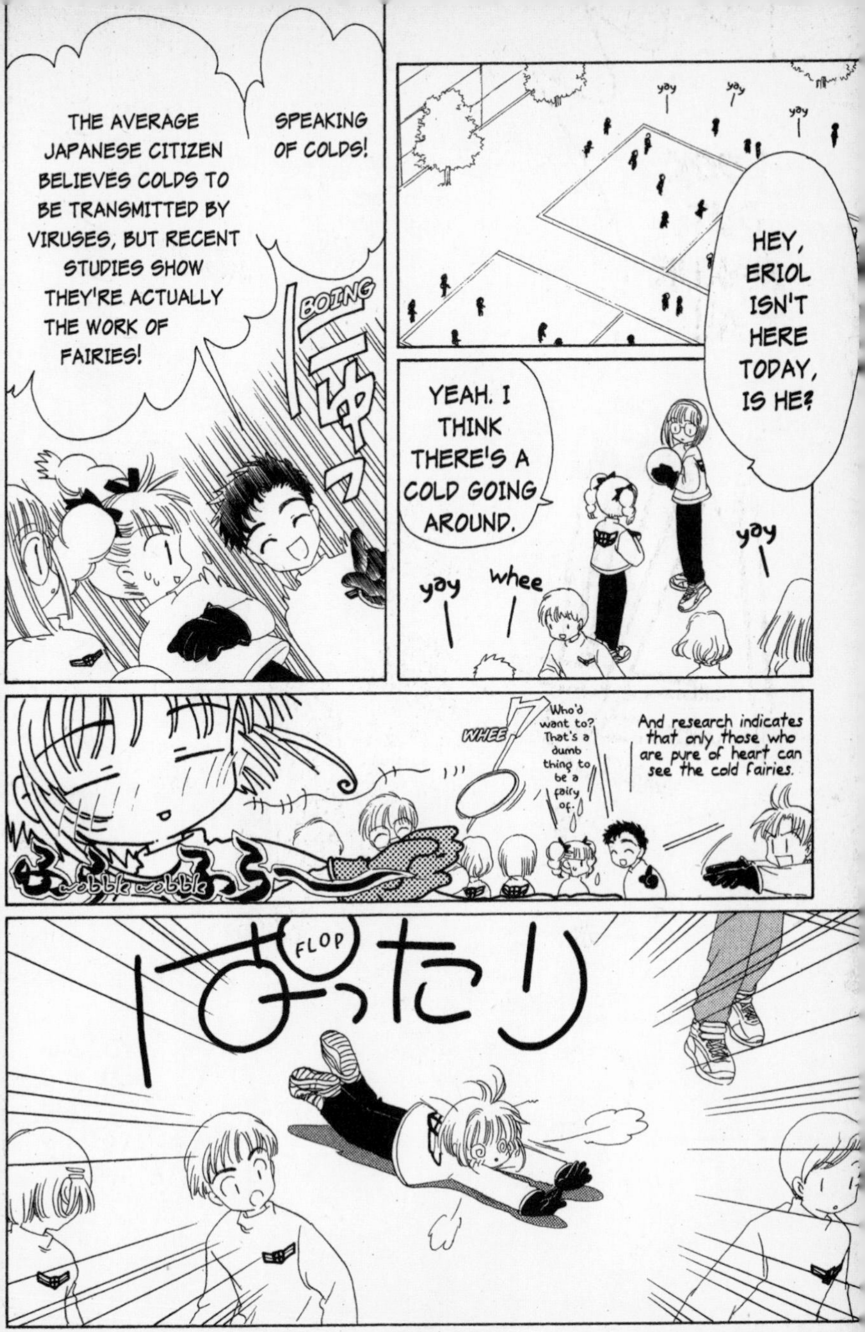
yay
yay
yay
HEY, ERIOL ISN'T HERE TODAY, IS HE?
YEAH. I THINK THERE'S A COLD GOING AROUND.
yay
whee
yay
SPEAKING OF COLDS!
THE AVERAGE JAPANESE CITIZEN BELIEVES COLDS TO BE TRANSMITTED BY VIRUSES, BUT RECENT STUDIES SHOW THEY'RE ACTUALLY THE WORK OF FAIRIES!
BOING
And research indicates that only those who are pure of heart can see the cold fairies.
Who'd want to? That's a dumb thing to be a fairy of.
WHEE
wobble wobble
FLOP

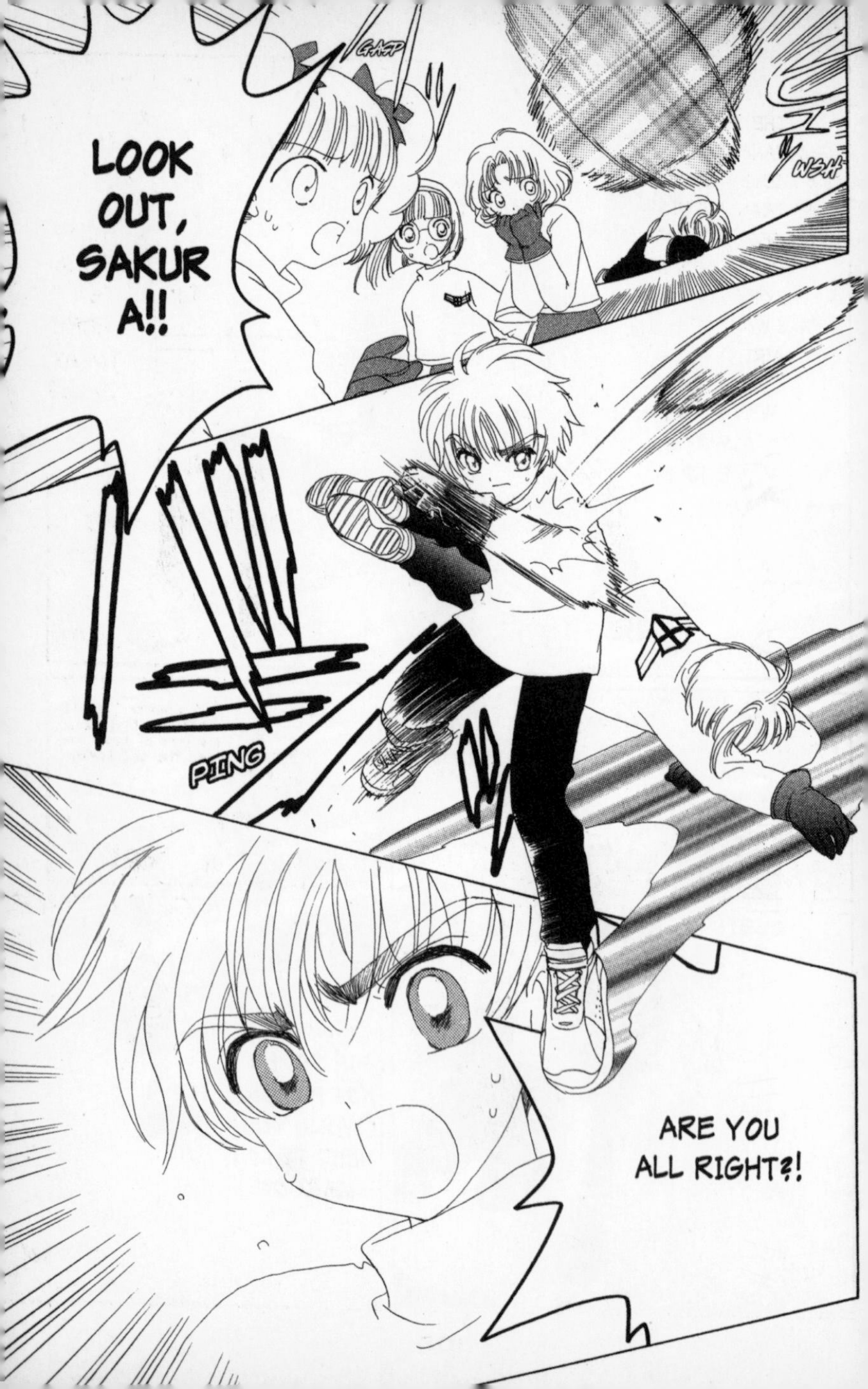
WSH
GASP
LOOK OUT, SAKURA!!
PING
ARE YOU ALL RIGHT?!

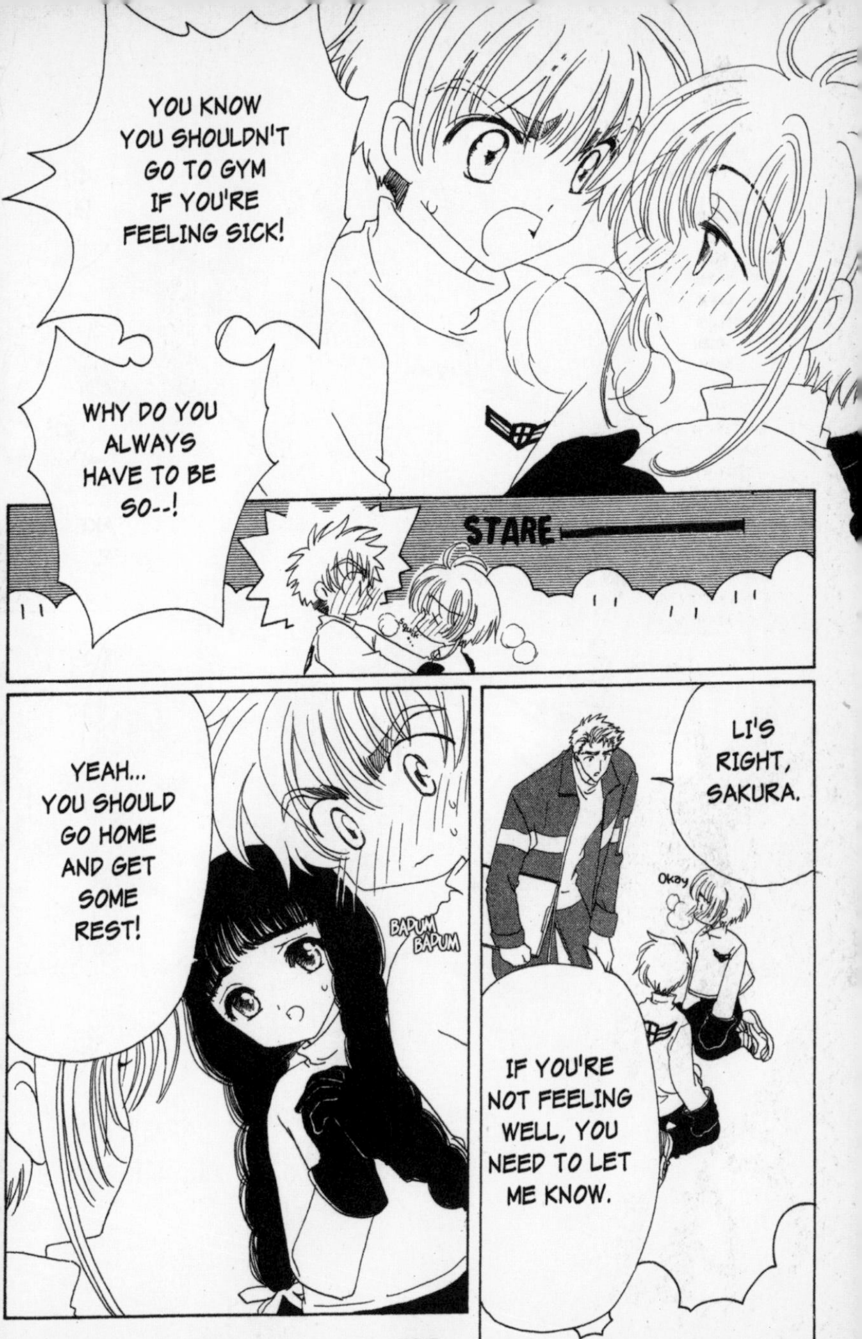

YOU KNOW YOU SHOULDN'T GO TO GYM IF YOU'RE FEELING SICK!
WHY DO YOU ALWAYS HAVE TO BE SO--!
STARE
LI'S RIGHT, SAKURA.
Okay
IF YOU'RE NOT FEELING WELL, YOU NEED TO LET ME KNOW.
YEAH... YOU SHOULD GO HOME AND GET SOME REST!
BADUM BADUM

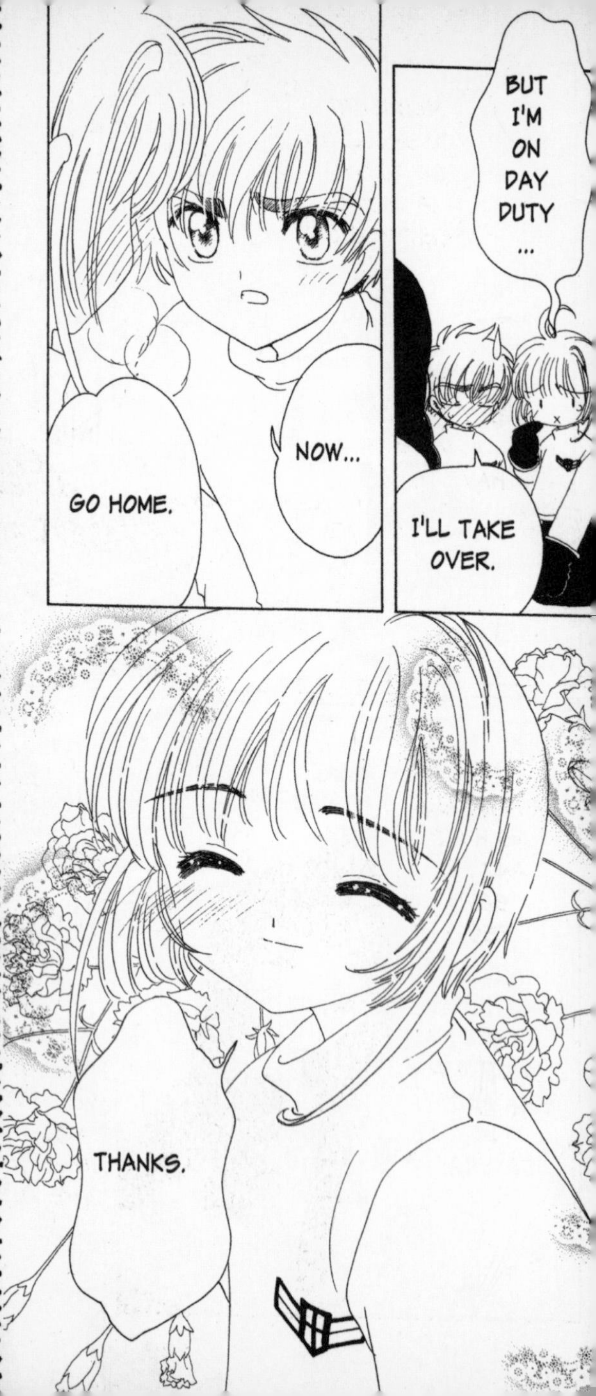
BUT I'M ON DAY DUTY ...
I'LL TAKE OVER.
NOW...
GO HOME.
THANKS.

23

SPINEL SUN
MASTER:
ERIOL HIIRAGIZAWA
BIRTHDAY:
SECRET
SYMBOL:
SUN
ASPECT:
DARK
EYES:
GREEN
BODY:
BLACK
MAGIC:
EASTERN MAGIC
FAVORITE FOOD:
SPICY STUFF
FAVORITE THING:
PEACE AND QUIET
LEAST FAVORITE THING:
ANYTHING NOISY
TEMPORARY FORM:
A BLACK KITTEN WITH TRANSPARENT WINGS

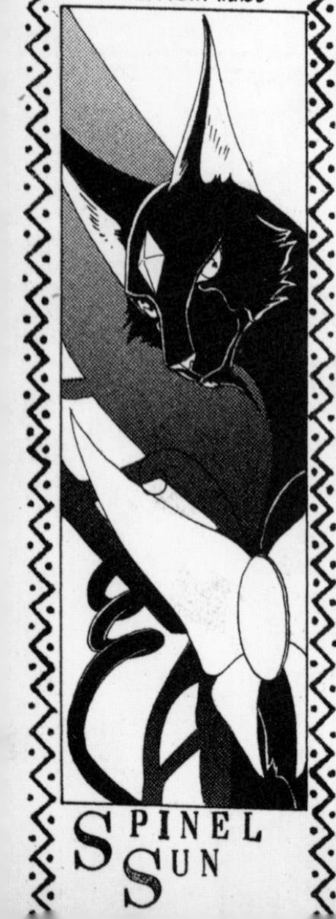

SPINEL SUN

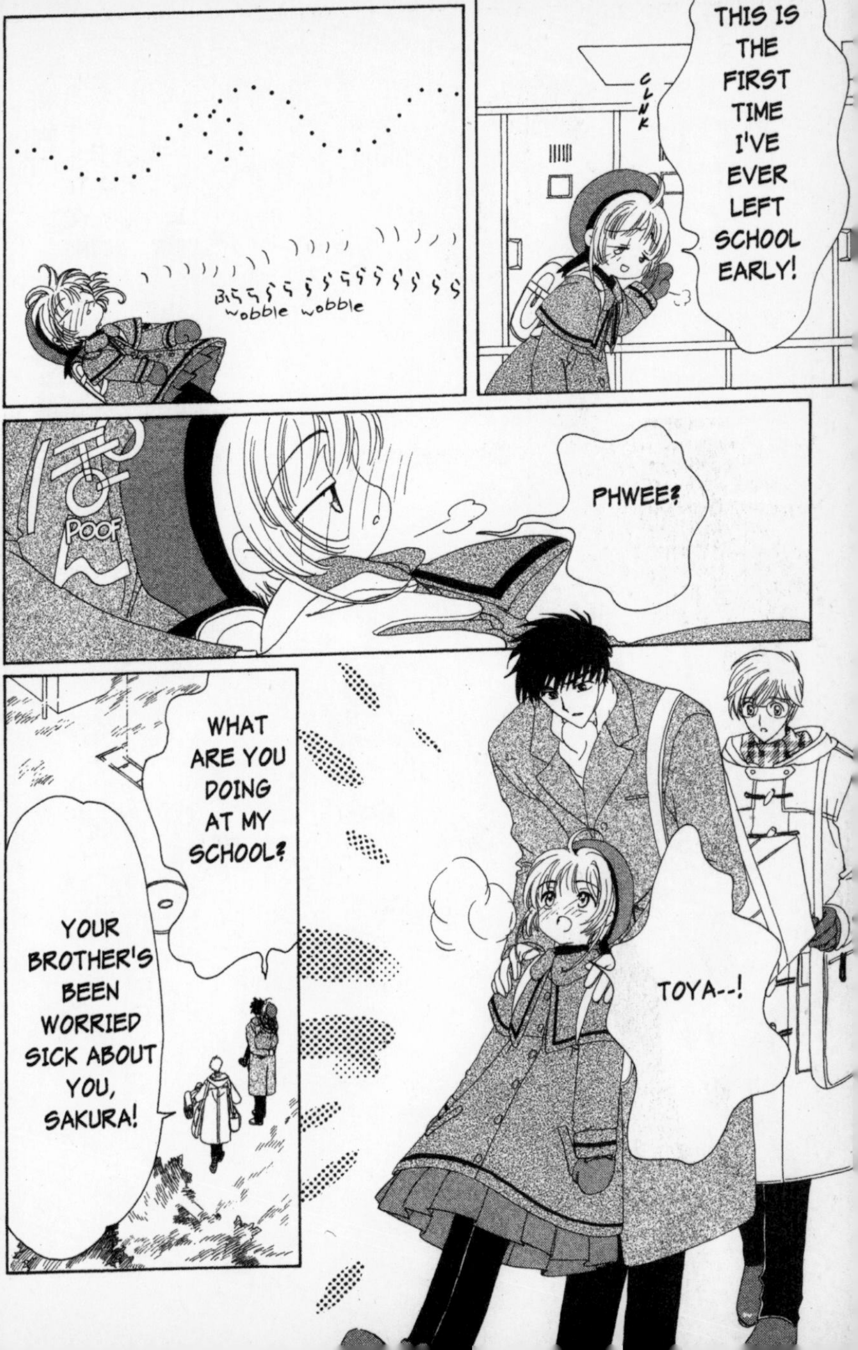
THIS IS THE FIRST TIME I'VE EVER LEFT SCHOOL EARLY!
CLNK
wobble wobble
PHWEE?
POOF
TOYA--!
WHAT ARE YOU DOING AT MY SCHOOL?
YOUR BROTHER'S BEEN WORRIED SICK ABOUT YOU, SAKURA!

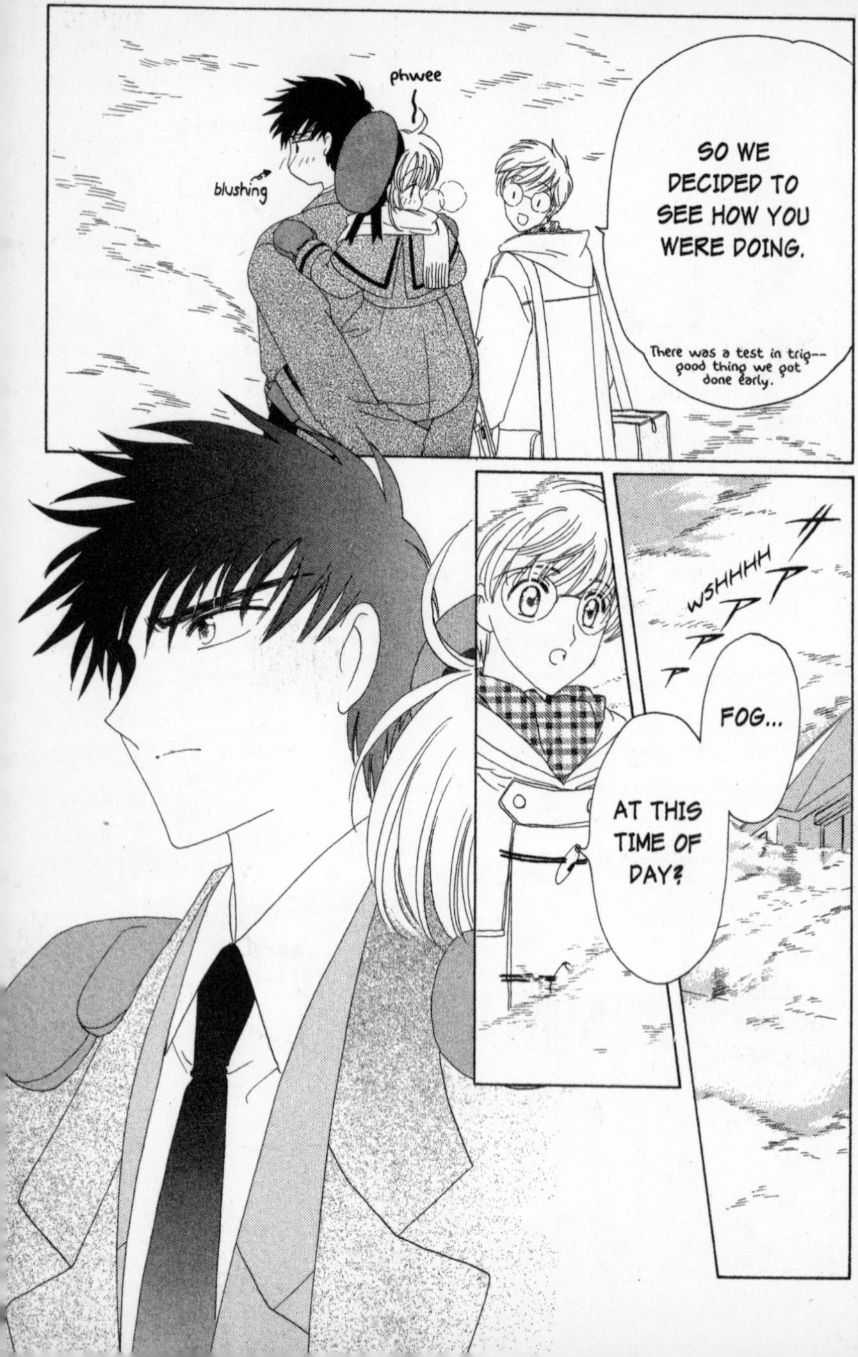
SO WE DECIDED TO SEE HOW YOU WERE DOING.
There was a test in trig--good thing we got done early.
phwee
blushing
WSHHHH
FOG...
AT THIS TIME OF DAY?

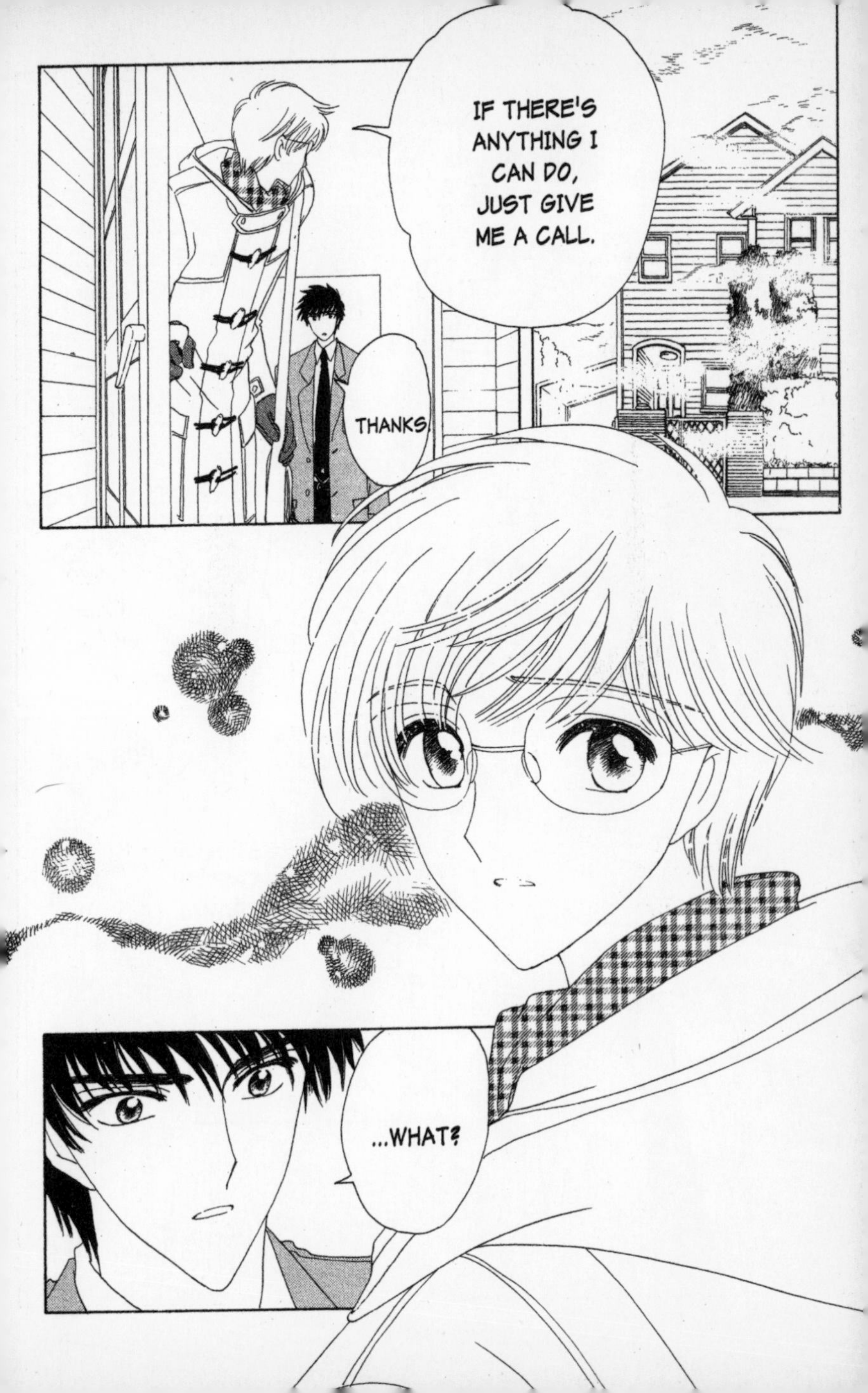
IF THERE'S ANYTHING I CAN DO, JUST GIVE ME A CALL.
THANKS.
...WHAT?

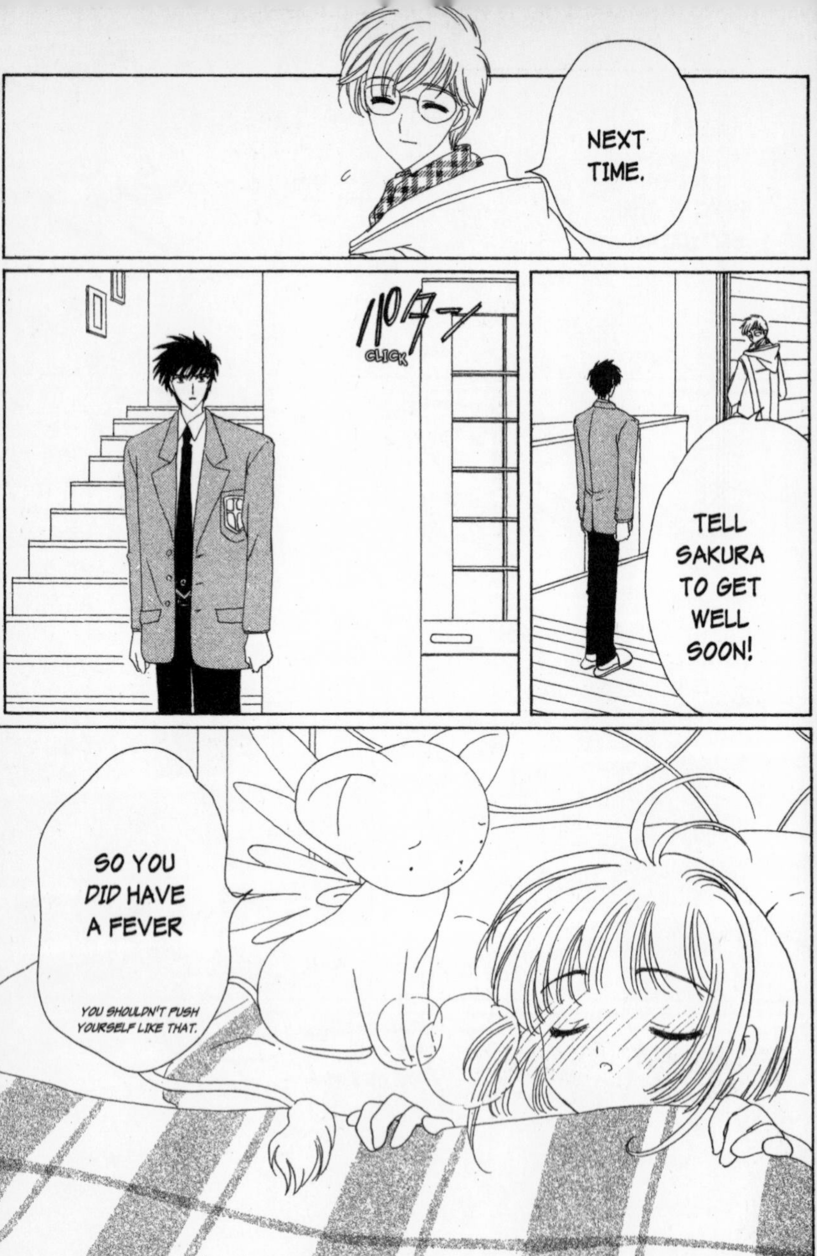
NEXT TIME.
TELL SAKURA TO GET WELL SOON!
パタン
CLICK
SO YOU DID HAVE A FEVER
YOU SHOULDN'T PUSH YOURSELF LIKE THAT.

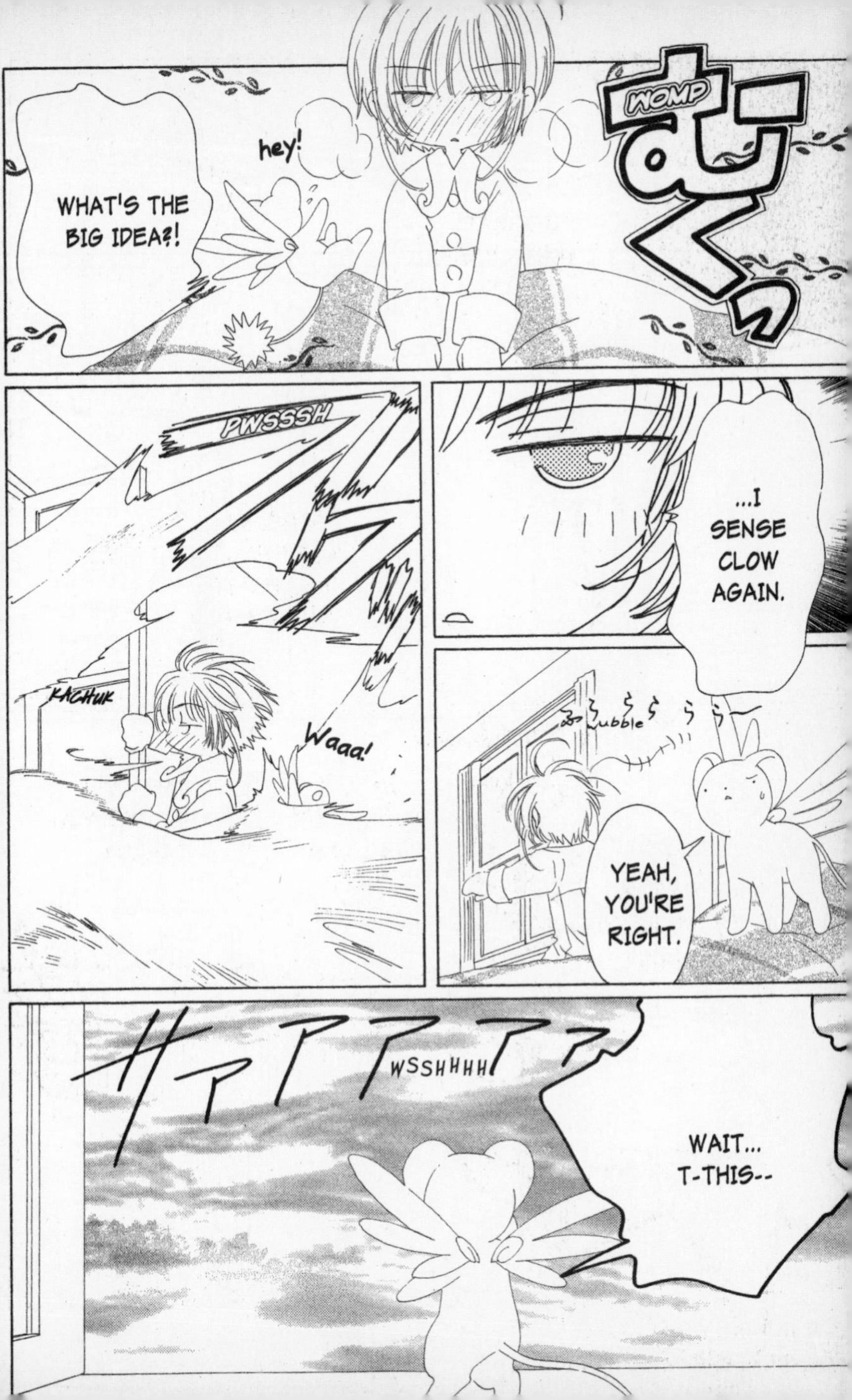
WOMP
hey!
WHAT'S THE BIG IDEA?!
...I SENSE CLOW AGAIN.
bubble
YEAH, YOU'RE RIGHT.
PWSSSH
KACHUK
Waaa!
WAIT... T-THIS--
WSSHHHH

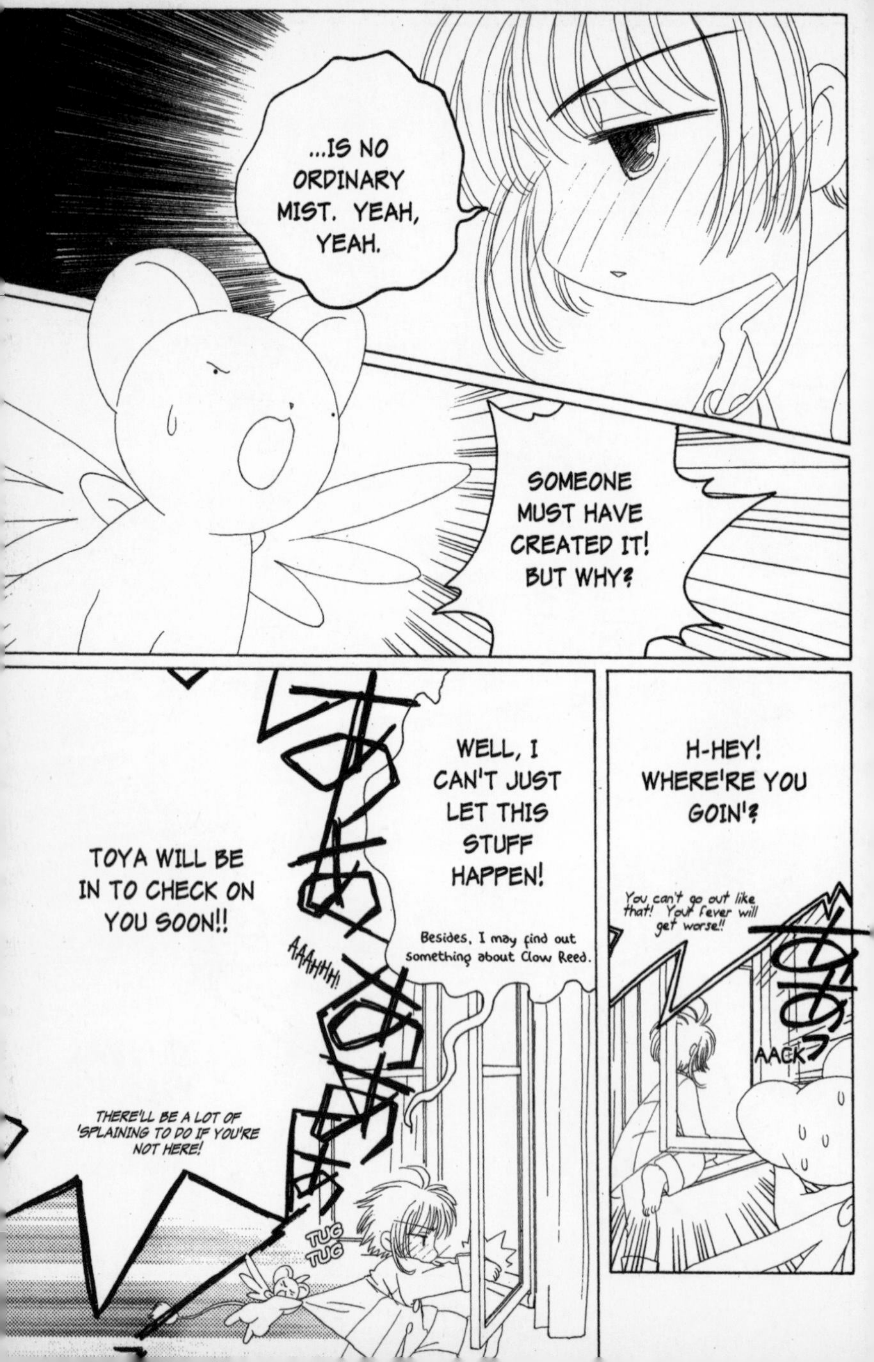
...IS NO ORDINARY MIST. YEAH, YEAH.
SOMEONE MUST HAVE CREATED IT! BUT WHY?
H-HEY! WHERE'RE YOU GOIN'?
You can't go out like that! Your fever will get worse!!
AACK
WELL, I CAN'T JUST LET THIS STUFF HAPPEN!
Besides, I may find out something about Clow Reed.
AAAHHH!
TOYA WILL BE IN TO CHECK ON YOU SOON!!
THERE'LL BE A LOT OF 'SPLAINING TO DO IF YOU'RE NOT HERE!
TUG TUG

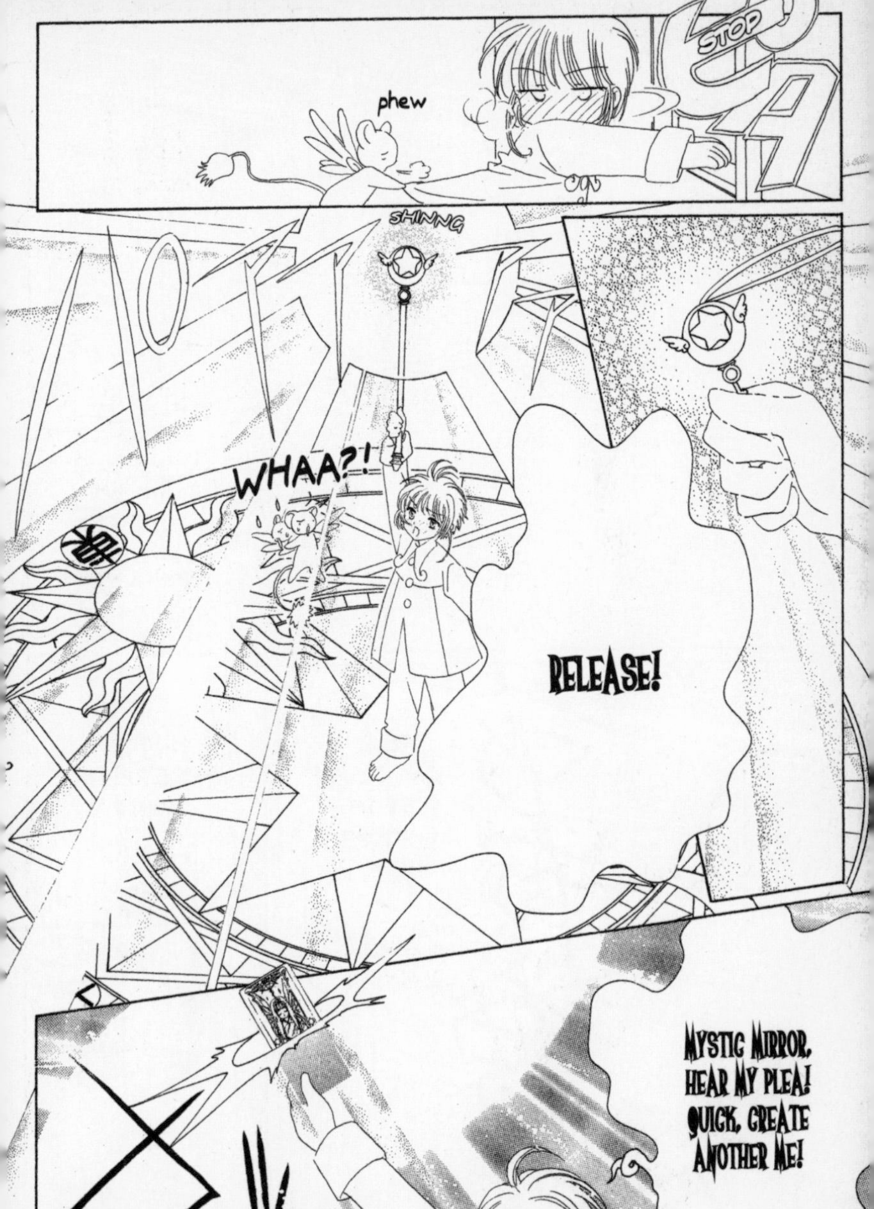
phew
RELEASE!
SHINNG
WHAA?!
MYSTIC MIRROR, HEAR MY PLEA! QUICK, CREATE ANOTHER ME!
FWSSH

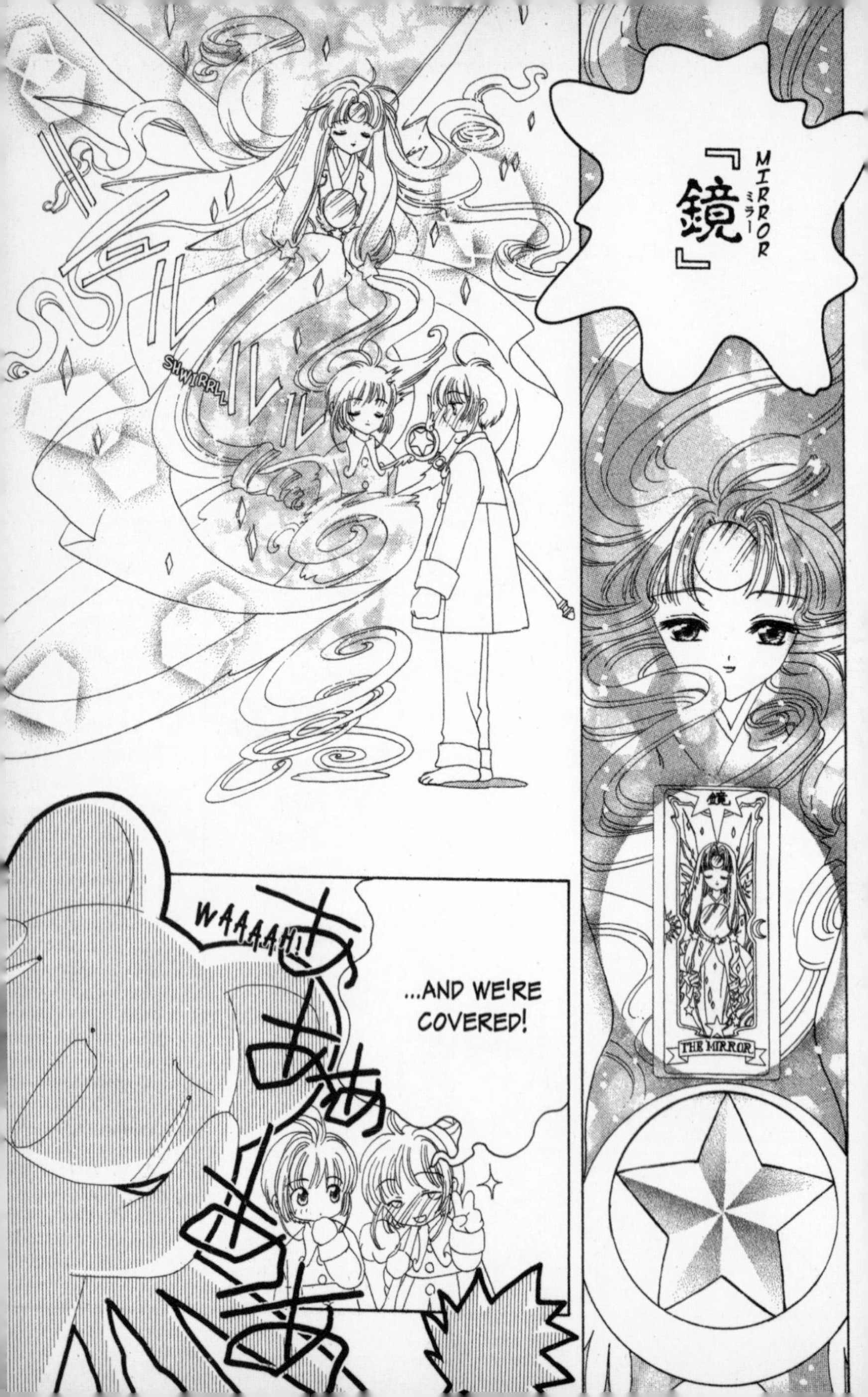
『鏡』
MIRROR
ミラー
THE MIRROR
SHWIRRLL
...AND WE'RE COVERED!
WAAAAAH!

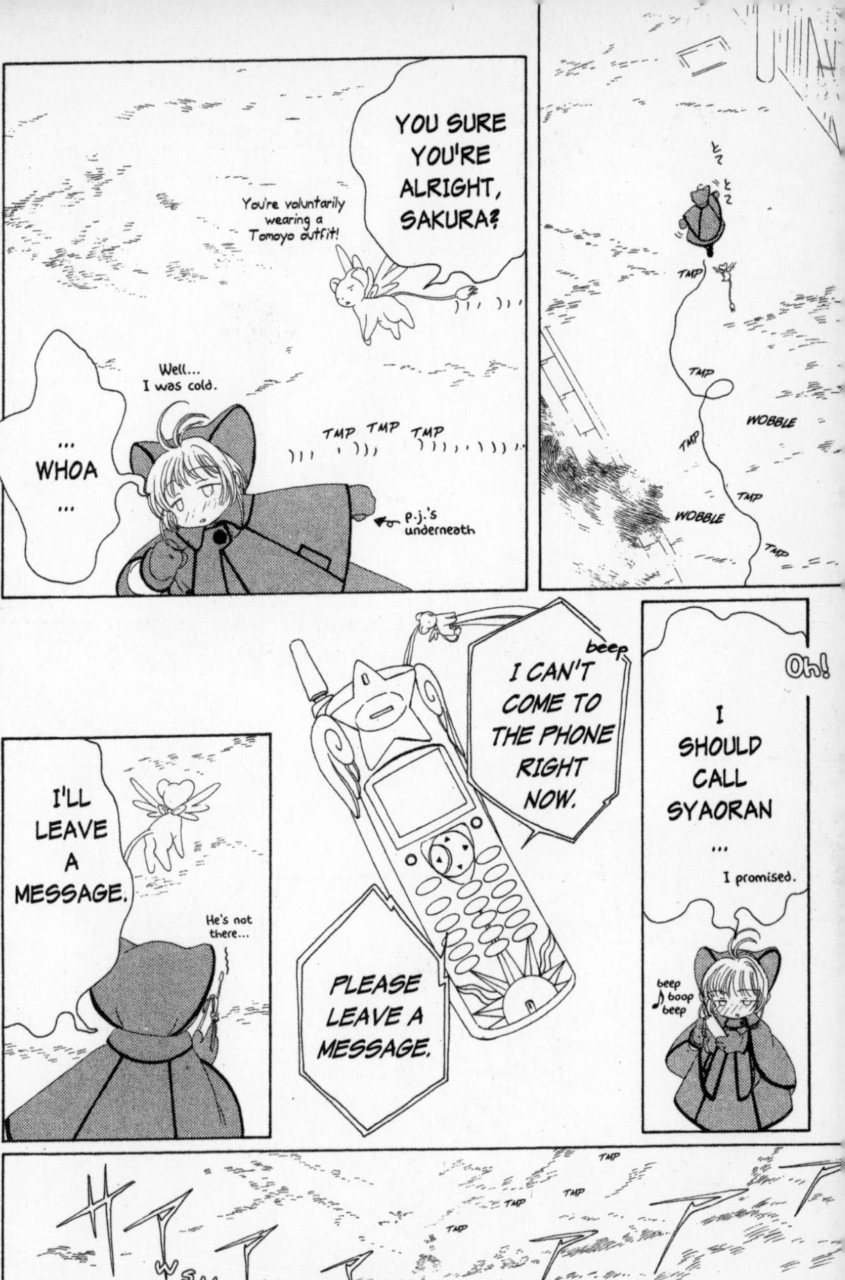
TMP
TMP
WOBBLE
TMP
TMP
WOBBLE
TMP
YOU SURE YOU'RE ALRIGHT, SAKURA?
You're voluntarily wearing a Tomoyo outfit!
Well... I was cold.
... WHOA ...
TMP TMP TMP
p.j.'s underneath
Oh!
I SHOULD CALL SYAORAN ...
I promised.
beep boop beep
beep
I CAN'T COME TO THE PHONE RIGHT NOW.
PLEASE LEAVE A MESSAGE.
I'LL LEAVE A MESSAGE.
He's not there...
TMP
TMP
TMP
TMP
WSHSHHHH

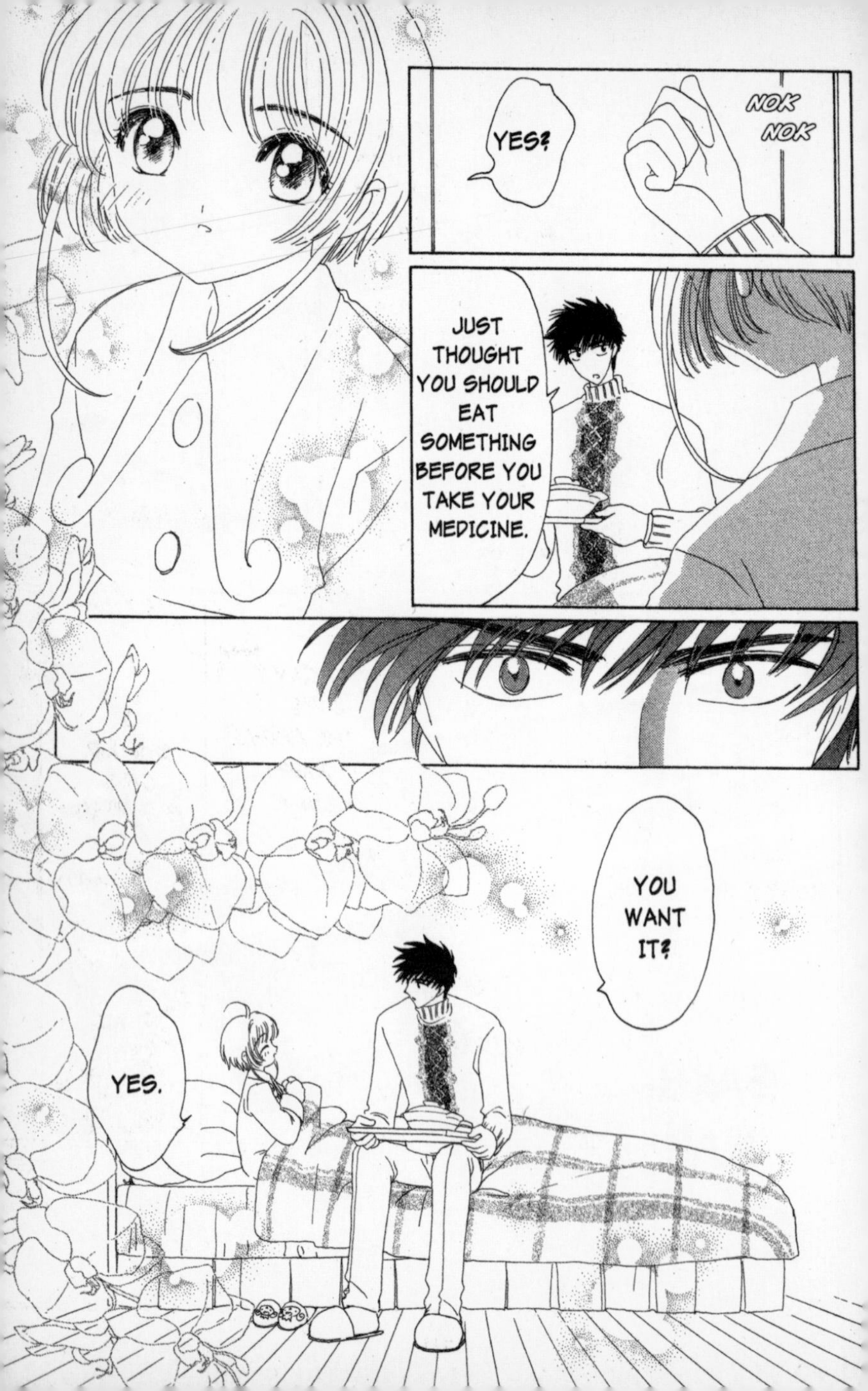
NOK NOK
YES?
JUST THOUGHT YOU SHOULD EAT SOMETHING BEFORE YOU TAKE YOUR MEDICINE.
YOU WANT IT?
YES.

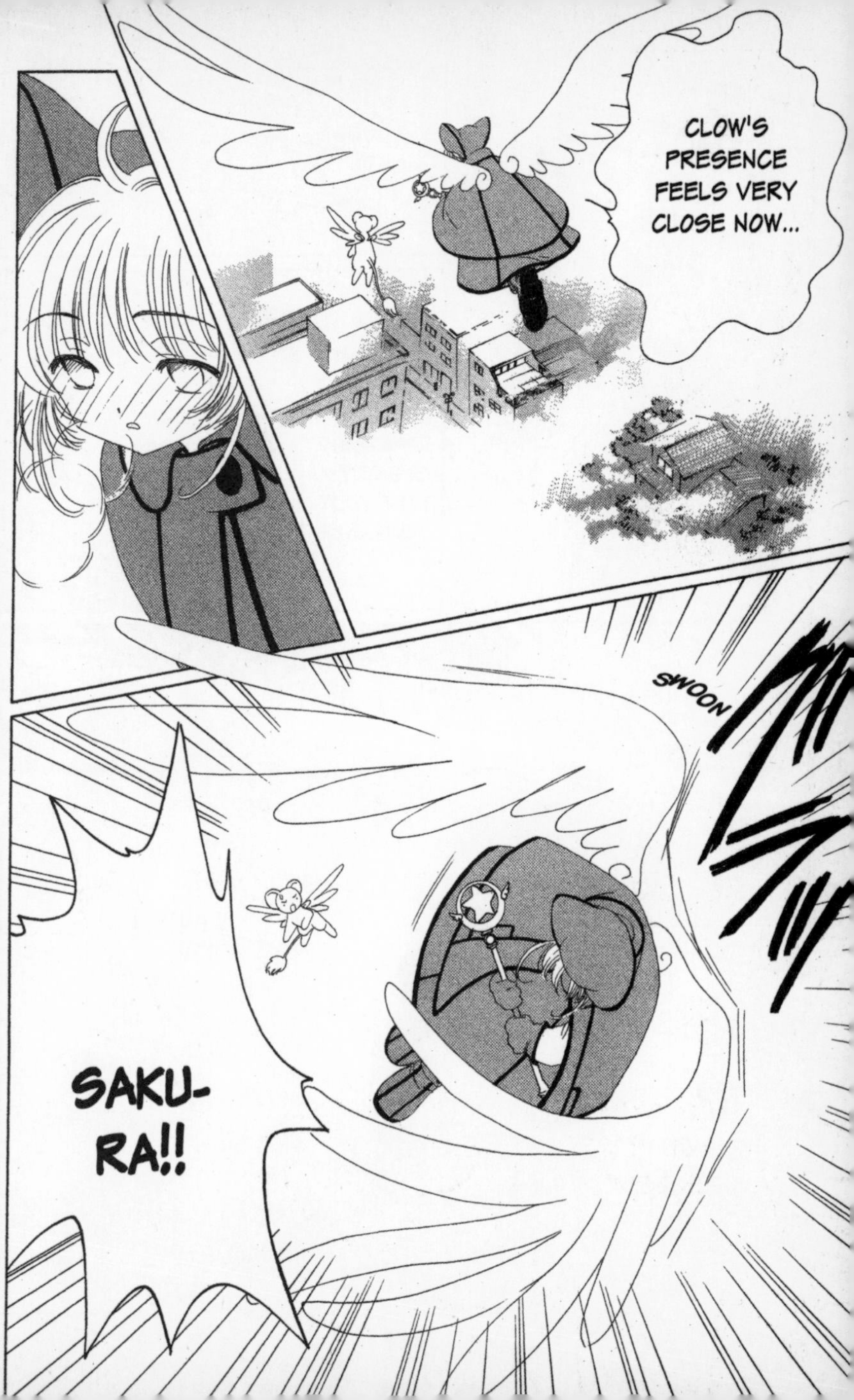
CLOW'S PRESENCE FEELS VERY CLOSE NOW...
SWOON
SAKU-RA!!

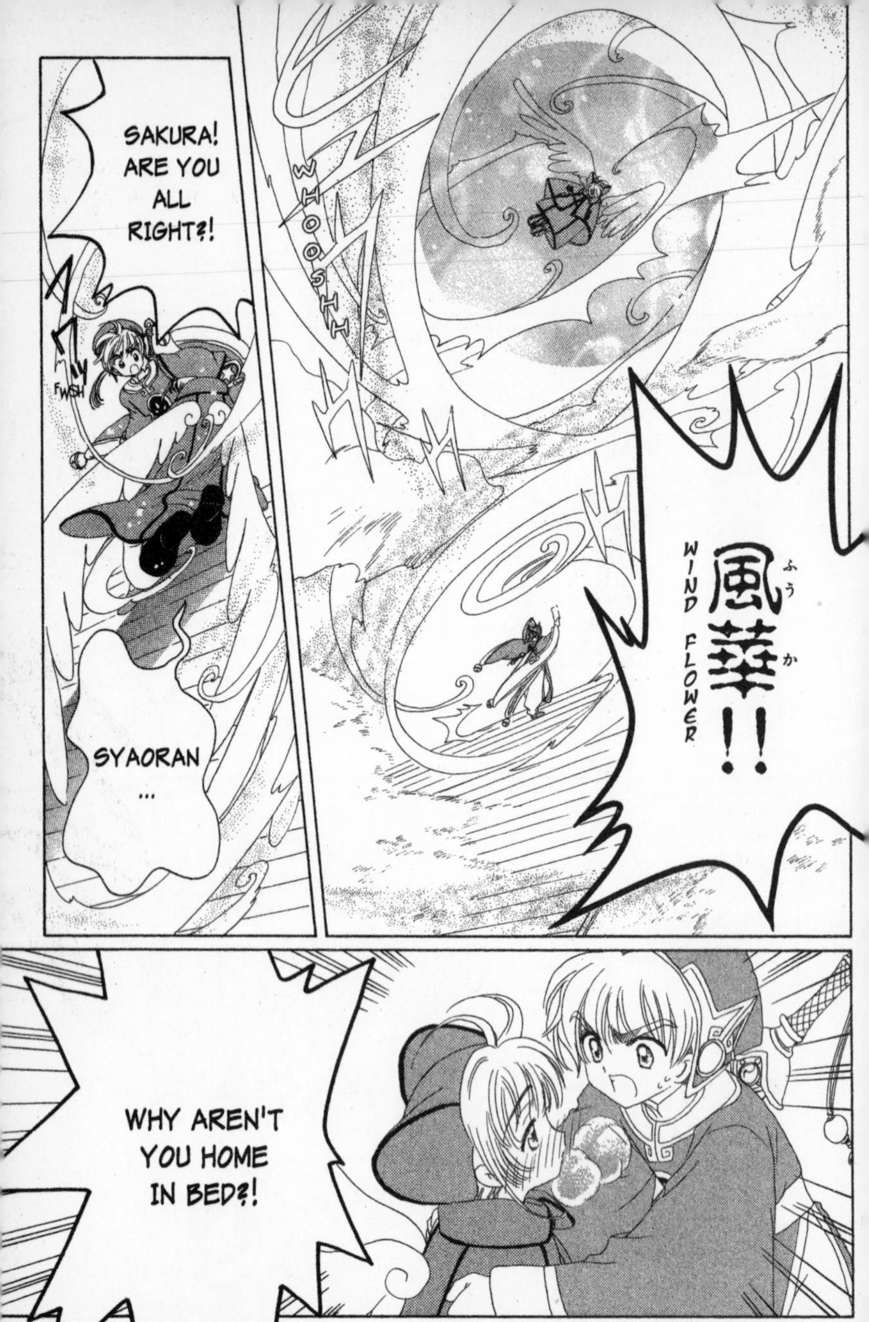
風華(ふうか)!!
WIND FLOWER
WHOOSH
SAKURA! ARE YOU ALL RIGHT?!
FWSH
SYAORAN ...
WHY AREN'T YOU HOME IN BED?!

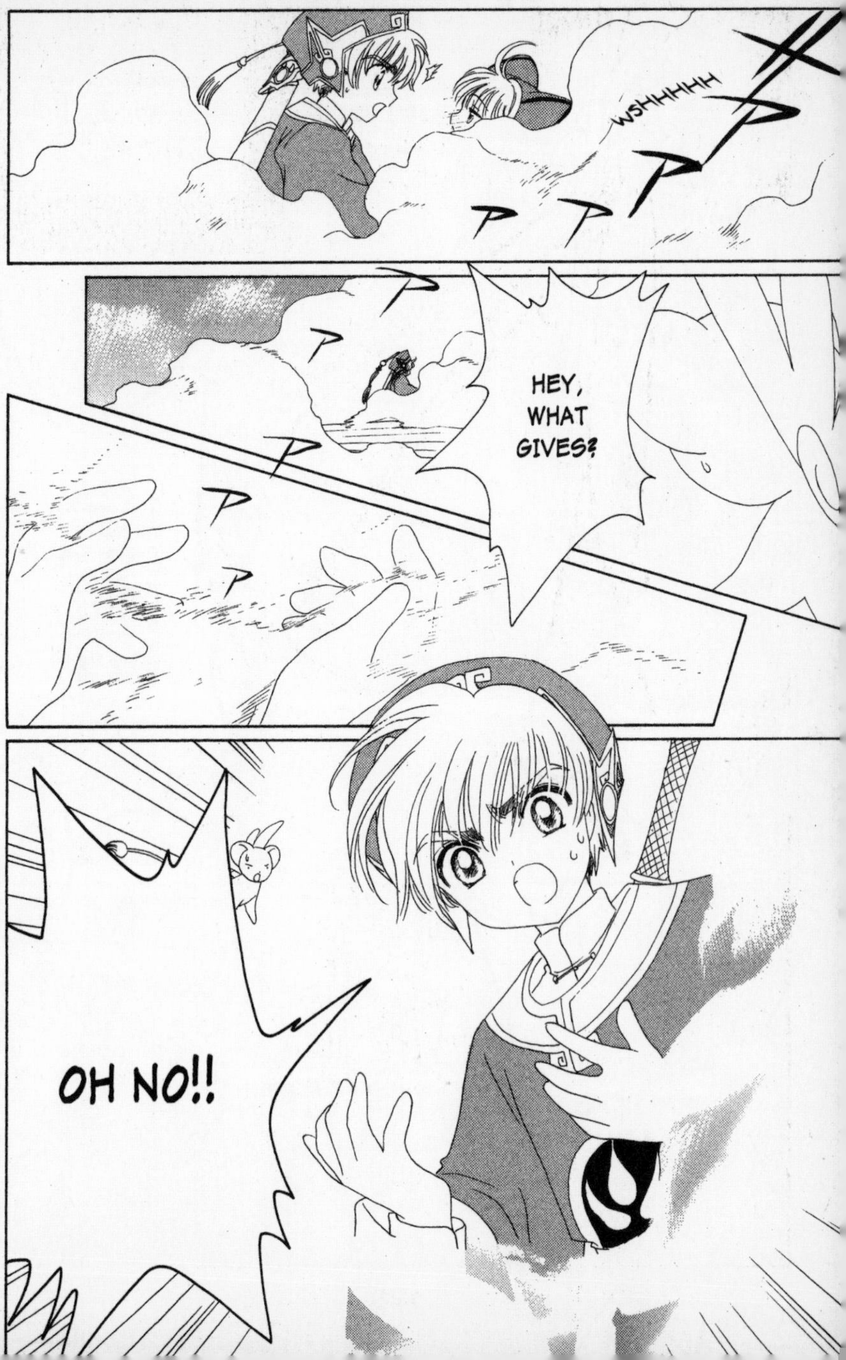
WSHHHHH
HEY, WHAT GIVES?
OH NO!!

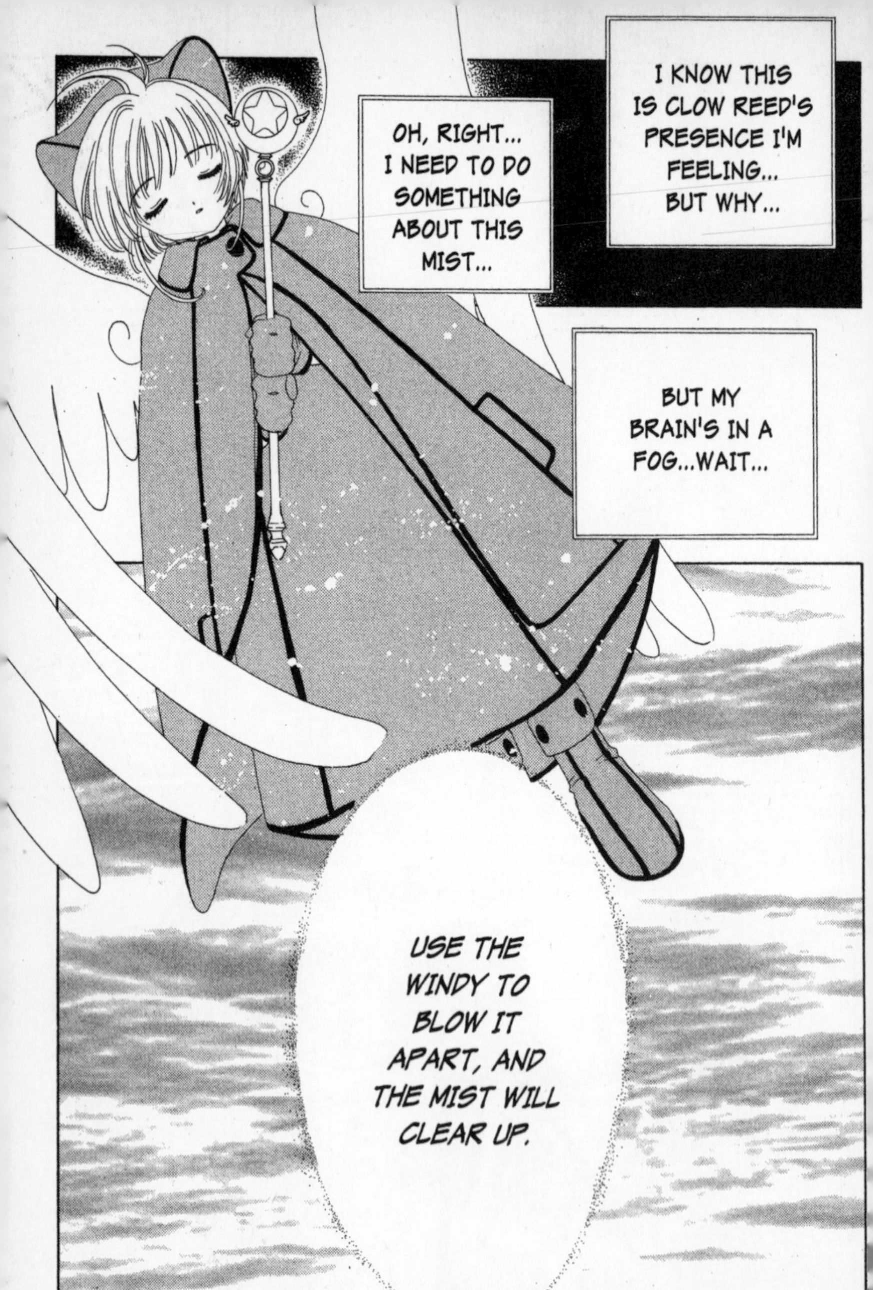
I KNOW THIS IS CLOW REED'S PRESENCE I'M FEELING... BUT WHY...
OH, RIGHT... I NEED TO DO SOMETHING ABOUT THIS MIST...
BUT MY BRAIN'S IN A FOG...WAIT...
USE THE WINDY TO BLOW IT APART, AND THE MIST WILL CLEAR UP.

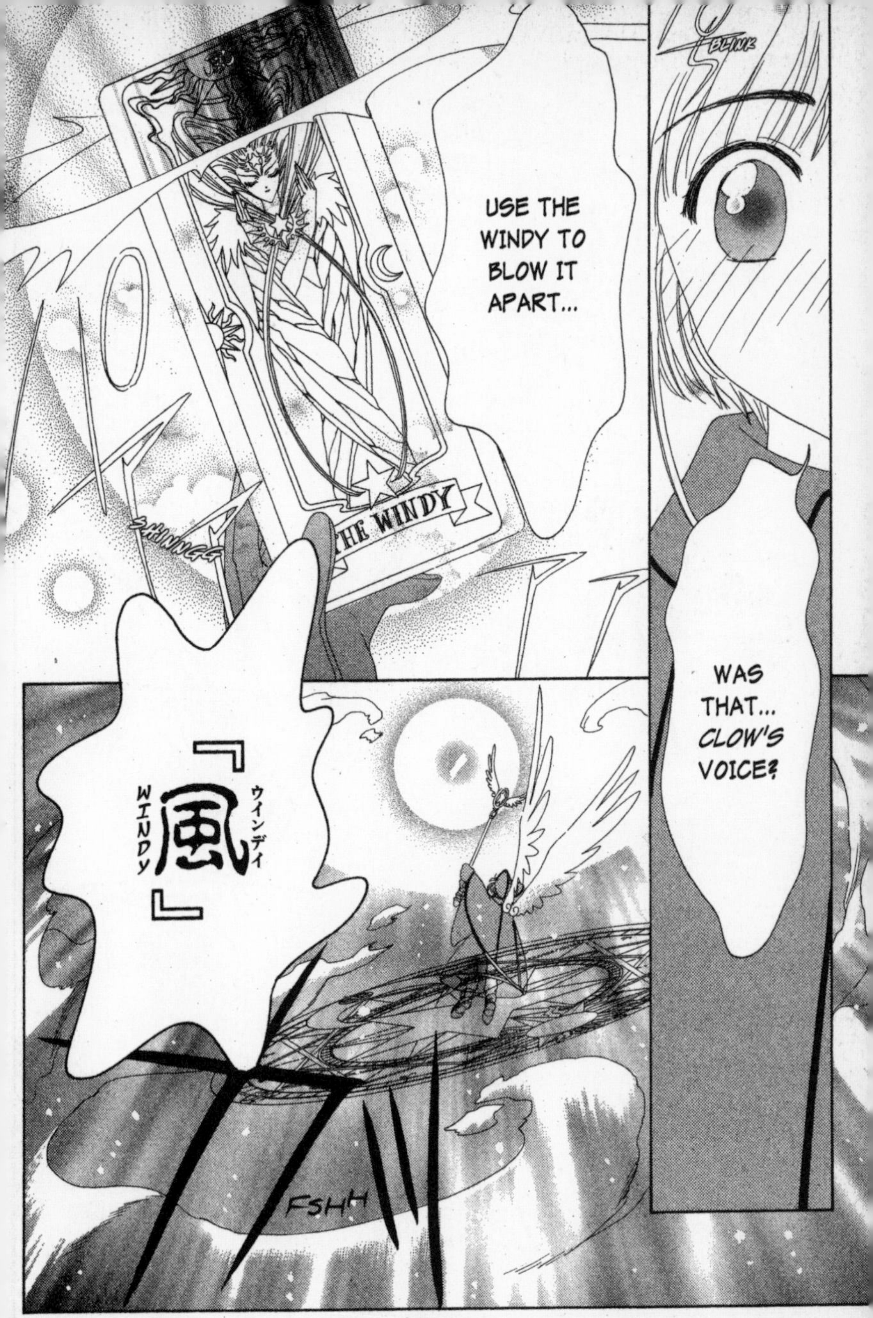
BLINK
WAS THAT... CLOW'S VOICE?
USE THE WINDY TO BLOW IT APART...
THE WINDY
SHINGG
「風」 ウインディ WINDY
FSHH

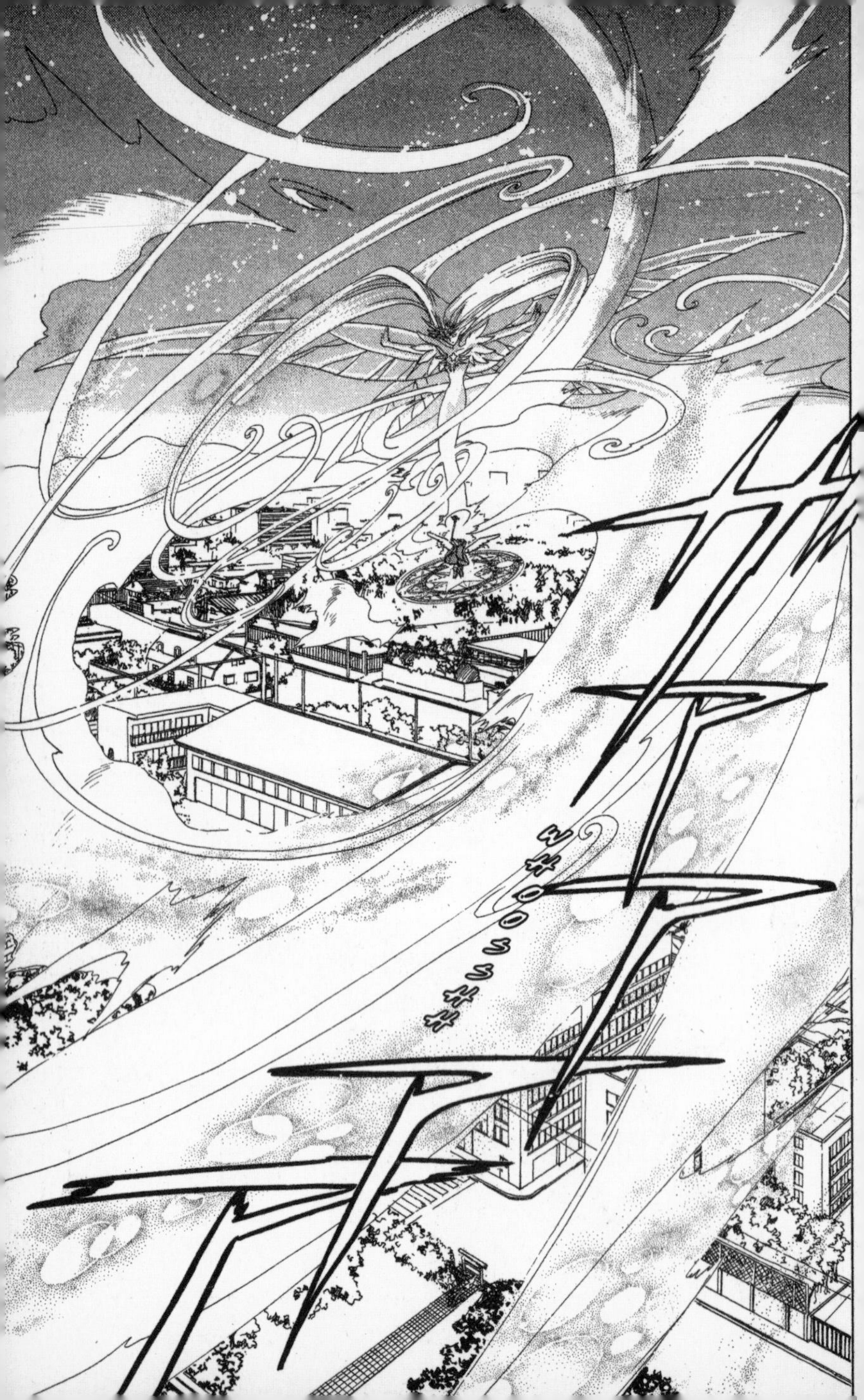
WHOOSSHH

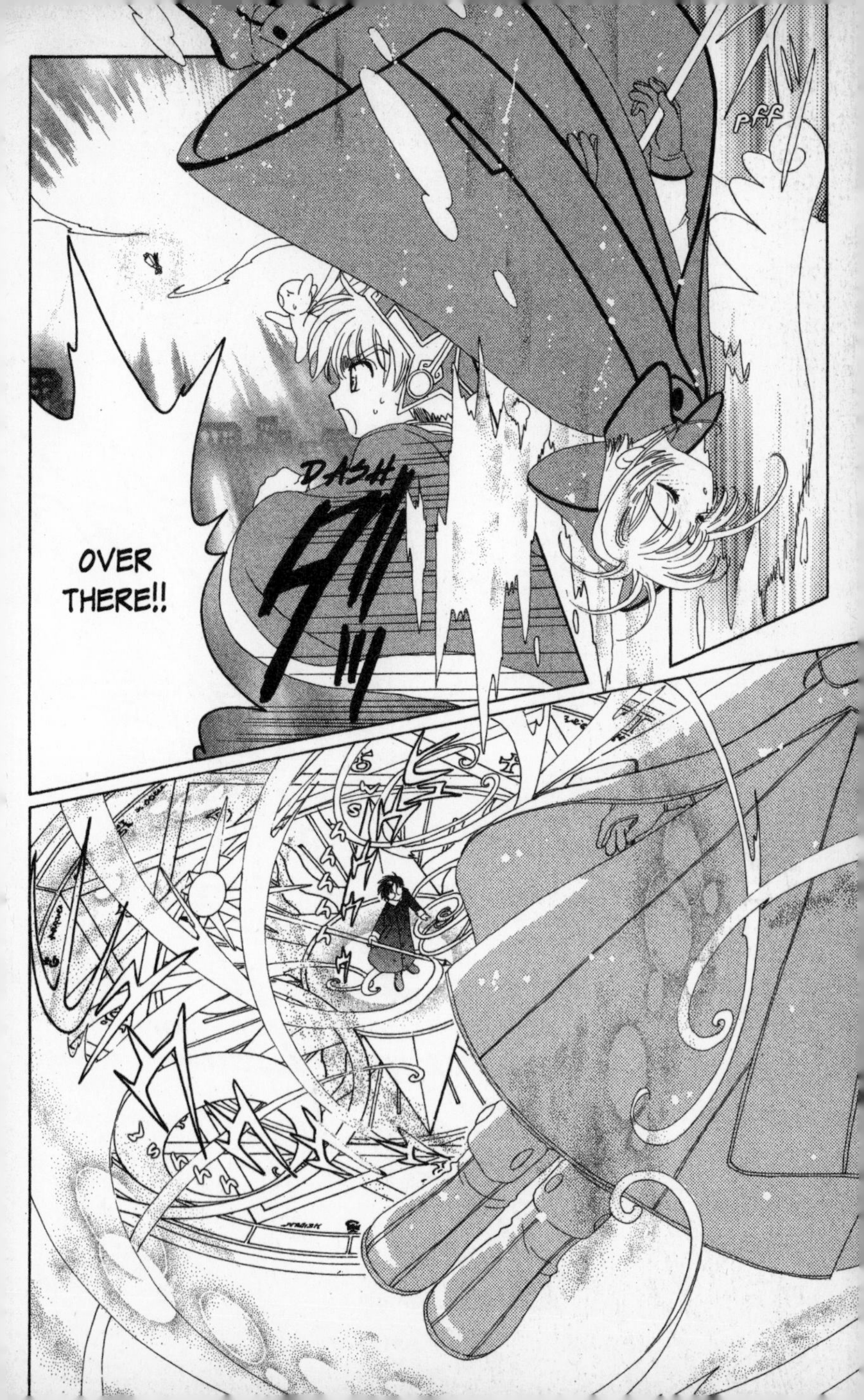
pff
DASH
OVER THERE!!

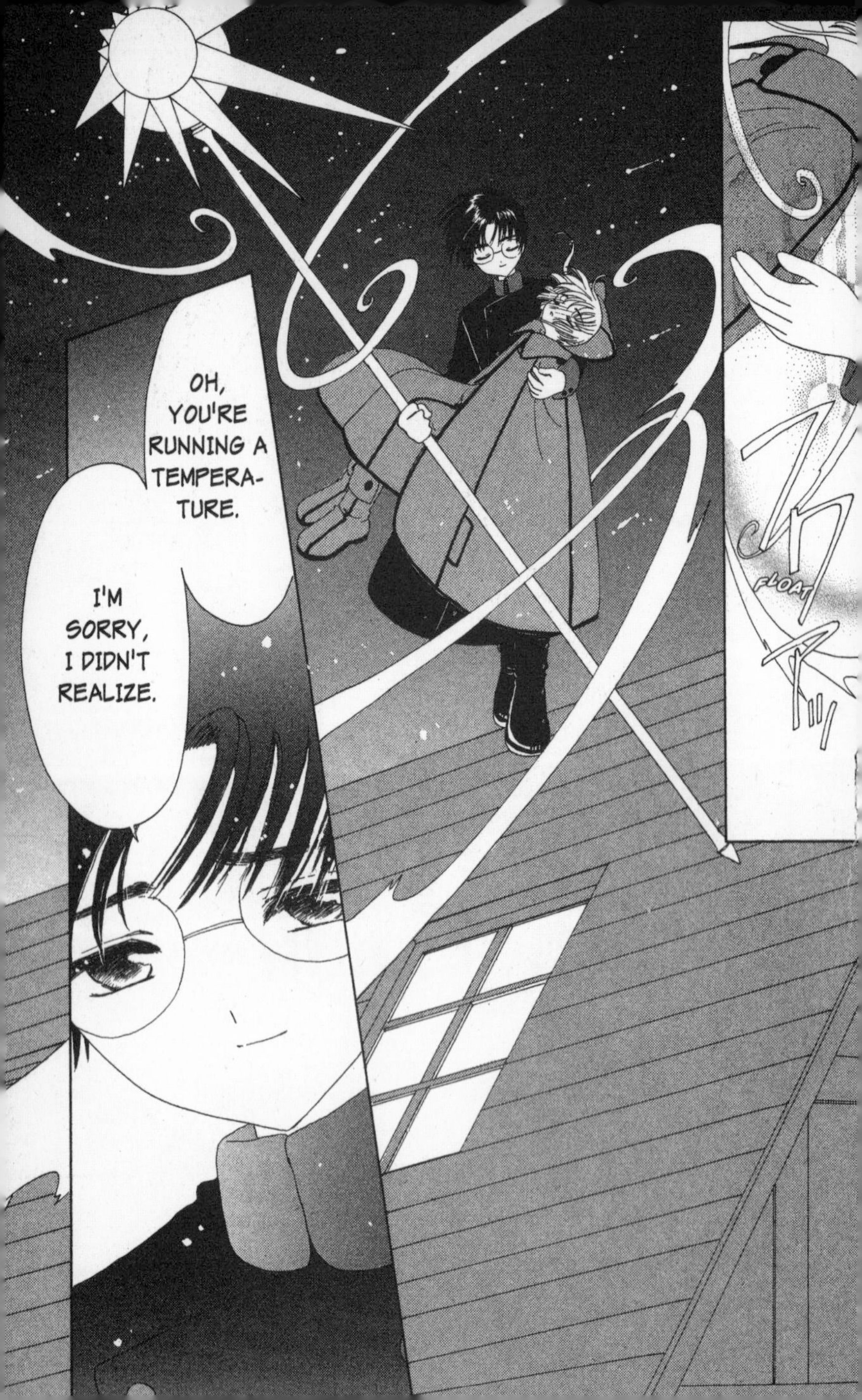
FLOAT
OH, YOU'RE RUNNING A TEMPERA-TURE.
I'M SORRY, I DIDN'T REALIZE.

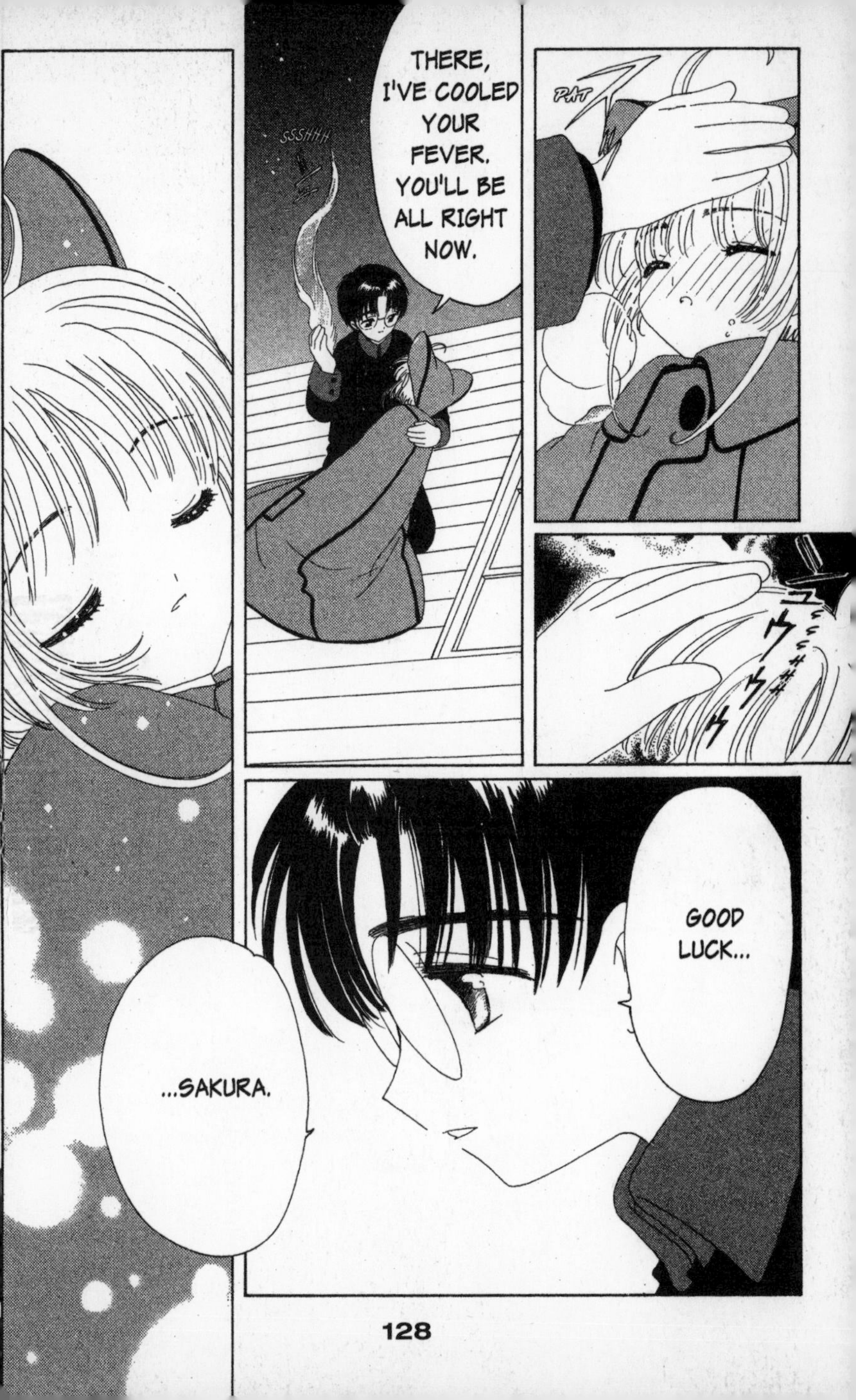
PAT
SSSHHH
THERE, I'VE COOLED YOUR FEVER. YOU'LL BE ALL RIGHT NOW.
GOOD LUCK...
...SAKURA.

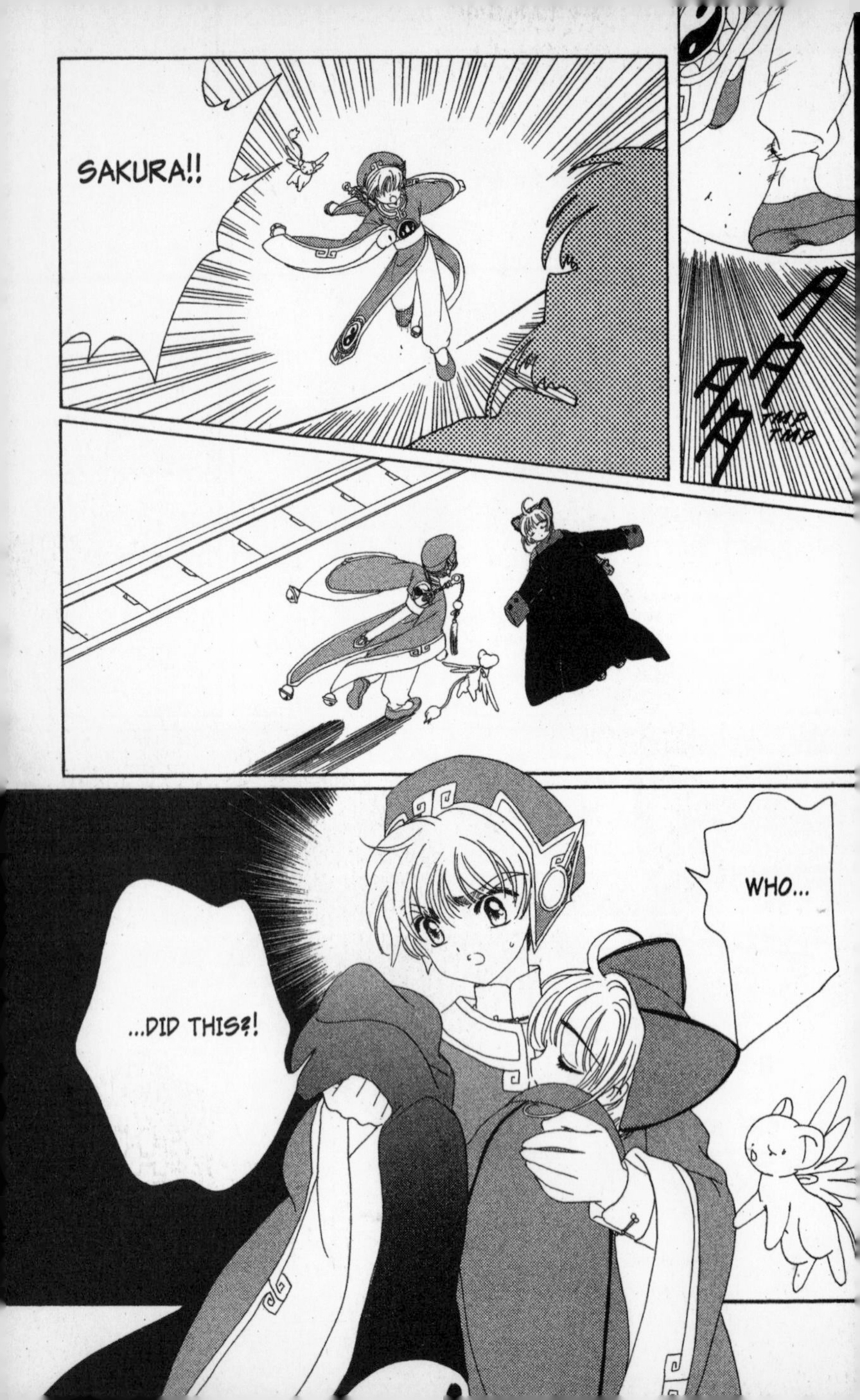
TMP TMP
SAKURA!!
WHO...
...DID THIS?!

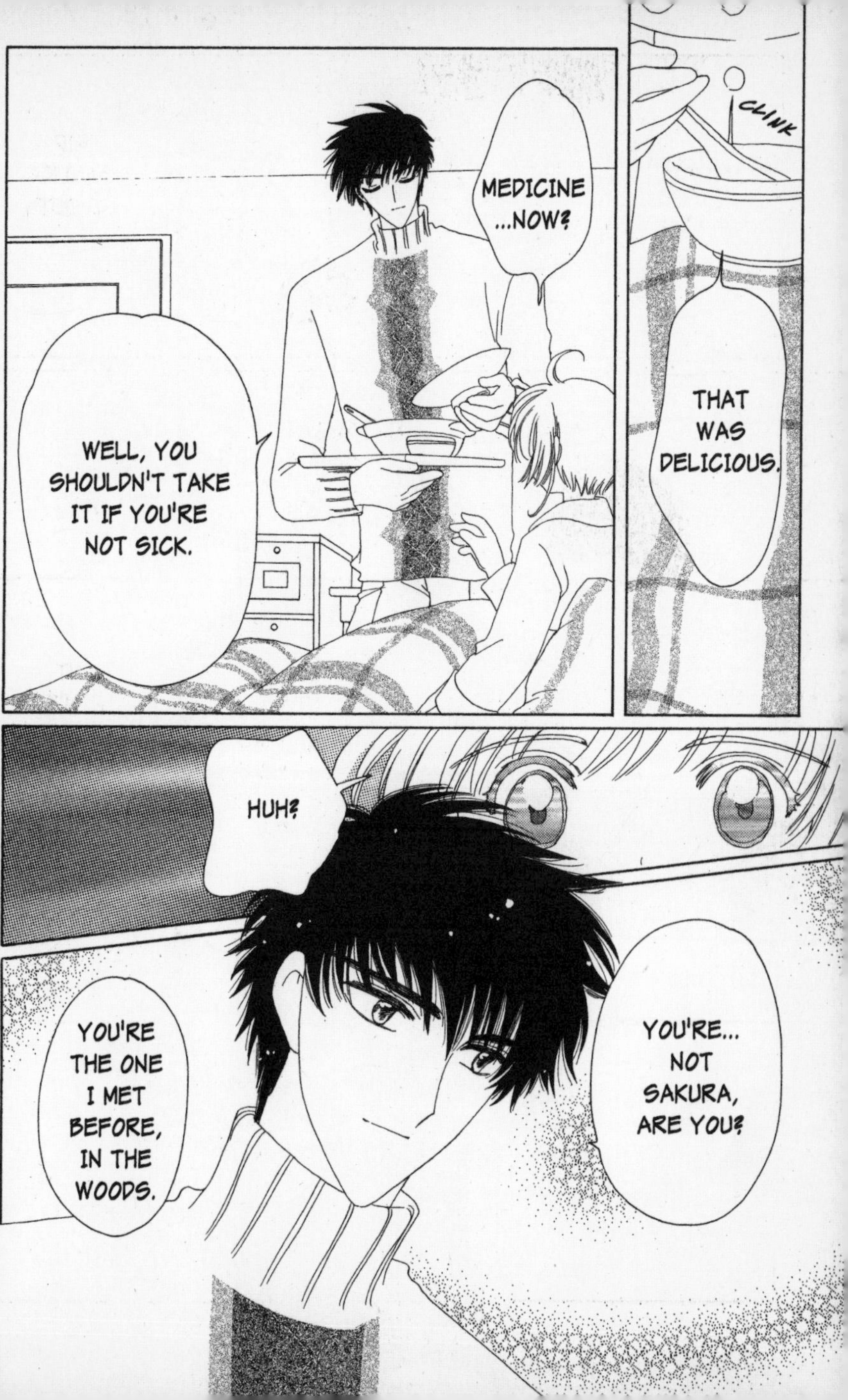
CLINK
THAT WAS DELICIOUS.
MEDICINE ...NOW?
WELL, YOU SHOULDN'T TAKE IT IF YOU'RE NOT SICK.
HUH?
YOU'RE... NOT SAKURA, ARE YOU?
YOU'RE THE ONE I MET BEFORE, IN THE WOODS.

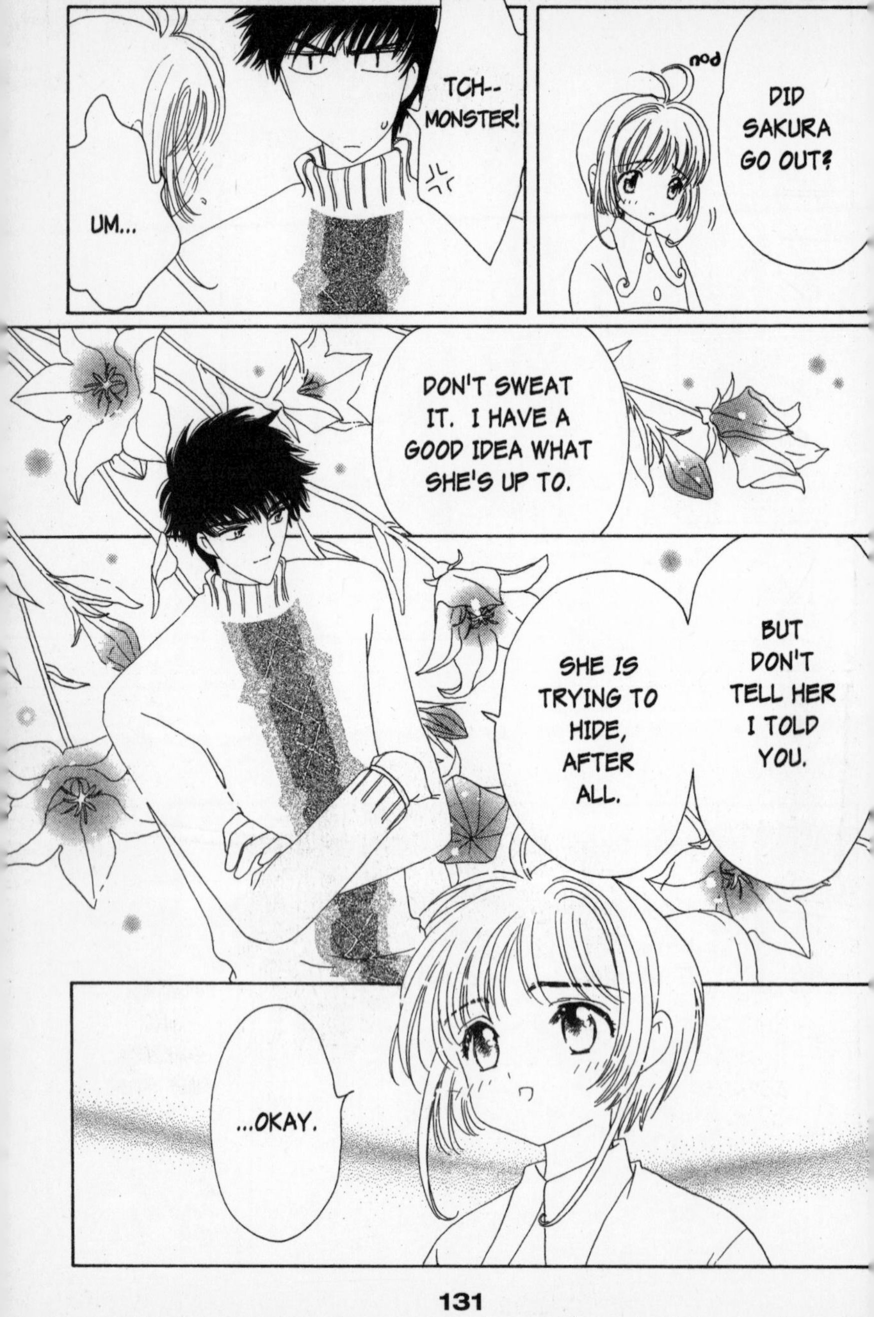
nod
DID SAKURA GO OUT?
TCH-- MONSTER!
UM...
DON'T SWEAT IT. I HAVE A GOOD IDEA WHAT SHE'S UP TO.
BUT DON'T TELL HER I TOLD YOU.
SHE IS TRYING TO HIDE, AFTER ALL.
...OKAY.

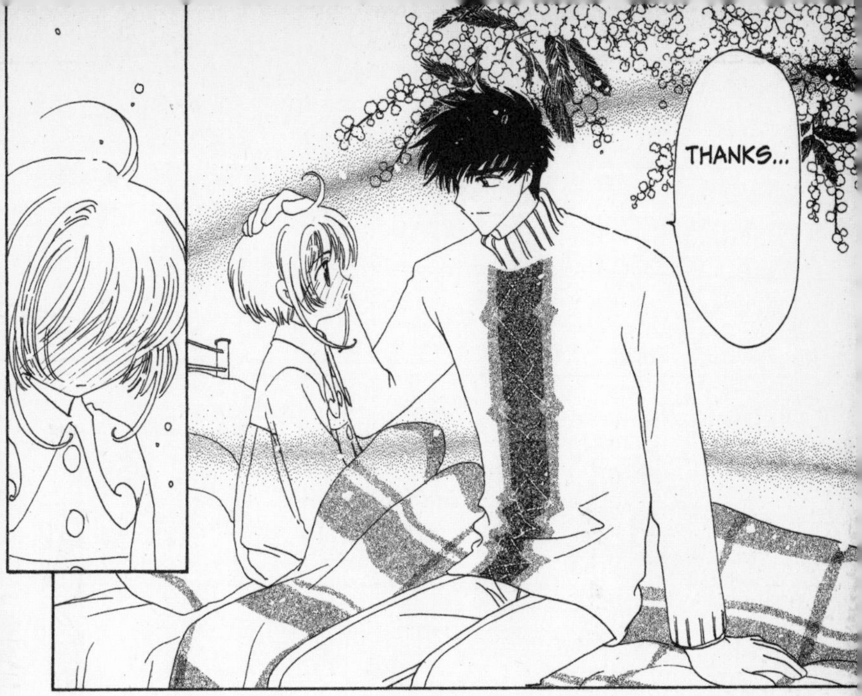
THANKS...

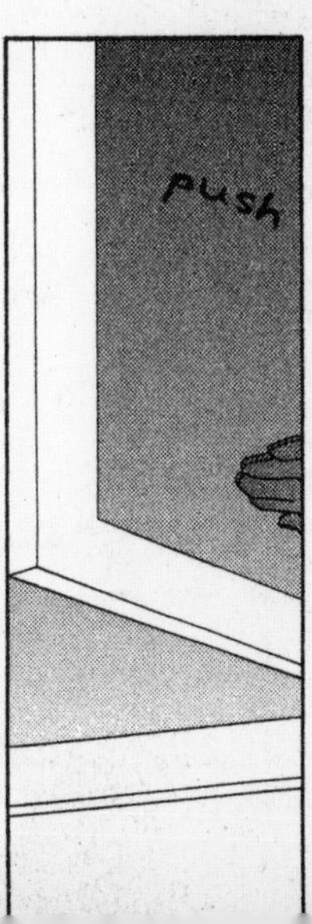
push

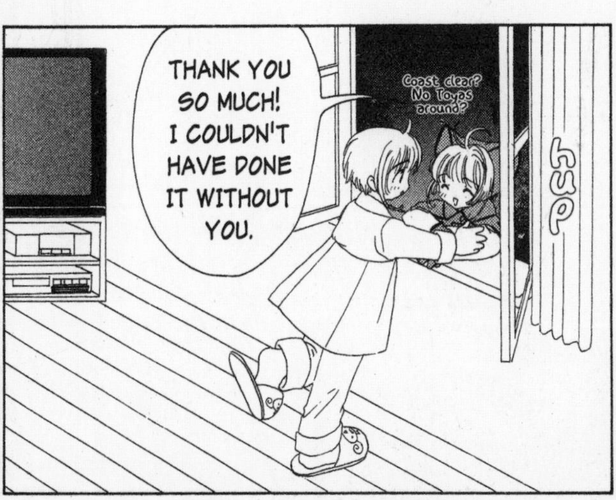
hup
Coast clear? No Toyas around?
THANK YOU SO MUCH! I COULDN'T HAVE DONE IT WITHOUT YOU.

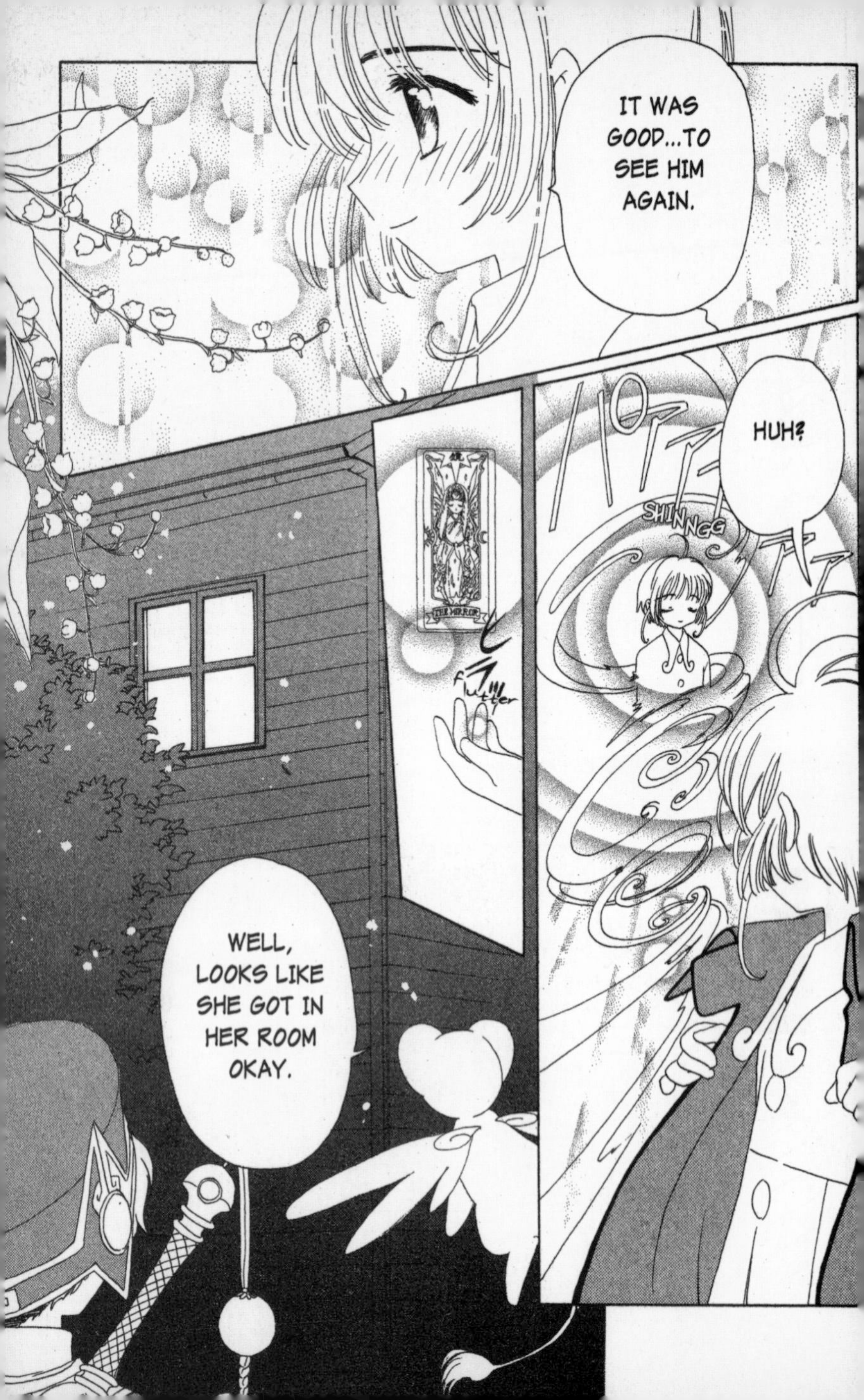
IT WAS GOOD...TO SEE HIM AGAIN.
HUH?
SHINNGG
flutter
WELL, LOOKS LIKE SHE GOT IN HER ROOM OKAY.

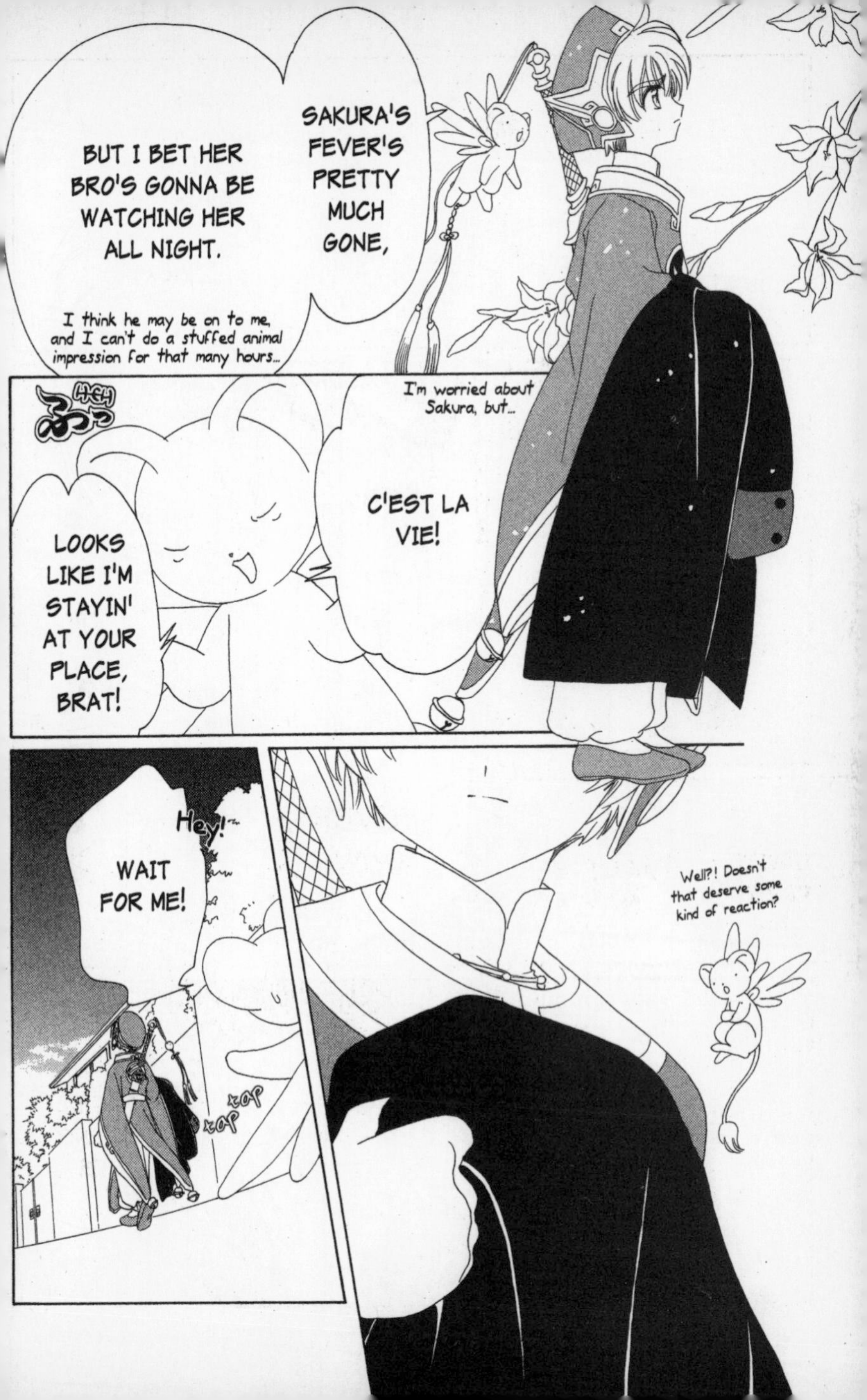
SAKURA'S FEVER'S PRETTY MUCH GONE,
BUT I BET HER BRO'S GONNA BE WATCHING HER ALL NIGHT.
I think he may be on to me, and I can't do a stuffed animal impression for that many hours...
I'm worried about Sakura, but...
C'EST LA VIE!
LOOKS LIKE I'M STAYIN' AT YOUR PLACE, BRAT!
ふっ
HEH
Well?! Doesn't that deserve some kind of reaction?
Hey!
WAIT FOR ME!
tap
tap

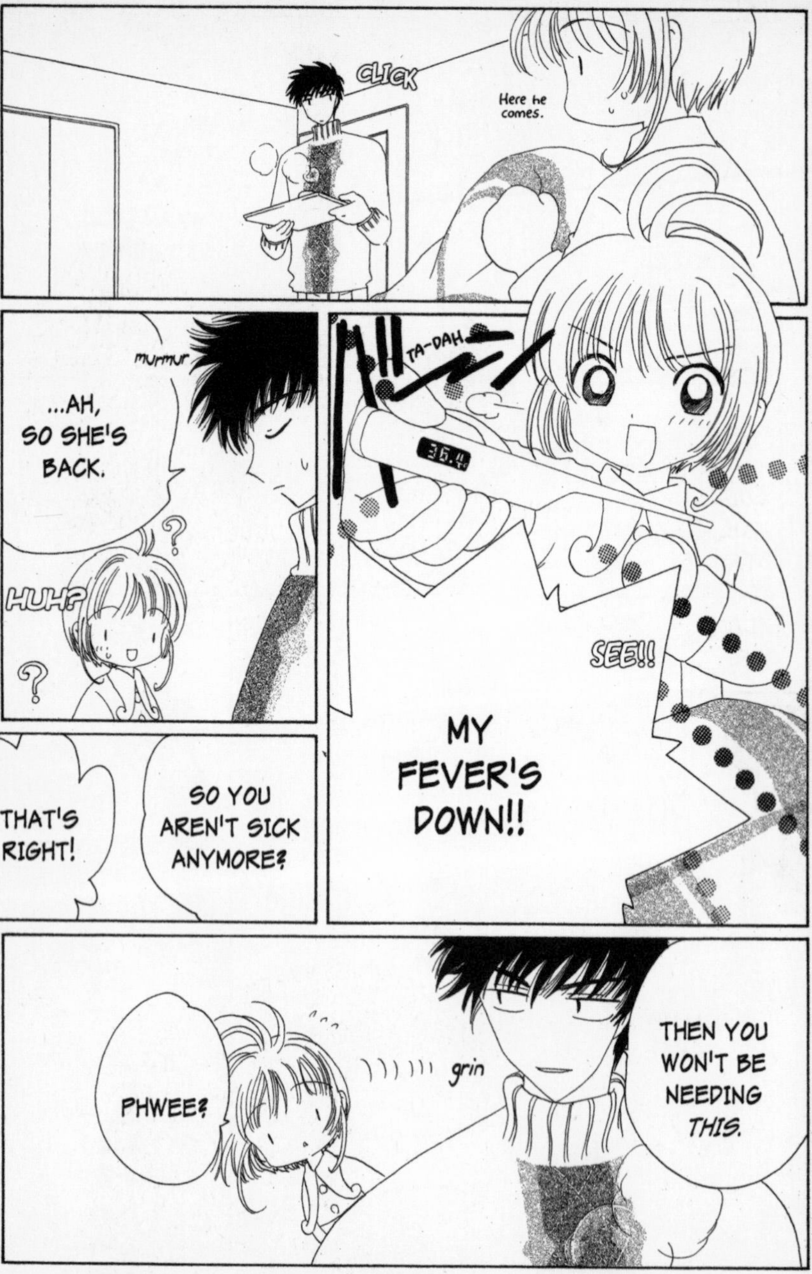
Here he comes.
CLICK
TA-DAH
36.4
SEE!!
MY FEVER'S DOWN!!
murmur
...AH, SO SHE'S BACK.
HUH?
SO YOU AREN'T SICK ANYMORE?
THAT'S RIGHT!
THEN YOU WON'T BE NEEDING *THIS.*
grin
PHWEE?

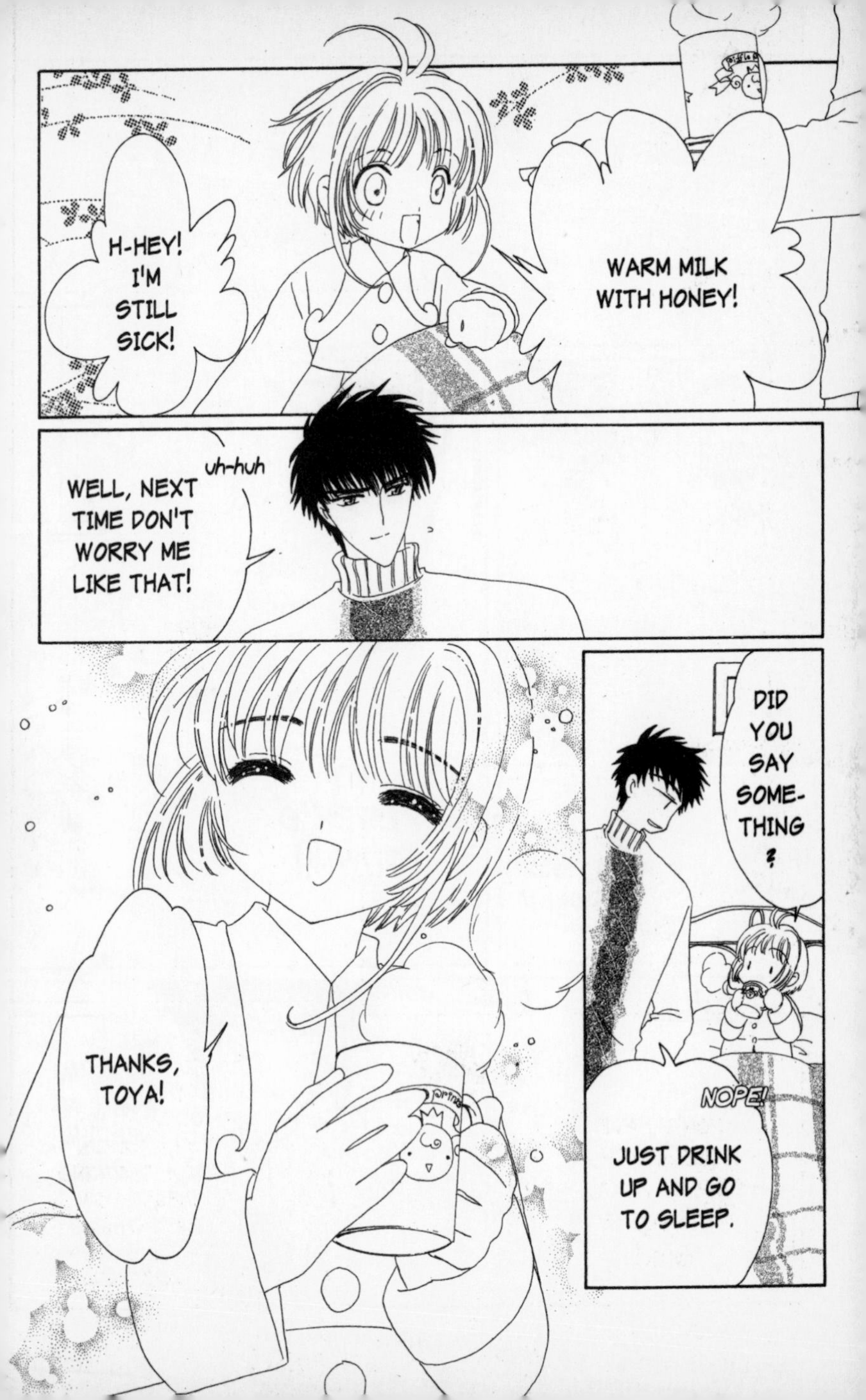
WARM MILK WITH HONEY!
H-HEY! I'M STILL SICK!
WELL, NEXT TIME DON'T WORRY ME LIKE THAT!
uh-huh
DID YOU SAY SOME-THING?
NOPE!
JUST DRINK UP AND GO TO SLEEP.
THANKS, TOYA!

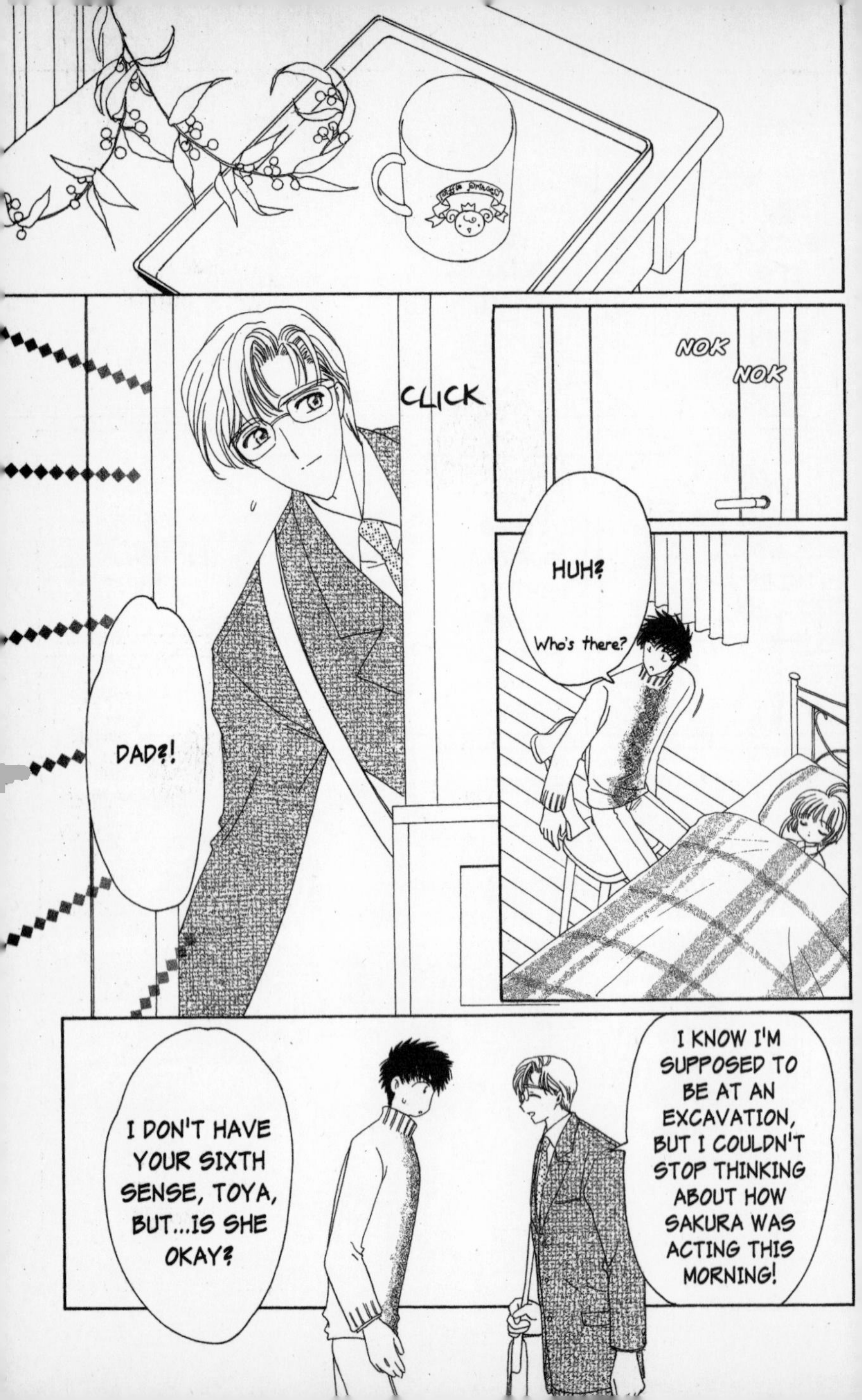
NOK
NOK
HUH?
Who's there?
CLICK
DAD?!
I KNOW I'M SUPPOSED TO BE AT AN EXCAVATION, BUT I COULDN'T STOP THINKING ABOUT HOW SAKURA WAS ACTING THIS MORNING!
I DON'T HAVE YOUR SIXTH SENSE, TOYA, BUT...IS SHE OKAY?

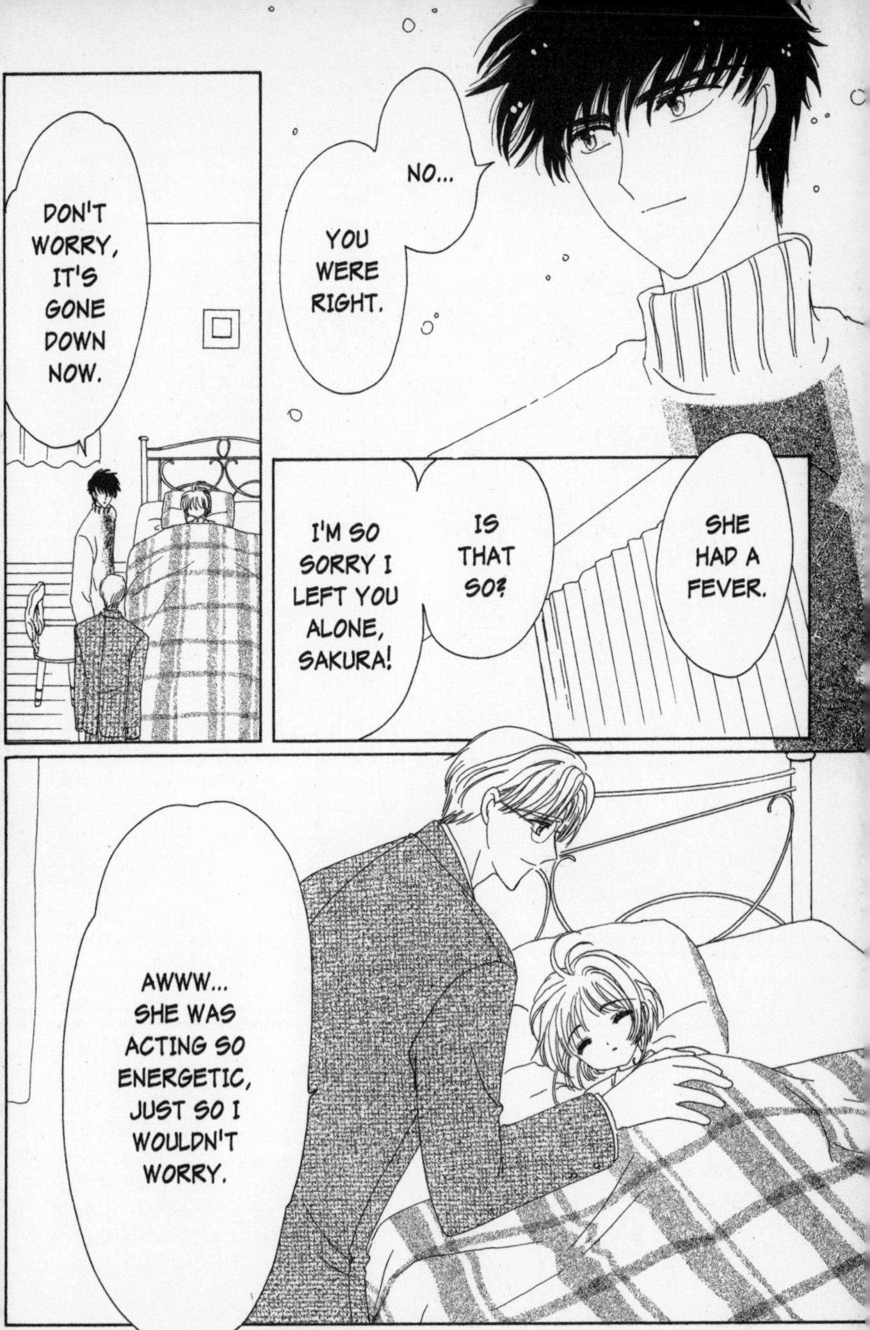
NO... YOU WERE RIGHT.
SHE HAD A FEVER.
IS THAT SO?
I'M SO SORRY I LEFT YOU ALONE, SAKURA!
DON'T WORRY, IT'S GONE DOWN NOW.
AWWW... SHE WAS ACTING SO ENERGETIC, JUST SO I WOULDN'T WORRY.

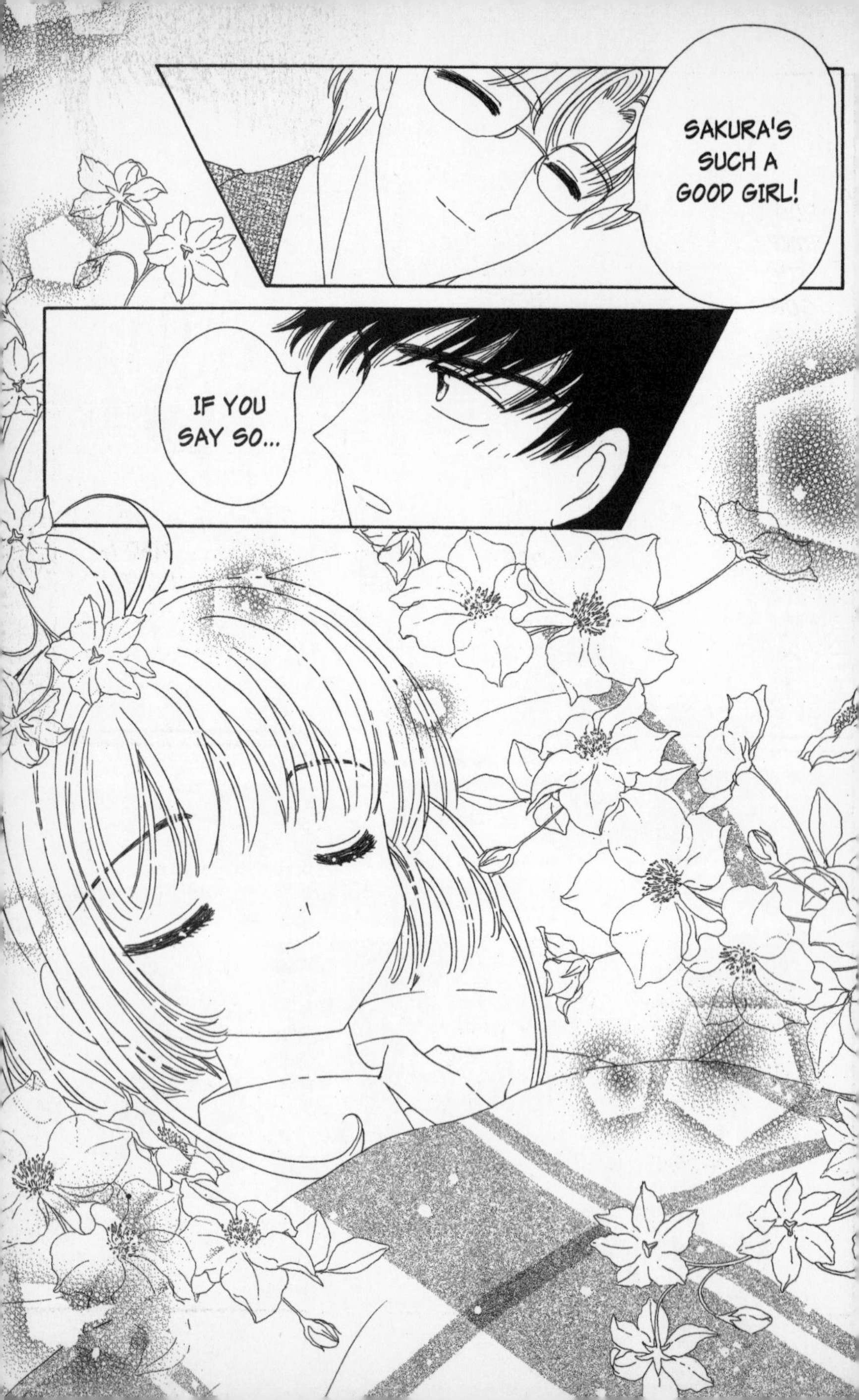
SAKURA'S SUCH A GOOD GIRL!
IF YOU SAY SO...

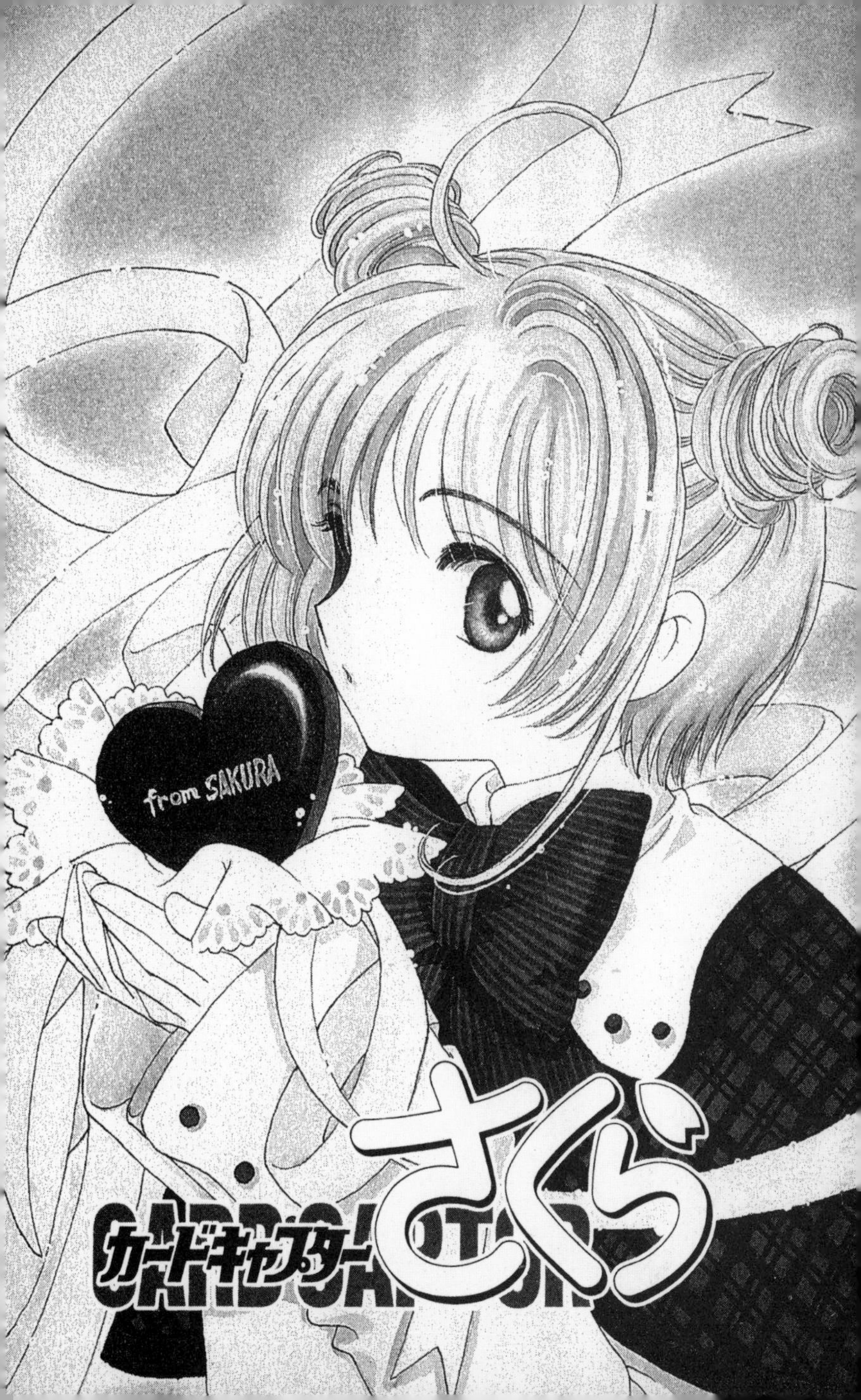
from SAKURA
カードキャプターさくら
CARD CAPTOR

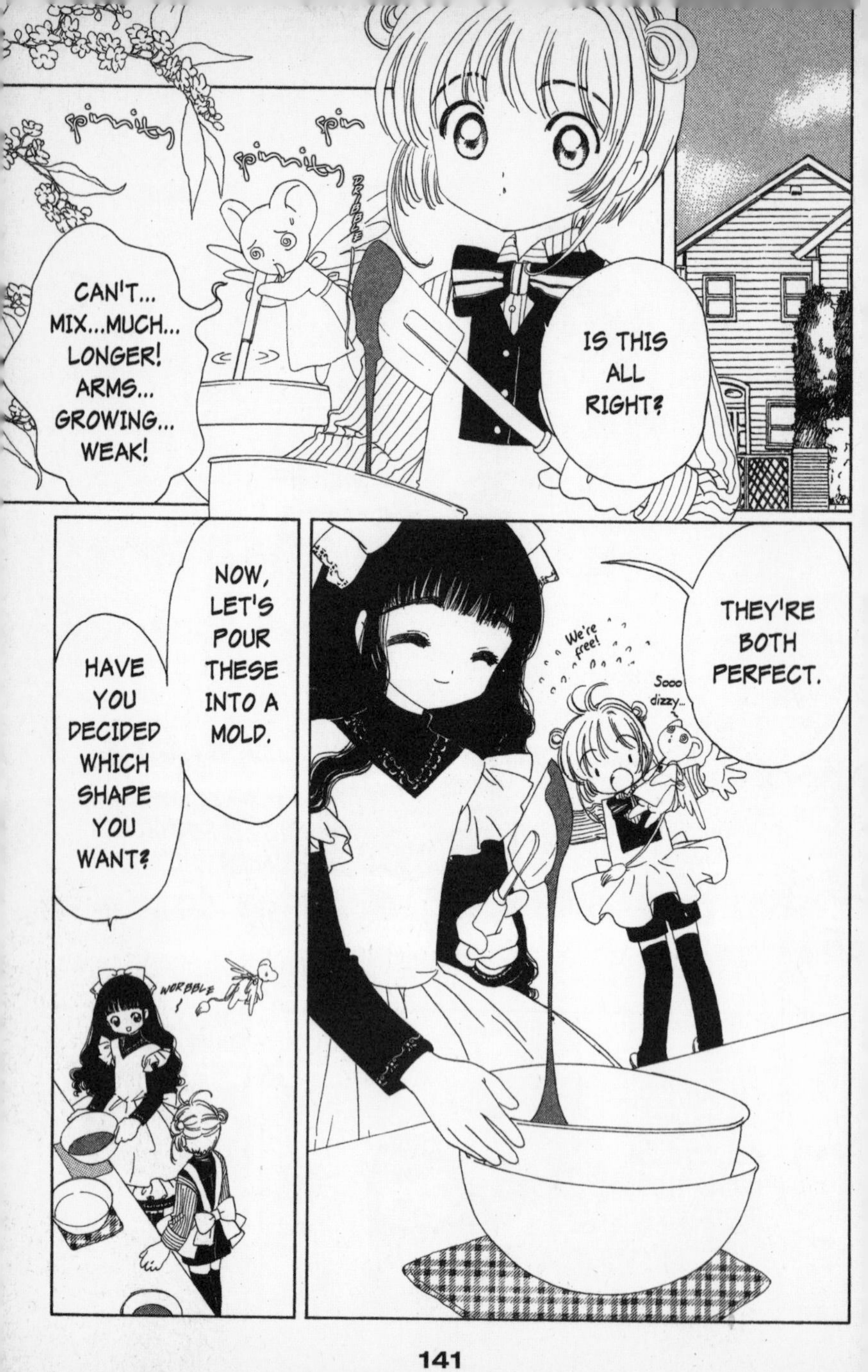

spin
spinnity
spinnity
DRIBBLE
IS THIS ALL RIGHT?
CAN'T... MIX...MUCH... LONGER! ARMS... GROWING... WEAK!
THEY'RE BOTH PERFECT.
Sooo dizzy...
We're free!
NOW, LET'S POUR THESE INTO A MOLD.
HAVE YOU DECIDED WHICH SHAPE YOU WANT?
WOBBLE

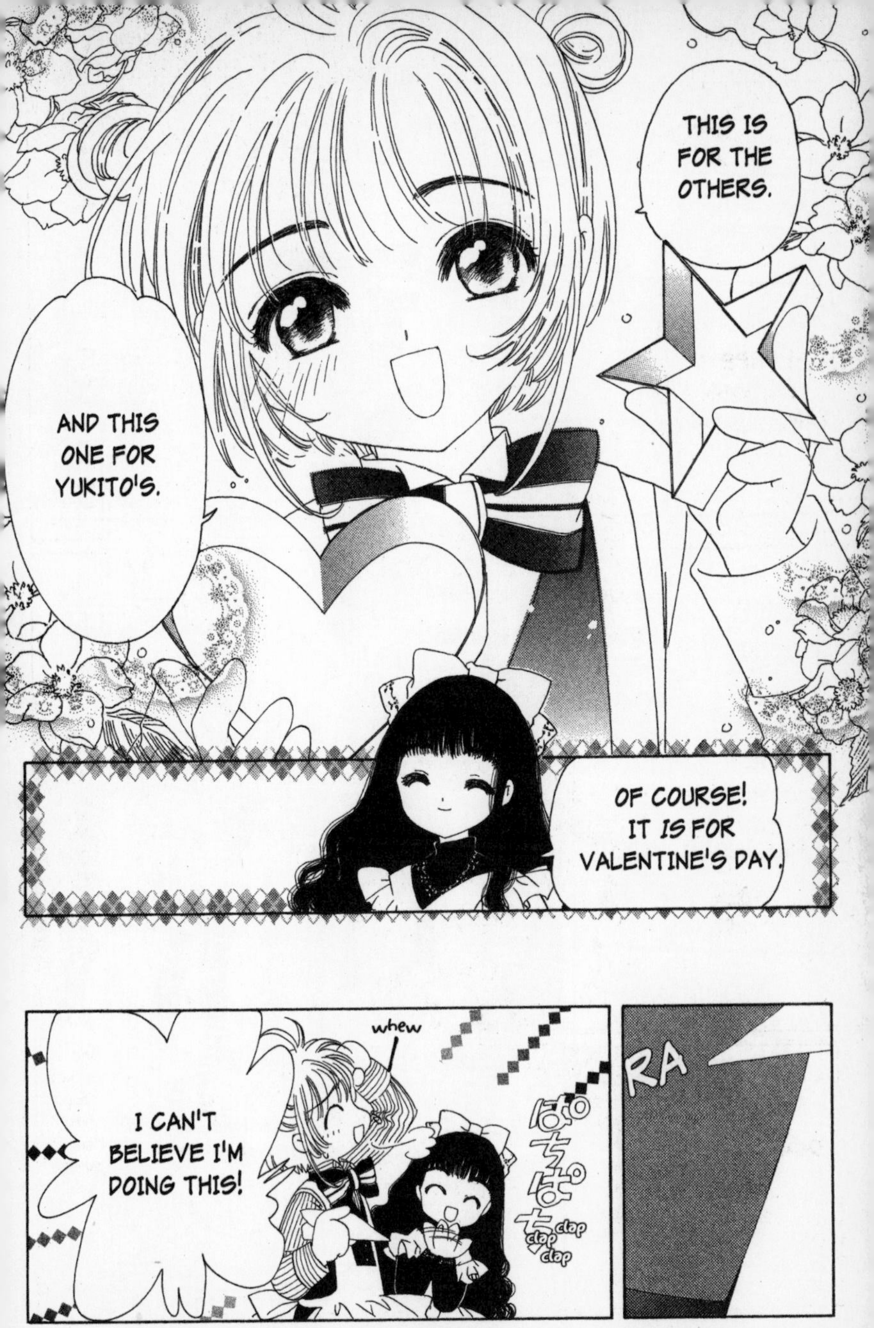
THIS IS FOR THE OTHERS.
AND THIS ONE FOR YUKITO'S.
OF COURSE! IT *IS* FOR VALENTINE'S DAY.
RA
whew
I CAN'T BELIEVE I'M DOING THIS!
ぱちぱち
clap clap clap

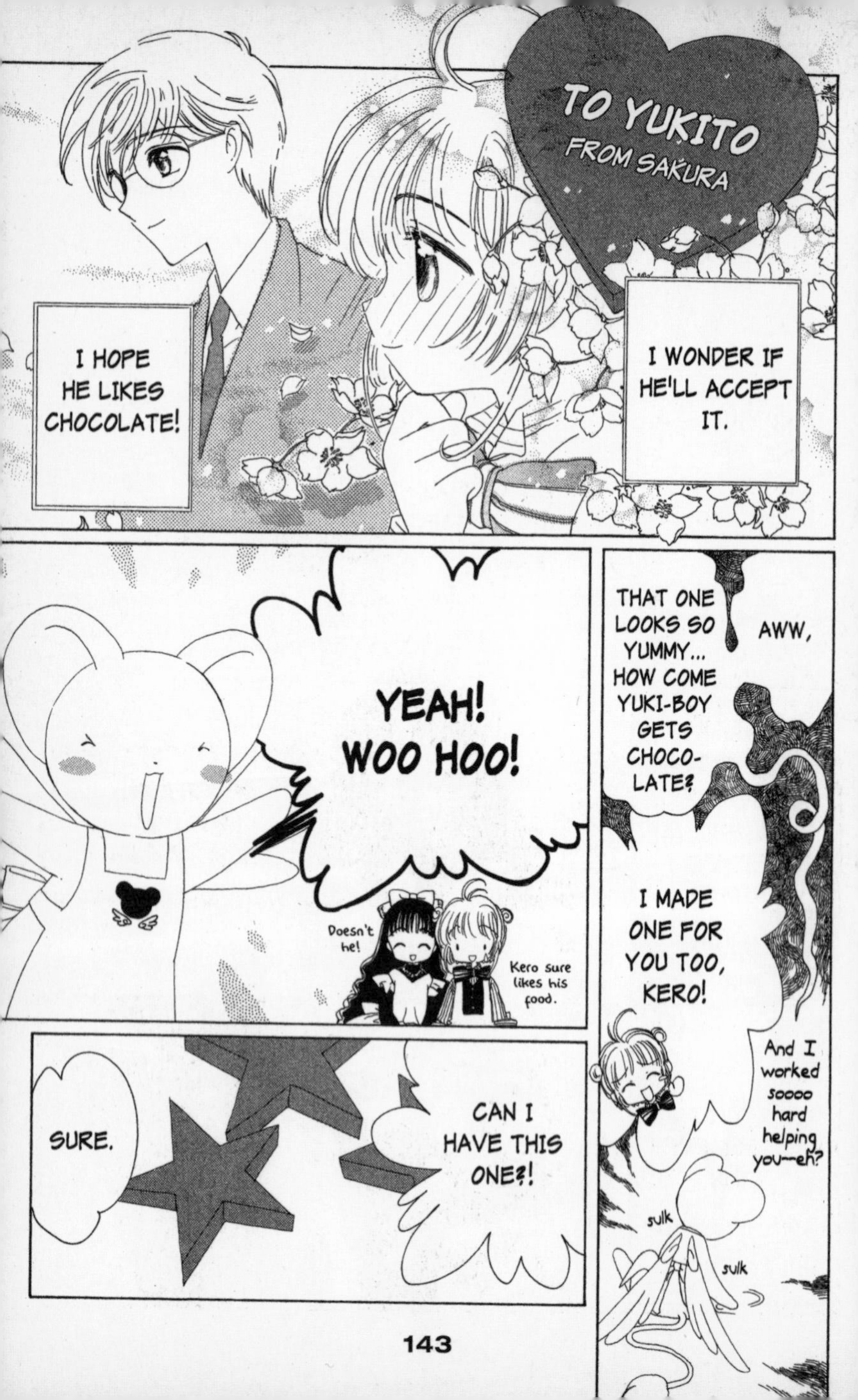
TO YUKITO FROM SAKURA
I WONDER IF HE'LL ACCEPT IT.
I HOPE HE LIKES CHOCOLATE!
AWW,
THAT ONE LOOKS SO YUMMY... HOW COME YUKI-BOY GETS CHOCO-LATE?
I MADE ONE FOR YOU TOO, KERO!
And I worked soooo hard helping you—eh?
sulk
sulk
YEAH! WOO HOO!
Kero sure likes his food.
Doesn't he!
CAN I HAVE THIS ONE?!
SURE.

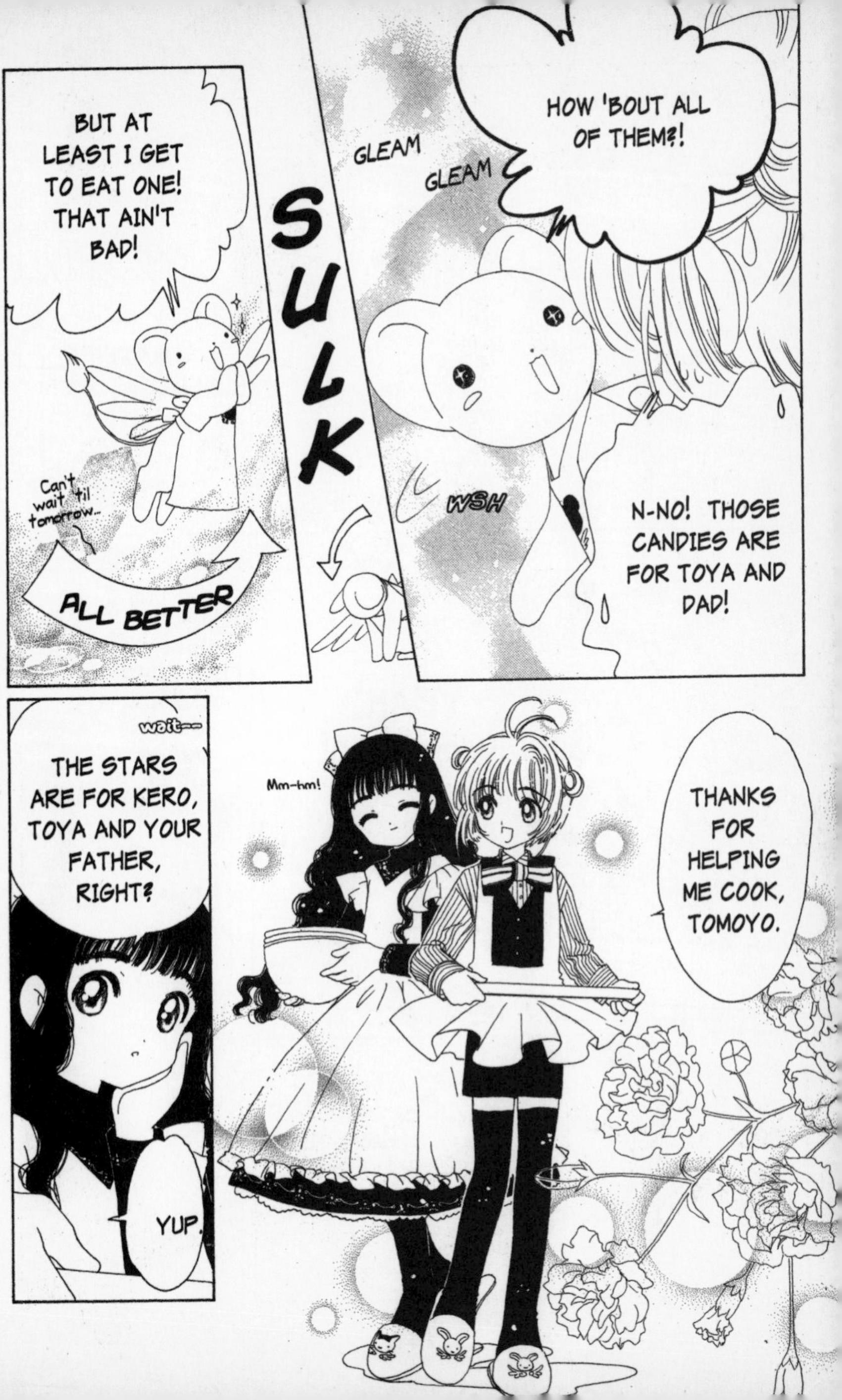
HOW 'BOUT ALL OF THEM?!
GLEAM
GLEAM
WSH
N-NO! THOSE CANDIES ARE FOR TOYA AND DAD!
SULK
BUT AT LEAST I GET TO EAT ONE! THAT AIN'T BAD!
Can't wait 'til tomorrow...
ALL BETTER
THANKS FOR HELPING ME COOK, TOMOYO.
Mm-hm!
wait---
THE STARS ARE FOR KERO, TOYA AND YOUR FATHER, RIGHT?
YUP.

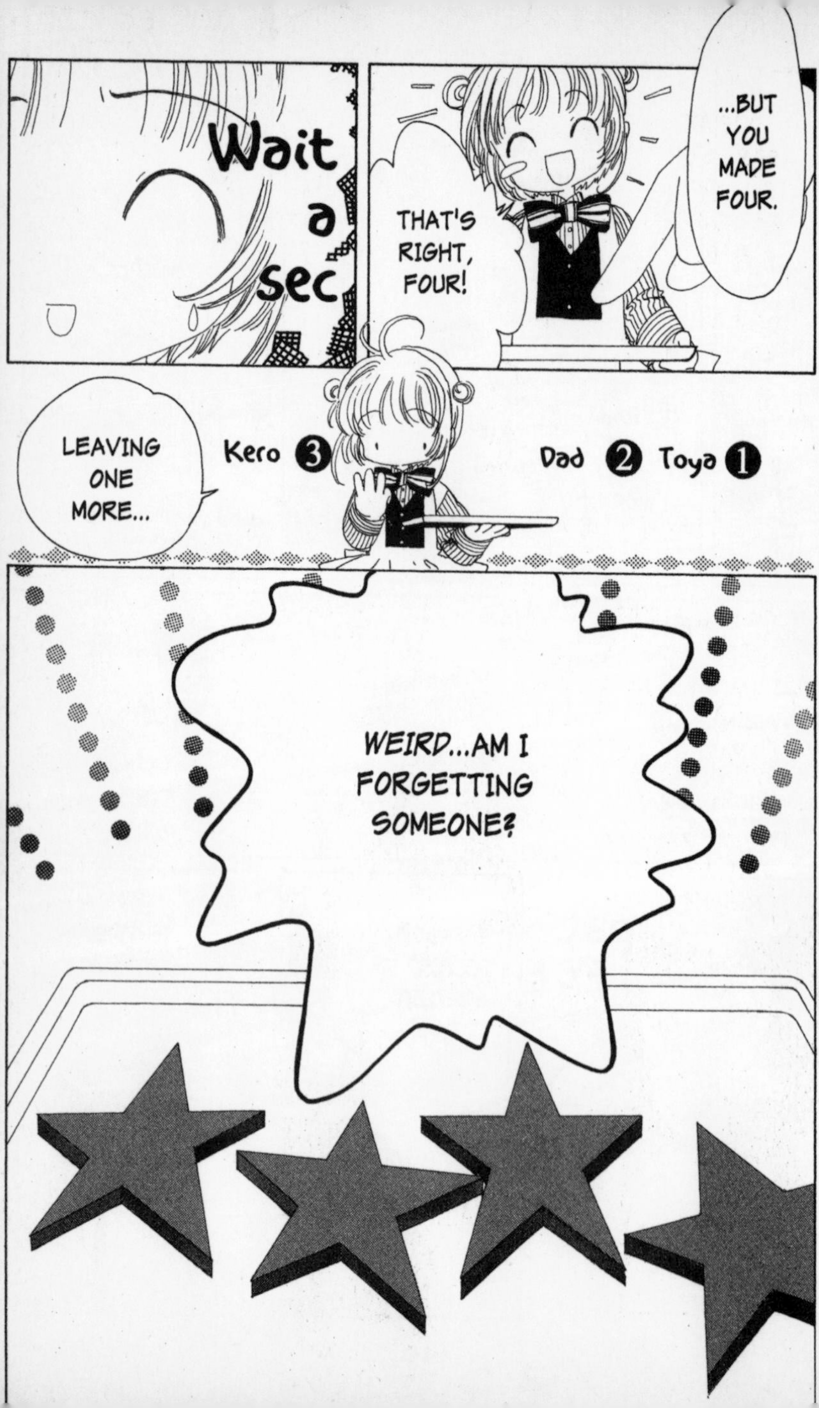
...BUT YOU MADE FOUR.
THAT'S RIGHT, FOUR!
Wait a sec
Toya 1
Dad 2
Kero 3
LEAVING ONE MORE...
WEIRD...AM I FORGETTING SOMEONE?

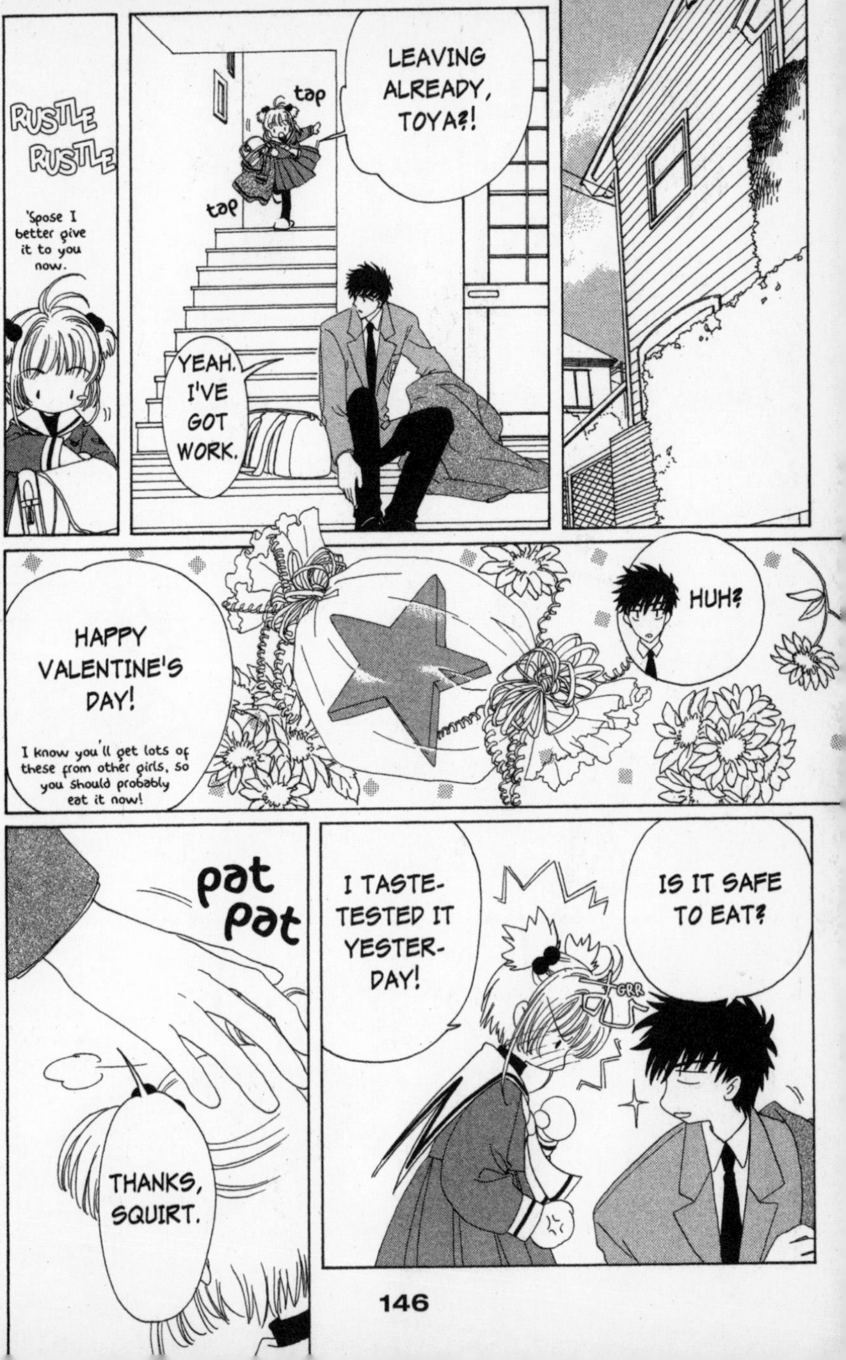
LEAVING ALREADY, TOYA?!
tap
tap
YEAH. I'VE GOT WORK.
RUSTLE RUSTLE
'Spose I better give it to you now.
HUH?
HAPPY VALENTINE'S DAY!
I know you'll get lots of these from other girls, so you should probably eat it now!
IS IT SAFE TO EAT?
I TASTE-TESTED IT YESTERDAY!
GRR
pat pat
THANKS, SQUIRT.

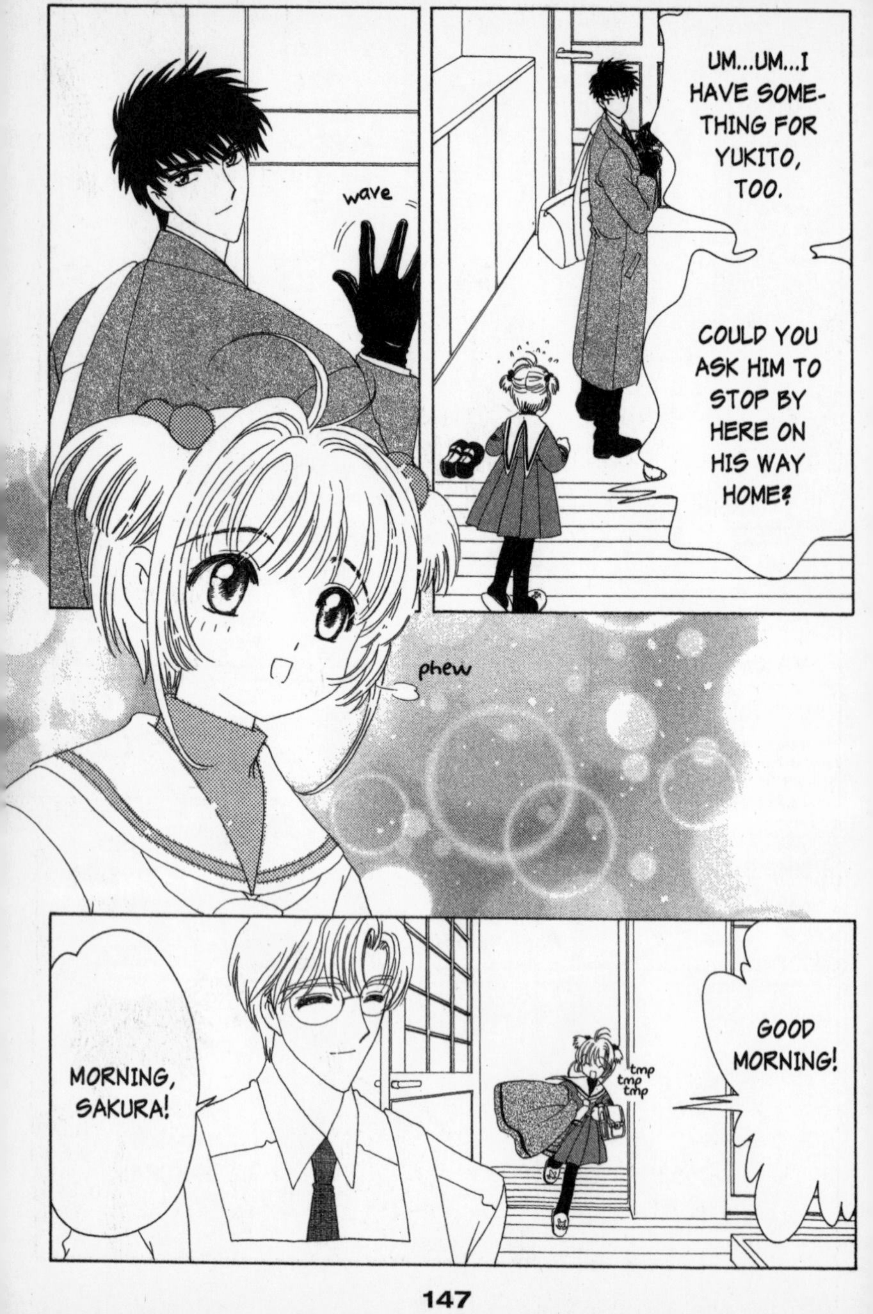
UM...UM...I HAVE SOME-THING FOR YUKITO, TOO.
COULD YOU ASK HIM TO STOP BY HERE ON HIS WAY HOME?
wave
phew
GOOD MORNING!
tmp tmp tmp
MORNING, SAKURA!

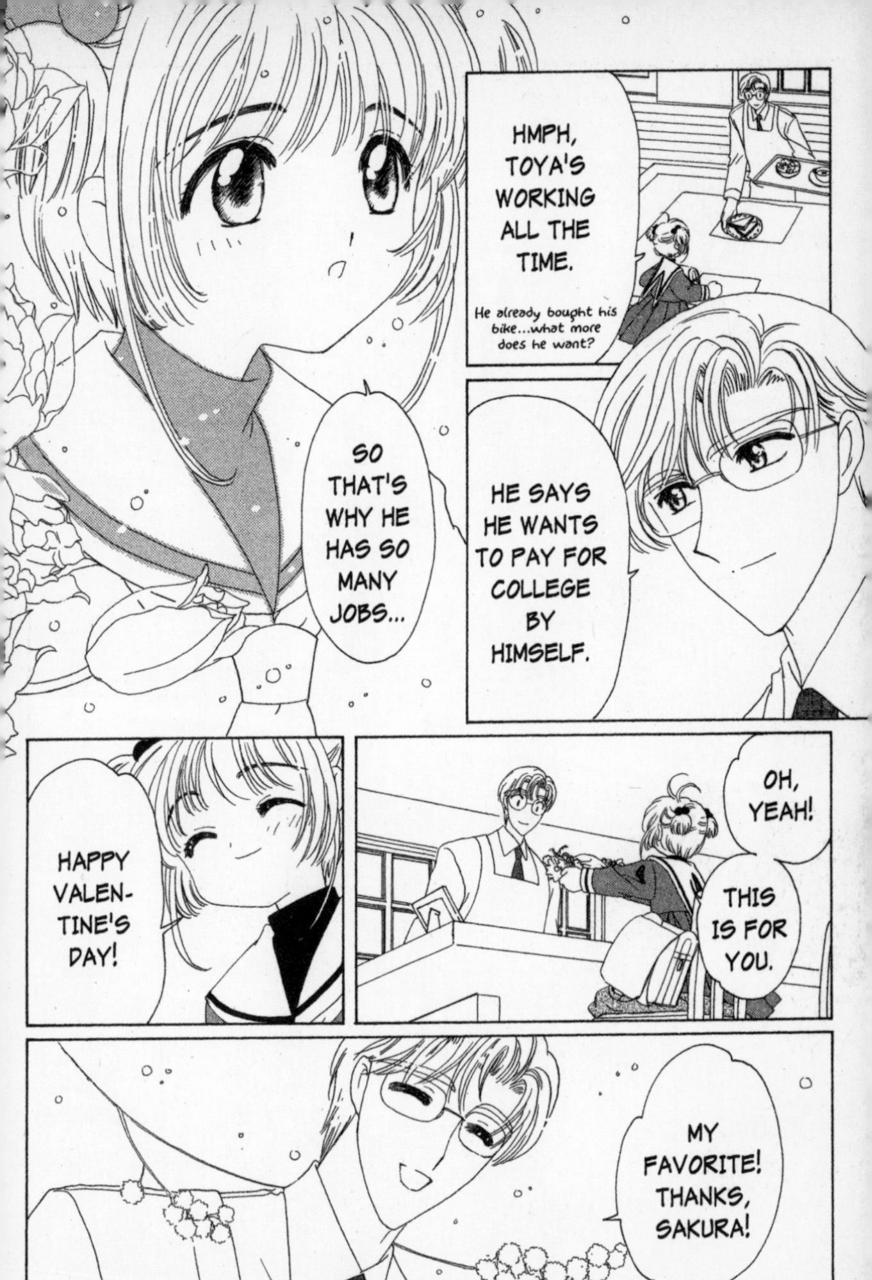
HMPH, TOYA'S WORKING ALL THE TIME.
He already bought his bike...what more does he want?
HE SAYS HE WANTS TO PAY FOR COLLEGE BY HIMSELF.
SO THAT'S WHY HE HAS SO MANY JOBS...
OH, YEAH!
THIS IS FOR YOU.
HAPPY VALEN-TINE'S DAY!
MY FAVORITE! THANKS, SAKURA!

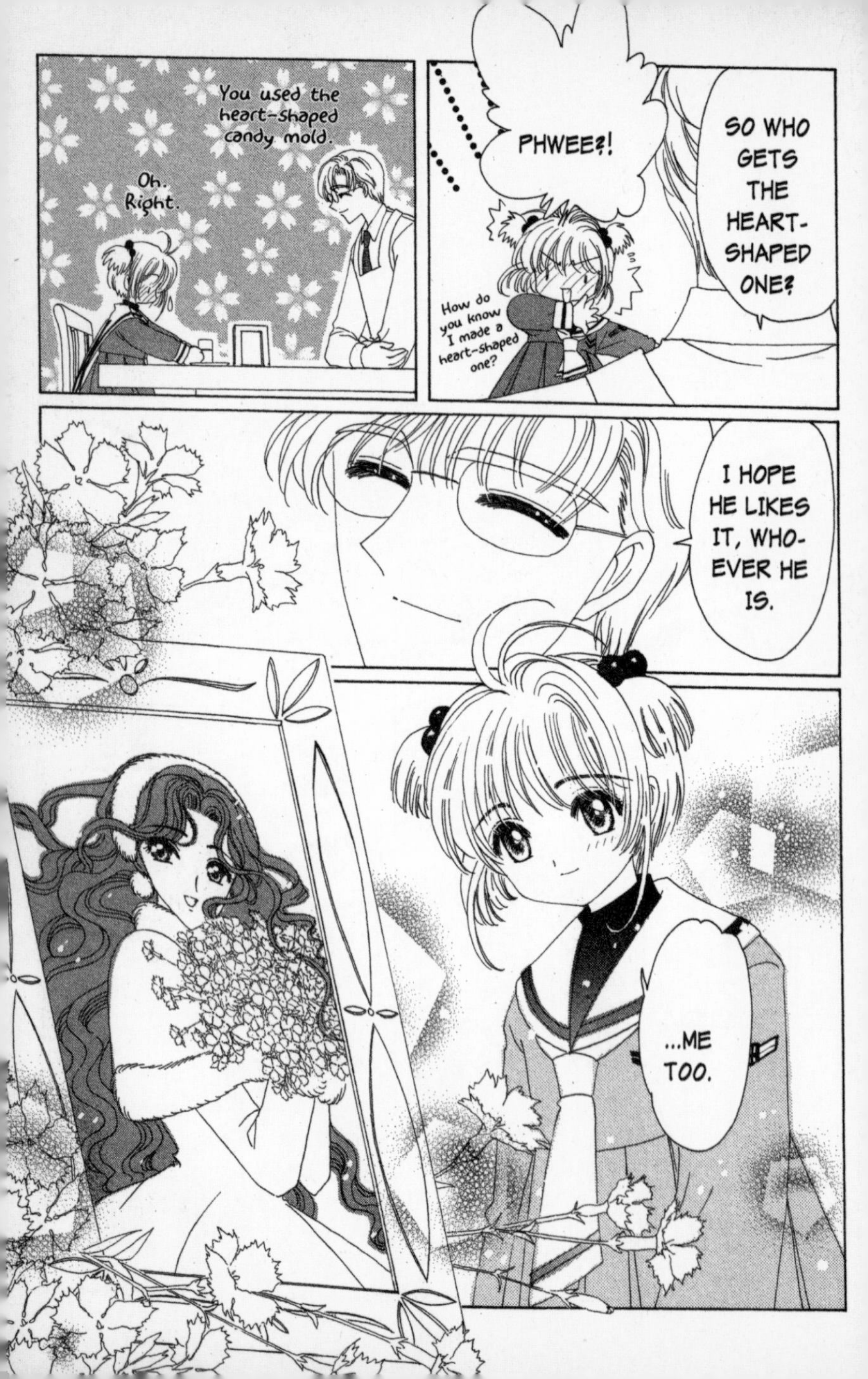
SO WHO GETS THE HEART-SHAPED ONE?
PHWEE?!
How do you know I made a heart-shaped one?
You used the heart-shaped candy mold.
Oh. Right.
I HOPE HE LIKES IT, WHO-EVER HE IS.
...ME TOO.

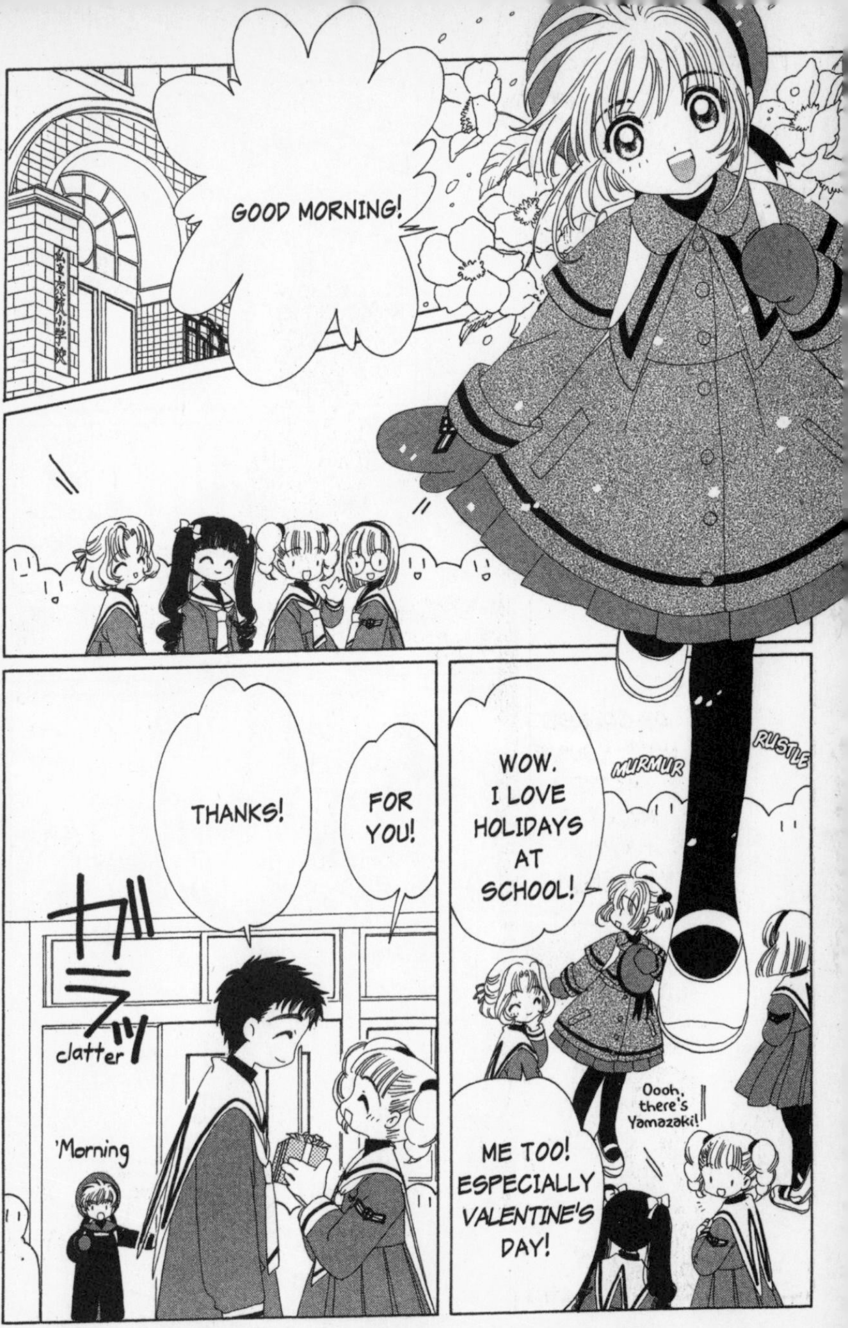
GOOD MORNING!
RUSTLE
MURMUR
WOW. I LOVE HOLIDAYS AT SCHOOL!
Oooh, there's Yamazaki!
ME TOO! ESPECIALLY VALENTINE'S DAY!
FOR YOU!
THANKS!
ガラッ
clatter
'Morning

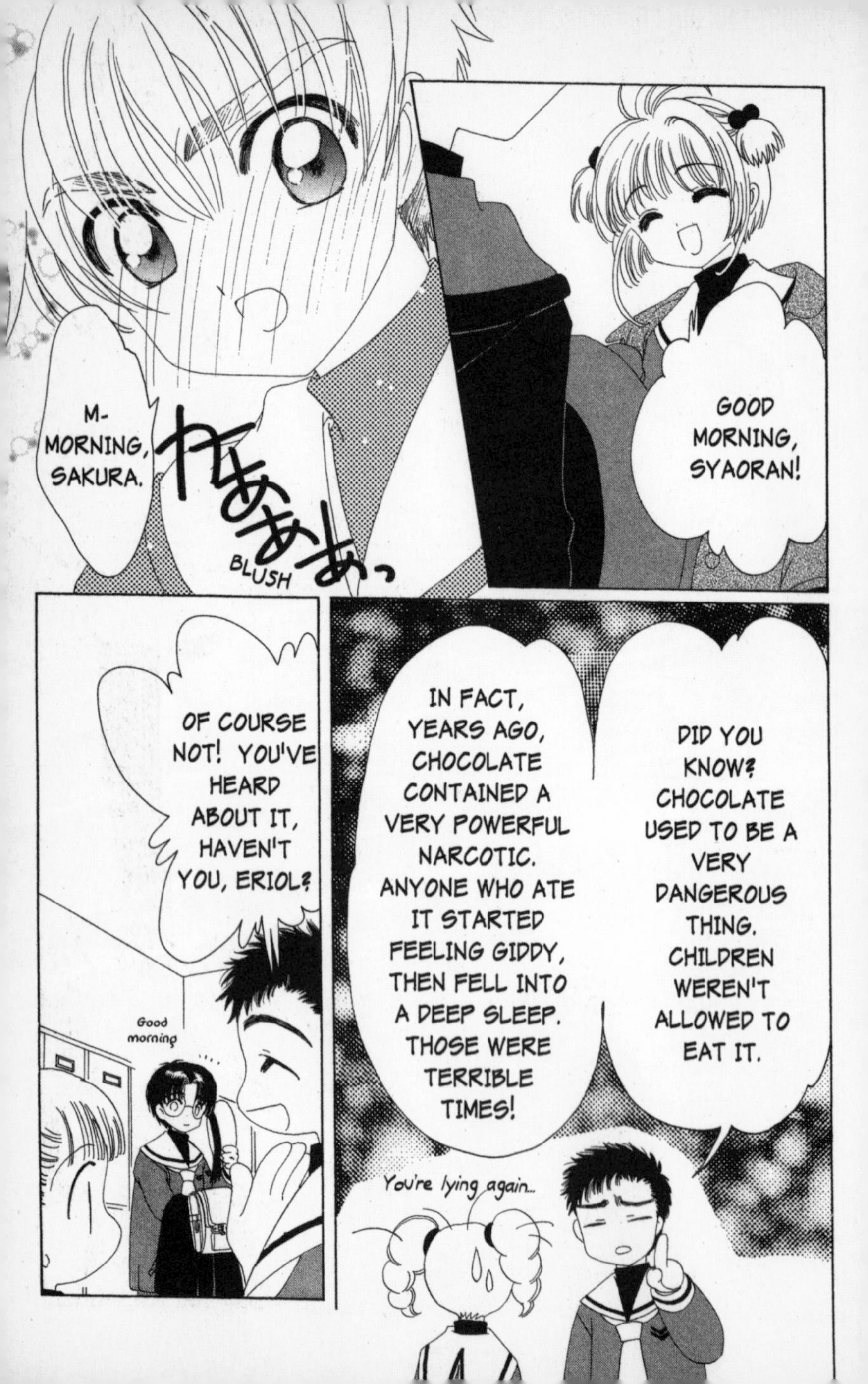
GOOD MORNING, SYAORAN!
M- MORNING, SAKURA.
かぁあぁっ
BLUSH
DID YOU KNOW? CHOCOLATE USED TO BE A VERY DANGEROUS THING. CHILDREN WEREN'T ALLOWED TO EAT IT.
IN FACT, YEARS AGO, CHOCOLATE CONTAINED A VERY POWERFUL NARCOTIC. ANYONE WHO ATE IT STARTED FEELING GIDDY, THEN FELL INTO A DEEP SLEEP. THOSE WERE TERRIBLE TIMES!
You're lying again...
OF COURSE NOT! YOU'VE HEARD ABOUT IT, HAVEN'T YOU, ERIOL?
Good morning

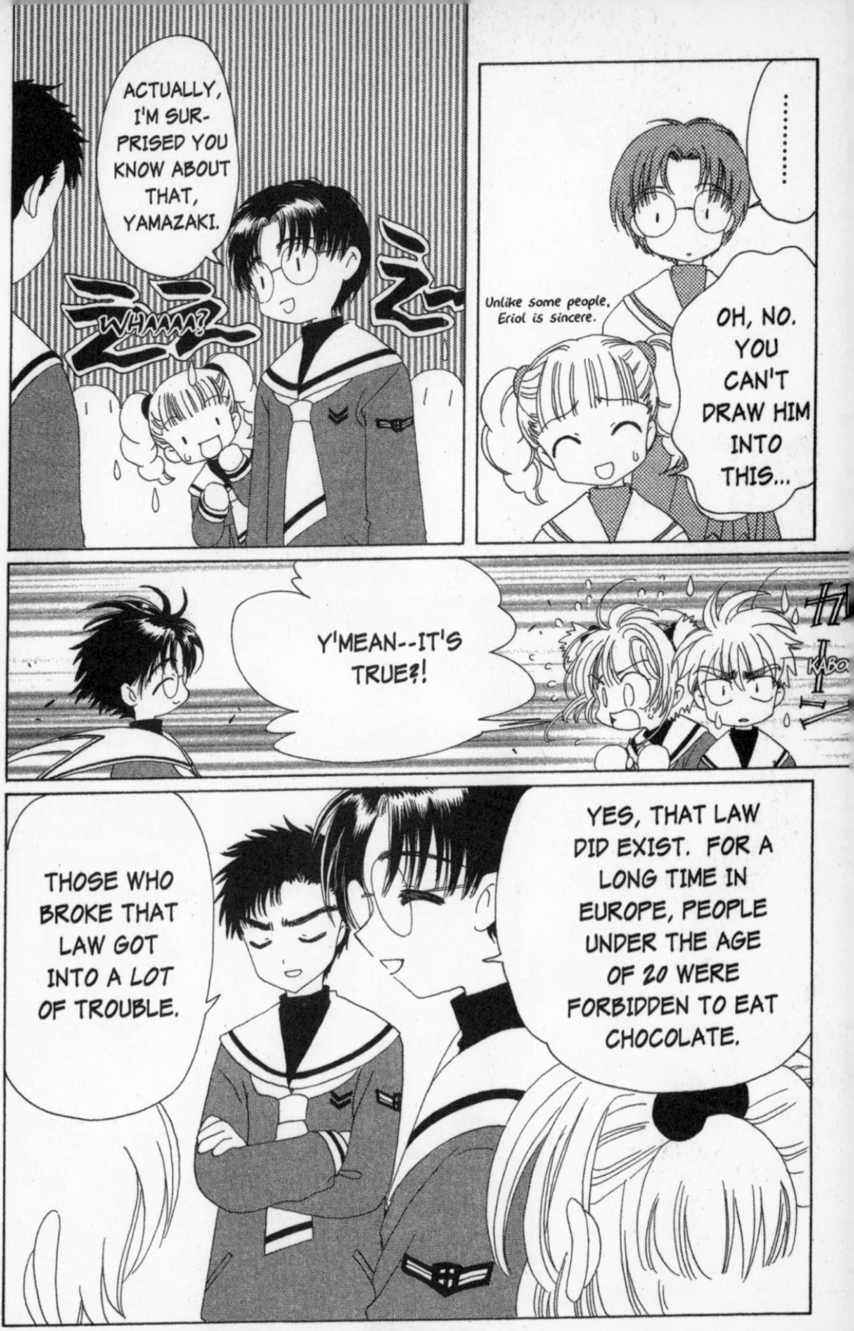

......
OH, NO. YOU CAN'T DRAW HIM INTO THIS...
Unlike some people, Eriol is sincere.
ACTUALLY, I'M SUR-PRISED YOU KNOW ABOUT THAT, YAMAZAKI.
WHAAAA?
Y'MEAN--IT'S TRUE?!
KABO
YES, THAT LAW DID EXIST. FOR A LONG TIME IN EUROPE, PEOPLE UNDER THE AGE OF 20 WERE FORBIDDEN TO EAT CHOCOLATE.
THOSE WHO BROKE THAT LAW GOT INTO A LOT OF TROUBLE.

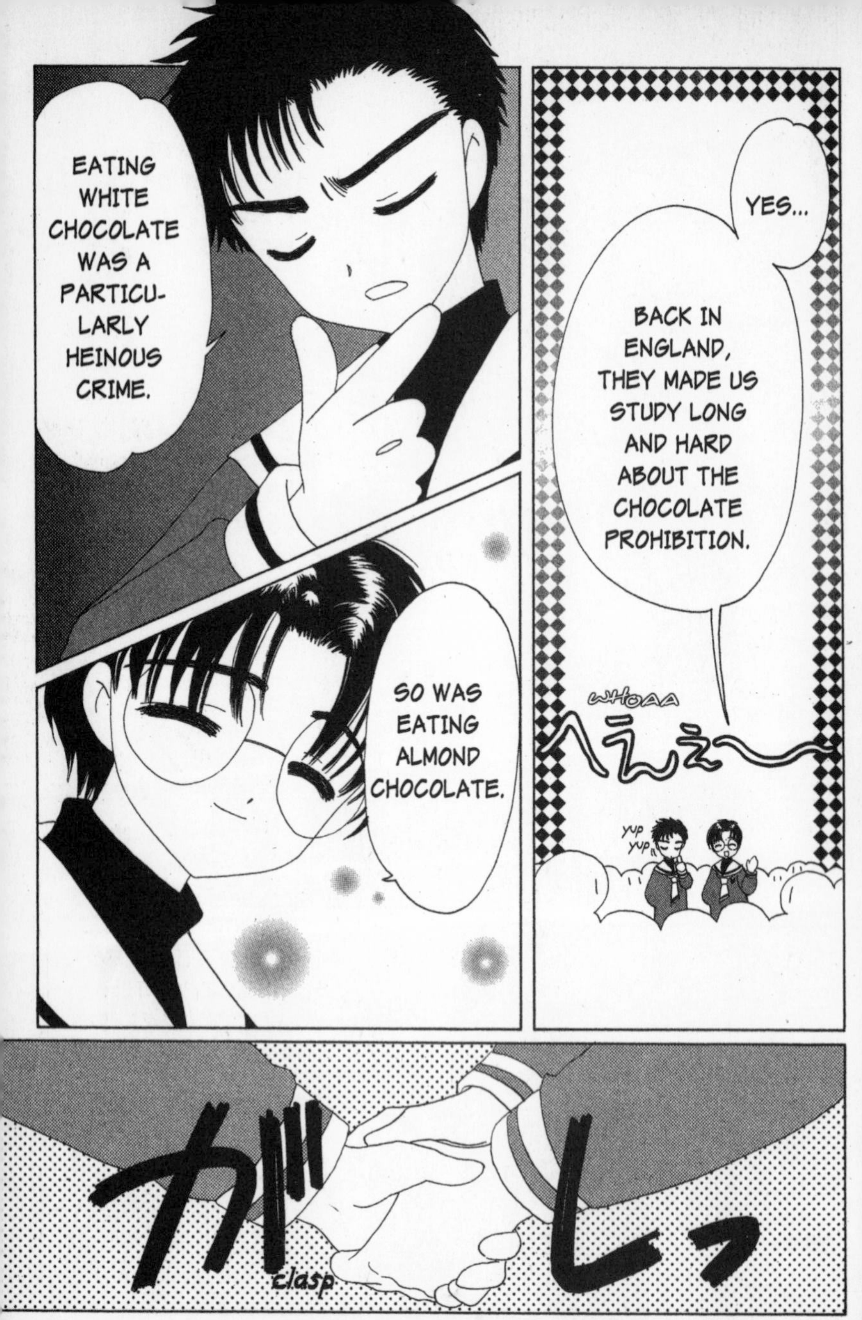
YES...
BACK IN ENGLAND, THEY MADE US STUDY LONG AND HARD ABOUT THE CHOCOLATE PROHIBITION.
WHOAA
へええ〜〜
yup yup
EATING WHITE CHOCOLATE WAS A PARTICU-LARLY HEINOUS CRIME.
SO WAS EATING ALMOND CHOCOLATE.
ガしっ
clasp

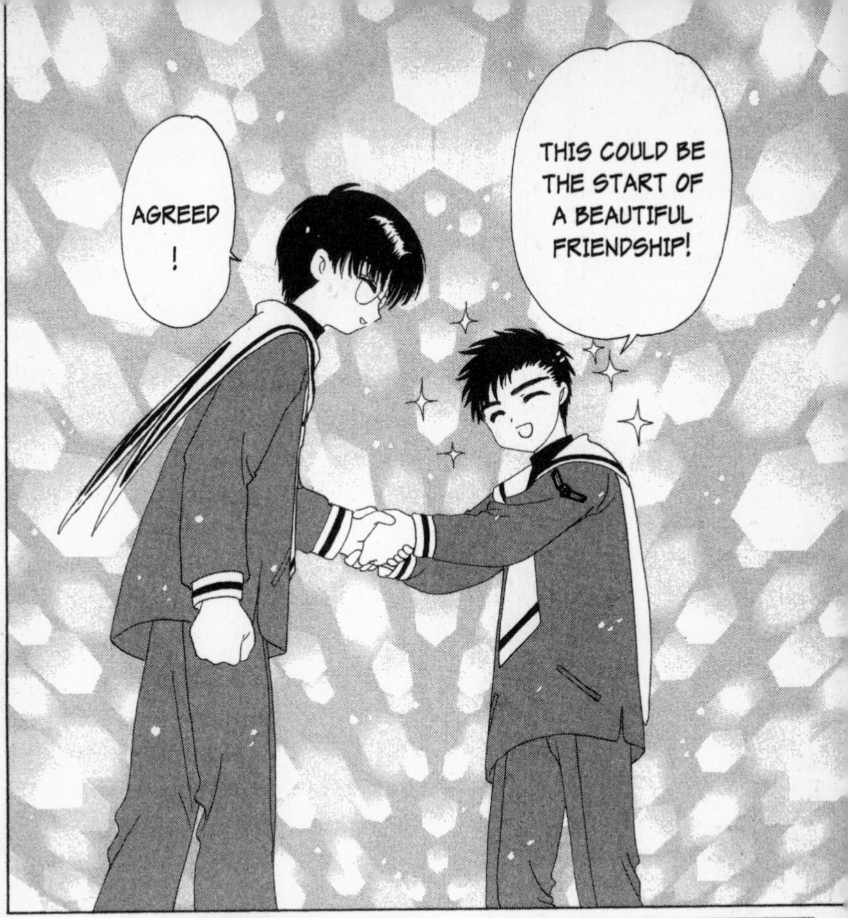
THIS COULD BE THE START OF A BEAUTIFUL FRIENDSHIP!
AGREED !

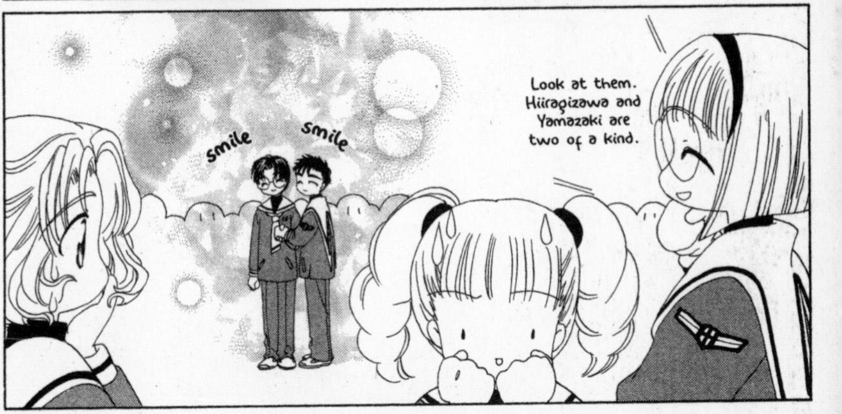
Look at them. Hiiragizawa and Yamazaki are two of a kind.
smile
smile

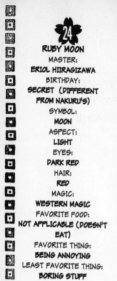

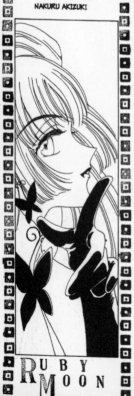

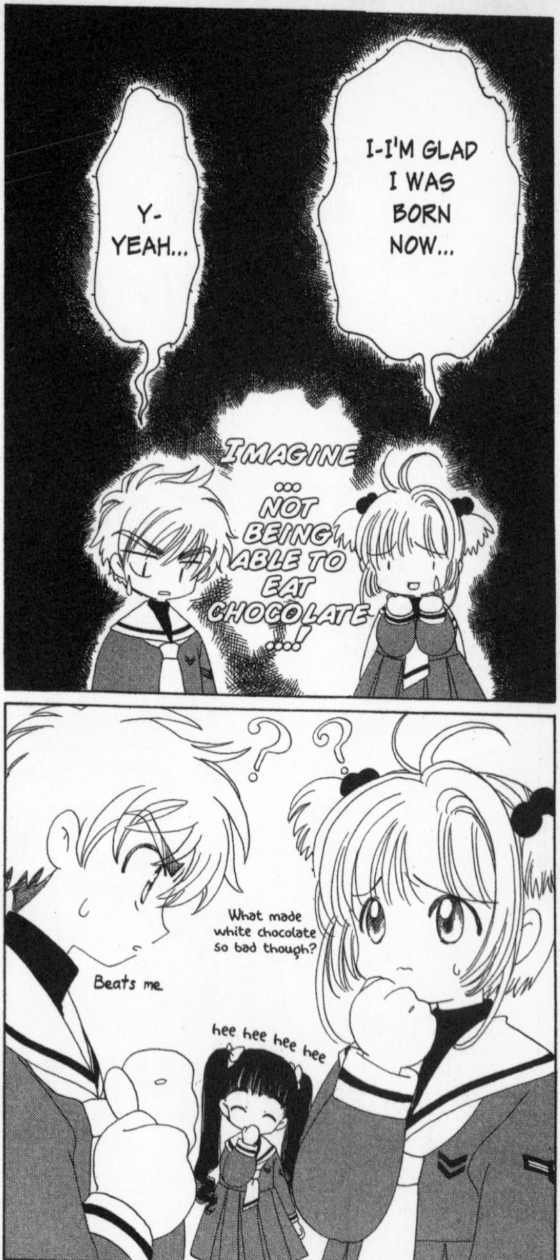
I-I'M GLAD I WAS BORN NOW...
Y- YEAH...
IMAGINE ... NOT BEING ABLE TO EAT CHOCOLATE ...!
What made white chocolate so bad though?
Beats me
hee hee hee hee

24

RUBY MOON

MASTER:
ERIOL HIIRAGIZAWA
BIRTHDAY:
SECRET (DIFFERENT FROM NAKURU'S)
SYMBOL:
MOON
ASPECT:
LIGHT
EYES:
DARK RED
HAIR:
RED
MAGIC:
WESTERN MAGIC
FAVORITE FOOD:
NOT APPLICABLE (DOESN'T EAT)
FAVORITE THING:
BEING ANNOYING
LEAST FAVORITE THING:
BORING STUFF
TEMPORARY FORM:
NAKURU AKIZUKI

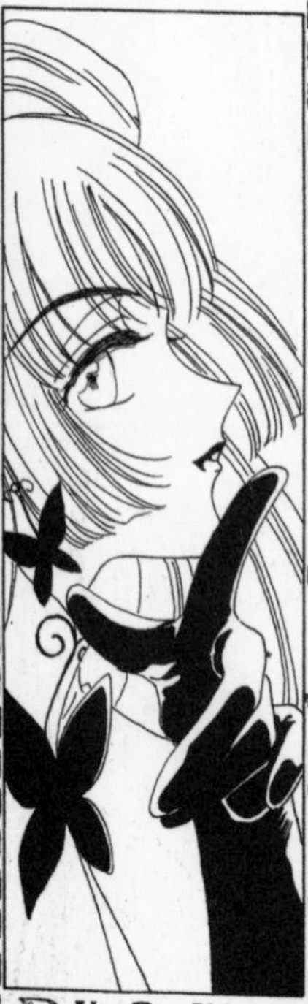

RUBY MOON

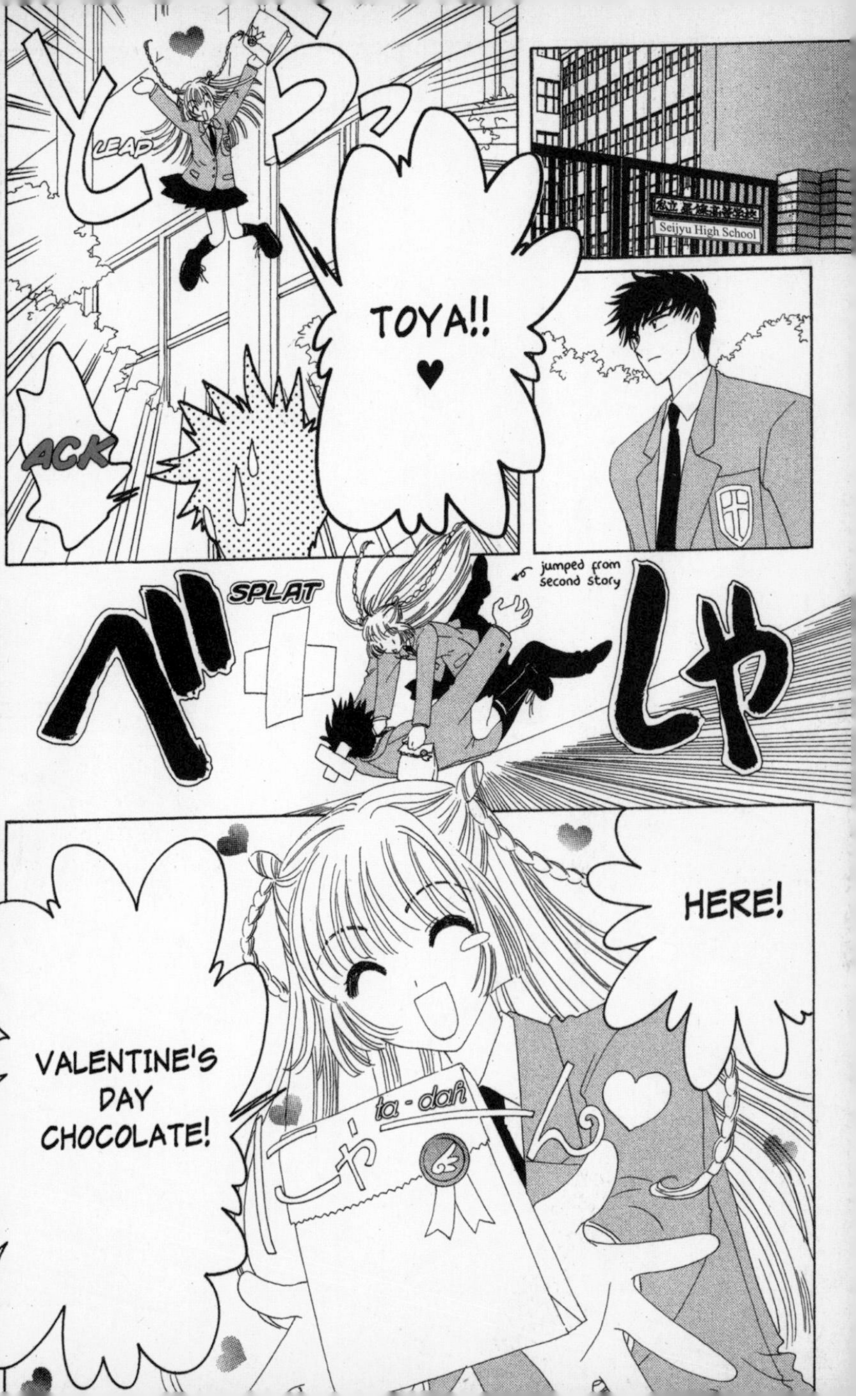
Seijyu High School
LEAP
TOYA!! ♥
ACK
jumped from second story
SPLAT
HERE!
VALENTINE'S DAY CHOCOLATE!
ta-dah

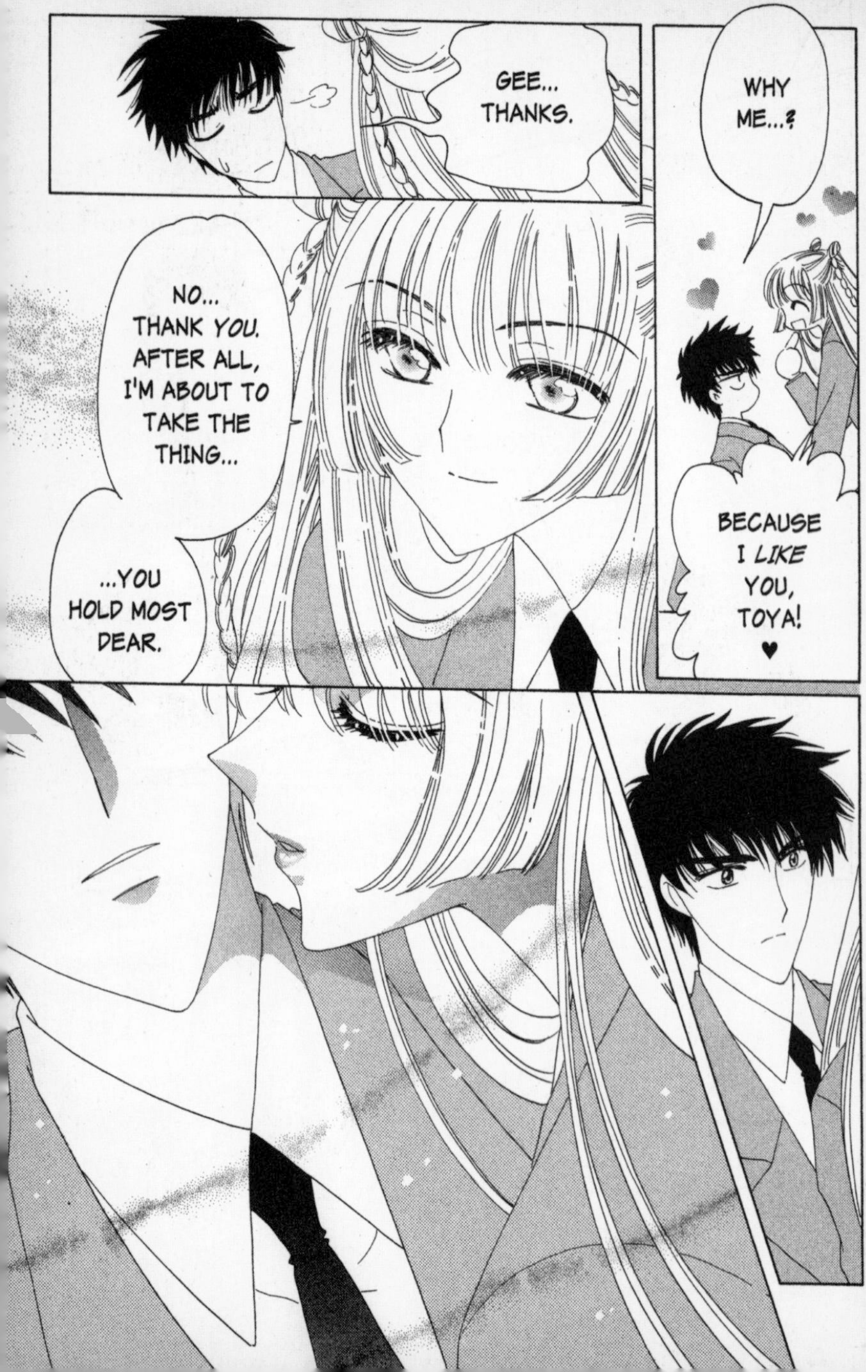
WHY ME...?
BECAUSE I *LIKE* YOU, TOYA! ♥
GEE... THANKS.
NO... THANK *YOU*. AFTER ALL, I'M ABOUT TO TAKE THE THING...
...YOU HOLD MOST DEAR.

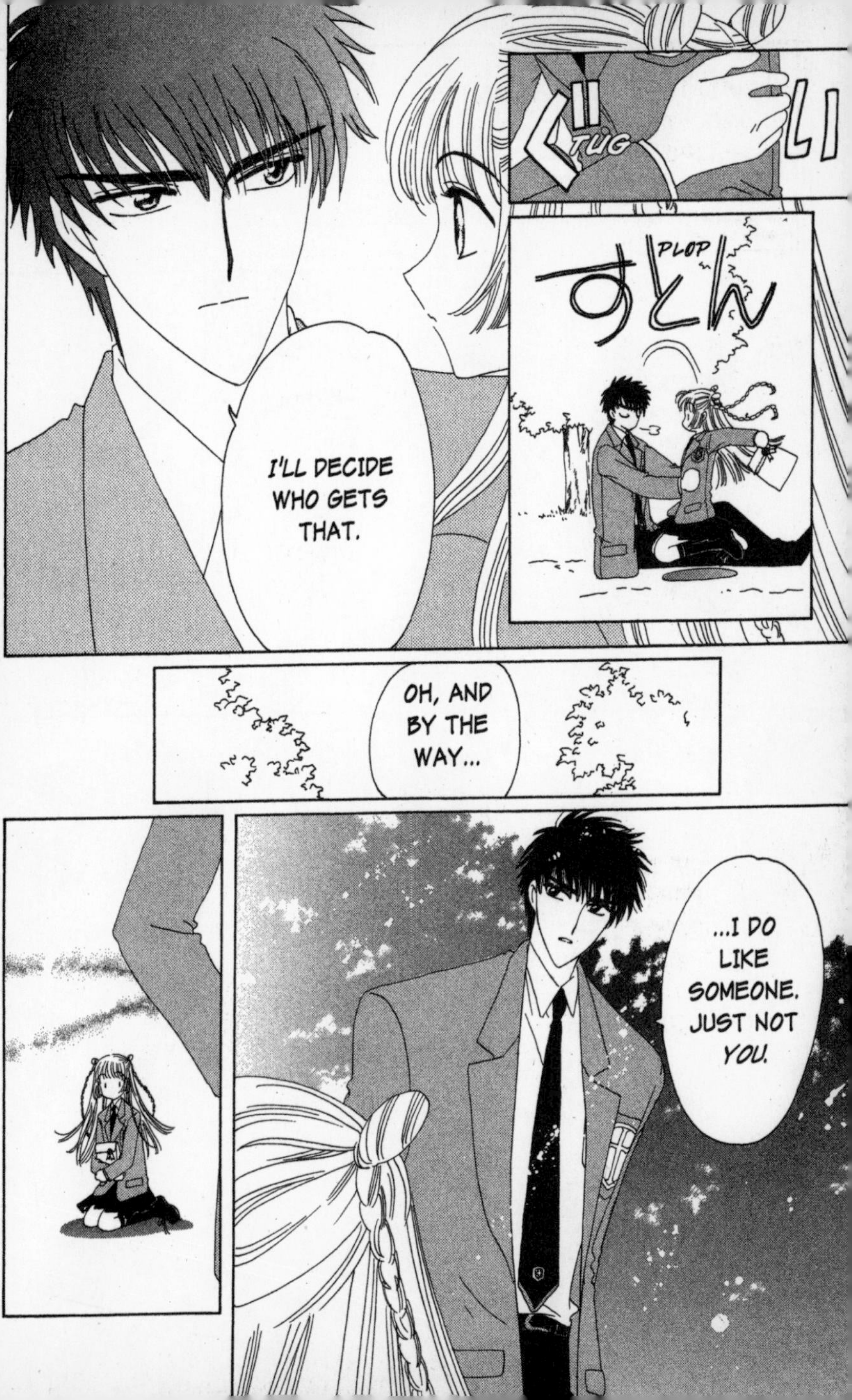
ぐい
TUG
すとん
PLOP
I'LL DECIDE WHO GETS THAT.
OH, AND BY THE WAY...
...I DO LIKE SOMEONE. JUST NOT YOU.

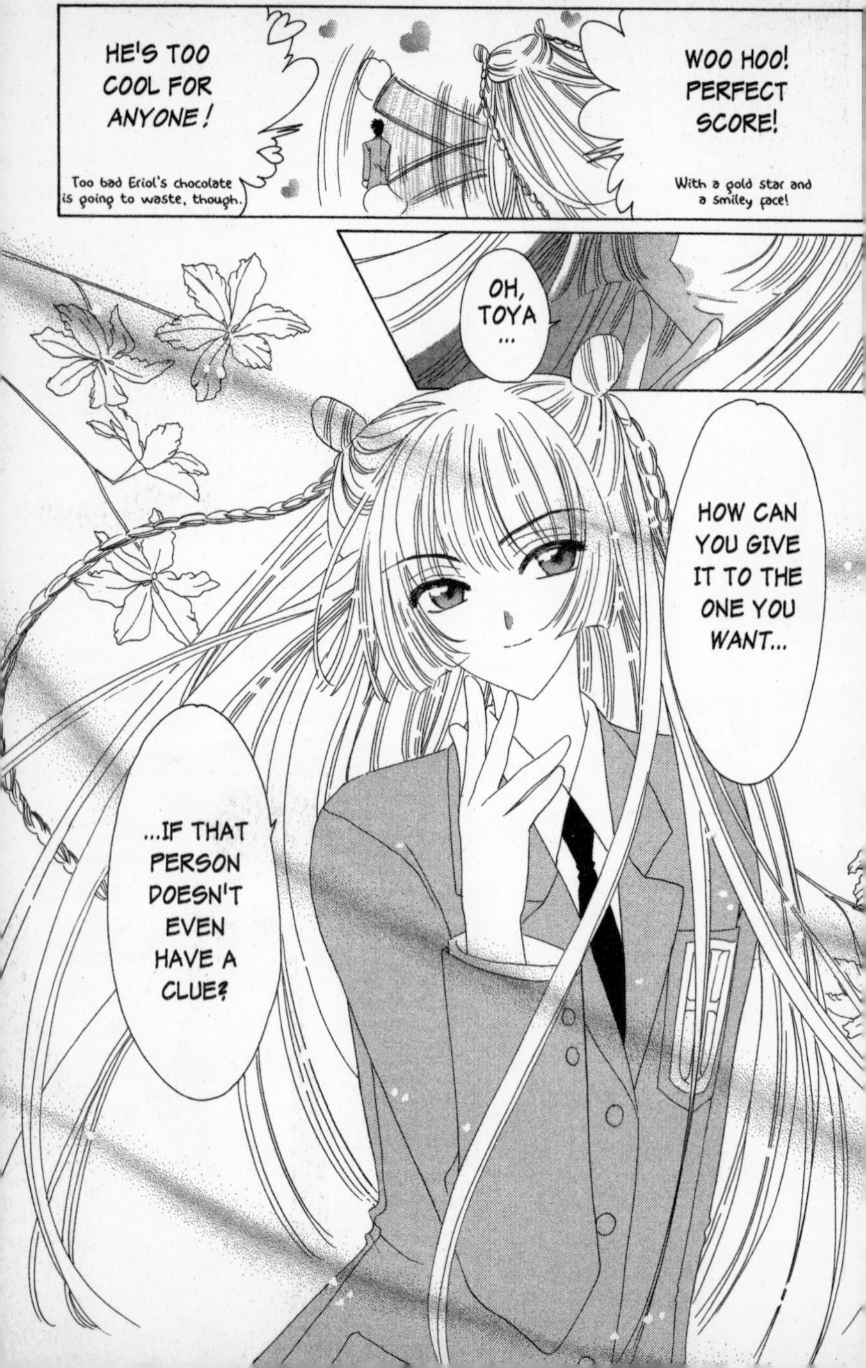
WOO HOO! PERFECT SCORE!
With a gold star and a smiley face!
HE'S TOO COOL FOR ANYONE!
Too bad Eriol's chocolate is going to waste, though.
OH, TOYA ...
HOW CAN YOU GIVE IT TO THE ONE YOU WANT...
...IF THAT PERSON DOESN'T EVEN HAVE A CLUE?

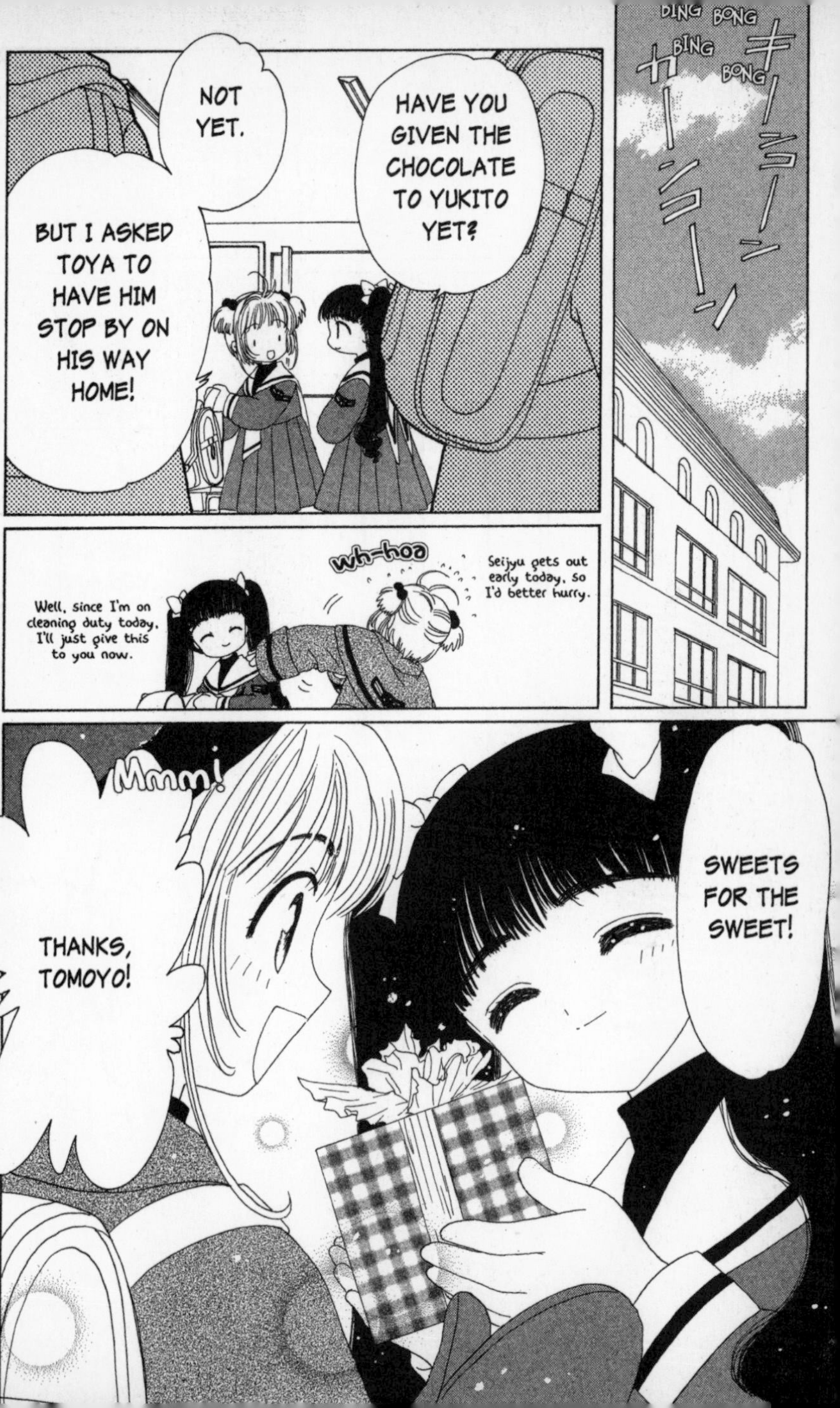
DING BONG
BING BONG
HAVE YOU GIVEN THE CHOCOLATE TO YUKITO YET?
NOT YET.
BUT I ASKED TOYA TO HAVE HIM STOP BY ON HIS WAY HOME!
Seijyu gets out early today, so I'd better hurry.
wh-hoa
Well, since I'm on cleaning duty today, I'll just give this to you now.
SWEETS FOR THE SWEET!
Mmm!
THANKS, TOMOYO!

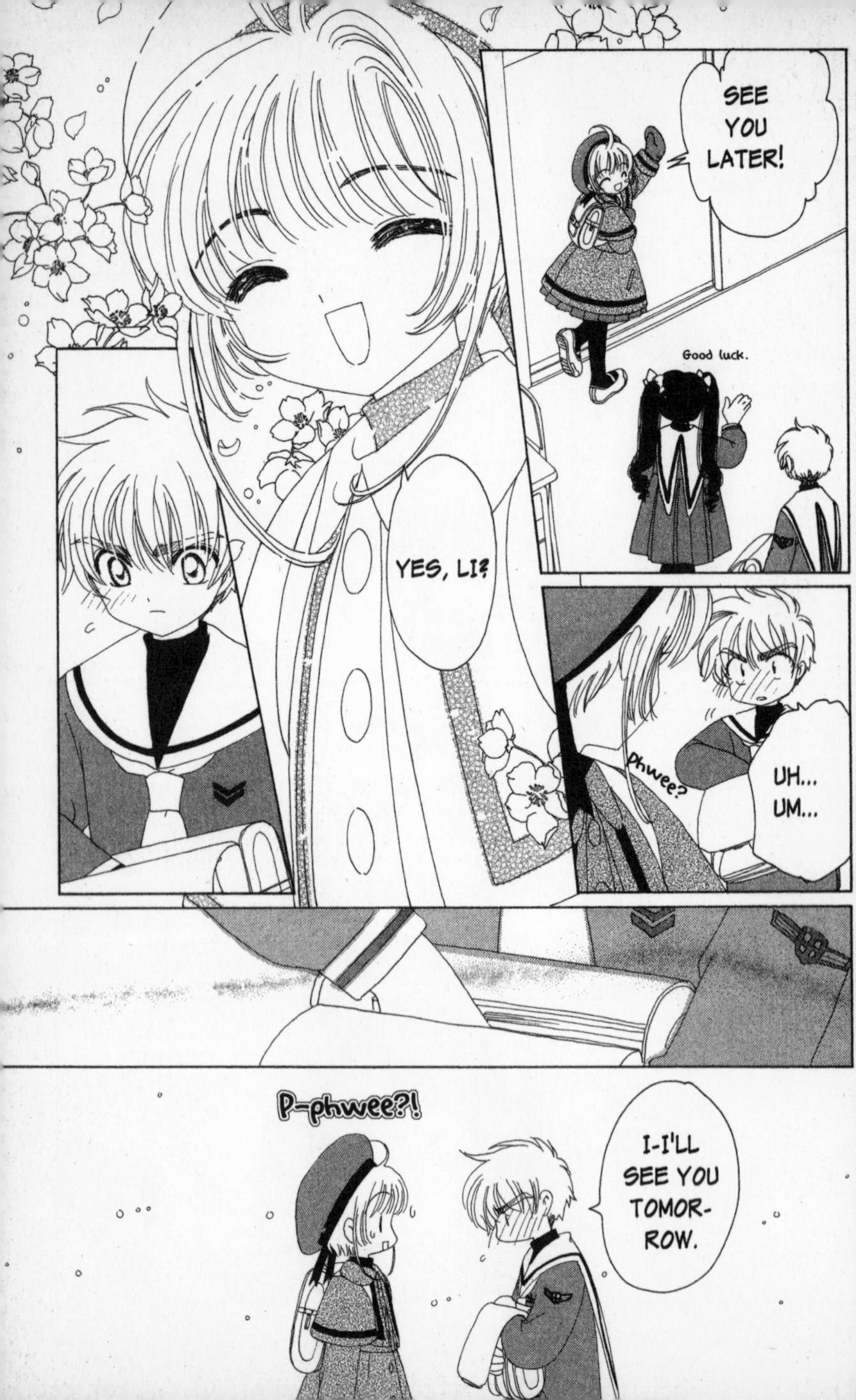
SEE YOU LATER!
Good luck.
Phwee?
UH... UM...
YES, LI?
I-I'LL SEE YOU TOMOR-ROW.
P-phwee?!

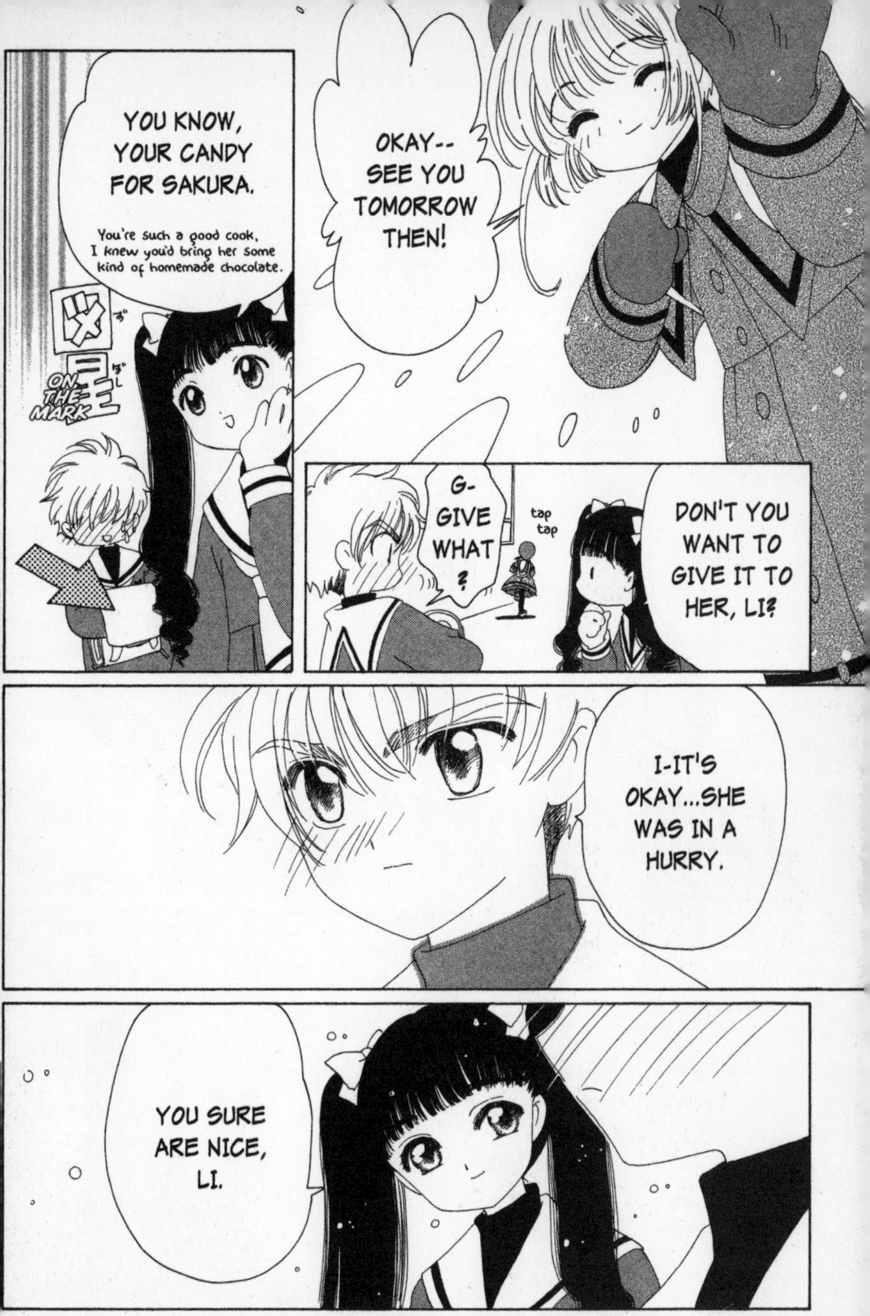
OKAY-- SEE YOU TOMORROW THEN!
DON'T YOU WANT TO GIVE IT TO HER, LI?
tap tap
G-GIVE WHAT?
YOU KNOW, YOUR CANDY FOR SAKURA.
You're such a good cook, I knew you'd bring her some kind of homemade chocolate.
ON THE MARK
I-IT'S OKAY...SHE WAS IN A HURRY.
YOU SURE ARE NICE, LI.

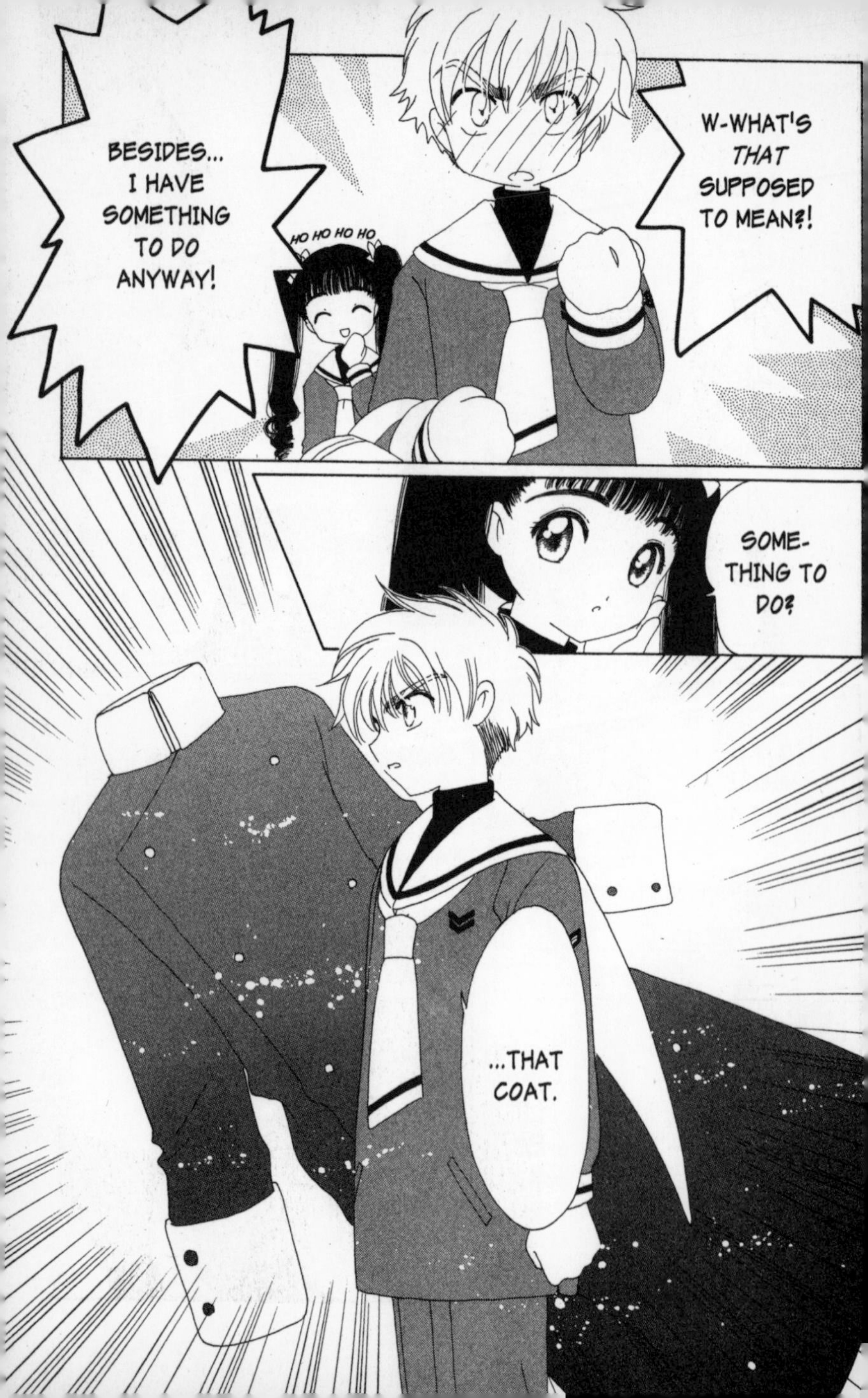
W-WHAT'S *THAT* SUPPOSED TO MEAN?!
BESIDES... I HAVE SOMETHING TO DO ANYWAY!
HO HO HO HO
SOME-THING TO DO?
...THAT COAT.

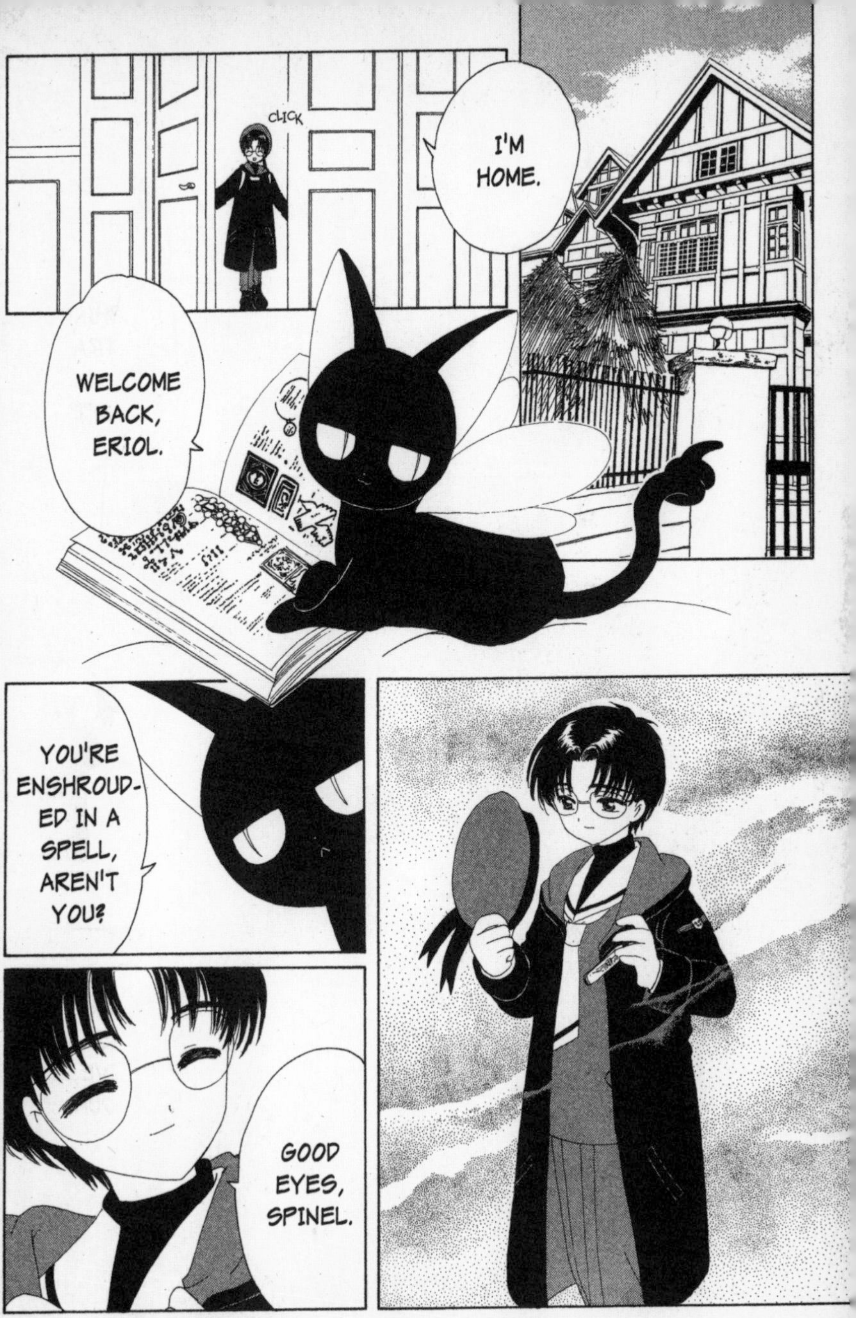
I'M HOME.
CLICK
WELCOME BACK, ERIOL.
YOU'RE ENSHROUD-ED IN A SPELL, AREN'T YOU?
GOOD EYES, SPINEL.

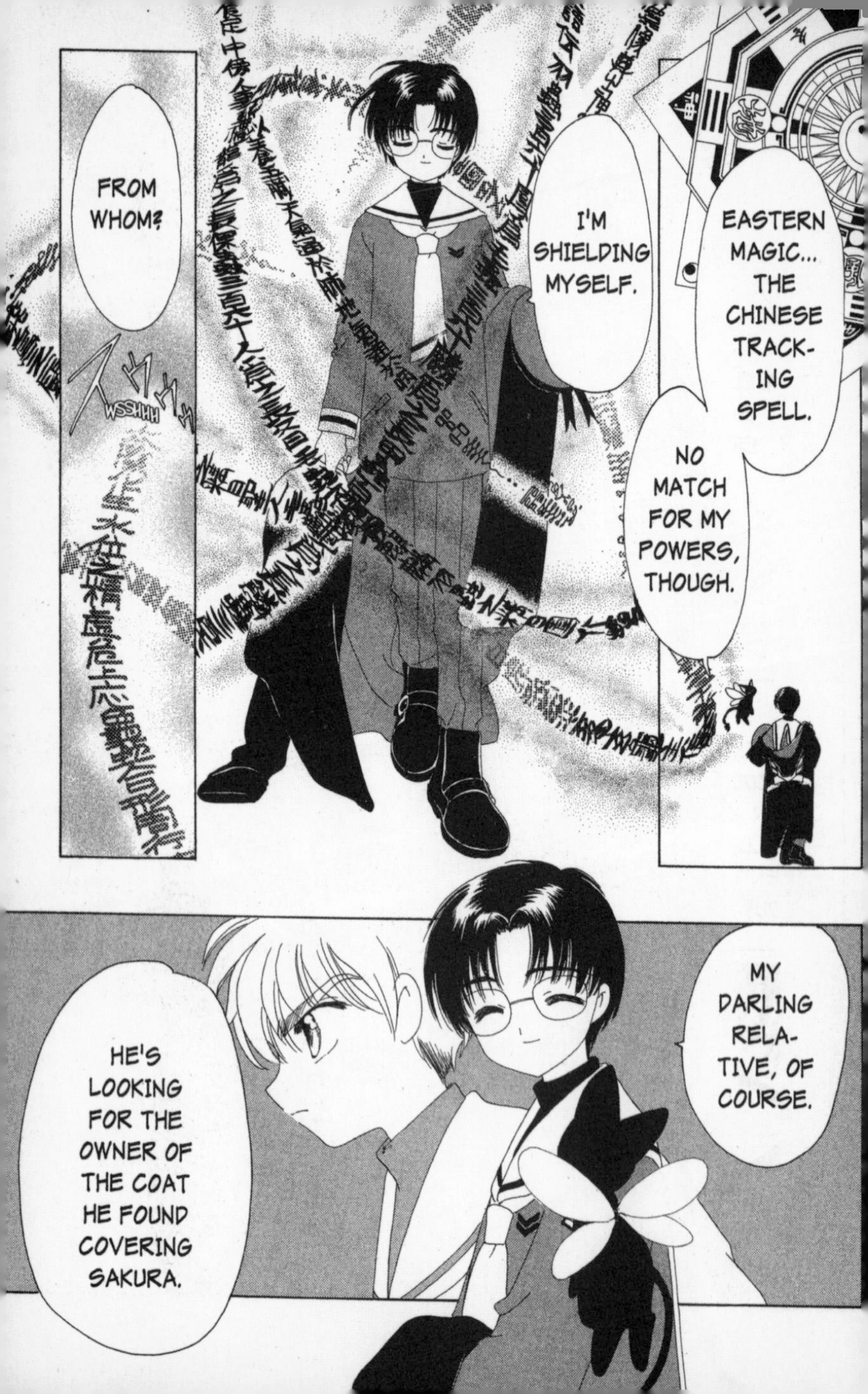
EASTERN MAGIC... THE CHINESE TRACK-ING SPELL.
NO MATCH FOR MY POWERS, THOUGH.
I'M SHIELDING MYSELF.
FROM WHOM?
WSSHHH
MY DARLING RELA-TIVE, OF COURSE.
HE'S LOOKING FOR THE OWNER OF THE COAT HE FOUND COVERING SAKURA.

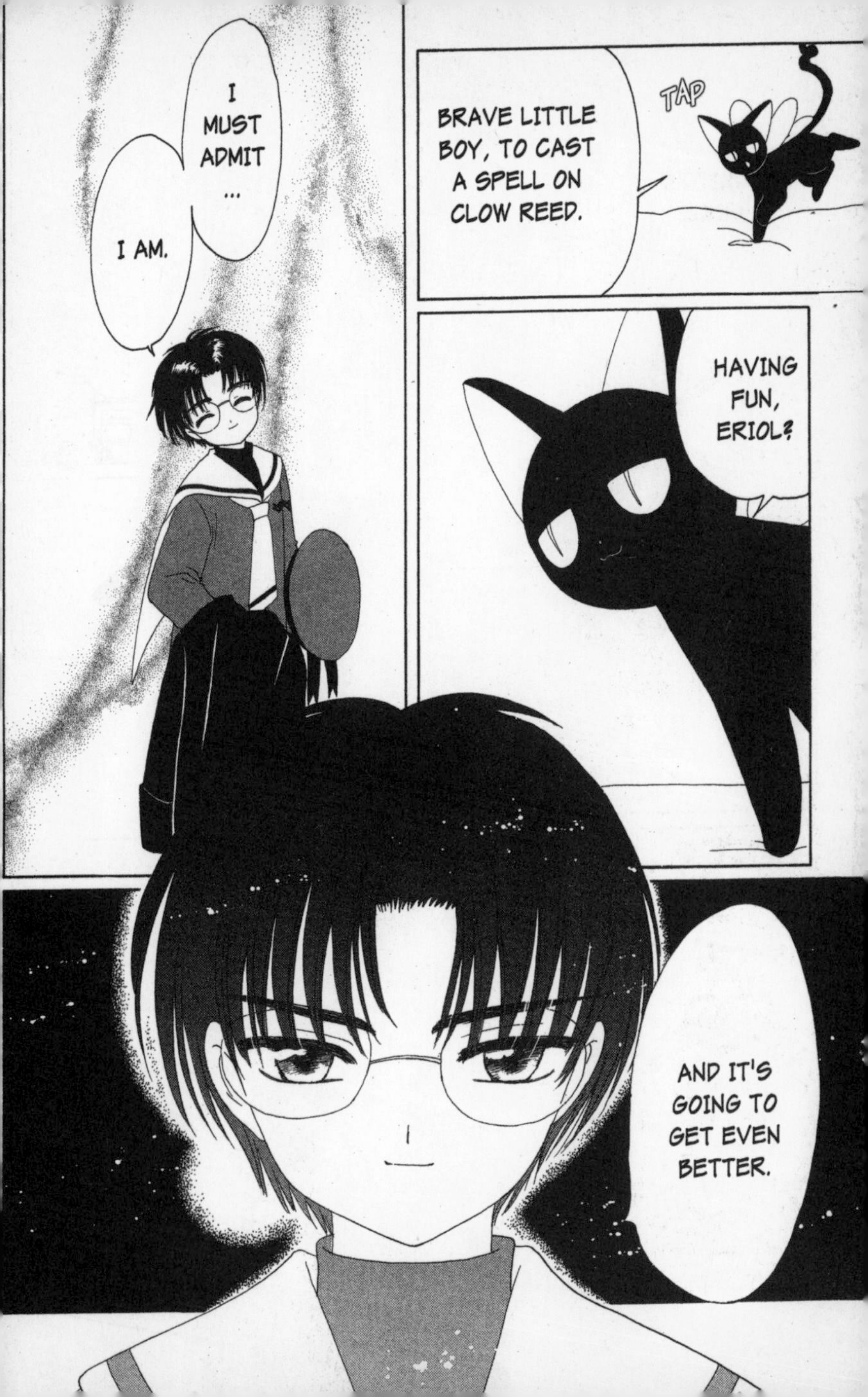
TAP
BRAVE LITTLE BOY, TO CAST A SPELL ON CLOW REED.
HAVING FUN, ERIOL?
I MUST ADMIT ...
I AM.
AND IT'S GOING TO GET EVEN BETTER.

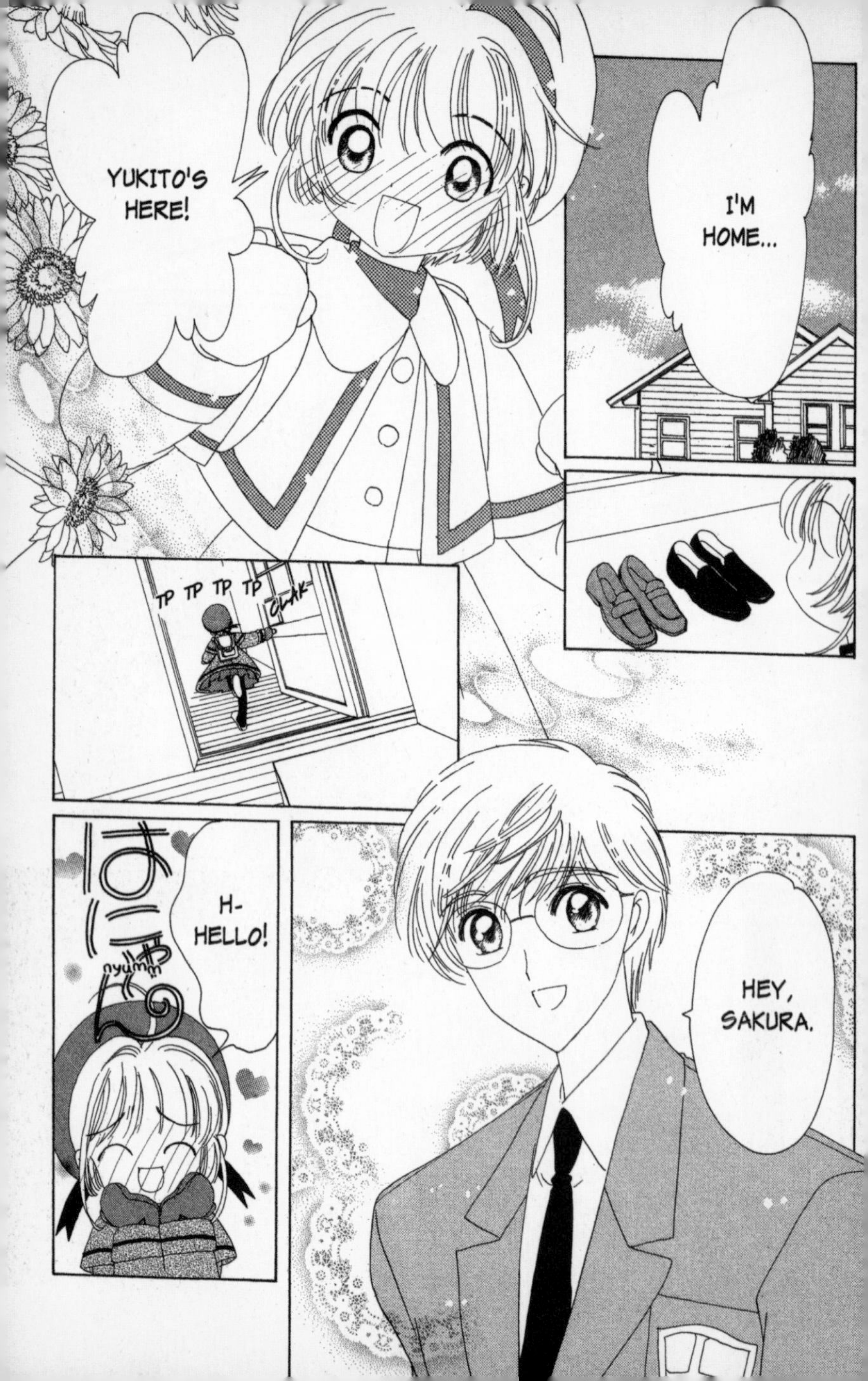
I'M HOME...
YUKITO'S HERE!
TP TP TP TP
CLAK
HEY, SAKURA.
H- HELLO!
はにゃ〜ん
nyumm

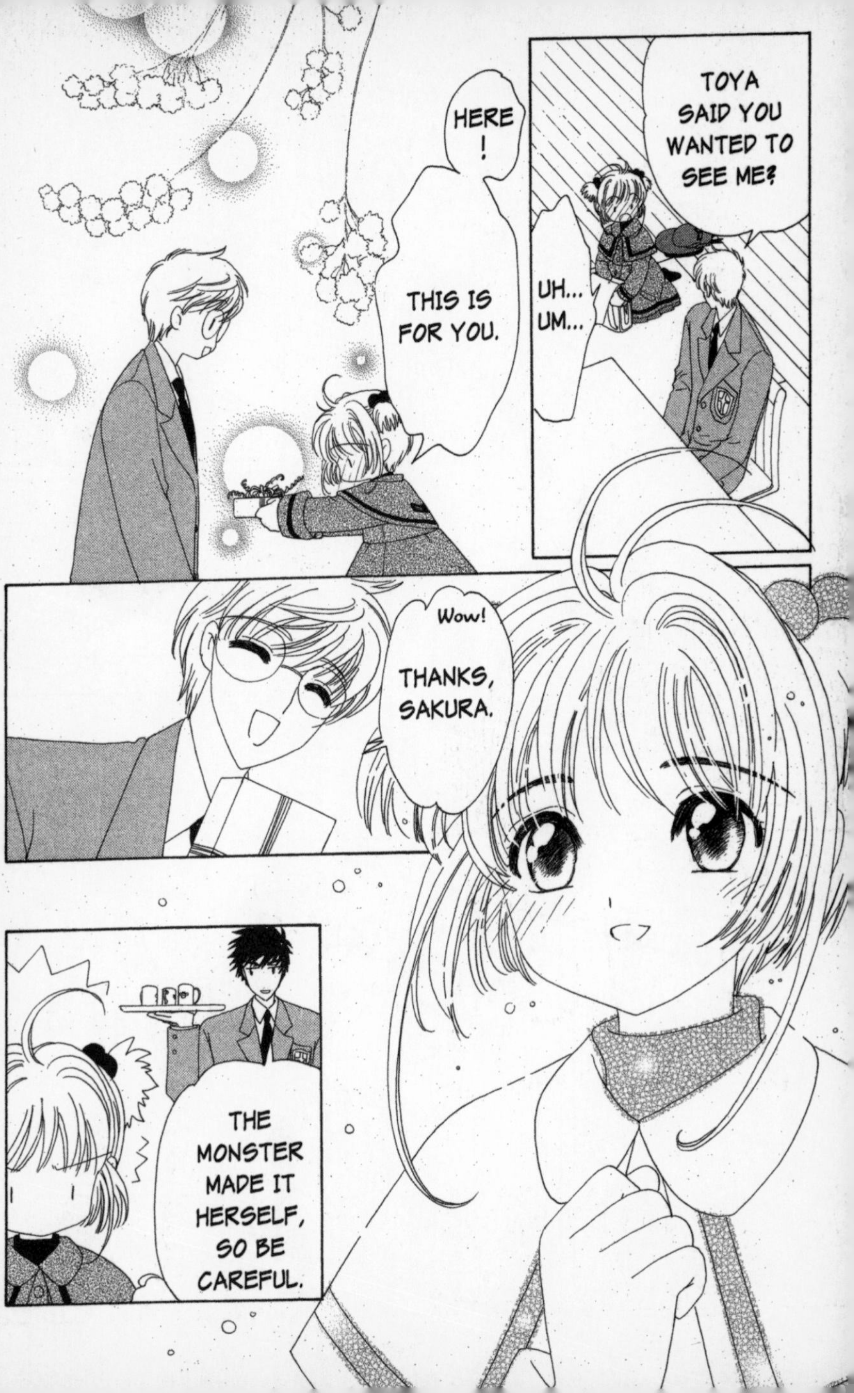
TOYA SAID YOU WANTED TO SEE ME?
UH... UM...
HERE!
THIS IS FOR YOU.
Wow!
THANKS, SAKURA.
THE MONSTER MADE IT HERSELF, SO BE CAREFUL.

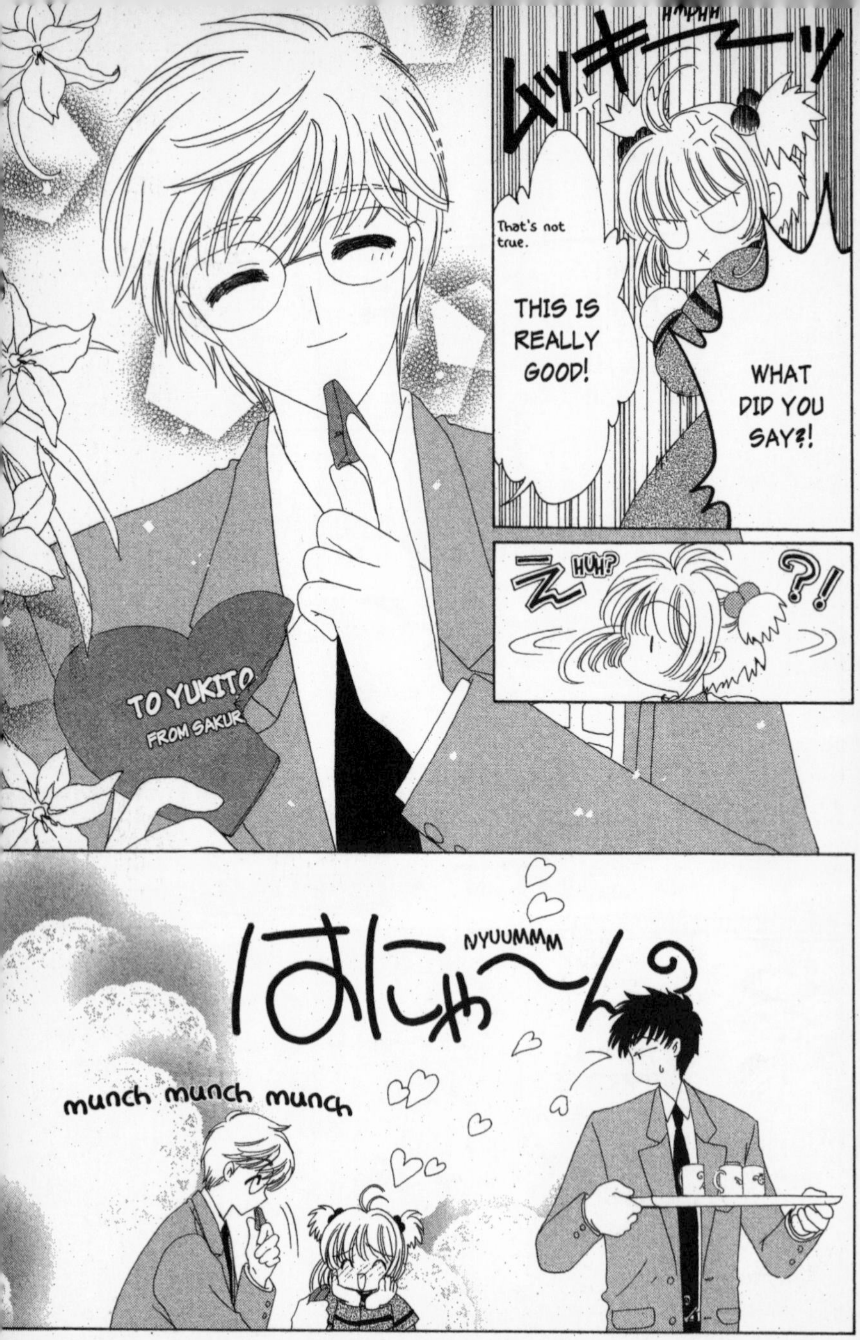
ムッキーッ
HMPHH
WHAT DID YOU SAY?!
That's not true.
THIS IS REALLY GOOD!
?!
え
HUH?
TO YUKITO
FROM SAKUR
はにゃ〜ん
NYUUMMM
munch munch munch

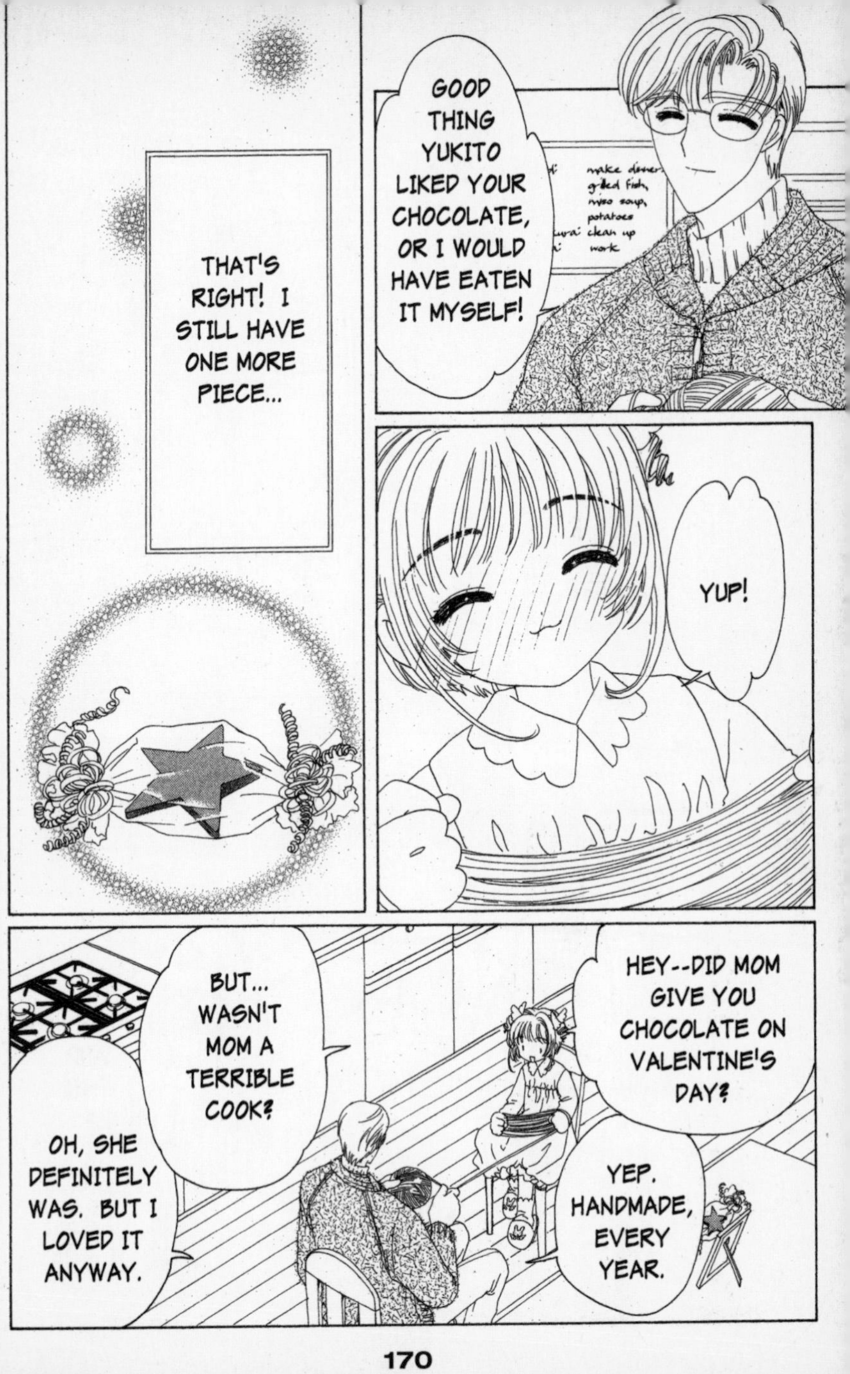
GOOD THING YUKITO LIKED YOUR CHOCOLATE, OR I WOULD HAVE EATEN IT MYSELF!
YUP!
THAT'S RIGHT! I STILL HAVE ONE MORE PIECE...
HEY--DID MOM GIVE YOU CHOCOLATE ON VALENTINE'S DAY?
YEP. HANDMADE, EVERY YEAR.
BUT... WASN'T MOM A TERRIBLE COOK?
OH, SHE DEFINITELY WAS. BUT I LOVED IT ANYWAY.

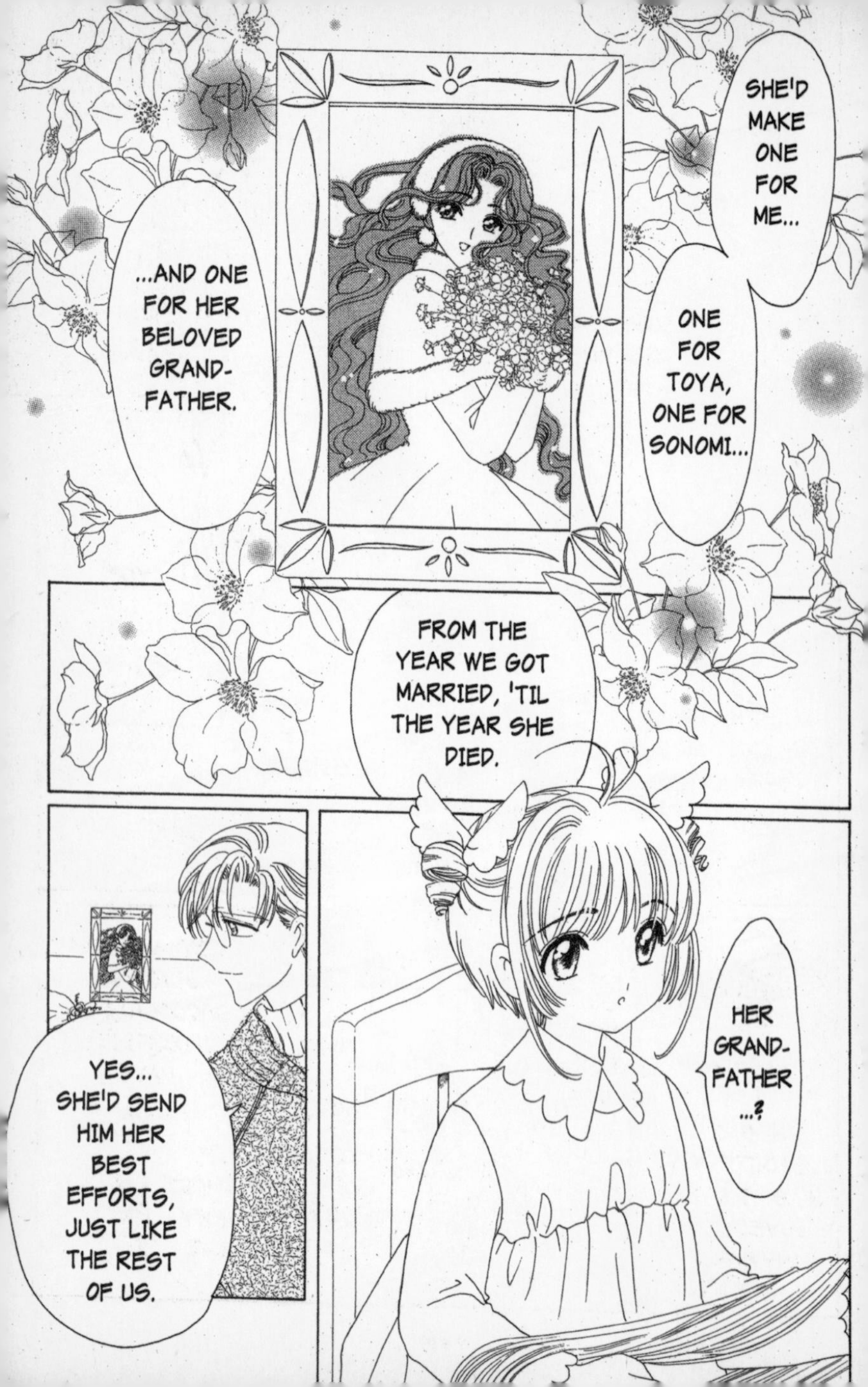
SHE'D MAKE ONE FOR ME...
ONE FOR TOYA, ONE FOR SONOMI...
...AND ONE FOR HER BELOVED GRAND-FATHER.
FROM THE YEAR WE GOT MARRIED, 'TIL THE YEAR SHE DIED.
HER GRAND-FATHER...?
YES... SHE'D SEND HIM HER BEST EFFORTS, JUST LIKE THE REST OF US.

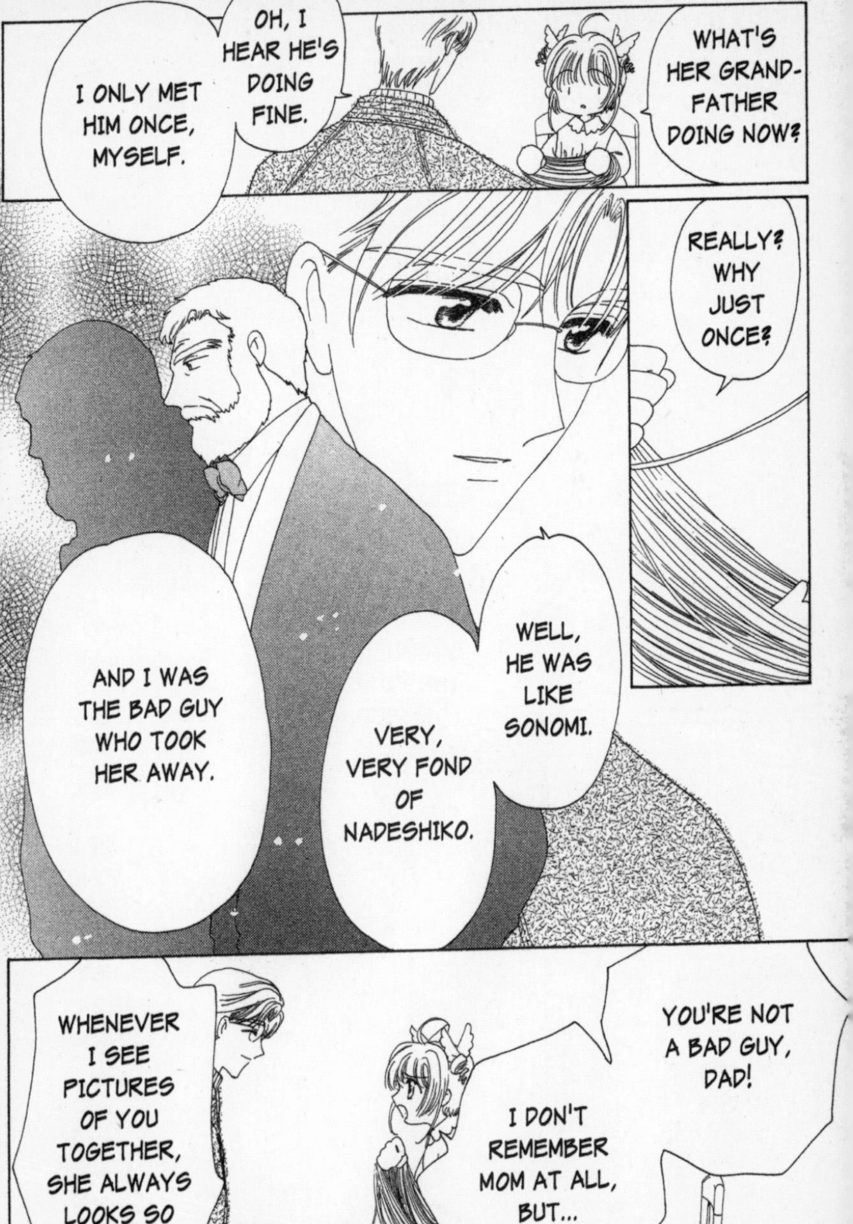
WHAT'S HER GRAND-FATHER DOING NOW?
OH, I HEAR HE'S DOING FINE.
I ONLY MET HIM ONCE, MYSELF.
REALLY? WHY JUST ONCE?
WELL, HE WAS LIKE SONOMI.
VERY, VERY FOND OF NADESHIKO.
AND I WAS THE BAD GUY WHO TOOK HER AWAY.
YOU'RE NOT A BAD GUY, DAD!
I DON'T REMEMBER MOM AT ALL, BUT...
WHENEVER I SEE PICTURES OF YOU TOGETHER, SHE ALWAYS LOOKS SO HAPPY!

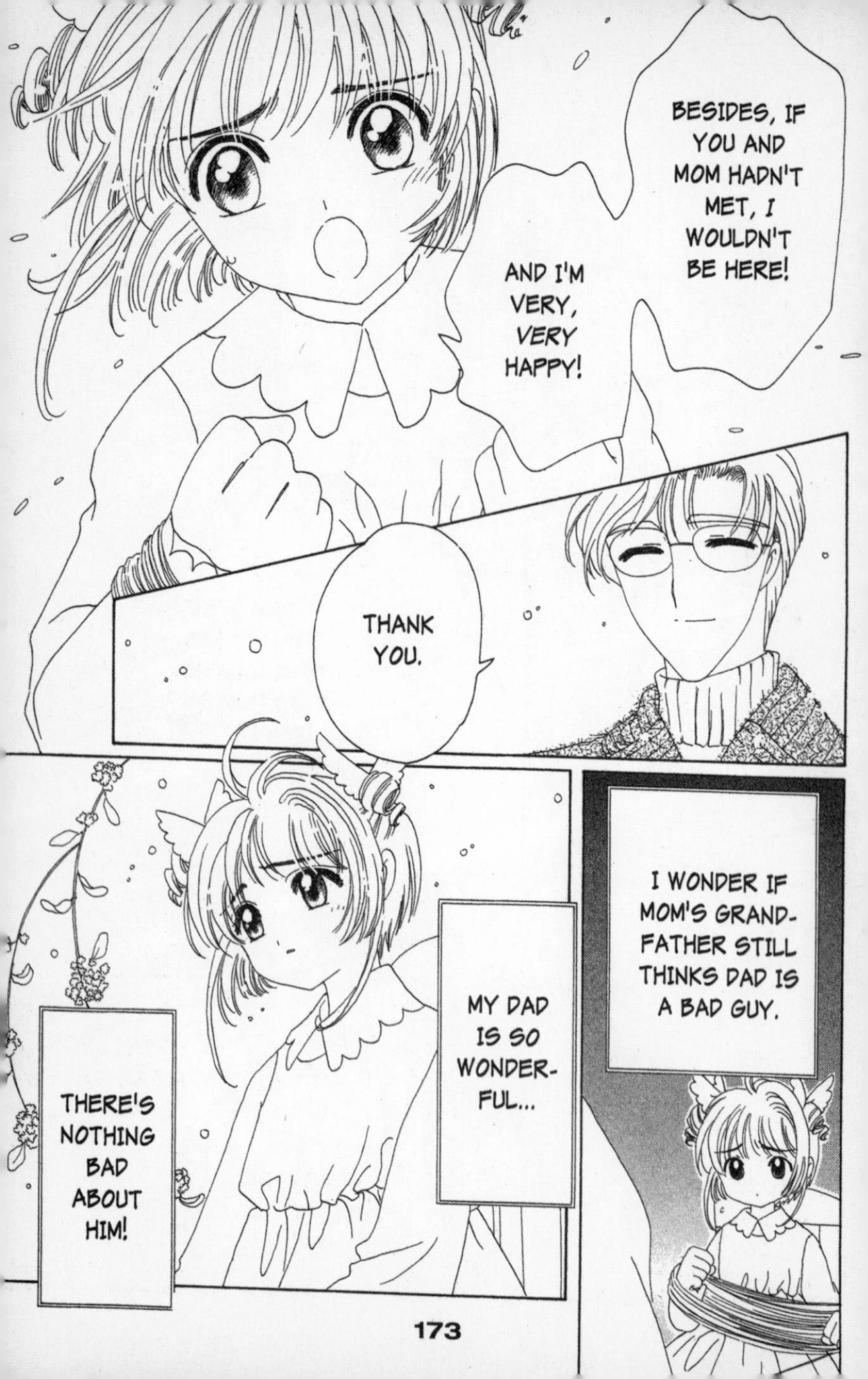
BESIDES, IF YOU AND MOM HADN'T MET, *I* WOULDN'T BE HERE!
AND I'M VERY, *VERY* HAPPY!
THANK YOU.
I WONDER IF MOM'S GRAND-FATHER STILL THINKS DAD IS A BAD GUY.
MY DAD IS SO WONDER-FUL...
THERE'S NOTHING BAD ABOUT HIM!

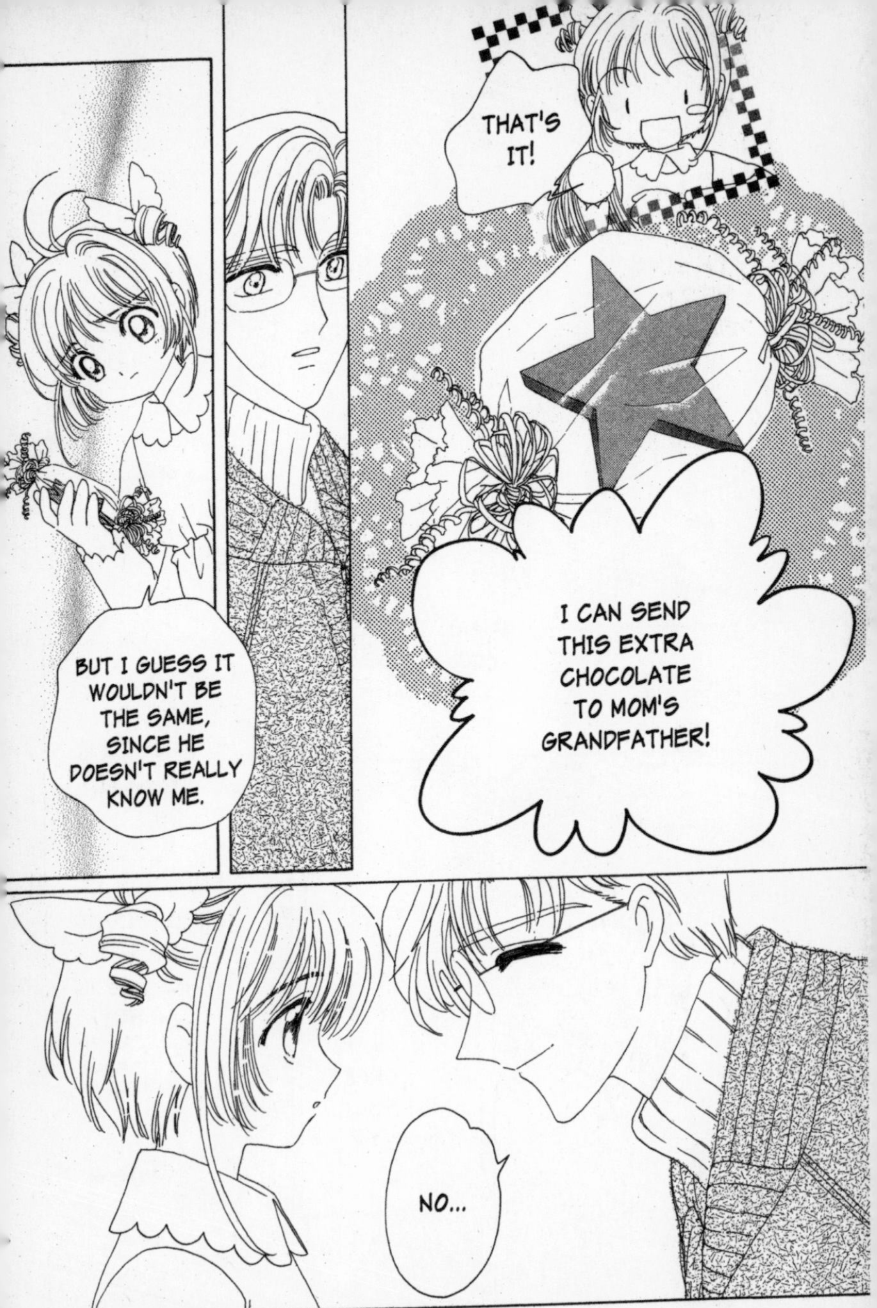
THAT'S IT!
I CAN SEND THIS EXTRA CHOCOLATE TO MOM'S GRANDFATHER!
BUT I GUESS IT WOULDN'T BE THE SAME, SINCE HE DOESN'T REALLY KNOW ME.
NO...

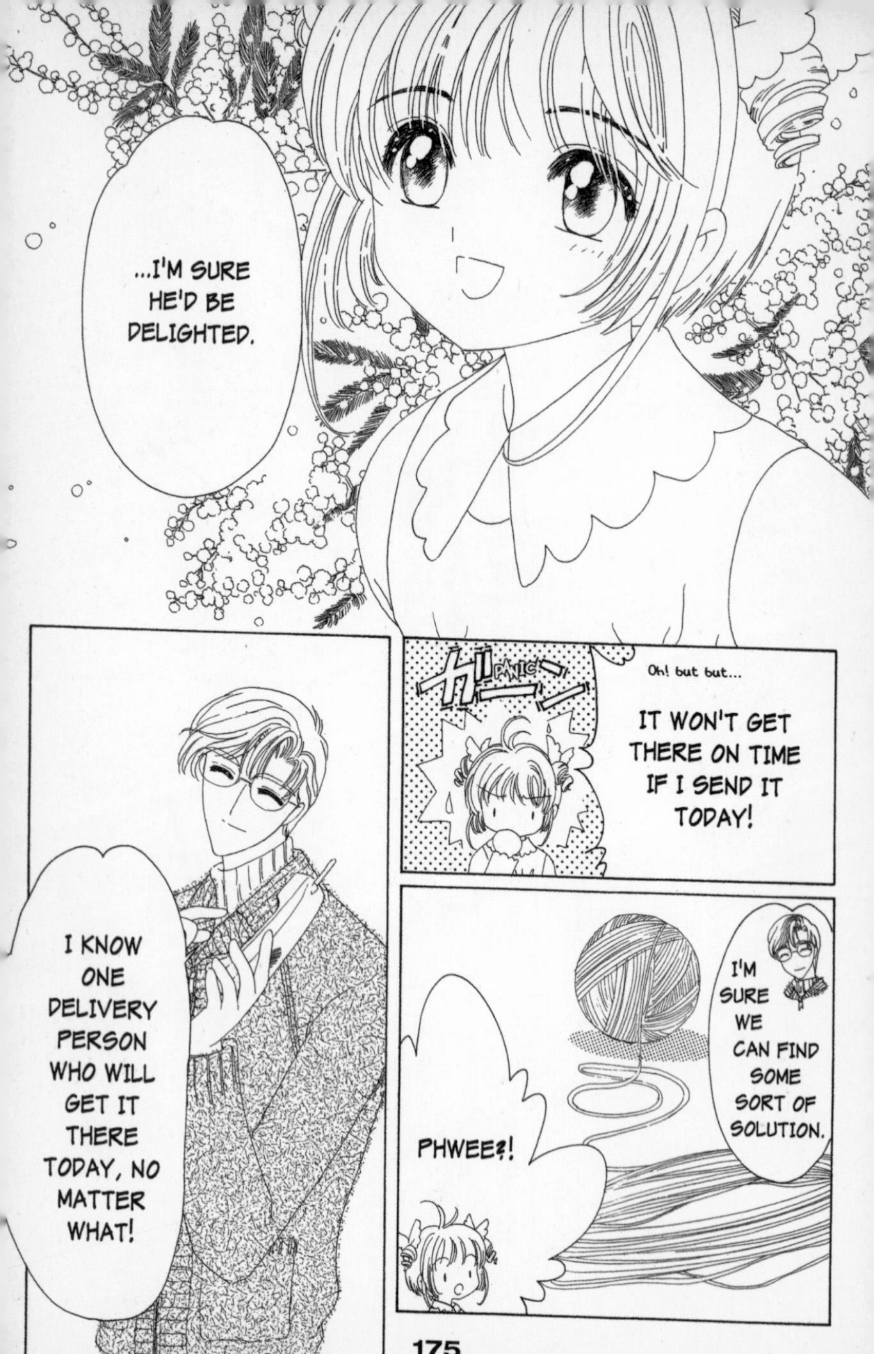
...I'M SURE HE'D BE DELIGHTED.
ガーン
PANIC
Oh! but but...
IT WON'T GET THERE ON TIME IF I SEND IT TODAY!
I'M SURE WE CAN FIND SOME SORT OF SOLUTION.
PHWEE?!
I KNOW ONE DELIVERY PERSON WHO WILL GET IT THERE TODAY, NO MATTER WHAT!

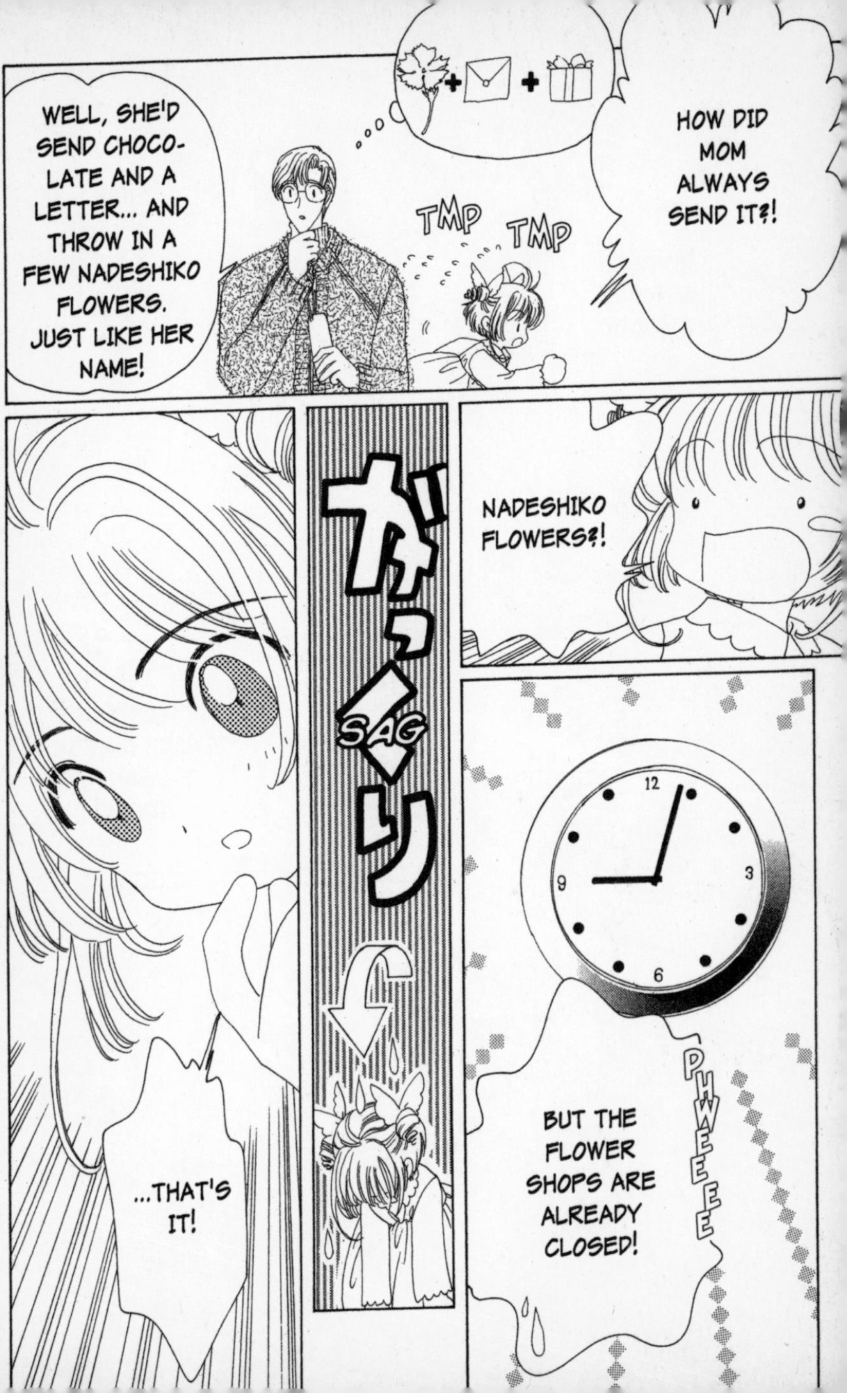
HOW DID MOM ALWAYS SEND IT?!
TMP
TMP
WELL, SHE'D SEND CHOCO-LATE AND A LETTER... AND THROW IN A FEW NADESHIKO FLOWERS. JUST LIKE HER NAME!
NADESHIKO FLOWERS?!
BUT THE FLOWER SHOPS ARE ALREADY CLOSED!
PHWEEE
がっくり
SAG
...THAT'S IT!

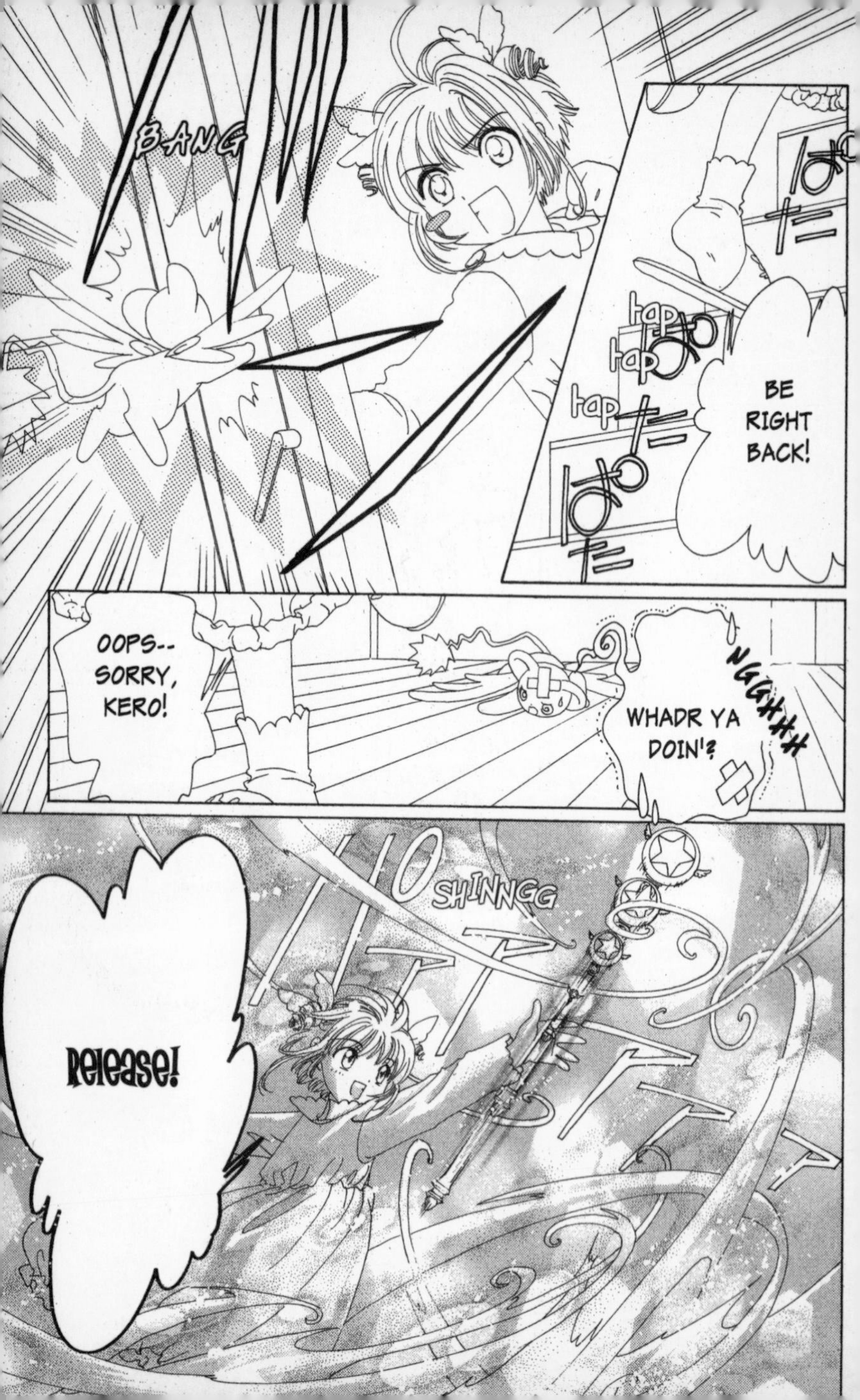
tap
tap
tap
BE RIGHT BACK!
BANG
NGGHHH
WHADR YA DOIN'?
OOPS-- SORRY, KERO!
SHINNGG
Release!

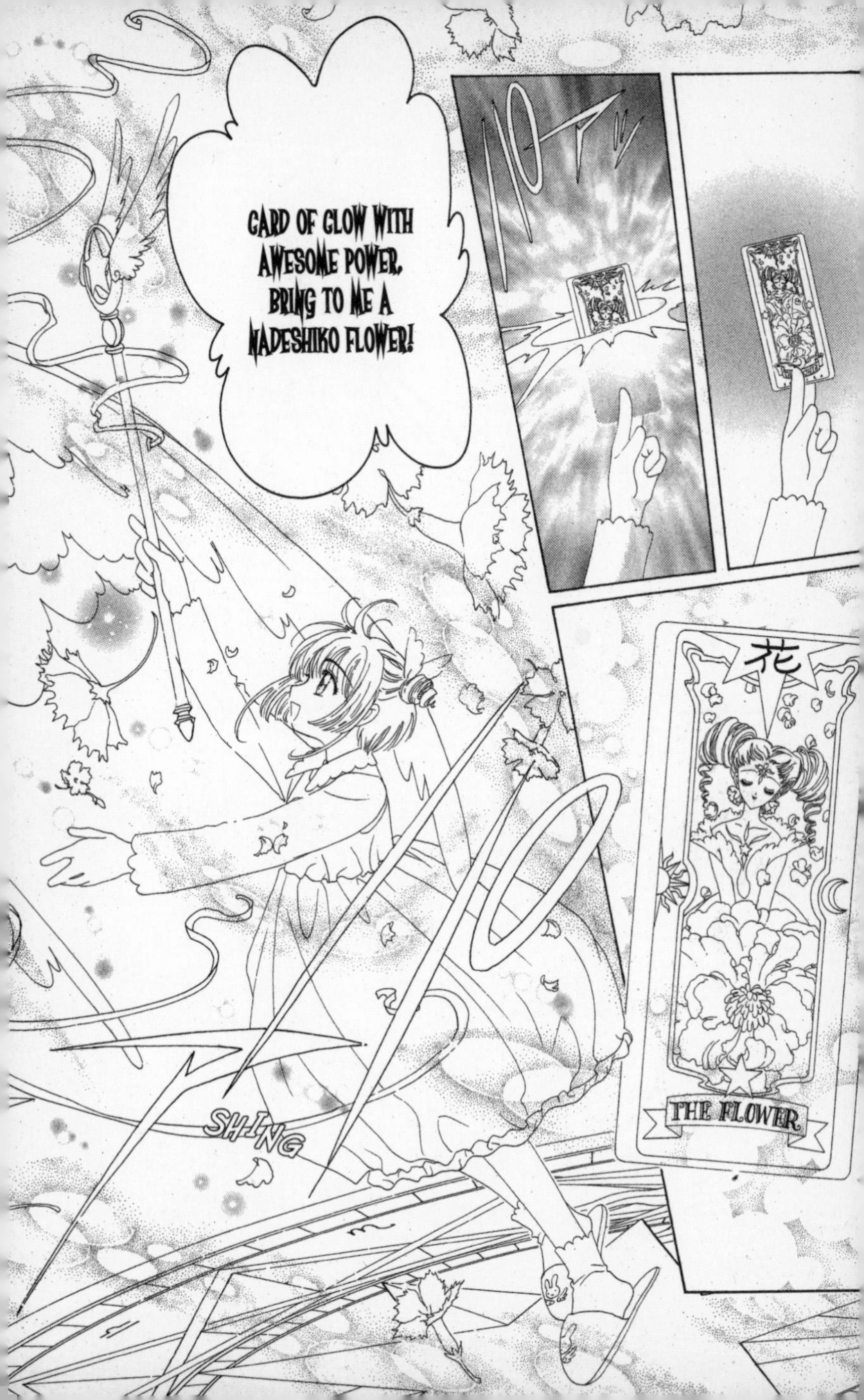
パアッ
花
THE FLOWER
CARD OF GLOW WITH AWESOME POWER, BRING TO ME A NADESHIKO FLOWER!
SHING

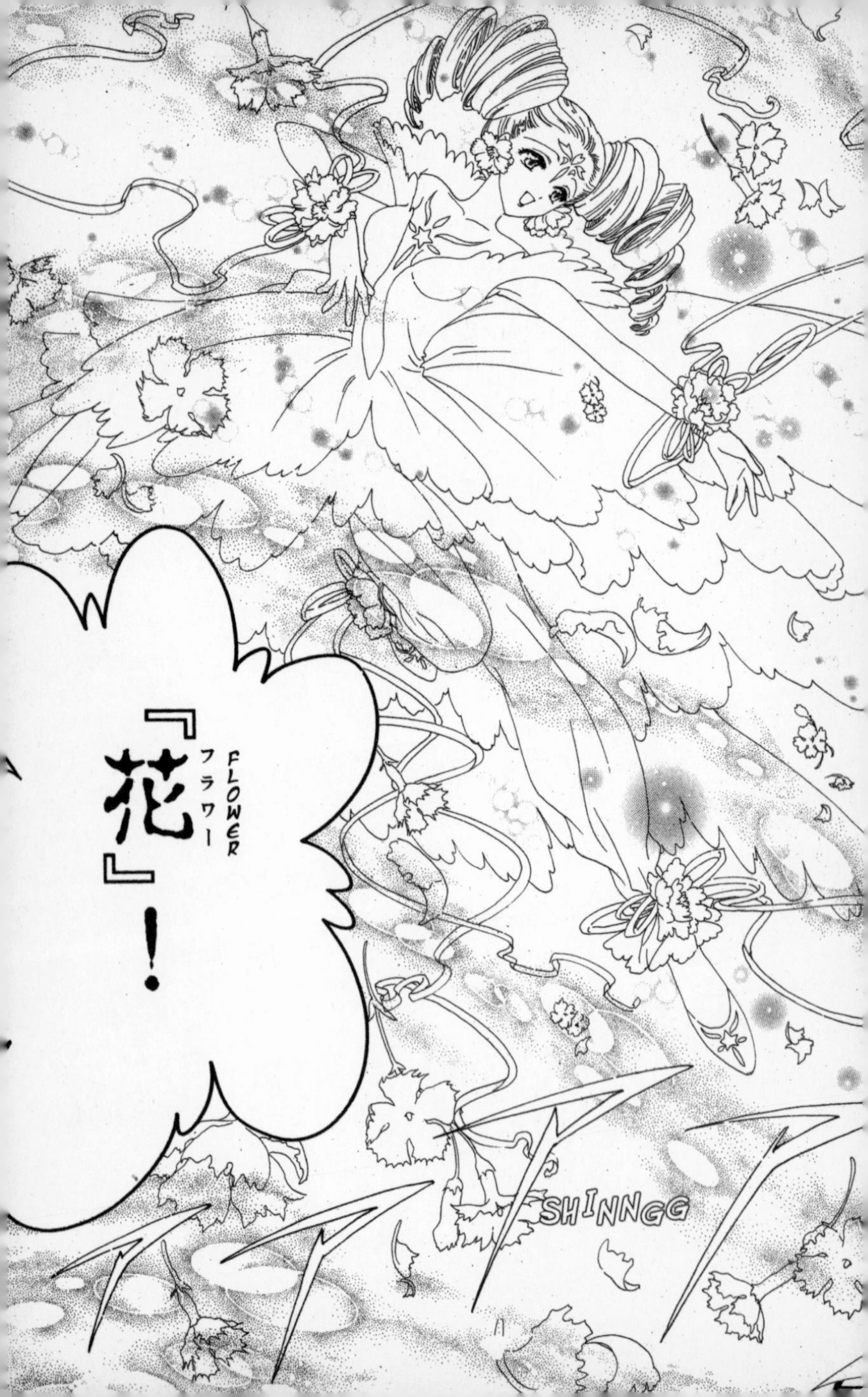
『花(フラワー FLOWER)』!
SHINNGG

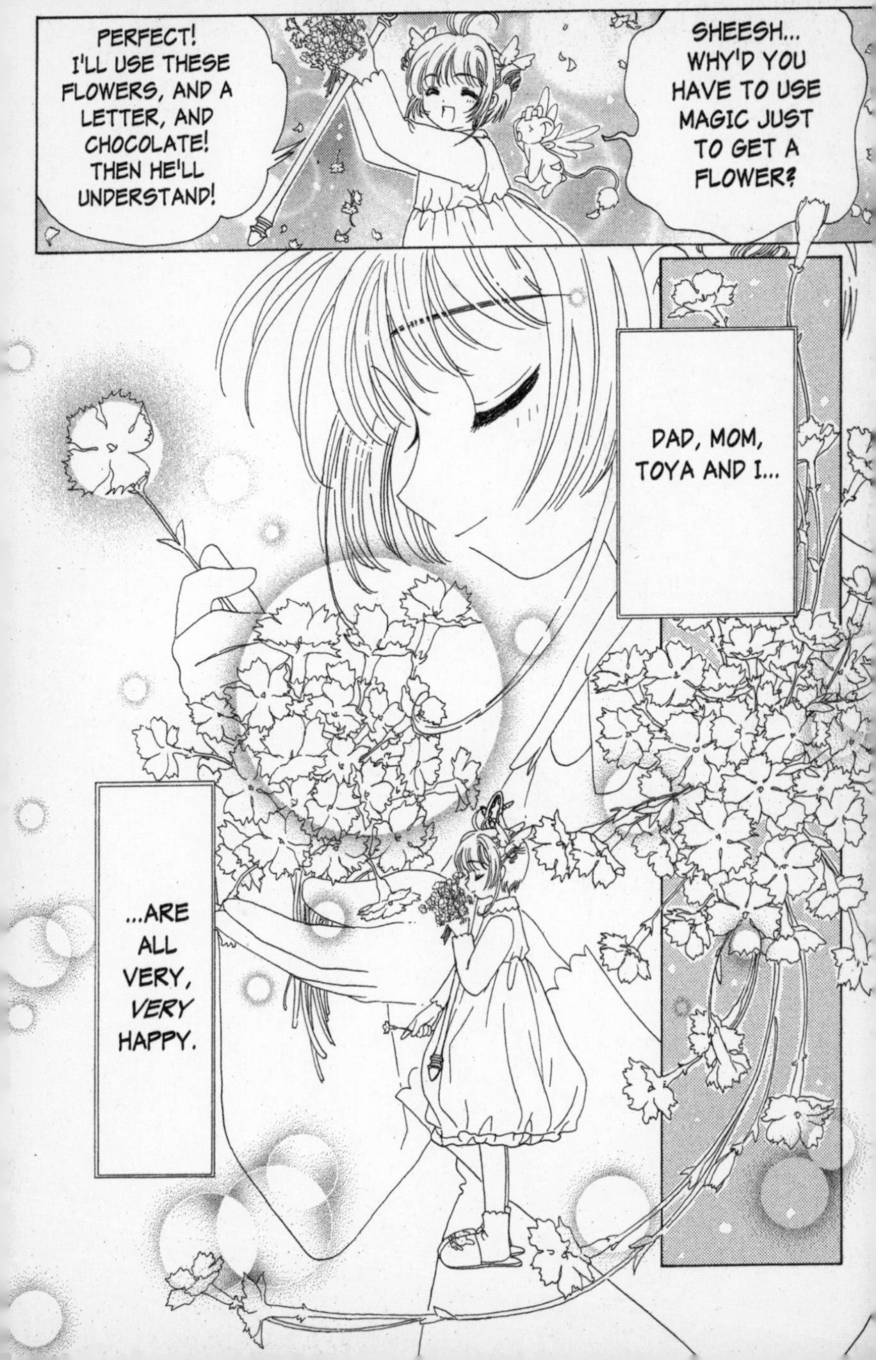
SHEESH... WHY'D YOU HAVE TO USE MAGIC JUST TO GET A FLOWER?
PERFECT! I'LL USE THESE FLOWERS, AND A LETTER, AND CHOCOLATE! THEN HE'LL UNDERSTAND!
DAD, MOM, TOYA AND I...
...ARE ALL VERY, *VERY* HAPPY.

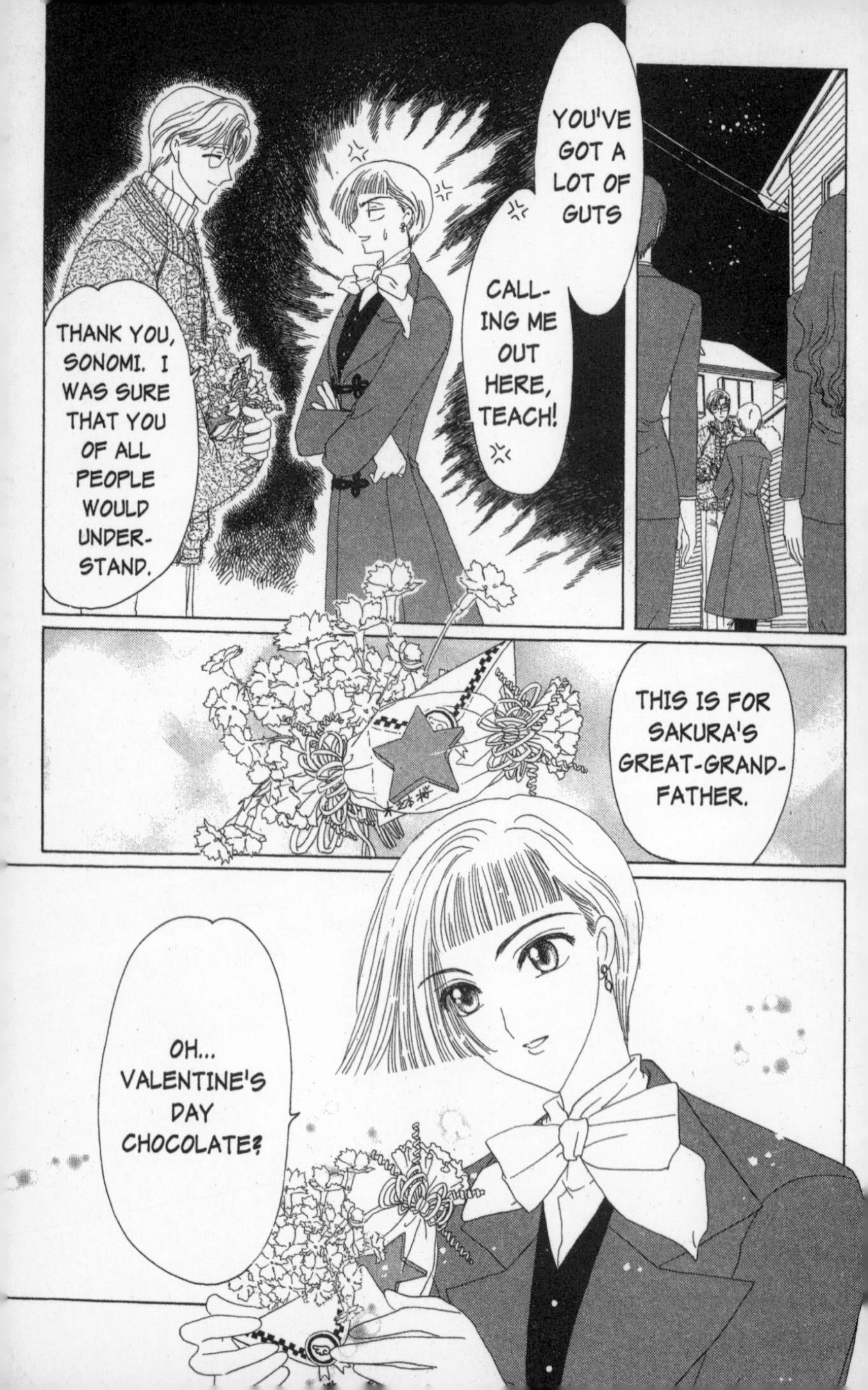
YOU'VE GOT A LOT OF GUTS
CALLING ME OUT HERE, TEACH!
THANK YOU, SONOMI. I WAS SURE THAT YOU OF ALL PEOPLE WOULD UNDERSTAND.
THIS IS FOR SAKURA'S GREAT-GRANDFATHER.
OH... VALENTINE'S DAY CHOCOLATE?

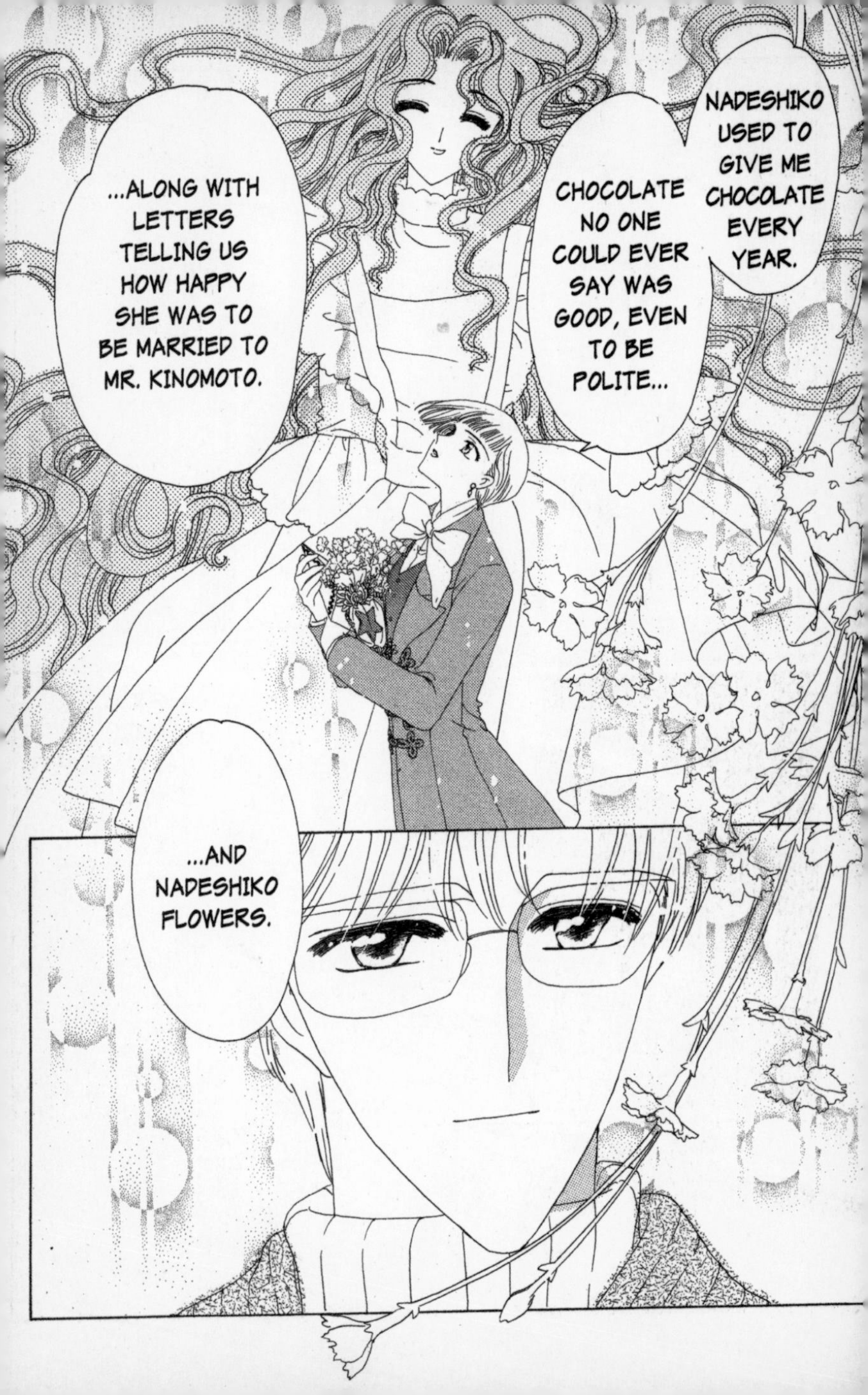
NADESHIKO USED TO GIVE ME CHOCOLATE EVERY YEAR.
CHOCOLATE NO ONE COULD EVER SAY WAS GOOD, EVEN TO BE POLITE...
...ALONG WITH LETTERS TELLING US HOW HAPPY SHE WAS TO BE MARRIED TO MR. KINOMOTO.
...AND NADESHIKO FLOWERS.

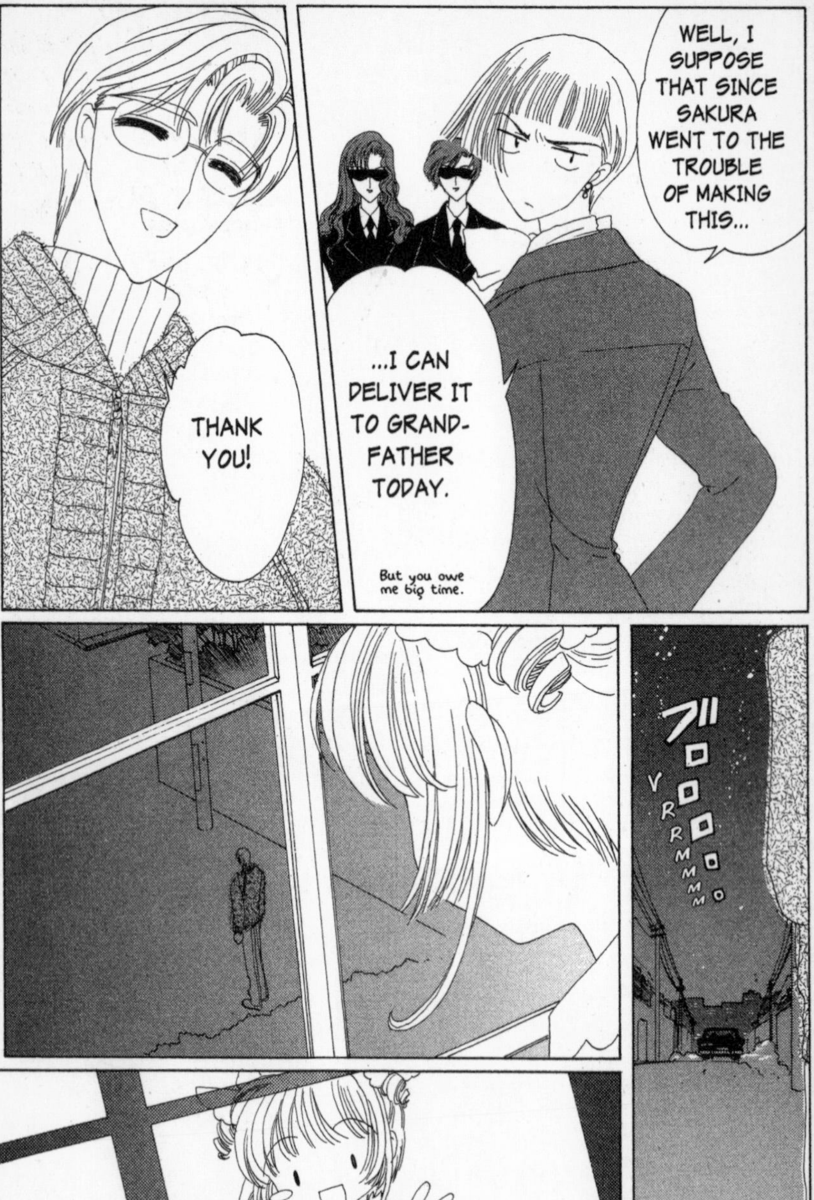
WELL, I SUPPOSE THAT SINCE SAKURA WENT TO THE TROUBLE OF MAKING THIS...
...I CAN DELIVER IT TO GRAND-FATHER TODAY.
But you owe me big time.
THANK YOU!
ブロロロロロ
VRRMMMM

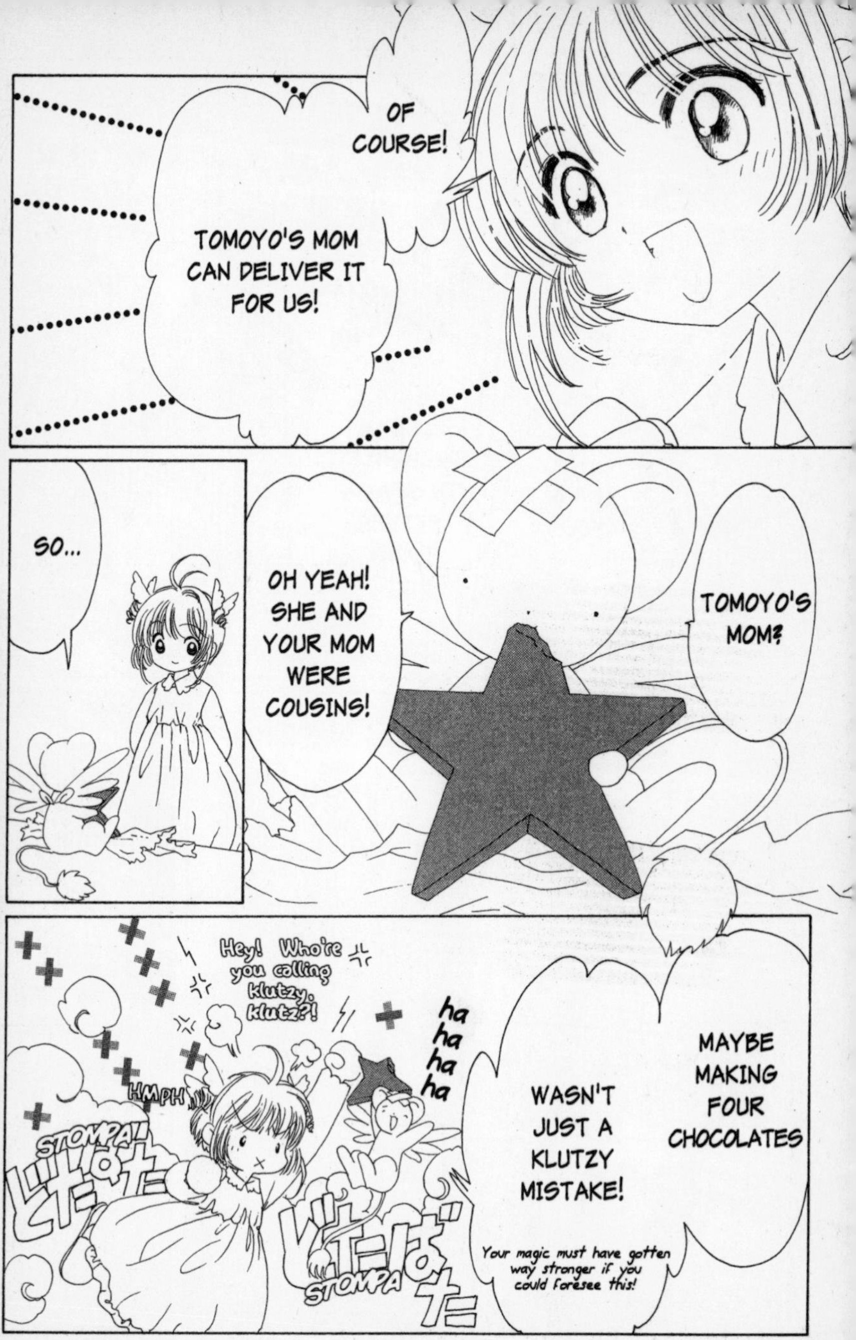
OF COURSE!
TOMOYO'S MOM CAN DELIVER IT FOR US!
TOMOYO'S MOM?
OH YEAH! SHE AND YOUR MOM WERE COUSINS!
SO...
MAYBE MAKING FOUR CHOCOLATES
WASN'T JUST A KLUTZY MISTAKE!
Your magic must have gotten way stronger if you could foresee this!
ha ha ha ha
Hey! Who're you calling klutzy, klutz?!
STOMPA
HMPH
STOMPA!!

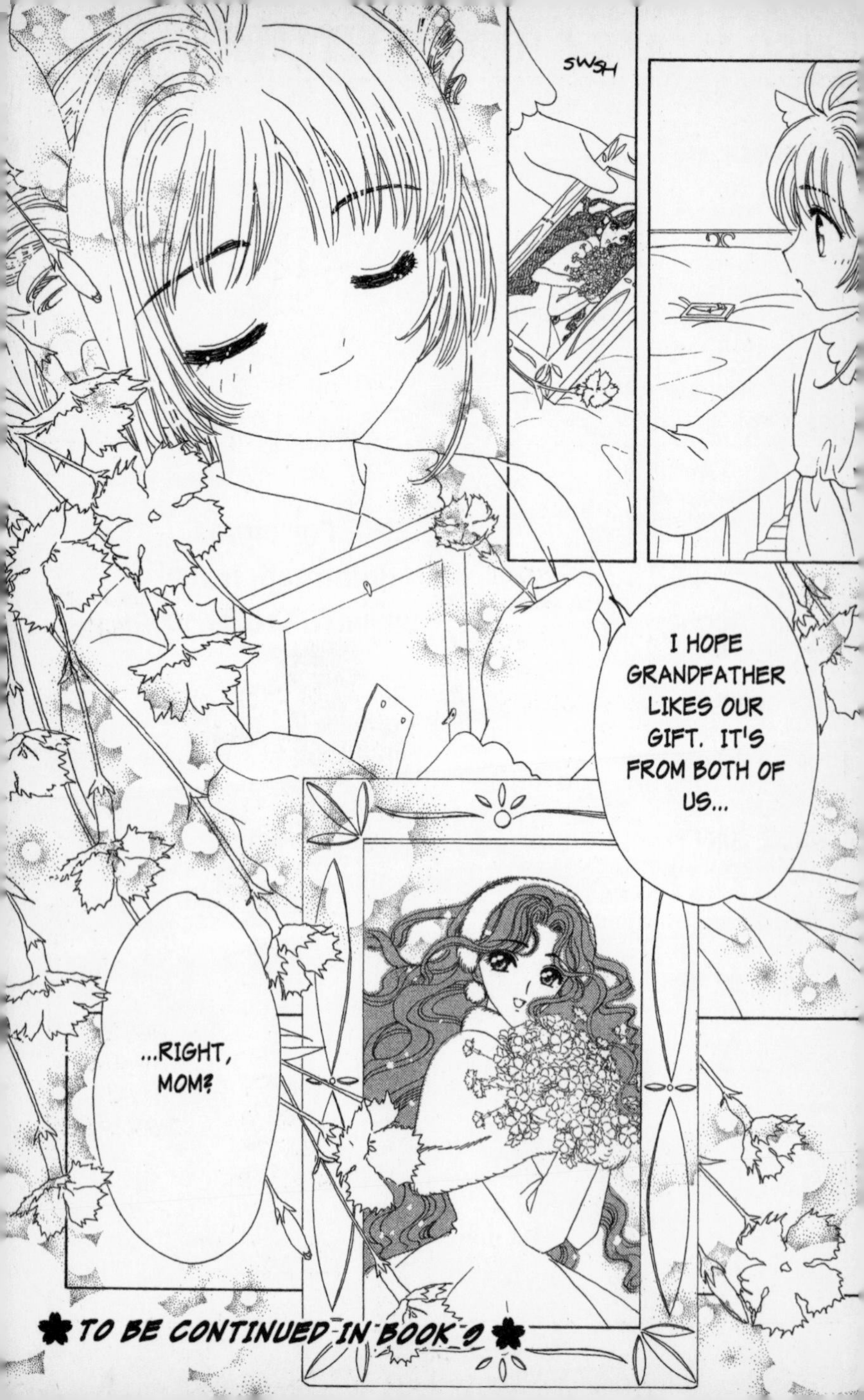
SWSH
I HOPE GRANDFATHER LIKES OUR GIFT. IT'S FROM BOTH OF US...
...RIGHT, MOM?
TO BE CONTINUED IN BOOK 9

ALSO AVAILABLE FROM 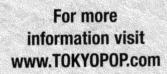TOKYOPOP®

ALSO AVAILABLE FROM ☻TOKYOPOP

12.20.03Y

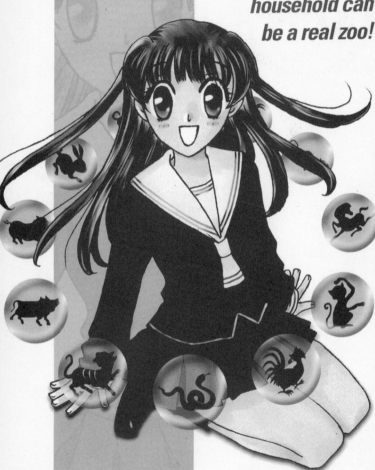

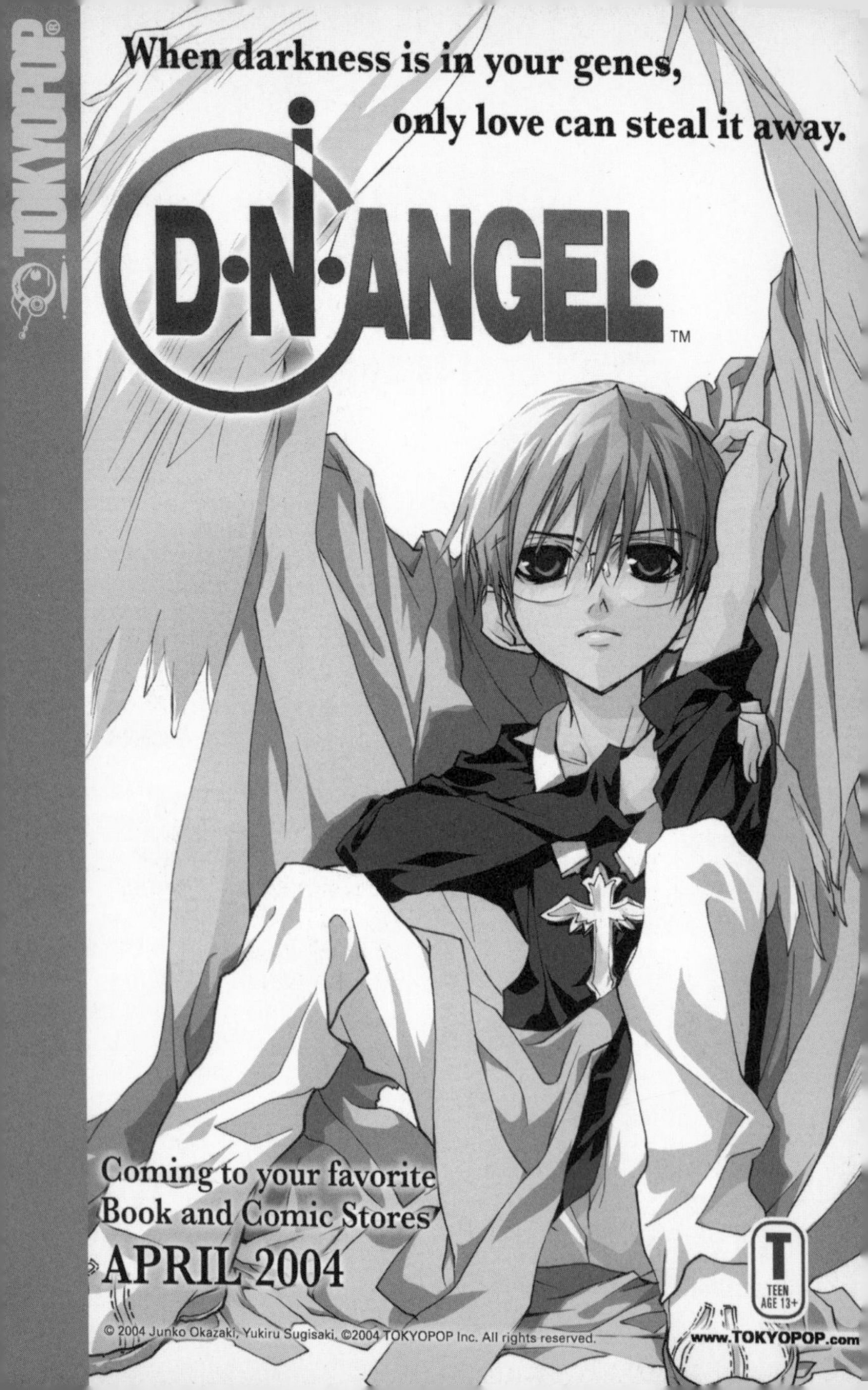

TOKYOPOP®
When darkness is in your genes,
only love can steal it away.
D·N·ANGEL™
Coming to your favorite
Book and Comic Stores
APRIL 2004
T
TEEN
AGE 13+
© 2004 Junko Okazaki, Yukiru Sugisaki. ©2004 TOKYOPOP Inc. All rights reserved.
www.TOKYOPOP.com

STOP!

This is the back of the book. You wouldn't want to spoil a great ending!

This book is printed "manga-style," in the authentic Japanese right-to-left format. Since none of the artwork has been flipped or altered, readers get to experience the story just as the creator intended. You've been asking for it, so TOKYOPOP® delivered: authentic, hot-off-the-press, and far more fun!

DIRECTIONS

If this is your first time reading manga-style, here's a quick guide to help you understand how it works.

1
2
3
4
5
6
7
8
9
10

It's easy... just start in the top right panel and follow the numbers. Have fun, and look for more 100% authentic manga from TOKYOPOP®!

100% AUTHENTIC MANGA
品質第一公式商品

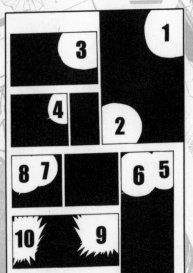

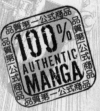

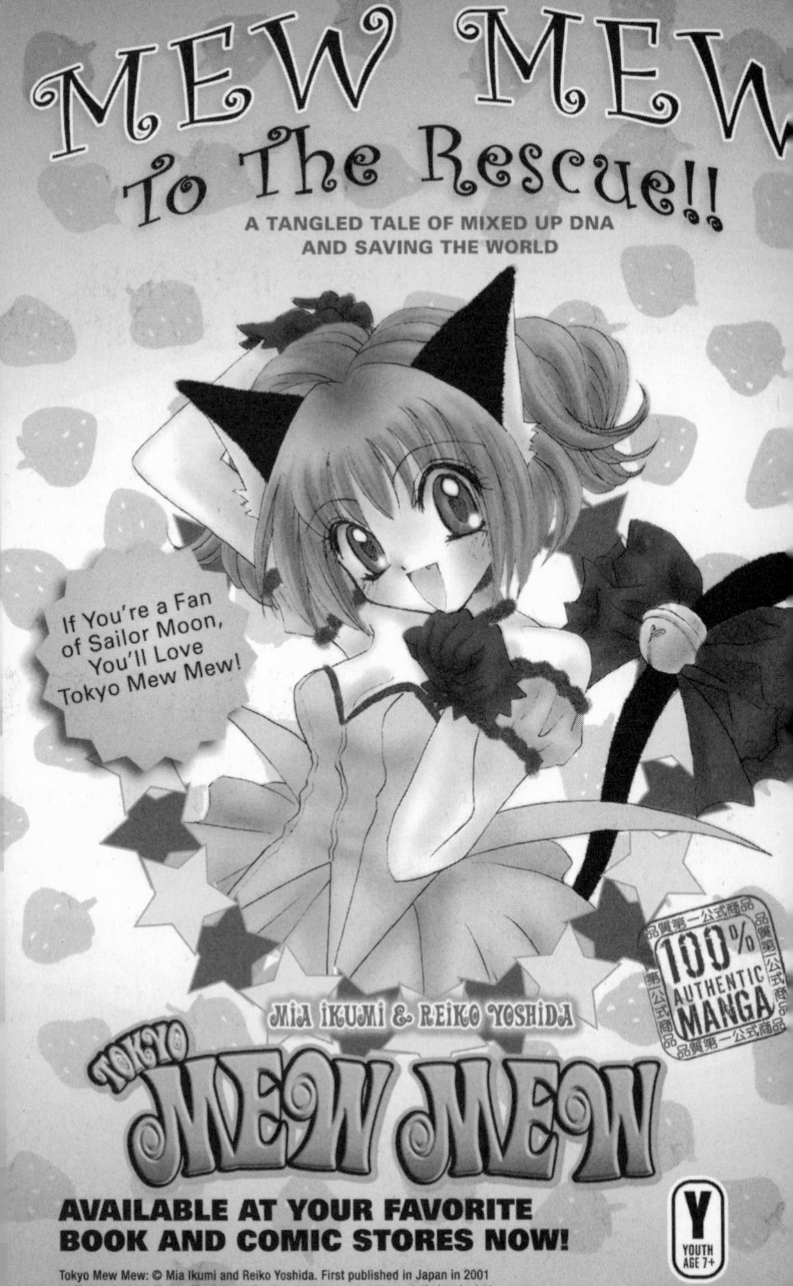
MEW MEW
To The Rescue!!
A TANGLED TALE OF MIXED UP DNA
AND SAVING THE WORLD
If You're a Fan of Sailor Moon, You'll Love Tokyo Mew Mew!
品質第一公式商品
100% AUTHENTIC MANGA
MIA IKUMI & REIKO YOSHIDA
TOKYO MEW MEW
AVAILABLE AT YOUR FAVORITE
BOOK AND COMIC STORES NOW!
Y
YOUTH AGE 7+
www.TOKYOPOP.c

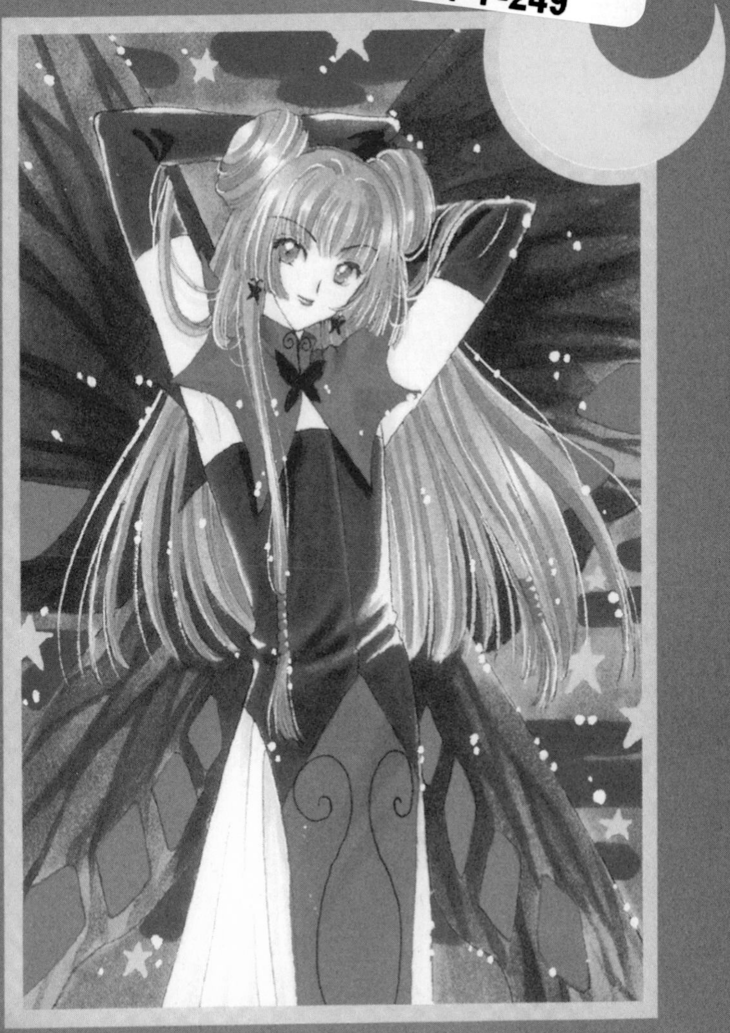

CLAMP